THE WISDEN GUIDE TO
INTERNATIONAL CRICKET 2013

EDITED BY STEVEN LYNCH

First published in the UK in 2012 by
John Wisden & Co
An imprint of Bloomsbury Publishing Plc
50 Bedford Square, London WC1B 3DP
www.wisden.com
www.bloomsbury.com

ISBN: 978 1 4081 7221 6

Cover by Greg Heinimann
Inside photographs © Getty Images

A CIP catalogue record for this book is available from the British Library.

This book is produced using paper that is made from wood
grown in managed, sustainable forests. It is natural, renewable and
recyclable. The logging and manufacturing processes conform to the
environmental regulations of the country of origin.

Typeset in Mendoza Roman and Frutiger
by Saxon Graphics Ltd, Derby

Printed and bound in Great Britain by CPI Group (UK) Ltd, Croydon CR0 4YY

INTRODUCTION

Welcome to the **Wisden Guide to International Cricket 2013**, which includes – in words and pictures, facts and figures – details of 200 leading players from the ten Test teams, telling you *how* they play as well as where they come from. You will also find a rundown on the players from the leading non-Test nations, and a handy guide to upcoming international fixtures. To help you identify everyone on the field or in the dressing-room, there are also photographs and short descriptions of the international umpires, coaches and referees. Finally there is a section containing records for all international matches – Tests, one-dayers and Twenty20s – with a country-by-country breakdown too.

Many of the profiles in the book are edited versions from ESPN Cricinfo's player pages, used with their kind permission. We have tried to include every player likely to appear in Test cricket in 2013 – but, like all selectors, we will undoubtedly have left out someone who should have been included. Details of anyone who managed to escape our selectorial net can be found on www.cricinfo.com.

The statistics have been updated to **September 17, 2012**, the end of the international season in England. The abbreviation 'S/R' in the batting tables denotes runs per 100 balls; in the bowling it shows the balls required to take each wicket. A dash (–) in the records usually indicates that full statistics are not available (such as details of fours and sixes, or balls faced, in all domestic matches).

Thanks are due to Christopher Lane of Wisden, Charlotte Atyeo, Emily Sweet and Nick Humphrey at Bloomsbury, Rob Brown and the typesetters at Saxon, Greg Heinimann who designed the new cover, and Cricinfo's technical wizards Robin Abrahams and Travis Basevi.

Finally, I couldn't have managed without the support of my wife Karina, who puts up with this annual intervention into our lives with amazing patience, and our sons Daniel and Mark.

Steven Lynch
September 2012

CONTENTS

PLAYER INDEX

PLAYER INDEX

ABDUR RAZZAK

Full name	**Khan Abdur Razzak**
Born	**June 15, 1982, Khulna**
Teams	**Khulna**
Style	**Left-hand bat, slow left-arm orthodox spinner**
Test debut	**Bangladesh v Australia at Chittagong 2005-06**
ODI debut	**Bangladesh v Hong Kong at Colombo 2004**
T20I debut	**Bangladesh v Zimbabwe at Khulna 2006-07**

THE PROFILE Another of Bangladesh's seemingly never-ending supply of left-arm spinners, Abdur Razzak first made his mark when he helped unheralded Khulna to their first-ever National Cricket League title in 2001-02. Quite tall, with a high action, "Raj" played for the A team against Zimbabwe early in 2004, and made the most of his opportunity with 15 wickets, including 7 for 17 in the third encounter on the batting paradise of Dhaka's old Bangabandhu National Stadium. He has an uncanny ability to pin batsmen down, although his action has often been questioned, most recently late in 2008, when he was suspended by the ICC after tests showed he sometimes flexed his elbow by almost twice the permitted 15 degrees. After remedial work, he was cleared to resume playing in March 2009. He was immediately hurried back, playing in the World Twenty20 in England then taking seven wickets in Bangladesh's rare one-day clean sweep against a depleted West Indies side in the Caribbean in July. Razzak had played his first Test in April 2006, against Australia on a turning track at Chittagong (even the Aussies played three spinners), but failed to take a wicket, and has continued to struggle for penetration in Tests, although he took 15 wickets in a domestic first-class game in 2011-12. But he has become an automatic one-day selection, maintaining a miserly economy-rate, and currently tops his country's wicket-taking lists in ODIs and Twenty20s. He was the only Bangladeshi signed up for the first year of the Indian Premier League in 2008, although he did not return for the second season.

THE FACTS Abdur Razzak took 5 for 29 in an ODI against Zimbabwe at Mirpur in December 2009 ... He took 7 for 11 (10 for 62 in the match) for Khulna at Sylhet in 2003-04 ... Razzak took a hat-trick – Bangladesh's second in ODIs, after one by Shahadat Hossain in 2006 – against Zimbabwe at Mirpur in December 2010 ... His best first-class figures are 8 for 123 for Khulna v Barisal in October 2011 – he added 7 for 70 in the second innings ...

THE FIGURES to 17.09.12   **ESPNcricinfo.com**

Batting & Fielding	M	Inns	NO	Runs	HS	Avge	S/R	100	50	4s	6s	Ct	St
Tests	9	17	5	214	43	17.83	65.64	0	0	30	4	3	0
ODIs	133	84	32	657	35	12.63	71.41	0	0	45	16	29	0
T20Is	21	14	7	27	9	3.85	51.92	0	0	1	0	9	0
First-class	56	93	14	1643	83	20.79	62.09	0	8	–	–	18	0

Bowling	M	Balls	Runs	Wkts	BB	Avge	RpO	S/R	5i	10m
Tests	9	2133	1185	18	3–93	65.83	3.33	118.50	0	0
ODIs	133	6963	5204	185	5–29	28.12	4.48	37.63	3	0
T20Is	21	486	538	33	4–16	16.30	6.64	14.72	0	0
First-class	56	12725	5934	197	8–123	30.12	2.79	64.59	7	2

ABDUR REHMAN

Full name	**Abdur Rehman**
Born	**March 1, 1980, Sialkot, Punjab**
Teams	**Sialkot, Habib Bank, Somerset**
Style	**Left-hand bat, slow left-arm orthodox spinner**
Test debut	**Pakistan v South Africa at Karachi 2007-08**
ODI debut	**Pakistan v West Indies at Faisalabad 2006-07**
T20I debut	**Pakistan v South Africa at Johannesburg 2006-07**

THE PROFILE Abdur Rehman made his international debut late in 2006 at the ripe old age of 26 (elderly considering the usual subcontinental trait of ruthlessly exposing youth to the world's best), and immediately did well, with two wickets in each of his first three one-dayers against West Indies. He's not a huge turner of the ball, but is accurate and consistent, and can exploit the rough well. He first gave notice of his ability back in 1999, with five and six wickets in successive matches for the Under-19s, but opportunities were limited by Pakistan's several spinners, most of them better batsmen. Rehman kept himself in contention with good domestic performances: in 2006-07 he was the leading bowler as Habib Bank won the Pentangular Cup, with 11 in an important victory over Sind. He missed the 2007 World Cup, but was recalled for the one-day series against Sri Lanka in Abu Dhabi. Then, with Pakistan looking for variety, Rehman got a Test chance against South Africa at home at the end of 2007, and took eight wickets on his debut – unusually, he took 4 for 105 in each innings – and finished the short series with 11 victims. After three years out of the Test side he returned in 2010-11, and grabbed his chance with 29 wickets in six Tests, including six West Indian scalps on a Basseterre "bunsen" which he said he'd like to roll up and carry around with him. He continued to prosper in 2012, forming a potent spin partnership with Saeed Ajmal. Rehman took 6 for 25 and 5 for 40 in successive innings as England were whitewashed at the start of the year, although he found Sri Lanka's batsmen a tougher proposition later on.

THE FACTS Abdur Rehman had identical figures of 4 for 105 in each innings of his Test debut, the first instance of this since Willie Bates took 2 for 43 in both innings for England v Australia at Melbourne in 1881-82 ... Rehman took 6 for 25 against England in Abu Dhabi in January 2012 ... He claimed 9 for 65 (14 for 101 in the match) for Somerset v Worcestershire at Taunton in September 2012 ... Rehman made 96 for Habib Bank v National Bank in January 2006 ...

THE FIGURES to 17.09.12   **espncricinfo.com**

Batting & Fielding	M	Inns	NO	Runs	HS	Avge	S/R	100	50	4s	6s	Ct	St
Tests	17	22	3	289	60	15.21	42.68	0	1	34	8	6	0
ODIs	25	18	5	104	31	8.00	52.52	0	0	8	1	5	0
T20Is	7	4	2	15	7	7.50	88.23	0	0	0	0	6	0
First-class	124	168	19	2591	96	17.38	–	0	12	–	–	55	0

Bowling	M	Balls	Runs	Wkts	BB	Avge	RpO	S/R	5i	10m
Tests	17	5354	2301	81	6–25	28.40	2.57	66.09	2	0
ODIs	25	1344	949	21	2–20	45.19	4.23	64.00	0	0
T20Is	7	150	174	11	2–7	15.81	6.96	13.63	0	0
First-class	124	27482	11941	463	9–65	25.79	2.60	59.35	23	5

ADNAN AKMAL

Full name	**Adnan Akmal**
Born	**March 13, 1985, Lahore**
Teams	**Lahore, Sui Northern Gas**
Style	**Right-hand bat, wicketkeeper**
Test debut	**Pakistan v South Africa at Dubai 2010-11**
ODI debut	**Pakistan v Zimbabwe at Bulawayo 2011**
T20I debut	**No T20Is yet**

THE PROFILE   One of three brothers to play – and keep wicket – for Pakistan, Adnan Akmal is usually considered the best pure keeper of the trio. He replaced his elder brother Kamran behind the stumps in October 2010, and took eight catches in his fourth Test, in New Zealand: it was a surprise when Faisalabad's Mohammad Salman was preferred for the Tests and one-dayers in the West Indies and Ireland that followed the 2011 World Cup, in which Kamran had had a chequered time behind the stumps. Adnan, though, was back in favour by the time of the Zimbabwe tour in September, and gave a polished performance as Pakistan won the only Test. He then produced an important innings in what was his first one-day international, briefly batting alongside his other brother, Umar. He seemed to make the position his own with some polished performances with the gloves in 2012 – in Tests at least, with Kamran latterly returning in the limited-overs games. But for a miscommunication back in 2004, Adnan might have played for Pakistan much earlier. By mistake, both he and Kamran were called up for a national camp before a one-day tournament and, after much confusion over who was actually wanted, Kamran was the one retained – even though Bob Woolmer, Pakistan's coach at the time, apparently thought Adnan was the country's best keeper. He kept plugging away on the domestic scene, improving his batting – he has now made two first-class hundreds in the Quaid-e-Azam Trophy – and the continuing errors of Kamran kept him in the frame. Eventually, with Kamran out of favour, Adnan received the summons to join the national squad. While he was travelling to the Gulf his brother Umar stepped in as Pakistan's wicketkeeper in a one-day international.

THE FACTS   Adnan Akmal followed his brothers Kamran and Umar in keeping wicket in international matches for Pakistan ... Adnan took seven catches in an innings (11 in the match) for Lahore Blues v Karachi Blues at Karachi in December 2004 ... He scored 120 for Sui Northern Gas against Customs at Islamabad in November 2009...

THE FIGURES to 17.09.12   **ESPncricinfo.com**

Batting & Fielding	M	Inns	NO	Runs	HS	Avge	S/R	100	50	4s	6s	Ct	St
Tests	16	21	5	440	61	27.50	44.89	0	2	55	0	47	8
ODIs	5	4	1	62	27	20.66	69.66	0	0	3	0	3	0
T20Is	0	0	–	–	–	–	–	–	–	–	–	–	–
First-class	96	145	15	3047	120	23.43	–	2	11	–	–	338	15

Bowling	M	Balls	Runs	Wkts	BB	Avge	RpO	S/R	5i	10m
Tests	16	0	–	–	–	–	–	–	–	–
ODIs	5	0	–	–	–	–	–	–	–	–
T20Is	0	0	–	–	–	–	–	–	–	–
First-class	96	0	–	–	–	–	–	–	–	–

AHMED SHEHZAD

Full name	**Ahmed Shehzad**
Born	**November 23, 1991, Lahore**
Teams	**Lahore, Habib Bank**
Style	**Right-hand bat, occasional legspinner**
Test debut	**No Tests yet**
ODI debut	**Australia v Pakistan at Dubai 2008-09**
T20I debut	**Australia v Pakistan at Dubai 2008-09**

THE PROFILE Ahmed Shehzad originally based his game on that of Ricky Ponting – not a bad role model – and had some success with this aggressive style in his early international outings. A solidly built right-hander with the ability to hit over the top, Shehzad was still only 19 when he hit 115 in a one-day international against New Zealand in February 2011, and added another hundred a couple of months later – but in between he endured a disappointing World Cup, his top score from five innings being just 13. He had made his first-class debut in January 2007, just two months after his 15th birthday, and in August 2007 he made 167 as Pakistan Under-19s chased down 342 to beat England at Derby (the home attack included Steven Finn and Chris Woakes, who have both since played for England). Shehzad followed that with some impressive performances at home, scoring 315 runs – with a highest of 105 – as Australia's Under-19s were thrashed 5-0. Another century followed in a youth Test against Bangladesh, and he carried that form into a triangular tournament in Sri Lanka, which Pakistan won. Early in 2009 he made the Test squad for the home series against Sri Lanka, although he didn't actually play, then played his first one-day international in Dubai shortly afterwards. Since then he's been confined to the shorter formats, despite consistent runs at first-class level at home – in 2010-11 he averaged 102.71 from six matches with three centuries (one a double), and the following season made 970 runs at 44.

THE FACTS Ahmed Shehzad was 19 when he scored 115 against New Zealand at Hamilton in February 2011: only Shahid Afridi, Imran Nazir and Salim Elahi have scored centuries at a younger age for Pakistan in ODIs ... Shehzad scored 254 for Habib Bank at Faisalabad in October 2010, and shortly afterwards made 123 and 109 not out for them at Sialkot ... He made 167 for Pakistan v England in an Under-19 Test at Derby in 2007 ...

THE FIGURES to 17.09.12   **ESPncricinfo.com**

Batting & Fielding	M	Inns	NO	Runs	HS	Avge	S/R	100	50	4s	6s	Ct	St
Tests	0	0	–	–	–	–	–	–	–	–	–	–	–
ODIs	19	19	1	477	115	26.50	67.56	2	0	52	6	7	0
T20Is	8	8	0	145	54	18.12	105.83	0	1	21	2	3	0
First-class	39	65	3	2805	254	45.24	62.23	7	14	396	22	36	0

Bowling	M	Balls	Runs	Wkts	BB	Avge	RpO	S/R	5i	10m
Tests	0	0	–	–	–	–	–	–	–	–
ODIs	19	15	20	0	–	–	8.00	–	0	0
T20Is	8	0	–	–	–	–	–	–	–	–
First-class	39	826	578	8	4–20	72.25	4.19	103.25	0	0

AIZAZ CHEEMA

Full name	**Aizaz Bin Ilyas Cheema**
Born	**September 5, 1979, Sargodha**
Teams	**Lahore, Pakistan International Airlines**
Style	**Right-hand bat, right-arm fast-medium bowler**
Test debut	**Pakistan v Zimbabwe at Bulawayo 2011**
ODI debut	**Pakistan v Zimbabwe at Bulawayo 2011**
T20I debut	**Pakistan v Zimbabwe at Harare 2011**

THE PROFILE Aizaz Cheema had to wait until he was 31 to get the call to play for Pakistan. Even then it looked as if he might not fulfil his dream, as after he was selected for the tour of the West Indies early in 2011 he was withdrawn from the squad, apparently after a doctor decided he was not fit enough. But he did make it onto the plane for the tour of Zimbabwe in September 2011, and shone in his first Test with four wickets in both innings: his match figures of 8 for 103 were Pakistan's second-best on debut. He continued to do well, taking nine wickets in two matches in Bangladesh, but then managed only one England scalp in three spin-dominated Tests in the UAE early in 2012. Cheema initially won his place on the back of a splendid 2010-11 domestic season – 58 wickets at 14.74, most of them for PIA. That included four six-fors in the space of three matches – two of them in the same game against Habib Bank – followed by seven in each innings against Karachi Blues. He started as an out-and-out speedster, capable of breaking the 90mph barrier – Umar Akmal once called him the fastest bowler he had faced in domestic cricket, adding "he swings it at pace too" – but he has throttled back in recent years and now takes a lot of wickets with a cunning slower delivery. He also has a decent yorker and, like most Pakistani bowlers reared on unforgiving tracks, can reverse-swing the ball. Cheema celebrated his 32nd birthday during his Test debut in Harare, but says: "Honestly speaking I didn't feel this fit at the age of 21 or 22. I couldn't run then what I can run now."

THE FACTS Aizaz Cheema's match figures of 8 for 103 were the best by a Pakistan bowler on Test debut after Mohammad Zahid's 11 for 130 against New Zealand at Rawalpindi in 1996-97 ... Cheema was the 11th bowler to take four wickets in each innings of his first Test ... He took 7 for 65 and 7 for 45 for PIA v Karachi Blues at Karachi in January 2011 ... His best first-class figures are 7 for 24, for PIA at Islamabad in November 2007 ...

THE FIGURES *to 17.09.12* ▪▪▪▪ **cricinfo.com**

Batting & Fielding	M	Inns	NO	Runs	HS	Avge	S/R	100	50	4s	6s	Ct	St
Tests	7	5	5	1	1*	–	4.34	0	0	0	0	1	0
ODIs	14	6	3	26	9*	8.66	57.77	0	0	2	0	2	0
T20Is	5	1	1	0	0*	–	0.00	0	0	0	0	0	0
First-class	70	68	29	345	33	8.84	–	0	0	–	–	14	0

Bowling	M	Balls	Runs	Wkts	BB	Avge	RpO	S/R	5i	10m
Tests	7	1200	638	20	4–24	31.90	3.19	60.00	0	0
ODIs	14	658	593	23	4–43	25.78	5.40	28.60	0	0
T20Is	5	102	116	8	4–30	14.50	6.82	12.75	0	0
First-class	70	10163	5457	244	7–24	22.36	3.22	41.65	15	4

HASHIM **AMLA**

Full name	**Hashim Mahomed Amla**
Born	**March 31, 1983, Durban, Natal**
Teams	**Dolphins**
Style	**Right-hand bat, occasional right-arm medium-pacer**
Test debut	**South Africa v India at Kolkata 2004-05**
ODI debut	**South Africa v Bangladesh at Chittagong 2007-08**
T20I debut	**South Africa v Australia at Brisbane 2008-09**

THE PROFILE An elegant, wristy right-hander with a fine temperament, Hashim Amla was the first South African of Indian descent to reach the Test team. His elevation was hardly a surprise after he reeled off four centuries in his first eight innings in 2004-05, after captaining the Dolphins (formerly Natal) at the tender age of 21. He made his Test debut against India late in 2004, but was not an instant success, with serious questions emerging about his technique as he mustered only 36 runs in four innings against England shortly afterwards, struggling with an ungainly crouched stance and a bat coming down from somewhere in the region of gully. But he made his second chance count, with 149 against New Zealand at Cape Town in April 2006, followed by big hundreds against New Zealand (again) and India in 2007-08, before a fine undefeated 104 helped save the 2008 Lord's Test. He came into his own in India early in 2010 with a monumental 253 not out to set up victory at Nagpur, following by valiant twin centuries in defeat at Kolkata. He was dominant in England in 2012, stroking South Africa's first triple-century at The Oval and adding another important hundred in the win at Lord's that guaranteed top spot in the ICC's Test rankings. He then made 150 in an ODI at Southampton. Not originally seen as a one-day player, after slamming 140 against Bangladesh late in 2008 he made 80 not out and 97 in consecutive victories over Australia to make his place safe, then flourished to the extent that by September 2012 he had the highest average of anyone with 2000 ODI runs. Amla is a devout Muslim, whose beard rivals Mohammad Yousuf's as the most impressive in the game.

THE FACTS Amla made 311 not out, South Africa's first Test triple-century, against England at The Oval in 2012 ... He scored 253 not out at Nagpur, and 114 and 123 not out at Kolkata in the two-Test series in India in February 2010: his series average of 490 has been exceeded only by England's Wally Hammond (563.00 v New Zealand in 1932-33) ... Amla's older brother Ahmed also plays for the Dolphins ...

THE FIGURES *to 17.09.12*   **ESPNcricinfo.com**

Batting & Fielding	M	Inns	NO	Runs	HS	Avge	S/R	100	50	4s	6s	Ct	St
Tests	62	108	9	4946	311*	49.95	51.63	16	23	627	6	56	0
ODIs	62	60	6	3216	150	59.55	91.72	10	19	318	17	23	0
T20Is	10	10	1	198	47*	22.00	122.22	0	0	24	3	4	0
First-class	153	254	24	11690	311*	50.82	–	36	57	–	–	121	0

Bowling	M	Balls	Runs	Wkts	BB	Avge	RpO	S/R	5i	10m
Tests	62	42	28	0	–	–	4.00	–	0	0
ODIs	62	0	–	–	–	–	–	–	–	–
T20Is	10	0	–	–	–	–	–	–	–	–
First-class	153	321	236	1	1–10	236.00	4.26	321.00	0	0

JAMES **ANDERSON**

ENGLAND

Full name	**James Michael Anderson**
Born	**July 30, 1982, Burnley, Lancashire**
Teams	**Lancashire**
Style	**Left-hand bat, right-arm fast-medium bowler**
Test debut	**England v Zimbabwe at Lord's 2003**
ODI debut	**England v Australia at Melbourne 2002-03**
T20I debut	**England v Australia at Sydney 2006-07**

THE PROFILE When the force is with him, James Anderson is capable of irresistible spells, seemingly able to swing the ball round corners at an impressive speed. New Zealand were blown away at Nottingham in 2008 (Anderson 7 for 43); the following May the West Indians looked clueless in Durham, while back at Trent Bridge in 2010 Pakistan's inexperienced batsmen could hardly lay a bat on him (5 for 54 and 6 for 17). He followed that with 24 wickets in the 2010-11 Ashes triumph, and 18 in the summer of 2012, despite not quite hitting his best form. There is still the odd bad day, when the ball isn't coming out quite right and refuses to swing: he can then sometimes look downcast, and the purists start murmuring that he seems to be looking at the ground at the moment of delivery, rather than down the pitch at the target as the MCC coaching manual advocates. Anderson had played only occasionally for Lancashire when he was hurried into England's one-day squad in Australia in 2002-03 as cover for Andy Caddick. He didn't have a number – or even a name – on his shirt, but ten overs for 12 runs in century heat at Adelaide earned him a World Cup spot. There was a five-for in his debut Test, against Zimbabwe in 2003, and a one-day hat-trick against Pakistan ... but then a stress fracture sidelined him for most of 2006. By the end of the following year, though, Anderson looked the part of pack leader again. His batting also steadily improved: he went 54 Test innings before collecting a duck, an unlikely England record, and at Cardiff in 2009 he survived for 69 nail-chewing minutes to help stave off defeat by Australia. He is also a superb fielder.

THE FACTS Anderson was the first man to take an ODI hat-trick for England, against Pakistan at The Oval in 2003 ... He took the first six wickets to fall on his way to 7 for 43 for England v New Zealand at Nottingham in 2008 ... Anderson went 54 Test innings before being out for a duck at The Oval in 2009, an English record; only AB de Villiers (78), Aravinda de Silva (75) and Clive Lloyd (58) have started with more duckless innings in Tests ...

THE FIGURES to 17.09.12   **ESPN**cricinfo.com

Batting & Fielding	M	Inns	NO	Runs	HS	Avge	S/R	100	50	4s	6s	Ct	St
Tests	73	98	37	692	34	11.34	37.83	0	0	85	2	43	0
ODIs	164	65	34	204	20*	6.58	41.97	0	0	14	0	44	0
T20Is	19	4	3	1	1*	1.00	50.00	0	0	0	0	3	0
First-class	139	167	64	1038	37*	10.07	–	0	0	–	–	75	0

Bowling	M	Balls	Runs	Wkts	BB	Avge	RpO	S/R	5i	10m
Tests	73	16183	8391	276	7–43	30.40	3.11	58.63	12	1
ODIs	164	8112	6781	222	5–23	30.54	5.01	36.54	1	0
T20Is	19	422	552	18	3–23	30.66	7.84	23.44	0	0
First-class	139	27495	14351	524	7–43	27.38	3.13	52.47	25	3

ASAD SHAFIQ

Full name	**Asad Shafiq**
Born	**January 28, 1986, Karachi**
Teams	**Karachi, Pakistan International Airlines**
Style	**Right-hand bat, occasional legspinner**
Test debut	**Pakistan v South Africa at Abu Dhabi 2010-11**
ODI debut	**Pakistan v Bangladesh at Dambulla 2010**
T20I debut	**Pakistan v New Zealand at Hamilton 2010-11**

THE PROFILE A solid right-hander with a compact technique reminiscent of Javed Miandad, arguably Pakistan's finest batsman, Asad Shafiq is a product of the Karachi tape-ball circuit. He made a fine start in first-class cricket, scoring a double-century in only his seventh match and falling just short of 1000 runs in his debut summer of 2007-08, making 926 at 57.87. Second-season syndrome kicked in, and his average dipped to 21 the following year – although he performed better in one-day games – but he roared back in 2009-10 to put his name firmly in the selectors' sights: 1244 runs at a fraction under 50, with four more hundreds. He played his first one-day internationals during the Asia Cup in Sri Lanka in mid-2010, and although he missed the Tests in England that followed he played in the one-day games which rounded off that fractious tour, looking good in scoring 50 at Headingley and 40 at The Oval. A Test debut followed on a placid pitch in Abu Dhabi: Shafiq made an unhurried 61, and added 83 in his next Test, to help Pakistan to a ten-wicket victory over New Zealand at Hamilton. The five players who reached 50 in that match before him got out before making it to 60 but, as Cricinfo reported, "Shafiq moved into the sixties in style, using his feet to Martin Guptill and lofting the ball over midwicket for four." He sat out the first few matches of the 2011 World Cup before finally getting a game and hitting 78 not out against Zimbabwe: 46 followed against Australia, then 30 in the semi-final defeat by India to show that his earlier omission was a mistake. Shafiq nailed down a Test place in 2012, following a maiden century against Bangladesh late the previous year with some solid displays against England, then an impressive double of 75 and 100 not out against Sri Lanka at Pallekele in July.

THE FACTS Asad Shafiq scored 223 in only his seventh first-class match, for Karachi Whites at Faisalabad in December 2007 ... He scored 181, and put on 431 for the second wicket with Yasir Hameed – who scored 300 – for North West Frontier Province against Baluchistan at Peshawar in March 2008 ...

THE FIGURES *to 17.09.12*　　　　　**ESPncricinfo.com**

Batting & Fielding	M	Inns	NO	Runs	HS	Avge	S/R	100	50	4s	6s	Ct	St
Tests	16	24	3	894	104	42.57	42.38	2	6	104	5	13	0
ODIs	35	34	3	930	78*	30.00	69.81	0	7	81	4	6	0
T20Is	10	10	0	192	38	19.20	103.78	0	0	19	2	3	0
First-class	53	91	8	3499	223	42.15	50.43	10	13	433	16	41	0

Bowling	M	Balls	Runs	Wkts	BB	Avge	RpO	S/R	5i	10m
Tests	16	0	–	–	–	–	–	–	–	–
ODIs	35	0	–	–	–	–	–	–	–	–
T20Is	10	0	–	–	–	–	–	–	–	–
First-class	53	68	66	0	–	–	5.82	–	0	0

RAVICHANDRAN **ASHWIN**

Full name	**Ravichandran Ashwin**
Born	**September 17, 1986, Madras (now Chennai)**
Teams	**Tamil Nadu, Chennai Super Kings**
Style	**Right-hand bat, offspinner**
Test debut	**India v West Indies at Delhi 2011-12**
ODI debut	**India v Sri Lanka at Harare 2010**
T20I debut	**India v Zimbabwe at Harare 2010**

THE PROFILE A tall offspinner with a high action, Ravichandran Ashwin made a superb start in international cricket. From the word go his stats have been eye-catching: in his maiden first-class season, 2006-07, he took 31 wickets at less than 20, with 11 of them coming against Baroda in only his fourth game. He showed promise with the bat as well the following season, although he was restricted by injury, and made his maiden first-class hundred in 2009-10. He was signed by Chennai Super Kings for the first IPL in 2008, and by the third instalment in 2010 proved to be the most economical regular bowler on view, often taking the new ball, and going for 6.1 an over, miserly in Twenty20 terms. Ashwin continued to perform consistently for Tamil Nadu, and captained them to the domestic one-day title in 2008-09. He was awarded a central contract that season but, with Harbhajan Singh the offspinner in possession, it was a long time before the selectors gave him a chance, particularly in Tests – even after some crafty one-day displays. But when Ashwin did get into the five-day side, against West Indies late in 2011, he immediately made it count, taking nine wickets in his first match, then adding nine more – and a century – in his third. After his eighth Test, in September 2012, he already had 49 wickets, was forming a potent spin partnership with left-armer Pragyan Ojha ... and was making Harbhajan look like yesterday's man. Not the most graceful mover in the field, Ashwin is working on his mobility, and confesses to being something of a cricket nerd: "I'm a big, big cricket fanatic. I just cannot stop thinking, talking cricket."

THE FACTS Ashwin took 6 for 31 and 6 for 54 against New Zealand at Hyderabad in August 2012 ... He took 6 for 47 in his first Test, and made 103 in his third, both against West Indies in 2011-12 ... Ashwin took 5 for 65 and 6 for 64 for Tamil Nadu v Baroda in Chennai in January 2007, in only his fourth first-class match ... He took a wicket (Tatenda Taibu of Zimbabwe) with his third ball in Twenty20 internationals ...

THE FIGURES *to 17.09.12*   **ESPncricinfo.com**

Batting & Fielding	M	Inns	NO	Runs	HS	Avge	S/R	100	50	4s	6s	Ct	St
Tests	8	12	3	353	103	39.22	73.23	1	1	44	4	2	0
ODIs	40	22	8	264	38	18.85	86.55	0	0	22	1	5	0
T20Is	11	3	2	36	17*	36.00	124.13	0	0	5	0	2	0
First-class	42	57	15	1523	107*	36.26	59.63	3	8	221	5	17	0

Bowling	M	Balls	Runs	Wkts	BB	Avge	RpO	S/R	5i	10m
Tests	8	2564	1305	49	6-31	26.63	3.05	52.32	5	1
ODIs	40	2143	1708	56	3-24	30.50	4.78	38.26	0	0
T20Is	11	258	336	7	1-22	48.00	7.81	36.85	0	0
First-class	42	11058	5074	183	6-31	27.72	2.75	60.42	16	4

AZHAR ALI

Full name	**Azhar Ali**
Born	**February 19, 1985, Lahore**
Teams	**Lahore, Khan Research Laboratories**
Style	**Right-hand bat, legspinner**
Test debut	**Pakistan v Australia at Lord's 2010**
ODI debut	**Pakistan v Ireland at Belfast 2011**
T20I debut	**No T20Is yet**

THE PROFILE Azhar Ali made steady progress in domestic cricket after a stuttering start in which he played only eight first-class matches in five seasons after his 2001-02 debut. Promotion to open paid off, though, and he made 409 runs at 68 in 2006-07 – with his first two hundreds – and improved on that in each of his next two seasons, good going in a country where opening has long been difficult. Azhar has a compact and correct technique, and although he initially had a few problems against the shorter ball he seemed to have addressed them by the end of the 2010 England tour, during which he was unlucky to miss a maiden Test century at The Oval, stranded on 92 after more than four hours' batting. Azhar started that long trip batting at No. 3, after the selectors decided they could do without Younis Khan and Mohammad Yousuf (although Yousuf was eventually called up), and although his inexperience showed at first he played two important innings – 30 and 51 – as Pakistan beat Australia in the second Test at Headingley. Once the dust settled from a fractious tour, Azhar continued to do well in Tests, although he was still not seen as a one-day player. He finally cracked the three-figure barrier against Sri Lanka in October 2011, and secured his place the following year with 157 against England in February. He added 157 and 136 in Sri Lanka later in the year, not long after improving his one-day stats with 96 and 81 not out against them. "The England series gave me a lot of confidence," said Azhar. "I am carrying on from there."

THE FACTS Azhar Ali scored 157 against England at Dubai in February 2012 – and 157 v Sri Lanka in Colombo in June ... After not making a century in his first nine first-class matches, spread over five seasons, he scored nine in his next 17 games ... Azhar took 14 for 128 for Lahore Greens v Azad Jammu & Kashmir in a Quaid-e-Azam Trophy Grade 2 (not first-class) match in October 2000 ...

THE FIGURES to 17.09.12   **ESPn**cricinfo.com

Batting & Fielding	M	Inns	NO	Runs	HS	Avge	S/R	100	50	4s	6s	Ct	St
Tests	24	44	4	1811	157	45.27	39.94	4	13	184	3	15	0
ODIs	12	12	3	441	96	49.00	67.95	0	4	39	1	2	0
T20Is	0	0	–	–	–	–	–	–	–	–	–	–	–
First-class	84	139	15	4795	157	38.66	–	15	23	–	–	67	0

Bowling	M	Balls	Runs	Wkts	BB	Avge	RpO	S/R	5i	10m
Tests	24	90	54	1	1–4	54.00	3.60	90.00	0	0
ODIs	12	48	41	0	–	–	5.12	–	0	0
T20Is	0	0	–	–	–	–	–	–	–	–
First-class	84	1347	871	26	4–34	33.50	3.87	51.80	1	0

GEORGE **BAILEY**

AUSTRALIA

Full name	**George John Bailey**
Born	**September 7, 1982, Launceston**
Teams	**Tasmania**
Style	**Right-hand bat**
Test debut	**No Tests yet**
ODI debut	**Australia v West Indies at Kingstown 2011-12**
T20I debut	**Australia v India at Sydney 2011-12**

THE PROFILE George Bailey caused a stir – and a footnote in history – when he was named as Australia's Twenty20 captain early in 2012. He hadn't played international cricket before, so became the first man to skipper the full Australian side on debut since Dave Gregory back in the very first Test of all in 1877. Bailey got the job after some adroit leadership of Tasmania, where he took the reins in 2009-10 after three years as Daniel Marsh's deputy. Tasmania won the one-day FR Cup in Bailey's first year in charge, when he was second in the runscoring lists with 538 at 60 – he was called up for the Australian one-day squad to play the Chappell-Hadlee series against New Zealand, but didn't make the starting XI – and in 2010-11 they won the Sheffield Shield too. His early international results were encouraging, although there were, inevitably, murmurs from some who doubted his right to be in the side. Bailey had been a consistent performer in the Tasmanian middle order for some years: he made 673 Shield runs in 2008-09, after 734 the previous season. After his Twenty20 international baptism he was included in the ODI side too, and made some useful contributions throughout 2012 – including 65 against England at The Oval, then an important unbeaten 57 as Pakistan were downed in Sharjah at the end of August. In July John Inverarity, Australia's national selector, named Bailey, Peter Forrest and David Hussey as "the three we've invested opportunity in over the last few months" with a view to Test selection – which, given that Forrest then struggled in England and Hussey is 35, could well mean that Bailey is next in line for a baggy green cap.

THE FACTS Bailey was only the second man, after Dave Gregory in the first-ever Test in 1877, to captain Australia in his first international match ... He made 160 not out for Tasmania v Victoria at Hobart in February 2011 ... Bailey has played for Scotland, and scored 123 not out against Warwickshire at Edgbaston in 2010 ... His great-great-great-grandfather was part of the Australian team which toured England in 1878 without playing a Test ...

THE FIGURES *to 17.09.12*   ᴇsᴘᴨcricinfo.com

Batting & Fielding	M	Inns	NO	Runs	HS	Avge	S/R	100	50	4s	6s	Ct	St
Tests	0	0	–	–	–	–	–	–	–	–	–	–	–
ODIs	13	13	2	441	65	40.09	77.50	0	3	31	6	10	0
T20Is	7	7	2	119	42	23.80	116.66	0	0	9	3	2	0
First-class	83	149	15	5417	160*	40.42	55.98	14	27	–	–	77	0

Bowling	M	Balls	Runs	Wkts	BB	Avge	RpO	S/R	5i	10m
Tests	0	0	–	–	–	–	–	–	–	–
ODIs	13	0	–	–	–	–	–	–	–	–
T20Is	7	0	–	–	–	–	–	–	–	–
First-class	83	84	46	0	–	–	3.28	–	0	0

JONNY **BAIRSTOW**

Full name	**Jonathan Marc Bairstow**
Born	**September 26, 1989, Bradford**
Teams	**Yorkshire**
Style	**Right-hand bat, wicketkeeper**
Test debut	**England v West Indies at Lord's 2012**
ODI debut	**England v India at Cardiff 2011**
T20I debut	**England v West Indies at The Oval 2011**

THE PROFILE A star was born – or so it seemed – in the closing stages of the 2011 season. England looked up against it, needing 75 from 50 balls to win the final ODI against India at Cardiff, when the debutant Jonny Bairstow strolled in. Seemingly unfazed, he clouted 41 from 21 balls, including three sixes. The second one, off the medium-pacer Vinay Kumar, disappeared into the River Taff, and third sailed out of the ground too. "I think we've just found a player," said Alastair Cook. In 2012 Bairstow made his Test debut, and encountered a few problems against West Indian bouncers – but, recalled against South Africa when Kevin Pietersen was dropped, he lit up Lord's with two fine knocks of 95 and 54, full of his trademark whipped on-drives. The son of the former England player David Bairstow, Jonny is also a red-haired wicketkeeper, though good enough to play solely as a batsman. He was the inaugural Wisden Schools Cricketer of the Year in 2007, and signed a full-time contract with Yorkshire two years later. He made an immediate impression with 82 on first-class debut against Somerset in June, and added five more fifties that season. He went close to 1000 first-class runs in 2010, but a century still eluded him – something he put right in fine style against Nottinghamshire in May 2011, converting his maiden ton into 205. Three more hundreds followed, including one in 81 balls in a one-dayer against Middlesex not long before he got the England call. That stirring debut followed: the only sadness was that his father wasn't there to see it. David Bairstow took his own life early in 1998, when Jonny was just eight.

THE FACTS Bairstow made 205 for Yorkshire v Nottinghamshire at Trent Bridge in May 2005 ... He scored 41 not out from 21 balls in his first Twenty20 international, against India at Cardiff in September 2011 ... Bairstow hit 50 and 109 not out for England Lions v Sri Lanka A at Scarborough in August 2011 ... His late father David played four Tests and 21 ODIs for England between 1979 and 1984 ...

THE FIGURES *to 17.09.12* ≡**cricinfo.com**

Batting & Fielding	M	Inns	NO	Runs	HS	Avge	S/R	100	50	4s	6s	Ct	St
Tests	4	6	1	187	95	37.40	57.18	0	2	27	0	2	0
ODIs	7	6	1	119	41*	23.80	76.77	0	0	9	3	3	0
T20Is	10	7	3	110	60*	27.50	107.84	0	1	7	2	11	0
First-class	61	102	19	3861	205	46.51	–	7	26	–	–	122	5

Bowling	M	Balls	Runs	Wkts	BB	Avge	RpO	S/R	5i	10m
Tests	4	0	–	–	–	–	–	–	–	–
ODIs	7	0	–	–	–	–	–	–	–	–
T20Is	10	0	–	–	–	–	–	–	–	–
First-class	61	0	–	–	–	–	–	–	–	–

ADRIAN **BARATH**

Full name	**Adrian Boris Barath**
Born	**April 14, 1990, Chaguanas, Trinidad**
Teams	**Trinidad & Tobago**
Style	**Right-hand bat, occasional offspinner**
Test debut	**West Indies v Australia at Brisbane 2009-10**
ODI debut	**West Indies v Zimbabwe at Providence 2009-10**
T20I debut	**West Indies v Zimbabwe at Port-of-Spain 2009-10**

THE PROFILE Adrian Barath, a diminutive opener, was long seen as one of the Caribbean's brightest batting talents, and fulfilled that promise with a superb Test-debut century at Brisbane in November 2009. He was only 19, and became West Indies' youngest centurion, breaking a record previously held by George Headley. Barath cut and carved like a veteran – but unfortunately his team-mates could muster only 73 runs between them, and West Indies still lost heavily. Barath's batting is based on orthodoxy: "Normally players begin by hitting across the line, but I was playing straight without anyone teaching me," he explained. "Maybe it was because of TV. I used to watch a lot and try and emulate what I saw." One of the best examples of those he was watching, Brian Lara, became an early mentor to his fellow Trinidadian. Barath was originally chosen for the series against Bangladesh in mid-2009, but joined the senior players in boycotting the matches in a row over contracts. Earlier in 2009 he had showed his mettle by making 132 against England for West Indies A in St Kitts, sharing a partnership of 262 with Lendl Simmons. Not long after that Barath – who hit centuries in his second and third first-class matches when still a few months short of his 17th birthday – made a career-best 192 against the Leeward Islands. Barath had some injury problems after his stunning debut – he missed the 2011 World Cup after tweaking a hamstring – but returned to the side afterwards. He had a hard time in England in 2012, failing to build on some solid starts, and lost his place when Chris Gayle returned to the fold for the home series against New Zealand that followed. However, Barath remains one for the future.

THE FACTS Barath was the 12th man to make a century in his first Test for West Indies, scoring 104 v Australia at Brisbane in November 2009 ... At 19 years 228 days he was West Indies' youngest Test century-maker, beating George Headley (20 years 230 days in 1929-30) ... After making 73 on his first-class debut in January 2007 when still only 16, Barath hit 131 in his second match and 101 in his third ...

THE FIGURES to 17.09.12   **ESPNcricinfo.com**

Batting & Fielding	M	Inns	NO	Runs	HS	Avge	S/R	100	50	4s	6s	Ct	St
Tests	15	28	0	657	104	23.46	47.33	1	4	93	5	13	0
ODIs	14	14	1	394	113	30.30	64.37	1	1	43	3	3	0
T20Is	2	2	0	23	15	11.50	58.97	0	0	3	0	1	0
First-class	46	81	4	2714	192	35.24	–	7	14	–	–	32	0

Bowling	M	Balls	Runs	Wkts	BB	Avge	RpO	S/R	5i	10m
Tests	15	6	4	0	–	–	4.00	–	0	0
ODIs	14	0	–	–	–	–	–	–	–	–
T20Is	2	0	–	–	–	–	–	–	–	–
First-class	46	12	4	0	–	–	2.00	–	0	0

CARLTON **BAUGH**

Full name	**Carlton Seymour Baugh junior**
Born	**June 23, 1982, Kingston, Jamaica**
Teams	**Jamaica**
Style	**Right-hand bat, wicketkeeper**
Test debut	**West Indies v Australia at Port-of-Spain 2002-03**
ODI debut	**West Indies v Australia at Kingston 2002-03**
T20I debut	**West Indies v New Zealand at Auckland 2008-09**

THE PROFILE Jamaica's slender wicketkeeper/batsman Carlton Baugh has been a consistent scorer – he has 11 first-class hundreds to his name – at every level except the highest, where his attempts at aggression often cost him his wicket. He was tried as Ridley Jacobs's replacement as early as 2003, but did little with the bat beyond a neat 68 against England at Old Trafford the following year. The selectors turned to Trinidad's Denesh Ramdin, a better technical keeper than the rather manufactured Baugh, but on the face of it an inferior batsman: but Ramdin confounded the issue by producing several good innings, including 166 against England early in 2009. By then, though, Ramdin's keeping was going off the boil, and the following year he was dropped. After two run-heavy domestic seasons Baugh returned for the rain-soaked tour of Sri Lanka late in 2010, and did enough in his first Tests for more than six years to retain his place for the 2011 World Cup, even though he had played 24 ODIs in those intervening years without ever passing 30. However, Baugh injured a hamstring just before the tournament started and was replaced by Devon Thomas, who did well. But afterwards Thomas went down with chickenpox, and Baugh got the gloves back: he made an important 27 in a low-scoring first Test against India, which West Indies won, and 60 in another modest total in the third Test. But the big scores resolutely refused to come, and despite some slick displays behind the stumps Baugh lost his place again when the selectors returned to Ramdin for the 2012 England tour.

THE FACTS Baugh has reached 150 three times in first-class cricket, two of them for West Indies on tour: 158 not out v Free State at Bloemfontein in December 2003, and 150 not out v Derbyshire in August 2004 – he also made 152 for Jamaica v Trinidad in February 2005 ... Baugh took five catches in an innings – and eight in the match – for Jamaica v Barbados at Bridgetown in March 2008 ... His father Carlton also played for Jamaica ...

THE FIGURES to 17.09.12   **ESPN**cricinfo.com

Batting & Fielding	M	Inns	NO	Runs	HS	Avge	S/R	100	50	4s	6s	Ct	St
Tests	21	36	2	610	68	17.94	50.00	0	3	71	4	43	5
ODIs	47	35	11	482	49	20.08	67.03	0	0	37	7	39	12
T20Is	3	3	0	10	7	3.33	83.33	0	0	1	0	0	0
First-class	95	158	18	4569	158*	32.63	–	12	19	–	–	188	23

Bowling	M	Balls	Runs	Wkts	BB	Avge	RpO	S/R	5i	10m
Tests	21	0	–	–	–	–	–	–	–	–
ODIs	47	0	–	–	–	–	–	–	–	–
T20Is	3	0	–	–	–	–	–	–	–	–
First-class	95	0	–	–	–	–	–	–	–	–

MICHAEL **BEER**

Full name **Michael Anthony Beer**
Born **June 9, 1984, Malvern, Victoria**
Teams **Western Australia**
Style **Right-hand bat, slow left-arm orthodox spinner**
Test debut **Australia v England at Sydney 2010-11**
ODI debut **No ODIs yet**
T20I debut **No T20Is yet**

THE PROFILE A tall left-arm spinner who toiled at club level in Melbourne for several years without getting past Victoria's second eleven, Michael Beer moved to Perth during the 2010 off-season, aged 26, as Western Australia searched for a front-line spinner. He was soon tried in the state team, settling in well without looking likely to run through sides: he has a nice high action, but doesn't spin the ball a huge amount. Beer claimed three wickets on first-class debut – ironically against Victoria – then in his third match took five against the England tourists, although he also leaked runs at more than five an over. One of his victims was Kevin Pietersen, who was perceived to have a problem with left-arm spinners – but it was still a major shock when Beer was named in the squad for the third Test at Perth in December 2010, after only five first-class matches. Journalists and headline-writers had a field day: "In times of stress the English make a cup of tea, the Aussies go for a Beer," joked Vic Marks in *The Observer*. Beer didn't play at the WACA, or at the MCG, but he made his debut in the final Test at Sydney, traditionally a good ground for the spinners. He looked steady, but no world-beater, finishing with the wicket of Paul Collingwood for 112: his figures would have been appreciably better if he hadn't overstepped in his third over before having the prolific Alastair Cook caught at mid-on. Cook, 46 at the time, sailed on to 189. In his second Test, at Port-of-Spain in April 2012, Beer was given the new ball – and soon surprised Adrian Barath with a well-disguised arm ball. He looks set to push Nathan Lyon for a Test spot in 2013.

THE FACTS Beer played for Australia after only seven first-class matches, in which he'd taken 16 wickets ... In Trinidad in April 2012 Beer became the first spinner to open the bowling for Australia in the first innings of a Test since Bill O'Reilly at Trent Bridge in 1938 ... Beer took 7 for 46 for Western Australia v New South Wales at Perth in February 2012 ... He played a few club games for St Kilda in Melbourne alongside Shane Warne ...

THE FIGURES to 17.09.12   **espncricinfo.com**

Batting & Fielding	M	Inns	NO	Runs	HS	Avge	S/R	100	50	4s	6s	Ct	St
Tests	2	3	1	6	2*	3.00	21.42	0	0	0	0	1	0
ODIs	0	0	–	–	–	–	–	–	–	–	–	–	–
T20Is	0	0	–	–	–	–	–	–	–	–	–	–	–
First-class	24	36	16	227	29*	11.35	31.83	0	0	20	0	13	0

Bowling	M	Balls	Runs	Wkts	BB	Avge	RpO	S/R	5i	10m
Tests	2	406	117	3	2–56	59.33	2.63	135.33	0	0
ODIs	0	0	–	–	–	–	–	–	–	–
T20Is	0	0	–	–	–	–	–	–	–	–
First-class	24	4926	2433	62	7–46	39.24	2.96	79.45	1	0

IAN **BELL**

Full name	**Ian Ronald Bell**
Born	**April 11, 1982, Walsgrave, Coventry**
Teams	**Warwickshire**
Style	**Right-hand bat, right-arm medium-pace bowler**
Test debut	**England v West Indies at The Oval 2004**
ODI debut	**England v Zimbabwe at Harare 2004-05**
T20I debut	**England v Pakistan at Bristol 2006**

THE PROFILE Ian Bell was earmarked for greatness long before he was drafted into the England squad in New Zealand in 2001-02, aged 19, as cover for the injured Mark Butcher. Tenacious and technically sound, with a cover-drive to die for, Bell is in the mould of Michael Atherton, who was burdened with similar expectations on his debut a generation earlier and was similarly adept at leaving the ball outside off. Bell had played only 13 first-class matches when called into that England squad, and his form dipped at first. He finally made his Test debut against West Indies in August 2004, stroking 70 at The Oval, before returning the following summer to lift his average to an obscene 297 against Bangladesh. Such rich pickings soon ceased: Bell mustered just 171 runs in the 2005 Ashes. But he bounced back better for the experience, collecting 313 runs in Pakistan, including a classy century at Faisalabad. And when Pakistan toured in 2006, Bell repeated the dose, with elegant hundreds in each of the first three Tests. He improved his record against the Aussies in 2006-07 without going on to the big score, then in 2008 made 199 against South Africa at Lord's. He missed the start of the 2009 Ashes, returning only when Kevin Pietersen was injured, but has been very productive since: after 140 at Durban, plus two tons against Bangladesh, he hit a cathartic century in the Ashes triumph at Sydney in January 2011, and four hundreds – one a double – in the home summer against Sri Lanka and India. He had a quieter time in Tests in 2012, but made up for it with 126 against West Indies after being moved back up to open in one-dayers.

THE FACTS After three Tests, and innings of 70, 65 not out and 162 not out, Bell's average was 297.00; he raised that to 303.00 before Australia started getting him out – only Lawrence Rowe (336), David Lloyd (308) and "Tip" Foster (306) have ever had better averages in Test history ... Bell has made Test centuries on eight different English grounds (including Cardiff but, oddly, not yet his home ground of Edgbaston): no-one else has managed more than six ... Bell made 262 not out for Warwickshire v Sussex at Horsham in May 2004 ...

THE FIGURES to 17.09.12   **espncricinfo.com**

Batting & Fielding	M	Inns	NO	Runs	HS	Avge	S/R	100	50	4s	6s	Ct	St
Tests	80	135	17	5527	235	46.83	51.26	16	34	636	23	63	0
ODIs	119	115	10	3783	126*	36.02	74.54	2	23	360	20	38	0
T20Is	7	7	1	175	60*	29.16	119.86	0	1	21	2	4	0
First-class	210	351	39	14191	262*	45.48	–	39	74	–	–	149	0

Bowling	M	Balls	Runs	Wkts	BB	Avge	RpO	S/R	5i	10m
Tests	80	108	76	1	1–33	76.00	4.22	108.00	0	0
ODIs	119	88	88	6	3–9	14.66	6.00	14.66	0	0
T20Is	7	–	–	–	–	–	–	–	–	–
First-class	210	2827	1598	47	4–4	34.00	3.39	60.14	0	0

TINO **BEST**

Full name	**Tino La Bertram Best**
Born	**August 26, 1981, Richmond Gap, St Michael, Barbados**
Teams	**Barbados**
Style	**Right-hand bat, right-arm fast bowler**
Test debut	**West Indies v Australia at Bridgetown, 2003**
ODI debut	**West Indies v Bangladesh at Kingstown, 2004**
T20I debut	**No T20Is yet**

THE PROFILE If cricket had prizes for enthusiasm and lung-busting effort, Tino Best would win every time. He charges in, confident and energetic, and tries to bowl as fast as possible. In his early days he was likened to a previous Barbadian great, Wes Hall. Best is a bit less fast and a lot less tall, so the comparison is a flattering one – but he was originally capable of nudging the speedo over 90mph, and has tightened his control from his wild and woolly early days: he was banned from bowling in a Test in Sri Lanka in 2005 after delivering three beamers. He came to prominence in 2003, topping the domestic averages with 39 wickets, and played against Australia at home in Barbados that May, without taking a wicket. He impressed in England in 2004, at least with his enthusiasm – his figures, as West Indies slumped to seven defeats out of eight, weren't great, and he was memorably psyched out by Andrew Flintoff while batting at Lord's: jokingly advised to "Mind the windows, Tino," Best tried to blast the next ball into the pavilion, and was immediately stumped. He then injured his back and missed the rest of the tour. He had stints in the unauthorised Indian Cricket League and with Yorkshire, and briefly reappeared in West Indian colours in 2009, when the senior players fell out with the board. That seemed to be that, but he made a surprise return in England in 2012, after injuries to other bowlers, and biffed 95 – the best Test score by a No. 11 – at Edgbaston. He then did well at home against New Zealand, to show the Best might still be to come.

THE FACTS Best made 95, the highest Test score by a No. 11, against England at Edgbaston in June 2012 (the previous record was 75, by Zaheer Khan of India) ... Best was banned from bowling after sending down a beamer to Sri Lanka's Rangana Herath at Kandy in July 2005, only the third time this had happened in a Test ... Best took 4 for 35, still his best figures in ODIs, in his first match, against Bangladesh at Kingstown in May 2004 ... He took 7 for 33 (11 for 66 in the match) for Barbados v Windward Islands in January 2004 ...

THE FIGURES *to 17.09.12*

Batting & Fielding	M	Inns	NO	Runs	HS	Avge	S/R	100	50	4s	6s	Ct	St
Tests	16	25	4	291	95	13.85	56.28	0	1	37	3	2	0
ODIs	15	11	5	67	24	11.16	68.36	0	0	6	0	3	0
T20Is	0	0	–	–	–	–	–	–	–	–	–	–	–
First-class	92	122	22	1272	95	12.72	–	0	2	–	–	30	0

Bowling	M	Balls	Runs	Wkts	BB	Avge	RpO	S/R	5i	10m
Tests	16	2433	1484	34	4–46	43.64	3.65	71.55	0	0
ODIs	15	707	621	19	4–35	32.68	5.27	37.21	0	0
T20Is	0	0	–	–	–	–	–	–	–	–
First-class	92	12257	7599	275	7–33	27.63	3.71	44.57	10	0

RAVI **BOPARA**

Full name	**Ravinder Singh Bopara**
Born	**May 4, 1985, Forest Gate, London**
Teams	**Essex**
Style	**Right-hand bat, right-arm medium-pace bowler**
Test debut	**England v Sri Lanka at Kandy 2007-08**
ODI debut	**England v Australia at Sydney 2006-07**
T20I debut	**England v New Zealand at Manchester 2008**

THE PROFILE Ravi Bopara has had an up-and-down Test career. Uniquely he followed three successive ducks (against Sri Lanka late in 2007, including an embarrassing first-ball run-out) with three successive centuries against West Indies in 2009, despite being dropped after his maiden hundred in Barbados. Those hundreds meant he was inked in at No. 3 against Australia for the 2009 Ashes – helping usher Michael Vaughan into retirement – but his wristy technique proved too loose, and he made only 105 runs in seven innings before being dropped. His usually excellent fielding wavered too, as he dropped a couple of relative sitters, while his energetic medium-pacers proved toothless. He reacted to the chop by making 201 for Essex against Surrey, and was back for the chastening one-day series against Australia. After that, 60 against South Africa in the 2011 World Cup and 96 against India at The Oval in September helped secure a one-day place, but in 2012 he played one Test against South Africa then dropped out for personal reasons, only returning in the end-of-season one-dayers. Bopara has packed a lot in since he signed for Essex at 17 in 2002. A good county season in 2006 won him a place in the Academy squad which was based in Perth during that winter's Ashes whitewash. When Kevin Pietersen broke a rib in the first match of the one-day tournament, Bopara was summoned: not worried about having such big boots to fill, he made his debut in front of the Sydney Hill, and bowled Australia's "finisher", Michael Hussey, as England began the amazing turnaround that eventually won them that series.

THE FACTS Bopara hit 229 for Essex v Northamptonshire at Chelmsford in June 2007, putting on 320 for the third wicket with Grant Flower ... He made 104 (at Bridgetown), 143 (at Lord's) and 108 (at Chester-le-Street) in successive Test innings, all against West Indies, in 2009; his previous three Test innings had all been ducks ... Bopara scored 201 not out for Essex in the English 50-over competition at Leicester in June 2008 ...

THE FIGURES to 17.09.12   **ESPN**cricinfo.com

Batting & Fielding	M	Inns	NO	Runs	HS	Avge	S/R	100	50	4s	6s	Ct	St
Tests	13	19	1	575	143	31.94	52.89	3	0	71	2	6	0
ODIs	83	77	15	1899	96	30.62	75.68	0	10	161	19	25	0
T20Is	21	19	2	364	59	21.41	99.45	0	2	29	3	4	0
First-class	129	215	27	7895	229	41.99	53.20	22	30	–	–	74	0

Bowling	M	Balls	Runs	Wkts	BB	Avge	RpO	S/R	5i	10m
Tests	13	434	290	1	1–39	290.00	4.00	434.00	0	0
ODIs	83	965	745	20	4–38	37.25	4.63	48.25	0	0
T20Is	21	118	129	9	4–10	14.33	6.55	13.11	0	0
First-class	129	9088	5836	134	5–75	43.55	3.85	67.82	1	0

TRENT **BOULT**

Full name	**Trent Alexander Boult**
Born	**July 22, 1989, Rotorua**
Teams	**Northern Districts**
Style	**Right-hand bat, left-arm fast-medium bowler**
Test debut	**New Zealand v Australia at Hobart 2011-12**
ODI debut	**New Zealand v West Indies at Basseterre 2012**
T20I debut	**No T20Is yet**

THE PROFILE   Fast bowler Trent Boult has been viewed as an international prospect ever since he was included, as a 17-year-old, in the New Zealand A winter training squad in 2007. One reason the selectors like the look of him is that he's a left-armer, and New Zealand have always been fond of those, dating back to the likes of Richard Collinge, Graham Troup and Geoff Allott. Boult is also fairly quick, and has the potential to be a handy batsman too. He was chosen for the A-team tour of India late in 2008, making his first-class debut in Chennai before he'd played at home (his maiden wicket was Suresh Raina). Back in New Zealand some good one-day displays earned him a trip to Australia for the Chappell-Hadlee one-day series early in 2009, although he didn't actually play. A quiet home season with Northern Districts followed, but he came to the fore in 2010-11 with 32 wickets at 25.34, which helped earn him a national contract for the first time. And late in 2011 he got a Test chance when Daniel Vettori was injured – and played his part with four wickets in a rare Kiwi victory over Australia. He continued on the fringes of the side in 2012, the highlight coming when he knocked back Sachin Tendulkar's middle stump in the Hyderabad Test in August. Boult's favourite cricketer is Wasim Akram – a pretty good role model for an aspiring left-arm quick – and, cricket aside, he hopes to become a chef and open his own chain of restaurants across New Zealand.

THE FACTS   Boult took 5 for 58 for Northern Districts v Otago in Dunedin in November 2008, in his first first-class match in New Zealand (his third overall) ... In 2010-11 he took 5 for 48 against Wellington and 5 for 35 v Auckland ... In the 2007-08 Under-19 World Cup he took 7 for 20 as Malaysia, the hosts, were shot out for 47 in Johor ... Boult's brother Jonothon has also played for ND ...

THE FIGURES *to 17.09.12*   **ESPncricinfo.com**

Batting & Fielding	M	Inns	NO	Runs	HS	Avge	S/R	100	50	4s	6s	Ct	St
Tests	6	10	7	83	33*	27.66	65.87	0	0	8	3	2	0
ODIs	3	3	2	7	5	7.00	58.33	0	0	0	0	1	0
T20Is	0	0	–	–	–	–	–	–	–	–	–	–	–
First-class	32	42	13	391	46	13.48	45.57	0	0	44	12	14	0

Bowling	M	Balls	Runs	Wkts	BB	Avge	RpO	S/R	5i	10m
Tests	6	1037	621	17	3–29	36.52	3.59	61.00	0	0
ODIs	3	159	121	3	2–45	40.33	4.56	53.00	0	0
T20Is	0	0	–	–	–	–	–	–	–	–
First-class	32	5436	2668	96	5–35	27.79	2.94	56.62	5	0

DOUG **BRACEWELL**

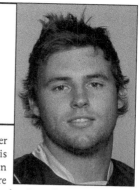

Full name	**Douglas Andrew John Bracewell**
Born	**September 28, 1990, Tauranga, Bay of Plenty**
Teams	**Central Districts, Delhi Daredevils**
Style	**Right-hand bat, right-arm fast-medium bowler**
Test debut	**New Zealand v Zimbabwe at Bulawayo 2011-12**
ODI debut	**New Zealand v Zimbabwe at Harare 2011-12**
T20I debut	**New Zealand v Zimbabwe at Harare 2011-12**

THE PROFILE Doug Bracewell, a brawny fast-medium bowler who is also a handy batsman, comes with a fine pedigree: his father Brendon bowled fast for New Zealand; his uncle John played for the national side and later coached them; two more uncles and a cousin also played first-class cricket. That all meant that Doug had a lot to live up to when he was himself promoted – on promise rather than performance – into the national side late in 2011. But he confirmed that promise by taking nine wickets for just 60 runs in the match as New Zealand pulled off a rare victory at Hobart in December, their first Test win in Australia for 26 years. Bracewell had not expected to be playing Tests so soon: on the preceding trip to Zimbabwe he was initially viewed as more of a one-day player. But he took four wickets in his first two Twenty20 internationals there, and three in his first two ODIs, then injuries to others let him in for the one-off Test at Bulawayo, and he took 5 for 85 in the second innings. Bracewell finished an impressive first year of Test cricket with 40 wickets in 11 matches. Ironically he found it harder going in limited-overs games after that promising start, although his batting – which once brought him 97 in a first-class match against Wellington – should ensure he remains in the mix. Bracewell is named after the great Australian batsman Doug Walters, one of his father's favourite players – although the son admits "I don't have a favourite Aussie." He was, unsurprisingly, spotted at an early age: he and his cousin Michael were in the squad for the Under-19 World Cup in 2010.

THE FACTS Bracewell took 6 for 40 on the final day – including Michael Clarke and Mike Hussey for ducks – at Hobart in December 2012, as New Zealand won a Test in Australia for the first time since 1985-86 ... He scored 97 for Central Districts v Wellington at Napier in November 2010 ... Bracewell's father Brendon won six Test caps for New Zealand as a fast bowler, while his uncle John played 41 as an offspinning allrounder, and later coached the national side ...

THE FIGURES to 17.09.12

cricinfo.com

Batting & Fielding	M	Inns	NO	Runs	HS	Avge	S/R	100	50	4s	6s	Ct	St
Tests	11	20	2	225	43	12.50	43.60	0	0	32	2	3	0
ODIs	6	4	1	14	8*	4.66	48.27	0	0	0	0	1	0
T20Is	8	3	1	31	20	15.50	172.22	0	0	0	3	3	0
First-class	29	45	6	750	97	19.23	49.96	0	3	110	8	10	0

Bowling	M	Balls	Runs	Wkts	BB	Avge	RpO	S/R	5i	10m
Tests	11	2011	1121	40	6–40	28.02	3.34	50.27	2	0
ODIs	6	336	281	7	3–55	40.14	5.01	48.00	0	0
T20Is	8	167	263	7	3–25	37.57	9.44	23.85	0	0
First-class	29	5036	2991	86	6–40	34.77	3.56	58.55	3	0

DARREN **BRAVO**

Full name	**Darren Michael Bravo**
Born	**February 6, 1989, Santa Cruz, Trinidad**
Teams	**Trinidad & Tobago**
Style	**Left-hand bat, occasional medium-pacer**
Test debut	**West Indies v Sri Lanka at Galle 2010-11**
ODI debut	**West Indies v India at Kingston 2009**
T20I debut	**West Indies v Zimbabwe at Port-of-Spain 2009-10**

THE PROFILE Darren Bravo is the younger half-brother of allrounder Dwayne, but although he can bowl a bit it is his batting – and quicksilver fielding, like Dwayne's – which aroused the interest of the selectors. A left-hander, Bravo junior has a style eerily reminiscent of Brian Lara – not a bad role model. "There are some similarities, like the batting technique, and they look alike a bit," said Chris Gayle, his first international captain. Bravo is actually a distant relative of Lara's, on his mother's side, and, like Lara, was born in Santa Cruz in Trinidad. "I go out there and play my game, the Darren Bravo game," he says, "and if in the eyes of the people it looks like Lara, then that is their judgment. At the end of the day it is just my game." Bravo scored 605 runs at 45 in 2008-09, his first full season for Trinidad & Tobago, including centuries against Barbados and the Windward Islands. This pushed him to the fringes of the West Indian side, and he made his debut alongside Dwayne in the short one-day series against India in June, scoring 19 and 21 in the only two innings the weather allowed him. Later in 2010 he made his Test debut in Sri Lanka, scoring half-centuries in all three matches, and really came of age the following year, extending his maiden Test century in October to 195 against Bangladesh, and following that up with lip-smacking innings of 136 and 166 against sterner foes, India. He had a few problems against the moving ball in England early in 2012, then picked up a groin injury that sidelined him for a while. However, given Bravo's flourishing backlift and penchant for the flashing cover-drive, those Lara comparisons are likely to hang around for a while yet.

THE FACTS Darren Bravo made his debut for West Indies, alongside his half-brother Dwayne, in the one-day series against India at home in June 2009 ... He made his first three Test centuries in the space of six weeks at the end of 2011: 195 against Bangladesh at Mirpur, then 136 and 166 in India in November ... After 12 Tests, Bravo had exactly the same batting record as Brian Lara – 941 runs at an average of 47.05 ...

THE FIGURES *to 17.09.12*   **ᴇＳＰＮ cricinfo.com**

Batting & Fielding	M	Inns	NO	Runs	HS	Avge	S/R	100	50	4s	6s	Ct	St
Tests	19	35	3	1420	195	44.37	46.34	3	7	154	18	14	0
ODIs	40	37	6	912	86	29.41	69.99	0	6	71	21	8	0
T20Is	5	5	0	102	42	20.40	107.36	0	0	11	3	0	0
First-class	47	80	5	2895	195	38.60	–	6	15	–	–	41	0

Bowling	M	Balls	Runs	Wkts	BB	Avge	RpO	S/R	5i	10m
Tests	19	0	–	–	–	–	–	–	–	–
ODIs	40	0	–	–	–	–	–	–	–	–
T20Is	5	0	–	–	–	–	–	–	–	–
First-class	47	52	28	1	1–9	28.00	3.23	52.00	0	0

DWAYNE **BRAVO**

Full name	**Dwayne John Bravo**
Born	**October 7, 1983, Santa Cruz, Trinidad**
Teams	**Trinidad, Chennai Super Kings**
Style	**Right-hand bat, right-arm fast-medium bowler**
Test debut	**West Indies v England at Lord's 2004**
ODI debut	**West Indies v England at Georgetown 2003-04**
T20I debut	**West Indies v New Zealand at Auckland 2005-06**

THE PROFILE A genuine allrounder (a rare breed in the Caribbean), Dwayne Bravo was born in Santa Cruz, like Brian Lara, and made his one-day debut in April 2004, on the tenth anniversary of Lara's 375. He won his first Test cap at Lord's three months later, aged 20, took three wickets with his medium-paced swingers, and displayed a cool, straight bat. West Indies lost the series, but at least they knew they had unearthed a special talent. Bravo hit his maiden century against South Africa in April 2005, and played an even better innings the following November, 113 at Hobart against the rampant Australians. He continued to chip in with useful runs, while a selection of slower balls makes him a handful in one-dayers, if less so in Tests. He's also electric in the field. Bravo missed the 2009 home Tests against England with a niggling ankle injury, then was left out for the Tests in England that followed – despite being fit enough to play in the IPL – although he did lift the side visibly in both one-day series. Back in Australia at the end of 2009, he made another century, at Adelaide. Earlier that year Bravo had been one of several players who boycotted the home series against Bangladesh as a contracts dispute festered, and he continues to flit between the international set-up and lucrative 20-over competitions: a decision to turn down a central contract cost him the West Indies vice-captaincy in 2011, not long before an injury in the first match ruled him out of the World Cup. He remained a limited-overs player only through much of 2012, although his bank balance was boosted by Twenty20 stints in Australia, Bangladesh and India.

THE FACTS Dwayne Bravo's second Test century – 113 at Hobart late in 2005 – came during a stand of 182 with his fellow-Trinidadian Denesh Ramdin, the day after Trinidad & Tobago qualified for the football World Cup for the first time ... Bravo averages 30.72 with the ball in Tests against Australia – but 81.66 v Pakistan ... He played 27 Tests before finally finishing on the winning side, against Sri Lanka at Port-of-Spain in April 2008 ... Bravo's half-brother Darren has also played for West Indies ...

THE FIGURES to 17.09.12

ESPncricinfo.com

Batting & Fielding	M	Inns	NO	Runs	HS	Avge	S/R	100	50	4s	6s	Ct	St
Tests	40	71	1	2200	113	31.42	48.59	3	13	269	21	41	0
ODIs	129	107	17	2165	112*	24.05	80.54	1	7	165	40	52	0
T20Is	27	24	7	470	66*	27.64	130.19	0	3	25	22	8	0
First-class	98	178	7	5242	197	30.65	–	8	29	–	–	84	0

Bowling	M	Balls	Runs	Wkts	BB	Avge	RpO	S/R	5i	10m
Tests	40	6466	3426	86	6–55	39.83	3.17	75.18	2	0
ODIs	129	5083	4487	146	4–19	30.73	5.29	34.81	0	0
T20Is	27	426	609	24	4–38	25.37	8.57	17.75	0	0
First-class	98	10865	5832	173	6–11	33.71	3.22	62.80	7	0

TIM **BRESNAN**

ENGLAND

Full name	**Timothy Thomas Bresnan**
Born	**February 28, 1985, Pontefract, Yorkshire**
Teams	**Yorkshire**
Style	**Right-hand bat, right-arm fast-medium bowler**
Test debut	**England v West Indies at Lord's 2009**
ODI debut	**England v Sri Lanka at Lord's 2006**
T20I debut	**England v Sri Lanka at Southampton 2006**

THE PROFILE The stocky Tim Bresnan was tipped for higher honours in 2001 after becoming Yorkshire's youngest player for 20 years. He quickly progressed to England's youth team, and played in two Under-19 World Cups. The potential took a few years to ripen, but in 2005 he was given more responsibility in a transitional Yorkshire team, and responded with 47 wickets with swinging deliveries which, if a shade short of truly fast, travel at a fair old rate. He can also bat, making three first-class centuries in 2007: he has reached 90 in Tests twice, too. A good start to the previous season had resulted in a place in a new-look one-day squad in June 2006, but Bresnan fell victim to the flashing blades of Sanath Jayasuriya and friends, took only two wickets in four appearances in what became a clean sweep for Sri Lanka, and then suffered a back injury. He responded well with the bat in 2007, although his form with the ball dipped a little (34 wickets at 34), before a return to bowling form the following year led to a one-day recall. He finally made his Test debut in May 2009, but failed to shine at first and had to make way for Andrew Flintoff in the Ashes series. But he returned to Yorkshire, worked on his fitness, and came back a better player ... and a good-luck charm too: England won the first 13 Tests in which Bresnan played, including the victories at Melbourne and Sydney which sealed the 2010-11 Ashes triumph, although the run – and his own superlative form – came to an end in mid-2012.

THE FACTS Bresnan made all three of his first-class centuries during 2007, including 126 not out for England A v India at Chelmsford ... He was on the winning side in his first 13 Tests, an England record: only Adam Gilchrist (15 for Australia) had more ... Bresnan's 80 v Australia at Centurion in October 2009 is the highest score by an England No. 8 in ODIs ... He took 5 for 42 for Yorkshire at Worcester in July 2005 ... Bresnan made his Yorkshire debut in a one-day game in 2001, when only 16 ...

THE FIGURES to 17.09.12   ESPNcricinfo.com

Batting & Fielding	M	Inns	NO	Runs	HS	Avge	S/R	100	50	4s	6s	Ct	St
Tests	16	14	3	399	91	36.27	42.58	0	3	47	1	7	0
ODIs	65	47	13	694	80	20.41	92.53	0	1	75	2	18	0
T20Is	21	12	6	79	23*	13.16	111.26	0	0	6	0	5	0
First-class	117	150	26	3473	126*	28.00	47.79	3	17	–	–	49	0

Bowling	M	Balls	Runs	Wkts	BB	Avge	RpO	S/R	5i	10m
Tests	16	3483	1713	57	5–48	30.05	2.95	61.10	1	0
ODIs	65	3231	2897	81	5–48	35.76	5.37	39.88	1	0
T20Is	21	400	493	16	3–10	30.81	7.39	25.00	0	0
First-class	117	20142	10289	328	5–42	31.36	3.06	61.41	6	0

STUART **BROAD**

Full name	**Stuart Christopher John Broad**
Born	**June 24, 1986, Nottingham**
Teams	**Nottinghamshire**
Style	**Left-hand bat, right-arm fast-medium bowler**
Test debut	**England v Sri Lanka at Colombo 2007-08**
ODI debut	**England v Pakistan at Cardiff 2006**
T20I debut	**England v Pakistan at Bristol 2006**

THE PROFILE Stuart Broad is an aggressive seamer with a strong high action and an ability to produce game-changing spells. He's at his best when pitching the ball up and nipping it away from the right-hander, but he is also adept at pulling his length back and peppering the ribs with a series of awkward short balls. Broad also has a classical batting technique, with a penchant for the back-foot drive. With time on his side, and a willingness to learn, he has the scope to develop into one of England's finest fast bowlers. Stuart made an impressive start to his international career, keeping a cool head in the mayhem of a Twenty20 match, then claiming an early wicket on his one-day debut. In the 2009 Ashes he was unimpressive at first, but kept his place, and silenced the critics with a superb spell to set up England's series-winning victory at The Oval. Broad can bat, too, and made up for a disappointing trot with a superb 169 – a long-overdue maiden first-class century – against Pakistan at Lord's in August 2010. After that came peaks and troughs: unrelated side injuries forced him home early from the Ashes tour and the 2011 World Cup, then a shoulder problem ended the home season prematurely. In between, though, he bowled magnificently at home against India, pitching the ball up more after struggling against Sri Lanka, and was named as England's Twenty20 captain. In 2012 he demolished West Indies with 11 wickets at Lord's, then worried South Africa with eight at Headingley. Runs, though, were rather thin on the ground.

THE FACTS Broad scored 169 – the highest by an England No. 9 in Tests – during a record eighth-wicket partnership of 332 with Jonathan Trott, against Pakistan at Lord's in 2010 ... After being part of Peter Siddle's Test hat-trick at Brisbane in November 2010, Broad took one himself against India at Trent Bridge in July 2011 ... Broad took 7 for 72 (11 for 165 in the match) against West Indies at Lord's in 2012 ... His father, Chris, played 25 Tests in the 1980s, scoring 1661 runs with six centuries – he's now a match referee (see page 219) ...

THE FIGURES to 17.09.12   ☰**sn**cricinfo.com

Batting & Fielding	M	Inns	NO	Runs	HS	Avge	S/R	100	50	4s	6s	Ct	St
Tests	50	68	9	1578	169	26.74	64.40	1	9	198	12	14	0
ODIs	93	50	17	415	45*	12.57	73.58	0	0	25	6	20	0
T20Is	38	15	7	62	18*	7.75	98.41	0	0	4	1	16	0
First-class	100	131	24	2635	169	24.62	59.18	1	16	–	–	30	0

Bowling	M	Balls	Runs	Wkts	BB	Avge	RpO	S/R	5i	10m
Tests	50	10608	5336	172	7–72	31.02	3.01	61.67	6	1
ODIs	93	4730	4079	148	5–23	27.56	5.17	31.95	1	0
T20Is	38	795	972	41	3–17	23.70	7.33	19.39	0	0
First-class	100	19007	10245	360	8–52	28.45	3.23	52.79	16	2

REGIS **CHAKABVA**

Full name	**Regis Wiriranai Chakabva**
Born	**September 20, 1987, Harare**
Teams	**Mashonaland Eagles**
Style	**Right-hand bat, wicketkeeper**
Test debut	**Zimbabwe v New Zealand at Bulawayo 2011-12**
ODI debut	**Zimbabwe v Kenya at Nairobi 2008-09**
T20I debut	**Zimbabwe v Pakistan at King City 2008-09**

THE PROFILE Regis Chakabva has long been considered a wicketkeeper of high promise, and a handy batsman too – and Tatenda Taibu's announcement during 2012 that he was retiring to devote himself to the church meant Chakabva should get an extended chance to show his worth. He had already displaced Taibu from behind the stumps in Tests, making his debut late in 2011, and in his second match – in New Zealand early the following year – he showed his class with the bat, despite his small stature, with a plucky 63 as Zimbabwe crumbled to an embarrassing defeat. Chakabva had played for the Under-19s back in 2005, but then slipped down the pecking order. One of the others tried was Alester Maregwede, but when he gave up keeping to concentrate on batting, Chakabva was picked for Zimbabwe A in 2007 after only four first-class matches; and when a Zimbabwean XI played in South Africa's one-day competition the following year he reeled off successive scores of 62, 66, 60 and 118. Taibu's return from an earlier retirement meant Chakabva played solely as a batsman for a while, but Taibu's ability to bowl handy medium-pace meant that Chakabva was often part of the squad. He made his international debut late in 2008, in a Twenty20 match in far-off Toronto, and a week later played his first ODI, in a triangular tournament in Nairobi. He didn't do much at first, and Taibu regained the gloves for Zimbabwe's Test recall in August 2011 – but Chakabva was still in the mix and, after some consistent displays for Mashonaland Eagles he soon won his first Test cap, and made 37 in a defiant stand of 86 with Malcolm Waller.

THE FACTS Chakabva made 131 for Northerns v Centrals in Harare in April 2009 ... He pulled off three stumpings in a Twenty20 match against a Bangladesh XI in Harare in June 2012 ... Chakabva scored 63 – more than a third of Zimbabwe's runs off the bat in the entire match – against New Zealand at Napier in January 2012 ...

THE FIGURES *to 17.09.12*   **ESPN**cricinfo.com

Batting & Fielding	M	Inns	NO	Runs	HS	Avge	S/R	100	50	4s	6s	Ct	St
Tests	2	4	0	108	63	27.00	39.70	0	1	9	0	2	0
ODIs	13	13	1	213	45	17.75	53.92	0	0	16	0	7	0
T20Is	2	2	0	1	1	0.50	11.11	0	0	0	0	0	0
First-class	53	92	6	2842	131	33.04	53.54	4	17	336	15	119	11

Bowling	M	Balls	Runs	Wkts	BB	Avge	RpO	S/R	5i	10m
Tests	2	0	–	–	–	–	–	–	–	–
ODIs	13	0	–	–	–	–	–	–	–	–
T20Is	2	0	–	–	–	–	–	–	–	–
First-class	53	18	19	0	–	–	6.33	–	0	0

SHIVNARINE **CHANDERPAUL**

Full name	**Shivnarine Chanderpaul**
Born	**August 16, 1974, Unity Village, Demerara, Guyana**
Teams	**Guyana**
Style	**Left-hand bat, occasional legspinner**
Test debut	**West Indies v England at Georgetown 1993-94**
ODI debut	**West Indies v India at Faridabad 1994-95**
T20I debut	**West Indies v New Zealand at Auckland 2005-06**

THE PROFILE Crouched and crabby, Shivnarine Chanderpaul proves there is life beyond the coaching handbook. He never seems to play in the V, or off the front foot, but uses soft hands, canny deflections and a whiplash pull to maintain a Test average nudging 50. Early on he struggled to convert fifties into hundreds, and also missed several matches through injury. That was rectified in 2000 when a large piece of floating bone was removed from his foot: suitably liberated, he set about rectifying his hundreds problem too, and now has 25 (22 against Australia, England, India and South Africa), including 104 as the Windies chased down a record 418 to beat the Aussies in Antigua in May 2003. The following year in England he ended his first bad trot by narrowly missing twin tons at Lord's. In 2005 he became captain during the first of several acrimonious disputes between the players and the board, and celebrated with 203 at home in Guyana. He stood down after struggling with bat and microphone in Australia, and was back to his limpet best in England in 2007, top-scoring in each of his five innings, and going more than 1000 minutes without being out in Tests for the third time in his career (he did it again in 2008). It's not all defence, though: he can blast with the best when he needs to. Chanderpaul became uncharacteristically vocal after high-level criticism of senior players in 2011. He was omitted from the one-day side, and was somewhat grudgingly restored to the Test team. Now West Indies' most-capped player, he continued to be a stumbling-block for opposition bowlers throughout 2012, passing 10,000 Test runs during the year.

THE FACTS Chanderpaul averages 65.74 in Tests against India, but only 28.77 v Zimbabwe ... He scored 303 not out for Guyana v Jamaica in January 1996 ... At Georgetown in April 2003 Chanderpaul reached his century against Australia in only 69 balls, the fourth-fastest in Test history by balls faced ... He became West Indies' most-capped player (133) against India in July 2011 (and celebrated with a century) ... Chanderpaul once shot a policeman in the hand in his native Guyana, mistaking him for a mugger ...

THE FIGURES to 17.09.12   **ESFN cricinfo.com**

Batting & Fielding	M	Inns	NO	Runs	HS	Avge	S/R	100	50	4s	6s	Ct	St
Tests	144	246	40	10342	203*	50.20	42.68	25	61	1126	33	62	0
ODIs	268	251	40	8778	150	41.60	70.74	11	59	722	85	73	0
T20Is	22	22	5	343	41	20.17	98.84	0	0	34	5	7	0
First-class	290	471	87	21332	303*	55.55	–		62	108	–	–	163	0

Bowling	M	Balls	Runs	Wkts	BB	Avge	RpO	S/R	5i	10m
Tests	144	1740	883	9	1–2	98.11	3.04	193.33	0	0
ODIs	268	740	636	14	3–18	45.42	5.15	52.85	0	0
T20Is	22	0	–	–	–	–	–	–	–	–
First-class	290	4694	2491	57	4–48	43.70	3.18	82.35	0	0

DINESH **CHANDIMAL**

Full name	**Lokuge Dinesh Chandimal**
Born	**November 18, 1989, Balapitiya**
Teams	**Nondescripts, Ruhuna**
Style	**Right-hand bat, wicketkeeper**
Test debut	**Sri Lanka v South Africa at Durban 2011-12**
ODI debut	**Sri Lanka v Zimbabwe at Bulawayo 2010**
T20I debut	**Sri Lanka v New Zealand at Providence 2009-10**

THE PROFILE Dinesh Chandimal is a batsman who can keep wicket, like one of his heroes Romesh Kaluwitharana. He's taller than the diminutive "Kalu", though, at 5ft 9ins (175cm), and collected a full national contract after a seamless run through Sri Lanka's age-group sides. First-class cricket also seemed to pose few terrors: he scored a century in his second match, against the New Zealand tourists in August 2009, and added two more in his next five games. He finished his first full home season with 895 runs at 52.64, and did well enough in limited-overs cricket to earn selection for the World Twenty20 in the West Indies early in 2010. He was also called up to keep wicket for the 50-overs team in a tri-series in Zimbabwe in June while Kumar Sangakkara took a rest. Still only 20, Chandimal did a passable impersonation of Sangakkara behind the stumps – and in front of them, too, spanking a superb 111 in only his second ODI, against India at Harare. Cricinfo observed: "He impressed with his shot-selection, his footwork and his aggressive bent of mind." He sat out the 2011 World Cup, but made a cool ODI century at Lord's not long afterwards. An injury to Prasanna Jayawardene gave Chandimal a Test chance in December 2011, which he grabbed with innings of 58 and 54, making it hard to leave him out. He duly retained his place as a batsman once Jayawardene returned, and hit 65 opening against Pakistan at Pallekele later in 2012.

THE FACTS Chandimal scored 111 in an ODI against India at Harare in June 2010, and 105 not out against England at Lord's in July 2011 ... He was only the second wicketkeeper, after Dilawar Hussain of India in 1933-34, to score two half-centuries on his Test debut ... Chandimal made 244 for Sri Lanka A v South Africa A in Colombo in August 2010 ... He scored 143 in an Under-19 Test against India when he was 17 ...

THE FIGURES *to 17.09.12*   **ESPNcricinfo.com**

Batting & Fielding	M	Inns	NO	Runs	HS	Avge	S/R	100	50	4s	6s	Ct	St
Tests	4	8	0	279	65	34.87	53.34	0	3	34	2	3	1
ODIs	45	44	8	1242	111	34.50	75.87	2	8	93	15	17	1
T20Is	11	10	0	168	56	16.80	100.00	0	1	13	2	0	0
First-class	39	63	7	3088	244	55.14	71.76	9	17	351	59	66	13

Bowling	M	Balls	Runs	Wkts	BB	Avge	RpO	S/R	5i	10m
Tests	4	0	–	–	–	–	–	–	–	–
ODIs	45	0	–	–	–	–	–	–	–	–
T20Is	11	0	–	–	–	–	–	–	–	–
First-class	39	12	5	0	–	–	2.50	–	0	0

ELTON **CHIGUMBURA**

Full name	**Elton Chigumbura**
Born	**March 14, 1986, Kwekwe**
Teams	**Mashonaland Eagles**
Style	**Right-hand bat, right-arm fast-medium bowler**
Test debut	**Zimbabwe v Sri Lanka at Harare 2004**
ODI debut	**Zimbabwe v Sri Lanka at Bulawayo 2004**
T20I debut	**Zimbabwe v Bangladesh at Khulna 2006-07**

THE PROFILE Elton Chigumbura, who was fast-tracked into the national side not long after his 18th birthday when several leading players fell out with the board, made his first-class debut in the Logan Cup when only 15. A genuine allrounder, he is a big hitter fond of the lofted drive, bowls at a sharp pace, and is an athletic fielder. He looked out of his depth in his first Test, in May 2004, but was more at home by the time of the Champions Trophy in England that September. Three years later he played a vital role in the shock victory over Australia at the inaugural World Twenty20, removing both openers and rotating the strike well as Zimbabwe squeaked home. Then, after a poor run, he pounded the Kenyans in Nairobi in 2009, smashing 79, 68, 43 and 36 in successive innings at a strike-rate well above 100, and picking up seven wickets for good measure. Early in 2010 Chigumbura took over as captain when Prosper Utseya stood down, but after a promising start – and a county stint with Northamptonshire – the responsibility seemed to affect him and his form fell away: in 20 matches in charge he failed to reach 50 and took only two wickets. He was replaced in 2011 by Brendan Taylor, but kept his place in the side, and chipped in with three important wickets in the historic Test-comeback victory over Bangladesh at Harare in August. But soon after that he injured his knee, and missed the Test against Pakistan that followed, then in New Zealand early in 2012 he was confined to the one-day team, in which he remains a dangerous hitter and handy bowling option.

THE FACTS Chigumbura scored 186 for Northerns v Westerns at Harare in April 2008 ... In May 2009 he hit 103 not out from 56 balls in a Twenty20 match for Northerns v Centrals at Bulawayo ... Chigumbura has the highest strike-rate of anyone who has scored 1000 runs in ODIs for Zimbabwe ... He took 6 for 24 against Sri Lanka A in a one-day match at Harare in July 2012 ...

THE FIGURES *to 17.09.12*   **ESPNcricinfo.com**

Batting & Fielding	M	Inns	NO	Runs	HS	Avge	S/R	100	50	4s	6s	Ct	St
Tests	7	13	0	192	71	14.76	40.16	0	1	29	3	2	0
ODIs	142	133	14	2837	79	23.84	83.05	0	14	226	82	45	0
T20Is	20	19	2	329	48	19.35	152.31	0	0	28	17	9	0
First-class	79	137	9	4353	186	34.00	–	5	29	–	–	35	0

Bowling	M	Balls	Runs	Wkts	BB	Avge	RpO	S/R	5i	10m
Tests	7	1033	595	12	5-54	49.58	3.45	86.08	1	0
ODIs	142	3722	3689	91	4-28	40.53	5.94	40.90	0	0
T20Is	20	246	355	15	4-31	23.66	8.65	16.40	0	0
First-class	79	9648	5289	182	5-33	29.06	3.28	53.01	4	0

MICHAEL **CLARKE**

Full name **Michael John Clarke**
Born **April 2, 1981, Liverpool, New South Wales**
Teams **New South Wales**
Style **Right-hand bat, left-arm orthodox spinner**
Test debut **Australia v India at Bangalore 2003-04**
ODI debut **Australia v England at Adelaide 2002-03**
T20I debut **Australia v New Zealand at Auckland 2004-05**

THE PROFILE Michael Clarke was being touted as an Australian captain before he'd even played a Test. And when he marked his debut with 151 against India in October 2004, his future looked even brighter than the yellow motorbike he received as Man of the Match. Another thrilling century followed on his home debut, and his first Test season ended with the Allan Border Medal. Then came the fall. Barely a year later he was dropped after 15 centuryless Tests. He was told to tighten his technique, especially early on against swing. Clarke remained a one-day regular, but had to wait until the low-key Bangladesh series early in 2006 to reclaim that Test spot. He cemented his place with two tons in the 2006-07 Ashes whitewash, did well in the World Cup, and has been a fixture ever since. In England in 2009 Clarke was the classiest batsman on show, finishing with two centuries and a near-miss (93). Soon afterwards he was entrusted with the Twenty20 captaincy, and took over as Test skipper too after the 2010-11 Ashes debacle. He soon showed himself to be a shrewd tactician, and the responsibility didn't seem to affect him: he creamed 329 not out against India at the SCG in January 2012, and two matches later added 210 at Adelaide. He started as a ravishing shotmaker who did not so much take guard as take off: he radiated a pointy-elbowed elegance reminiscent of the young Greg Chappell or Mark Waugh. His bouncy fielding and searing run-outs, often from square on, add to his value, while his slow left-armers can surprise (they once shocked six Indians in a Test). A cricket nut since he was in nappies, the young "Pup" honed his technique against the bowling machine at his dad's indoor centre.

THE FACTS Clarke scored a century on his Test debut, 151 v India at Bangalore in 2004-05, and the following month added another in his first home Test, 141 v New Zealand at Brisbane ... Clarke averages 65.66 in ODIs against Sri Lanka, but only 15.50 v Scotland (and 0.00 v Ireland) ... He took 6 for 9 in a Test against India at Mumbai in November 2004 ... He made 329 not out against India at Sydney in January 2012 ...

THE FIGURES to 17.09.12   **ESFn**cricinfo.com

Batting & Fielding	M	Inns	NO	Runs	HS	Avge	S/R	100	50	4s	6s	Ct	St
Tests	83	138	13	6097	329*	48.77	54.52	19	22	682	27	93	0
ODIs	221	202	42	7278	130	45.48	78.44	7	54	589	49	87	0
T20Is	34	28	5	488	67	21.21	103.17	0	1	29	10	13	0
First-class	145	247	22	10457	329*	46.47	–	35	38	–	–	152	0

Bowling	M	Balls	Runs	Wkts	BB	Avge	RpO	S/R	5i	10m
Tests	83	2076	1029	29	6–9	35.48	2.97	71.58	2	0
ODIs	221	2489	2079	56	5–35	37.12	5.01	44.44	1	0
T20Is	34	156	225	6	1–2	37.50	8.65	26.00	0	0
First-class	145	3256	1717	40	6–9	42.92	3.16	81.40	1	0

NICK **COMPTON**

Full name	**Nicholas Richard Denis Compton**
Born	**June 26, 1983, Durban, South Africa**
Teams	**Somerset**
Style	**Right-hand bat, occasional offspinner**
Test debut	**No Tests yet**
ODI debut	**No ODIs yet**
T20I debut	**No T20Is yet**

THE PROFILE Nick Compton is the grandson of the legendary Denis, who scintillated for England in a 20-year Test career that ended in 1957. Denis died when Nick was barely a teenager, although he does remember a practice session in the garden: "I was playing with a high elbow, hitting the ball back. He was sitting on the porch, with the ever-present glass of brandy, and he just said 'For God's sake, hit the bloody thing'." Compton junior was born in South Africa, after his father emigrated there, but returned to England in his teens, following his grandfather's footsteps to Lord's after studies at Harrow. After a few matches for Middlesex in the previous two seasons he sailed past 1000 runs in 2006, earned his county cap and an England A tour – but four middling seasons followed, during which he was sometimes dropped, and in 2011 he joined Somerset. It paid off with 1098 runs, including a maiden double-century, and he really flowered the following year, when he came closer than anyone to scoring 1000 first-class runs before the end of May without actually managing it – four figures ticked up on June 1. Compton usually opens or goes in at No. 3, and his game is based on a tight defensive technique, plus good judgment about which balls to play and which to leave. And, according to Cricinfo, "his powers of concentration would shame a security camera". Compton finished that 2012 season with 1494 runs at the heady average of 99.60 – even Grandad didn't quite match that in his record-breaking year of 1947 – and a place on the Indian tour after Andrew Strauss's retirement opened up a place at the top of the order.

THE FACTS In 2012 Compton reached 1000 first-class runs for the season on June 1 ... He scored 254 not out for Somerset v Durham at Chester-le-Street in May 2011, and two further double-centuries the following year ... Compton's grandfather Denis made 5807 runs at 50.06 in 78 Tests for England; in 1947 he made a record 3816 runs (and 18 centuries) in the English season ...

THE FIGURES to 17.09.12

ESPTI cricinfo.com

Batting & Fielding	M	Inns	NO	Runs	HS	Avge	S/R	100	50	4s	6s	Ct	St
Tests	0	0	–	–	–	–	–	–	–	–	–	–	–
ODIs	0	0	–	–	–	–	–	–	–	–	–	–	–
T20Is	0	0	–	–	–	–	–	–	–	–	–	–	–
First-class	96	164	23	6254	254*	44.35	48.20	16	27	–	–	49	0

Bowling	M	Balls	Runs	Wkts	BB	Avge	RpO	S/R	5i	10m
Tests	0	0	–	–	–	–	–	–	–	–
ODIs	0	0	–	–	–	–	–	–	–	–
T20Is	0	0	–	–	–	–	–	–	–	–
First-class	96	164	215	3	1–1	71.66	7.86	54.66	0	0

ALASTAIR **COOK**

Full name	**Alastair Nathan Cook**
Born	**December 25, 1984, Gloucester**
Teams	**Essex**
Style	**Left-hand bat, occasional offspinner**
Test debut	**England v India at Nagpur 2005-06**
ODI debut	**England v Sri Lanka at Manchester 2006**
T20I debut	**England v West Indies at The Oval 2007**

THE PROFILE   Wise judges were saying that the tall, dark and handsome Alastair Cook was destined for great things very early on. A left-hander strong on the pull, Cook was thrown in at the deep end by Essex the year after leaving Bedford School with a fistful of batting records, and has barely looked back since. He makes his runs with a languid ease reminiscent of David Gower, if slightly more stiff-legged. His early England career was full of successes, although a barren spell in 2010 – he looked vulnerable around off stump, with a tendency to play around the front pad – briefly threatened his place before a century against Pakistan at The Oval saved his skin. But the rest, as they say, is history: he piled up 766 runs in the 2010-11 Ashes triumph, then made a colossal 294 against India at Edgbaston. Cook was in the Caribbean with the A team when the original England SOS came early in 2006, after a crop of injuries: he flew to India and, unfazed, stroked 60 and an unbeaten 104 in a memorable debut at Nagpur. Cook lost his one-day place for a while, not helped by some occasionally ponderous fielding, and missed the 2011 World Cup, but returned afterwards, and showed signs that he could up the tempo if required. There were innings of 119 and 95 against Sri Lanka, successive tons against Pakistan in Abu Dhabi early in 2012, and two more at home later in the year. His Test form dipped a little, though, a slight worry for him as he contemplated life as Test skipper after the retirement of his long-time opening partner Andrew Strauss.

THE FACTS   Cook was the 16th England batsman to make a century on Test debut ... He made 766 runs against Australia in 2010-11, a number exceeded in an Ashes series only by Don Bradman (twice), Wally Hammond and Mark Taylor ... Cook's stand of 127 with Marcus Trescothick v Sri Lanka at Lord's in 2006 was the second-highest in Tests by unrelated players who share a birthday (they were both born on Christmas Day), behind 163 by Vic Stollmeyer and Kenneth Weekes (both born Jan 24) for West Indies at The Oval in 1939 ...

THE FIGURES to 17.09.12   ᴇѕᵖᵰcricinfo.com

Batting & Fielding	M	Inns	NO	Runs	HS	Avge	S/R	100	50	4s	6s	Ct	St
Tests	83	146	9	6555	294	47.84	48.00	20	29	749	7	73	0
ODIs	56	56	3	2121	137	40.01	79.28	5	13	238	4	17	0
T20Is	4	4	0	61	26	15.25	112.96	0	0	10	0	1	0
First-class	172	304	24	13194	294	47.12	52.62	38	64	–	–	159	0

Bowling	M	Balls	Runs	Wkts	BB	Avge	RpO	S/R	5i	10m
Tests	83	6	1	0	–	–	1.00	–	0	0
ODIs	56	0	–	–	–	–	–	–	–	–
T20Is	4	0	–	–	–	–	–	–	–	–
First-class	172	270	205	6	3–13	34.16	4.55	45.00	0	0

ED **COWAN**

Full name	**Edward James McKenzie Cowan**
Born	**June 16, 1982, Paddington, Sydney**
Teams	**Tasmania, Gloucestershire**
Style	**Left-hand bat**
Test debut	**Australia v India at Melbourne 2011-12**
ODI debut	**No ODIs yet**
T20I debut	**No T20Is yet**

THE PROFILE Ed Cowan, a patient and correct left-hander – something of a throwback to an earlier type of opening batsman – looked to be drifting out of first-class cricket after playing only three times for New South Wales in 2008-09. But a move to Tasmania was just what he needed: in his first season there he made 957 runs at 53, the second-highest aggregate in that summer's Sheffield Shield, including a career-best 225 against South Australia. He followed that with a hundred for Australia A, then hit a purple patch – four centuries in four matches – at the start of the 2011-12 home season. That got him into the Boxing Day Test against India, and he made a watchful start, batting almost five hours for 68. In the third Test at Perth he dropped anchor while David Warner exploded at the other end – they eventually put on 214, of which Cowan's share was 74. In the Caribbean it was a similar story: patient starts, few failures (only two single-figure scores in his first seven Tests), but no breakthrough big hundred. He captained Australia A in England in 2012, making a century against Derbyshire before being out for 99 against the England Lions (and adding 73 in the other "Test"). The 2012-13 home season will be an important one for Cowan, one of the most thoughtful characters in Australian cricket – and one of the game's best users of Twitter. He has already written a book (a diary of a season), has a degree, and worked as an analyst for an investment bank. He played a few matches for Oxford University in 2003, and scored 137 not out for the British Universities against the touring Zimbabweans.

THE FACTS Cowan scored 225 for Tasmania against South Australia at Hobart in November 2009 ... He scored 137 not out, his maiden first-class hundred, for British Universities against Zimbabwe at Edgbaston in 2003 ... Cowan fielded for Australia as a substitute before he had played for NSW: called from the Members' Bar, he was on the SCG for about five minutes against Pakistan in 2004-05 ...

THE FIGURES to 17.09.12   **ESPN**cricinfo.com

Batting & Fielding	M	Inns	NO	Runs	HS	Avge	S/R	100	50	4s	6s	Ct	St
Tests	7	12	0	358	74	29.83	41.82	0	3	40	0	14	0
ODIs	0	0	–	–	–	–	–	–	–	–	–	–	–
T20Is	0	0	–	–	–	–	–	–	–	–	–	–	–
First-class	74	132	9	5037	225	40.95	47.17	15	19	–	–	58	00

Bowling	M	Balls	Runs	Wkts	BB	Avge	RpO	S/R	5i	10m
Tests	7	0	–	–	–	–	–	–	–	–
ODIs	0	0	–	–	–	–	–	–	–	–
T20Is	0	0	–	–	–	–	–	–	–	–
First-class	74	18	33	0	–	–	11.00	–	0	0

PAT **CUMMINS**

Full name	**Patrick James Cummins**
Born	**May 8, 1993, Westmead, Sydney**
Teams	**New South Wales**
Style	**Right-hand bat, right-arm fast bowler**
Test debut	**Australia v South Africa at Johannesburg 2011-12**
ODI debut	**Australia v South Africa at Centurion 2011-12**
T20I debut	**Australia v South Africa at Cape Town 2011-12**

THE PROFILE Few have had as meteoric a rise as pacey Pat Cummins. He made his initial mark in the Twenty20 Big Bash in 2010-11, taking 3 for 29 against Tasmania in his first match: he finished with 11 wickets and a fine economy-rate of 6.5 runs per over. There was a first-class debut too: his third game was the Sheffield Shield final in which, still only 17, he bowled 48 overs in eventual winners Tasmania's first innings, taking 3 for 118. Cummins then became the youngest player to be given a central contract for Australia, and was selected for the upcoming tour of South Africa, after doing well for New South Wales in the Champions League T20. He was an instant success at international level, too, taking 3 for 25 in his first Twenty20 game, and 3 for 28 in his maiden ODI. Cummins missed the first Test in South Africa in November 2011 – when Australia were skittled for 47 – but in the second became, at 18, their second-youngest debutant. He claimed 6 for 79 in the second innings, a spell which included an impressive working-over of Jacques Kallis. Then Cummins strode in with his side still 18 short of the victory that would square the series ... and nervelessly biffed 13 of them, including the winning boundary. Then, though, the bandwagon stopped. He picked up a heel niggle, and missed the 2011-12 home season. Back for the limited-overs series in England in July 2012, he injured his side, before returning against Pakistan in the UAE in September. Australia have deemed Cummins so important to the national side's future that the team performance manager has drawn up a three-year plan for his management and development.

THE FACTS Cummins was 18 years 185 days old when he made his Test debut – the only younger man to play for Australia was 17-year-old Ian Craig in 1952-53 ... Cummins took 6 for 79 in his first Test, the best debut figures by an Australian fast bowler since Tony Dodemaide's 6 for 58 in 1987-88 ...

THE FIGURES *to 17.09.12*   **ESPncricinfo.com**

Batting & Fielding	M	Inns	NO	Runs	HS	Avge	S/R	100	50	4s	6s	Ct	St
Tests	1	2	1	15	13*	15.00	68.18	0	0	2	0	1	0
ODIs	5	3	2	21	11*	21.00	95.45	0	0	3	0	0	0
T20Is	5	3	1	9	7	4.50	112.50	0	0	0	0	1	0
First-class	4	6	3	25	13*	8.33	47.16	0	0	3	0	1	0

Bowling	M	Balls	Runs	Wkts	BB	Avge	RpO	S/R	5i	10m
Tests	1	264	117	7	6–79	16.71	2.65	37.71	1	0
ODIs	5	216	214	7	3–28	30.57	5.94	30.85	0	0
T20Is	5	114	118	10	3–15	11.80	6.21	11.40	0	0
First-class	4	1080	534	16	6–79	33.37	2.96	67.50	1	0

MARCHANT **DE LANGE**

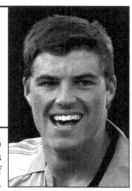

Full name	**Marchant de Lange**
Born	**October 13, 1990, Tzaneen, Limpopo**
Teams	**Titans, Kolkata Knight Riders**
Style	**Right-hand bat, right-arm fast bowler**
Test debut	**South Africa v Sri Lanka at Durban 2011-12**
ODI debut	**South Africa v New Zealand at Auckland 2011-12**
T20I debut	**South Africa v New Zealand at Hamilton 2011-12**

THE PROFILE   A genuinely fast bowler whose short run-up dates from his days throwing the javelin on the junior athletics circuit, Marchant de Lange hails from the northern town of Tzaneen, most famous as the home of Modjadji, the Rain Queen. De Lange was discovered at the local academy, and made his first-class debut for Easterns in 2010-11. The lofty de Lange was soon earmarked as one of the next generation of South African quicks: he consistently threatens 90mph on the speed-gun, and can extract good bounce, like his similarly tall Titans team-mate Morne Morkel. However, he faces a battle to oust either Morkel or Dale Steyn from the new-ball spots in Tests for the time being, although he did make a great start to his international career: chosen for South Africa A in November 2011, de Lange took 5 for 56 against the Australian tourists, which led to his inclusion in the senior squad. He made his Test debut on Boxing Day 2011 after Vernon Philander was injured and, bowling with pace and hostility on an unhelpful pitch, de Lange claimed 7 for 81 (Steyn went wicketless), although Sri Lanka survived to record their first victory on South African soil. He was unlucky to miss out when Philander was fit again for the next match, but toured New Zealand shortly afterwards, and started his 50-overs career in equally impressive style with 4 for 46 in a comfortable victory at Auckland. Another Test cap followed, at Wellington, but he managed only one wicket (the former Titans wicketkeeper Kruger van Wyk) there. A back injury cut short his tour of England later in 2012, but de Lange remains very much one to watch.

THE FACTS   Marchant de Lange's figures of 7 for 81 on Test debut have been bettered for South Africa only by Lance Klusener (8 for 64 v India in 1996-97) and Alf Hall (7 for 63 v England in 1922-23) ... de Lange took 6 for 36 and 5 for 26 for Easterns v Boland at Benoni in January 2011 ... He took 5 for 56 – including four wickets in 11 balls – for South Africa A v Australians at Potchefstroom in December 2011 ...

THE FIGURES to 17.09.12   **ᴇꜱᴘⁿ cricinfo.com**

Batting & Fielding	M	Inns	NO	Runs	HS	Avge	S/R	100	50	4s	6s	Ct	St
Tests	2	2	0	9	9	4.50	47.36	0	0	2	0	1	0
ODIs	1	0	–	–	–	–	–	–	–	–	–	0	0
T20Is	2	0	–	–	–	–	–	–	–	–	–	0	0
First-class	18	23	3	204	35	10.20	68.91	0	0	25	9	8	0

Bowling	M	Balls	Runs	Wkts	BB	Avge	RpO	S/R	5i	10m
Tests	2	448	277	9	7–81	30.77	3.70	49.77	1	0
ODIs	1	54	46	4	4–46	11.50	5.11	13.50	0	0
T20Is	2	48	79	3	2–36	26.33	9.87	16.00	0	0
First-class	18	3157	1928	67	7–81	28.77	3.66	47.11	4	1

NARSINGH **DEONARINE**

Full name	**Narsingh Deonarine**
Born	**August 16, 1983, Albion, Berbice, Guyana**
Teams	**Guyana**
Style	**Left-hand bat, offspinner**
Test debut	**West Indies v South Africa at Georgetown 2004-05**
ODI debut	**West Indies v India at Dambulla 2005**
T20I debut	**West Indies v Australia at Hobart 2009-10**

THE PROFILE In many respects Narsingh Deonarine is a carbon copy of his distinguished Guyana team-mate Shivnarine Chanderpaul. Both are small, wiry left-handers, although Deonarine is rather chunkier and not quite so open and unorthodox at the crease. He also affects the anti-glare patches under the eyes that Chanderpaul borrowed from baseball. Deonarine also started as a handy offspinner, with an easy delivery not unlike Carl Hooper's. It was his bowling which first helped him into the regional team in 2005, and he toured Sri Lanka later that year after several senior players dropped out following a contracts dispute. When the seniors returned, however, there was no place for Deonarine – and for four years it looked as if that was his solitary flirtation with the international game. But in 2008-09 he topped 1000 runs for Guyana, finishing as the leading scorer in the regional tournament, and was recalled for the tour of England: although he didn't make the side there, he did in Australia, scoring 82 at Perth. Some handy innings followed against South Africa in mid-2010, to suggest that Guyana might be providing much of the West Indian middle-order fibre for a while yet, but Deonarine's career stalled later that year when he was cut from the board's contracts list, a no-nonsense press release stating that his fitness was "regrettably unacceptable for an international cricketer". He worked on that, started bowling more, and was back for the England tour in 2012: he played in the final Test, and kept his place for the New Zealand series that followed at home, making 79 as the first Test was won then taking six wickets with his offbreaks in another victory in the second.

THE FACTS Deonarine scored 198 for Guyana v Combined Campuses & Colleges at Georgetown in March 2009: that season he was the leading runscorer in the West Indian domestic tournament with 1068 ... Deonarine's maiden first-class century was 100 for West Indies B v India A at Bridgetown in March 2003 ... He took 7 for 26 as Guyana bowled Barbados out for 58 at Bridgetown in March 2012 ...

THE FIGURES *to 17.09.12* ▄▄cricinfo.com

Batting & Fielding	M	Inns	NO	Runs	HS	Avge	S/R	100	50	4s	6s	Ct	St
Tests	14	22	2	588	82	29.40	40.52	0	4	66	6	12	0
ODIs	20	19	3	510	65*	31.87	69.48	0	4	42	7	6	0
T20Is	7	6	1	49	36*	9.80	98.00	0	0	4	0	0	0
First-class	100	171	19	5673	198	37.32	–	8	38	–	–	66	0

Bowling	M	Balls	Runs	Wkts	BB	Avge	RpO	S/R	5i	10m
Tests	14	1169	531	19	4–37	27.94	2.72	61.52	0	0
ODIs	20	321	312	6	2–18	52.00	5.83	53.50	0	0
T20Is	7	36	50	0	–	–	8.33	–	0	0
First-class	100	7997	3676	122	7–26	30.13	2.75	65.54	3	0

JADE **DERNBACH**

Full name	**Jade Winston Dernbach**
Born	**April 3, 1986, Johannesburg, South Africa**
Teams	**Surrey**
Style	**Right-hand bat, right-arm fast-medium bowler**
Test debut	**No Tests yet**
ODI debut	**England v Sri Lanka at The Oval 2011**
T20I debut	**England v Sri Lanka at Bristol 2011**

THE PROFILE Jade Dernbach was born in South Africa, but his family came to England when he was 14, and he considers himself very English: "I don't owe anything to South Africa. I was just born there, did a bit of schooling there. My whole cricket career has been based in the UK." And his professional cricket has been for Surrey, as a fast-medium bowler of modest pace but a lot of variety. His speciality is the slower ball, which Surrey's manager Chris Adams describes as "an X-factor delivery – it has a very special variance, dynamite and unusual, an exceptional disguise". If that sounds a lot to live up to, the man they call "Dirtbag" has largely managed it so far. He made his first-team debut at 17, and matured quickly to be Surrey's leading first-class wicket-taker in 2006 with 46. A spell in Australia, playing grade cricket in Sydney, helped improve his allround game, and his first hint of international recognition came in 2009, when he was called up to the ECB Fast Bowling Programme in Florida and Chennai. He was part of the Performance squad which shadowed the successful main one during the 2010-11 Ashes tour, and was playing for the England Lions in the West Indies when he was called up for the World Cup as a replacement for the injured Ajmal Shahzad. England departed the competition almost immediately he arrived, but Dernbach stayed in the reckoning, and made his international debut at home in 2011. He took 4 for 22 in a Twenty20 game against India, but wickets were rarer in the 50-overs games. Still, Dernbach had established himself as a handy back-up performer, and earned an incremental England contract.

THE FACTS Dernbach took 6 for 47 for Surrey at Leicester in June 2009 ... He took a wicket (Sanath Jayasuriya of Sri Lanka) with his eighth delivery in Twenty20 internationals, and three days later took one with his ninth ball in ODIs (Angelo Mathews) ... Dernbach's bowling arm is covered in tattoos – "everything from Chinese script to a fish," according to *The Sun* newspaper ...

THE FIGURES to 17.09.12   **ESP11**cricinfo.com

Batting & Fielding	M	Inns	NO	Runs	HS	Avge	S/R	100	50	4s	6s	Ct	St
Tests	0	0	–	–	–	–	–	–	–	–	–	–	–
ODIs	18	5	1	15	5	3.75	57.69	0	0	1	0	3	0
T20Is	12	1	0	3	3	3.00	75.00	0	0	0	0	6	0
First-class	73	93	34	561	56*	9.50	–	0	1	–	–	10	0

Bowling	M	Balls	Runs	Wkts	BB	Avge	RpO	S/R	5i	10m
Tests	0	0	–	–	–	–	–	–	–	–
ODIs	18	913	920	25	4–45	36.80	6.04	36.52	0	0
T20Is	12	244	276	14	4–22	19.71	6.78	17.42	0	0
First-class	73	11537	6538	203	6–47	32.20	3.40	56.83	9	0

AB de VILLIERS

SOUTH AFRICA

Full name	**Abraham Benjamin de Villiers**
Born	**February 17, 1984, Pretoria**
Teams	**Titans, Royal Challengers Bangalore**
Style	**Right-hand bat, wicketkeeper, occ. medium-pacer**
Test debut	**South Africa v England at Port Elizabeth 2004-05**
ODI debut	**South Africa v England at Bloemfontein 2004-05**
T20I debut	**South Africa v Australia at Johannesburg 2005-06**

THE PROFILE A batsman of breathtaking chutzpah and enterprise, as well as the skills and the temperament required to back up his creative intent. A superb fielder, also perfectly at ease donning pads and gloves. A fine rugby player, golfer, and tennis player. All AB de Villiers needs to show off his abundant gifts is a ball ... just about any ball. Few drive as sweetly and to the boundary as regularly, and – in South Africa, at any rate – even fewer possess the silkily snappy footwork required to put spinners in their place. He adjusts seamlessly to all formats, averaging almost 50 in both Tests and ODIs. His potential was recognised years before he made the leap to senior international level as an opening batsman against England in 2004-05. After a slump in 2006 and 2007, de Villiers returned to the straight and narrow early in 2008 with a blistering 103 not out off 109 balls against West Indies at Durban. Later that year came an undefeated 217 at Ahmedabad, South Africa's first double-century against India he bettered that, statistically anyway, with 278 not out (a national record at the time) against Pakistan in November 2010. South Africans do not take easily to the precociously talented, but it helps if they do not come across all precocious. Such is the case with de Villiers, whose lazy smile under an every-which-way thatch of blond hair has helped convince the nation that he's worth feeding despite all that talent. He obviously convinced the selectors, anyway, because he was appointed limited-overs captain in 2011. His workload was increased when Mark Boucher's eye injury meant de Villiers had to keep wicket in Tests, too. He did well in England in 2012, but this may prove to be an unsustainable extra burden.

THE FACTS de Villiers scored 278 not out against Pakistan at Abu Dhabi in November 2010 ... He made 217 not out at Ahmedabad in April 2008, after India had been bowled out for 76 ... He averages 81.42 in Tests against Sri Lanka, but 17.25 in four matches against Bangladesh ... de Villiers went a Test-record 78 innings before falling for a duck, against Bangladesh in November 2008 ... His record includes five ODIs for the Africa XI ...

THE FIGURES to 17.09.12   **ESPncricinfo.com**

Batting & Fielding	M	Inns	NO	Runs	HS	Avge	S/R	100	50	4s	6s	Ct	St
Tests	77	129	14	5618	278*	48.85	54.92	13	29	649	42	108	1
ODIs	132	127	22	5168	146	49.21	93.15	13	29	478	88	109	3
T20Is	39	38	7	693	79*	22.35	119.48	0	4	52	21	35	4
First-class	102	173	19	7481	278*	48.57	57.12	16	43	–	–	156	2

Bowling	M	Balls	Runs	Wkts	BB	Avge	RpO	S/R	5i	10m
Tests	77	198	99	2	2–49	49.50	3.00	99.00	0	0
ODIs	132	12	22	0	–	–	11.00	–	0	0
T20Is	39	0	–	–	–	–	–	–	–	–
First-class	102	228	133	2	2–49	66.50	3.50	114.00	0	0

MAHENDRA SINGH **DHONI**

Full name	**Mahendra Singh Dhoni**
Born	**July 7, 1981, Ranchi, Bihar**
Teams	**Jharkhand, Chennai Super Kings**
Style	**Right-hand bat, wicketkeeper**
Test debut	**India v Sri Lanka at Chennai 2005-06**
ODI debut	**India v Bangladesh at Chittagong 2004-05**
T20I debut	**India v South Africa at Johannesburg 2006-07**

THE PROFILE The odds against a Virender Sehwag clone emerging from the backwaters of Jharkhand were highly remote – until MS Dhoni arrived (a one-time railway ticket collector, his first love was football). His batting is swashbuckling, and his wicketkeeping usually secure. A rapid hundred as East Zone clinched the Deodhar Trophy, an audacious 60 in the Duleep Trophy final, and two tons against Pakistan A established him as a clinical destroyer of bowling attacks, and in just his fifth ODI – against Pakistan in April 2005 – Dhoni cracked a dazzling 148, putting even Sehwag in the shade. He followed that with 183 against Sri Lanka in November, beating Adam Gilchrist's highest ODI score by a wicketkeeper. He made an instant impact in Tests, too, pounding 148 at Faisalabad in his fifth match, when India were struggling to avoid the follow-on. His keeping improved, and he quickly became key in a revitalised side. He stepped up to captain India to the inaugural World Twenty20 title in September 2007, and was then the most expensive signing ($1.5m) for the inaugural IPL in 2008. He took over as full-time Test captain when Anil Kumble retired that November, rubber-stamping victory over Australia then defeating England and New Zealand. He won eight of his first 11 Tests – an unprecedented start for an Indian skipper – then turned his attention to 50-over cricket, leading from the front with the bat to make sure the 2011 World Cup was won. After that, though, he was criticised as India slumped to 4-0 Test whitewashes in England and Australia – but he remained calm, and continued to lead with panache (in one-day games at least) throughout 2012.

THE FACTS Dhoni's unbeaten 183 against Sri Lanka at Jaipur in November 2005 is the highest score in ODIs by a wicketkeeper, and included 120 in boundaries (10 sixes and 15 fours) ... Of players with 4000 runs in ODIs, only Michael Bevan (53.88) has a higher average than Dhoni's 51.17 ... The only other Indian to score a century in an ODI in which he kept wicket is Rahul Dravid ... Dhoni's record includes three ODIs for the Asia XI ...

THE FIGURES to 17.09.12   ᴇsᴘⁿcricinfo.com

Batting & Fielding	M	Inns	NO	Runs	HS	Avge	S/R	100	50	4s	6s	Ct	St
Tests	69	109	13	3692	148	38.45	60.00	5	26	395	66	194	30
ODIs	211	188	53	6908	183*	51.17	88.42	7	46	531	139	199	66
T20Is	33	31	12	587	48*	30.85	109.51	0	0	34	17	15	5
First-class	110	175	16	5854	148	36.81	–	8	40	–	–	302	49

Bowling	M	Balls	Runs	Wkts	BB	Avge	RpO	S/R	5i	10m
Tests	69	78	58	0	–	–	4.46	–	0	0
ODIs	211	12	14	1	1–14	14.00	7.00	12.00	0	0
T20Is	33	0	–	–	–	–	–	–	–	–
First-class	110	108	78	0	–	–	4.33	–	0	0

TILLEKERATNE **DILSHAN**

Full name	**Tillekeratne Mudiyanselage Dilshan**
Born	**October 14, 1976, Kalutara**
Teams	**Bloomfield, Basnahira, Royal Challengers Bangalore**
Style	**Right-hand bat, offspinner**
Test debut	**Sri Lanka v Zimbabwe at Bulawayo 1999-2000**
ODI debut	**Sri Lanka v Zimbabwe at Bulawayo 1999-2000**
T20I debut	**Sri Lanka v England at Southampton 2006**

THE PROFILE Tillekeratne Mudiyanselage Dilshan, who started life as Tuwan Mohamad Dilshan before converting to Buddhism, is a light-footed right-hander and an electric fielder who made an unbeaten 163 against Zimbabwe in only his second Test in November 1999. Technically sound, comfortable against pace, with quick feet and strong wrists, Dilshan has talent in abundance. But that bright start was followed by a frustrating time when he was shovelled up and down the order, and in and out of the side. After a lean series against England in 2001 he didn't play another Test until late 2003. He returned determined to play his own aggressive game, and was immediately successful. He continued to do well, and was one of four centurions in an innings victory over India in July 2008. He put a lean one-day trot behind him just in time for the 2007 World Cup, then against Bangladesh at Chittagong in January 2009 hit 162 and 143 then wrapped up the match with four wickets. Later that year Dilshan lit up the World Twenty20 in England with some spectacular batting, including his own trademark cheeky scoop over the shoulder. He made ten international centuries in 2009, although the following year was rather less spectacular. On the march to the 2011 World Cup final he was in fine form, scoring two centuries, and inherited the captaincy shortly afterwards when Kumar Sangakkara stepped down. Dilshan led from the front in England, making a superb 193 in the Lord's Test, but a run of defeats cost him the job early the following year. He remained an important member of the side, though, hitting two Test centuries against Pakistan in mid-2012.

THE FACTS Dilshan's 193 in 2011 was Sri Lanka's highest score in a Test at Lord's ... He hit 168 against Bangladesh in Colombo in September 2005, putting on 280 with Thilan Samaraweera, a Sri Lankan fifth-wicket record in Tests ... Dilshan made his first ODI century in the record total of 443 for 9 against the Netherlands at Amstelveen in July 2006 ... He made 200 not out while captaining North Central Province v Central in Colombo in February 2005 ...

THE FIGURES to 17.09.12   **ESFΠ** cricinfo.com

Batting & Fielding	M	Inns	NO	Runs	HS	Avge	S/R	100	50	4s	6s	Ct	St
Tests	81	133	11	5028	193	41.21	65.91	14	21	621	24	86	0
ODIs	248	223	32	6715	160*	35.15	86.54	13	27	696	44	96	1
T20Is	38	37	6	917	104*	29.58	124.59	1	5	112	17	18	2
First-class	219	357	22	13068	200*	39.00	–	35	55	–	–	350	23

Bowling	M	Balls	Runs	Wkts	BB	Avge	RpO	S/R	5i	10m
Tests	81	2629	1340	32	4–10	41.87	3.05	82.15	0	0
ODIs	248	3985	3190	67	4–4	47.61	4.80	59.47	0	0
T20Is	38	150	185	5	2–4	37.00	7.40	30.00	0	0
First-class	219	5385	2670	76	5–49	35.13	2.97	70.85	1	0

J-P **DUMINY**

Full name	**Jean-Paul Duminy**
Born	**April 14, 1984, Strandfontein, Cape Town**
Teams	**Cape Cobras, Deccan Chargers**
Style	**Left-hand bat, occasional offspinner**
Test debut	**South Africa v Australia at Perth 2008-09**
ODI debut	**South Africa v Sri Lanka at Colombo 2004-05**
T20I debut	**South Africa v Bangladesh at Cape Town 2007-08**

THE PROFILE Slightly built but stylish, left-hander Jean-Paul Duminy had trouble finding a place in South Africa's strong middle order – but when an injury to Ashwell Prince finally let him into the Test side in Australia late in 2008, more than four years after his one-day debut, he certainly made it count. First Duminy stroked a nerveless 50 not out as his side made light of a target of 414 to start with victory at Perth, then he set up a series-winning triumph at Melbourne with a superb 166, most of it coming during an eye-popping ninth-wicket stand of 180 with Dale Steyn. A four-hour 73 followed in the return series in a defeat at Durban: Duminy had arrived, a fact confirmed by a big-money IPL contract. He had first featured in a one-day series in Sri Lanka in 2004. He struggled there, scoring only 29 runs in five attempts, and dropped off the national radar for a couple of years. But he continued to score heavily at home, and was given an extended one-day run after the 2007 World Cup, showing signs of developing into a late-innings "finisher": he batted into the final over in three successive victories against West Indies. A horror run in Tests in 2009-10 – only one score above 11 in nine innings – cost him his place, but Duminy remained a one-day fixture, missing a century against Ireland during the 2011 World Cup by just one run. He returned to the Test side after more than two years with 103 against New Zealand at Wellington in March 2012, then batted tidily in England later in the year. He is also a superb fielder, while his part-time offbreaks occasionally come in handy.

THE FACTS Duminy scored 169 as Cape Cobras followed on against the Eagles at Stellenbosch in February 2007 ... He scored 200 not out – with nine sixes – for the Cobras against the Dolphins at Paarl in December 2010 ... Both Duminy's ODI hundreds have come at Zimbabwe's expense ... Against Ireland in 2011 he became only the second man (after Adam Gilchrist) to be out for 99 in a World Cup match ...

THE FIGURES *to 17.09.12*　　　　　　　　**ESPN**cricinfo.com

Batting & Fielding	M	Inns	NO	Runs	HS	Avge	S/R	100	50	4s	6s	Ct	St
Tests	16	26	5	789	166	37.57	43.32	2	4	92	6	14	0
ODIs	94	85	20	2601	129	40.01	83.60	2	15	163	30	39	0
T20Is	37	35	9	846	96*	32.53	123.14	0	4	69	26	16	0
First-class	73	119	21	4998	200*	51.00	49.95	15	25	–	–	55	0

Bowling	M	Balls	Runs	Wkts	BB	Avge	RpO	S/R	5i	10m
Tests	16	875	510	12	3–89	42.50	3.49	72.91	0	0
ODIs	94	1234	1032	27	3–31	38.22	5.01	45.70	0	0
T20Is	37	120	165	6	1–3	27.50	8.25	20.00	0	0
First-class	73	3108	1757	43	5–108	40.86	3.39	72.27	1	0

FAF **DU PLESSIS**

Full name	**Francois du Plessis**
Born	**July 13, 1984, Pretoria**
Teams	**Titans, Chennai Super Kings**
Style	**Right-hand bat, legspinner**
Test debut	**No Tests yet**
ODI debut	**South Africa v India at Cape Town 2010-11**
T20I debut	**South Africa v England at Chester-le-Street 2012**

THE PROFILE Francois du Plessis, usually known as Faf, could well have joined the South African player drain to England after signing as a Kolpak with Lancashire in 2008. However, he produced a stunning display in the MTN40 competition at home in 2010-11 – he topped the run-charts with 567, including three centuries, from ten matches – and was called up to the national one-day squad. He made his debut in the home series against India shortly before the World Cup, making 60 in his first innings, and was included in the World Cup squad – although in India he was part of a misfiring middle order that was one cause of South Africa's quarter-final loss to New Zealand. Du Plessis, who has a liking for big scores, played in the Lancashire leagues before proving a popular signing at Old Trafford. He's a superb fielder – probably South Africa's best since Jonty Rhodes – and Lancashire fans still go misty-eyed over a sensational catch in the Twenty20 Cup quarter-final against Middlesex in 2008. He's also a handy legspinner, but batting is very much his strong suit: he can score all around the wicket, and possesses a peachy off-drive. Du Plessis has been a consistent performer in the 50-overs side: after two early failures he failed to reach double figures only once in his next 18 innings, which included a run-a-ball 72 against Sri Lanka at Bloemfontein in January 2012 and an unbeaten 66 from just 49 deliveries in New Zealand the following month. Good form while captaining South Africa A ensured him a place on the one-day leg of the triumphant England tour later in 2012, and a Test cap is not out of the question.

THE FACTS Du Plessis scored 176 for Titans v Lions at Centurion in November 2008 ... He made 144, sharing a stand of 292 with Dean Elgar, while captaining South Africa A v Sri Lanka A at Durban in July 2012 ... du Plessis made 177 in an Under-19 Test against England at Chelmsford in August 2003 ... He played for Lancashire in 2008 and 2009 ...

THE FIGURES *to 17.09.12*   **ESPNcricinfo.com**

Batting & Fielding	M	Inns	NO	Runs	HS	Avge	S/R	100	50	4s	6s	Ct	St
Tests	0	0	–	–	–	–	–	–	–	–	–	–	–
ODIs	26	24	4	563	72	28.15	88.38	0	4	49	4	12	0
T20Is	2	2	0	12	8	6.00	133.33	0	0	1	0	0	0
First-class	77	126	11	4381	176	38.09	–	8	29	–	–	75	0

Bowling	M	Balls	Runs	Wkts	BB	Avge	RpO	S/R	5i	10m
Tests	0	0	–	–	–	–	–	–	–	–
ODIs	26	132	123	2	1–8	61.50	5.59	66.00	0	0
T20Is	2	0	–	–	–	–	–	–	–	–
First-class	77	2444	1387	41	4–39	33.82	3.40	59.60	0	0

FIDEL **EDWARDS**

Full name	**Fidel Henderson Edwards**
Born	**February 6, 1982, Gays, St Peter, Barbados**
Teams	**Barbados**
Style	**Right-hand bat, right-arm fast bowler**
Test debut	**West Indies v Sri Lanka at Kingston 2002-03**
ODI debut	**West Indies v Zimbabwe at Harare 2003-04**
T20I debut	**West Indies v South Africa at Johannesburg 2007-08**

THE PROFILE Fidel Edwards had an extraordinary start in international cricket, the kind that can either haunt or add lustre to a career. He was spotted in the nets by Brian Lara early in 2003, and called up for his Test debut after only one match for Barbados: he promptly took 5 for 36 against Sri Lanka. He added five in his first overseas Test, and six in his debut one-dayer. Edwards has a slingy round-arm action which leaves him vulnerable to back strains, and indeed he missed most of 2010 after surgery to correct a slipped disc – but he roared back in mid-2011 with 19 wickets in three Tests against India. When he's fit, though, his unusual action and slippery pace has troubled many a distinguished batsman. Edwards bowls fast, can swing the ball and reverse it too, but insists that he doesn't go for out-and-out pace – which is just as well, because he has learned that pace without control leads straight to the boundary at international level. In Antigua in June 2006 he had India's Virender Sehwag in all kinds of trouble before a hamstring twanged. And he hurried England's batsmen up in 2007, taking nine wickets in two Tests and ten – including 5 for 45 at Lord's – as West Indies won the one-day series 2-1. After that he grabbed eight more, including both openers in both innings, in the first Test against Australia at Kingston in May 2008. But between November 2011 and May 2012, though, he took only nine wickets in six Tests, and lost his place. He's not much of a batsman, yet twice hung on tenaciously to deny England series-levelling victories in the Caribbean early in 2009.

THE FACTS Edwards had played only one first-class match – taking one wicket – before his Test debut against Sri Lanka at Kingston in June 2003, when he took 5 for 36 … He later took 6 for 22 on his ODI debut, against Zimbabwe at Harare in November 2003 … Edwards opened the bowling in Tests several times with his half-brother Pedro Collins … Edwards averages 21.45 with the ball in Tests against Sri Lanka, but 90.36 in eight matches against South Africa … Unoriginally, his nickname is "Castro" …

THE FIGURES to 17.09.12 **espncricinfo.com**

Batting & Fielding	M	Inns	NO	Runs	HS	Avge	S/R	100	50	4s	6s	Ct	St
Tests	54	87	28	392	30	6.64	28.16	0	0	48	2	9	0
ODIs	50	22	14	73	13	9.12	45.62	0	0	5	0	4	0
T20Is	17	4	2	10	7*	5.00	111.11	0	0	1	0	5	0
First-class	83	128	46	593	40	7.23	–	0	0	–	–	14	0

Bowling	M	Balls	Runs	Wkts	BB	Avge	RpO	S/R	5i	10m
Tests	54	9391	6064	158	7–87	38.37	3.87	59.43	11	0
ODIs	50	2138	1812	60	6–22	30.20	5.08	35.63	2	0
T20Is	17	318	434	14	3–23	31.00	8.18	22.71	0	0
First-class	83	11656	7537	228	7–87	33.05	3.87	51.12	13	1

ELIAS SUNNY

Full name	**Mohammad Elias Sunny**
Born	**August 2, 1986, Dhaka**
Teams	**Dhaka**
Style	**Left-hand bat, slow left-arm orthodox spinner**
Test debut	**Bangladesh v West Indies at Chittagong 2011-12**
ODI debut	**Bangladesh v Pakistan at Mirpur 2011-12**
T20I debut	**Bangladesh v Ireland at Belfast 2012**

THE PROFILE   He may be one of Bangladesh's production line of slow left-armers, but Elias Sunny has more than one string to his bow. He's a livewire in the field, and is also a better batsman than most of his rivals: his three first-class centuries include 176, back in 2005, although he has not yet had much chance with the bat at international level. In the 2010-11 Bangladesh domestic season Sunny finished in the top ten of both sets of averages, with 498 runs at 45 and 24 wickets at 26. He made his first-class debut at 17, but with so many other spinners around it took him almost a decade to break into the national set-up. When he did, towards the end of 2011, he made it count: he shrugged off the disappointment of having two early catches dropped to run through the West Indian batting at Chittagong, and finished with 6 for 94. *Wisden* observed that he "flighted the ball craftily", despite a slightly round-arm action, and he became only the third Bangladeshi (after Javed Omar and Mohammad Ashraful in 2001) to lift the match award on debut. An untimely stomach upset kept him out of the next Test, but he was back when Pakistan visited, and persisted manfully to take three of the five wickets that fell as they ran up nearly 600. Then, when Bangladesh toured the cricketing outposts of Europe in mid-2012, Sunny collected a cheap five-for against Ireland to keep his name in the frame. He started playing cricket with a taped-up tennis ball in the Hajaribagh district of Dhaka – and remains much in demand on the popular tape-ball circuit.

THE FACTS   Elias took 6 for 94 in his first Test in October 2011: only two left-arm spinners (Alf Valentine of West Indies and England's James Langridge) have had better debut figures ... Sunny took 5 for 13, Bangladesh's best figures in Twenty20 internationals, against Ireland at Belfast in July 2012 ... His best first-class figures are 7 for 79 (13 for 107 in the match) for Dhaka v Sylhet in October 2008 ... Sunny hit 176 for Chittagong v Barisal in February 2005, sharing a fourth-wicket stand of 365 with Ehsanul Haque ...

THE FIGURES *to 17.09.12*   **espncricinfo.com**

Batting & Fielding	M	Inns	NO	Runs	HS	Avge	S/R	100	50	4s	6s	Ct	St
Tests	3	5	1	38	20*	9.50	27.33	0	0	4	1	1	0
ODIs	2	2	1	1	1	1.00	16.66	0	0	0	0	0	0
T20Is	6	3	2	4	2*	4.00	66.66	0	0	0	0	3	0
First-class	61	97	12	1980	176	23.29	41.18	3	8	–	–	32	0

Bowling	M	Balls	Runs	Wkts	BB	Avge	RpO	S/R	5i	10m
Tests	3	623	353	12	6–94	29.41	3.39	51.91	1	0
ODIs	2	96	82	3	2–36	27.33	5.12	32.00	0	0
T20Is	6	120	110	9	5–13	12.22	5.50	13.33	1	0
First-class	61	12320	5741	224	7–79	25.62	2.79	55.00	11	1

SHAMINDA **ERANGA**

Full name	**Ranaweera Mudiyanselage Shaminda Eranga**
Born	**June 23, 1986, Chilaw**
Teams	**Chilaw Marians, Uva**
Style	**Right-hand bat, right-arm fast-medium bowler**
Test debut	**Sri Lanka v Australia at Colombo 2011**
ODI debut	**Sri Lanka v Australia at Hambantota 2011**
T20I debut	**Sri Lanka v India at Pallekele 2012**

THE PROFILE A brisk fast-medium bowler who can nudge 90mph on the speed-gun, Shaminda Eranga made a spectacular start in international cricket, dismissing Brad Haddin with his second ball in ODIs (and adding Ricky Ponting a few overs later). A month later, called up for the third Test against Australia, he went one better, taking a wicket with his first ball, a widish delivery which Shane Watson obligingly sliced to backward point. Eranga will hope to last longer than the only other Sri Lankan to strike with his first ball in a Test – Chamila Gamage, who did it in 2002, won only one more cap and finished with just five wickets. Eranga had that many after his first Test, adding Michael Clarke, Mike Hussey and Haddin (again) to a distinguished bag to finish with 4 for 65 in the first innings. He was spotted in 2006 at an all-island pace-bowling competition by the former Test fast bowler Champaka Ramanayake. Eranga, who is also a handy tailend batsman with a first-class century to his name, joined the Chilaw Marians, and did enough to earn a place in the national development squad. He made his debut for Sri Lanka A in 2010, and was in the squad that faced West Indies late that year. "This young lad is fit and looks a willing horse," observed Aravinda de Silva, Sri Lanka's chief selector. In 2011, after some good displays for the A team on tour in England – he took seven wickets in the match against Durham – Eranga was flown back to Sri Lanka to join up with the main squad for the Australian series. A shoulder injury reduced his effectiveness in 2012, but he was recalled for his Twenty20 international debut in August 2012 – and again took a wicket (Gautam Gambhir) in his first over.

THE FACTS Eranga was the second Sri Lankan (after Chamila Gamage) to take a wicket with his first ball in a Test match, dismissing Australia's Shane Watson at Colombo in September 2011 ... The previous month Eranga had struck with his second ball in ODIs, and next year took a wicket with his fourth ball in a Twenty20 international ... Eranga scored 100 not out for Chilaw Marians v Sinhalese Sports Club in February 2012 ...

THE FIGURES to 17.09.12   **ESPn**cricinfo.com

Batting & Fielding	M	Inns	NO	Runs	HS	Avge	S/R	100	50	4s	6s	Ct	St
Tests	1	1	0	12	12	12.00	30.76	0	0	2	0	1	0
ODIs	3	3	1	3	2	1.50	27.27	0	0	0	0	1	0
T20Is	1	1	0	6	6	6.00	85.71	0	1	0	0	0	0
First-class	41	55	21	869	100*	25.55	61.80	1	4	78	33	24	0

Bowling	M	Balls	Runs	Wkts	BB	Avge	RpO	S/R	5i	10m
Tests	1	254	127	5	4–65	25.40	3.00	50.80	0	0
ODIs	3	114	99	4	2–38	24.75	5.21	28.50	0	0
T20Is	1	24	30	2	2–30	15.00	7.50	12.00	0	0
First-class	41	4053	2627	77	5–86	34.11	3.88	52.63	1	0

PAKISTAN

FAISAL IQBAL

Full name	**Faisal Iqbal**
Born	**December 30, 1981, Karachi, Sind**
Teams	**Karachi, Pakistan International Airlines**
Style	**Right-hand bat, occasional right-arm medium-pacer**
Test debut	**Pakistan v New Zealand at Auckland 2000-01**
ODI debut	**Pakistan v Sri Lanka at Lahore 1999-2000**
T20I debut	**No T20Is yet**

THE PROFILE A gutsy middle-order batsman with a sound defence and attitude to boot, Faisal Iqbal was a prolific junior performer, but his elevation to the national squad was criticised as nepotism – he's the nephew of the great Javed Miandad, the coach when Faisal made his Test debut in 2000-01. But he silenced the critics with three pleasing knocks then, and a counter-attacking 83 off 85 balls against Australia in Colombo in October 2002. He was particularly impressive against Shane Warne, using his feet superbly to seize the momentum, and did it all with a swagger reminiscent of his uncle. However, he couldn't do it again in that series, or in South Africa shortly afterwards, and lost his place. Recalled against India at Karachi in January 2006 when Inzamam-ul-Haq was injured, Faisal made an attractive maiden Test hundred, with some assured back-foot play and composed defence, to help Pakistan to a comfortable series-clinching win. Another good season in 2008-09, which included his second double-century, ensured he stayed in the mix, but after the Sydney Test of January 2010 – which Pakistan somehow lost after taking a first-innings lead of 206 – Faisal was one of those jettisoned. That seemed to be that, but he remained a consistent runscorer at home, and after he averaged nearly 50 in the domestic season he was recalled for the Sri Lankan tour in June 2012, although he didn't actually get into the side. "I have been surviving only because of my mental toughness," he said. "In the past I have been playing mainly as a replacement, which is why I wasn't able to cement a permanent place. But now I think I can make it."

THE FACTS Faisal Iqbal's maiden Test century, 139 at Karachi in January 2006, helped Pakistan defeat India by a record margin of 341 runs, even though they were 0 for 3 after the first over of the match ... He made 200 not out for PIA v Sui Southern Gas in January 2009 ... Faisal made 100 not out v Zimbabwe at Harare in November 2002: in 17 other ODIs his highest score is 32 ... His uncle Javed Miandad is Pakistan's leading scorer, with 8832 runs from 124 Tests ...

THE FIGURES to 17.09.12   **ESPNcricinfo.com**

Batting & Fielding	M	Inns	NO	Runs	HS	Avge	S/R	100	50	4s	6s	Ct	St
Tests	26	44	2	1124	139	26.76	44.16	1	8	136	5	22	0
ODIs	18	16	2	314	100*	22.42	60.50	1	0	24	4	3	0
T20Is	0	0	–	–	–	–	–	–	–	–	–	–	–
First-class	174	272	28	9842	200*	40.33	–	21	55	–	–	146	0

Bowling	M	Balls	Runs	Wkts	BB	Avge	RpO	S/R	5i	10m
Tests	26	6	7	0	–	–	7.00	–	0	0
ODIs	18	18	33	0	–	–	11.00	–	0	0
T20Is	0	0	–	–	–	–	–	–	–	–
First-class	174	210	143	1	1–6	143.00	4.08	210.00	0	0

CALLUM **FERGUSON**

Full name	**Callum James Ferguson**
Born	**November 21, 1984, North Adelaide, South Australia**
Teams	**South Australia, Pune Warriors**
Style	**Right-hand bat, right-arm medium-pacer**
Test debut	**No Tests yet**
ODI debut	**Australia v New Zealand at Melbourne 2008-09**
T20I debut	**Australia v New Zealand at Sydney 2008-09**

THE PROFILE After a few stutters, Callum Ferguson came of age in 2008-09. Easy to watch, more of an accumulator than a big hitter, he had suffered from getting out when set, but came back from a season of English club cricket more determined to cash in. His 644 first-class runs in the season that followed included two hundreds (his first for nearly four years) and, despite being lightly built, he showed some power too, with 401 one-day runs at almost a run a ball. He was called up for the Chappell-Hadlee one-dayers against New Zealand in February 2009, and made a rapid 55 not out in the last match: he continued this good start in South Africa, before kicking off the ODIs in England in September with 71 not out at The Oval and 55 at Lord's. All this was a welcome return to form: Ferguson had shone in 2004-05, his debut season, with 733 Shield runs – including 93 in his second match and a maiden century in his fourth – while the rest of South Australia's strokemakers struggled. But over the next three seasons he struggled to reproduce that form, before the retirements of Darren Lehmann and Matthew Elliott meant more responsibility. There was a setback in October 2009, when he badly injured his right knee while fielding in the Champions Trophy final victory over New Zealand. Ferguson needed reconstructive surgery and missed the whole of the next home season. He was back in 2010-11, and was soon recalled to the national side – but 46 against England at Sydney in February was not enough to earn him a World Cup place, and he missed the later tour of Sri Lanka too. But he remained in the mix, and was part of the squad that took on Pakistan in the UAE in September 2012, although he didn't actually get a game.

THE FACTS Ferguson made 132 for South Australia v Queensland at Brisbane in November 2008 ... In January 2002 he scored 258 not out for South Australia Under-19s v Queensland ... Ferguson scored 93 (v Queensland) in his second first-class match in 2004-05, and 103 (v New South Wales) in his fourth, in 2004-05 ...

THE FIGURES to 17.09.12   **ESPN cricinfo.com**

Batting & Fielding	M	Inns	NO	Runs	HS	Avge	S/R	100	50	4s	6s	Ct	St
Tests	0	0	–	–	–	–	–	–	–	–	–	–	–
ODIs	30	25	9	663	71*	41.43	85.32	0	5	64	0	7	0
T20Is	3	3	0	16	8	5.33	84.21	0	0	1	0	1	0
First-class	63	117	9	3832	132	35.48	56.46	7	23	–	–	27	0

Bowling	M	Balls	Runs	Wkts	BB	Avge	RpO	S/R	5i	10m
Tests	0	0	–	–	–	–	–	–	–	–
ODIs	30	0	–	–	–	–	–	–	–	–
T20Is	3	0	–	–	–	–	–	–	–	–
First-class	63	42	38	0	–	–	5.42	–	0	0

DILHARA **FERNANDO**

SRI LANKA

Full name	**Congenige Randhi Dilhara Fernando**
Born	**July 19, 1979, Colombo**
Teams	**Sinhalese Sports Club, Uva**
Style	**Right-hand bat, right-arm fast-medium bowler**
Test debut	**Sri Lanka v Pakistan at Colombo 2000**
ODI debut	**Sri Lanka v South Africa at Paarl 2000-01**
T20I debut	**Sri Lanka v England at Southampton 2006**

THE PROFILE When Dilhara Fernando burst onto the international scene, young and raw, he was seen as the long-term replacement for Chaminda Vaas as the cutting edge of Sri Lanka's attack. However, he has been in and out of the side and – although his natural pace means he is usually in the selectors' minds – he has been something of a serial under-achiever in recent years. Six months after his debut he was clocked at 91.9mph in Durban – hits the pitch hard, and moves the ball off the seam. He rattled India at Galle in 2001, taking five wickets and sending Javagal Srinath to hospital. At first he paid for an inconsistent line and length, but worked hard with the former Test opening bowler Rumesh Ratnayake: he also learnt the art of reverse swing, and developed a well-disguised slower one. But injuries intervened. Fernando was quick during the 2003 World Cup, but bowled a lot of no-balls, a problem he later blamed on a spinal stress fracture. He returned after six months, only for another fracture to be detected in January 2004. He reclaimed his place in the national squad later that year, and has been there or thereabouts ever since, although latterly he has found Test wickets elusive – in 11 matches between August 2007 and August 2011 he took only 17 at 67, almost double his career average. The no-ball problem does occasionally resurface: he was omitted after the first Test against Pakistan in March 2006 before returning later that year for the one-day series in England, which Sri Lanka swept 5–0. He was in the 2011 World Cup squad but didn't play, then toured England, where he appeared in two of the Tests before an injured knee ruled him out of the one-day series. He returned to reach 100 Test wickets against Pakistan in mid-2012.

THE FACTS Fernando took 6 for 27 against England in Colombo in September 2007: overall he averages 20.05 with the ball against England in ODIs, but 79.71 in 15 matches against South Africa ... He averages 19.28 with the ball in Tests against Bangladesh – but 49.66 against India, even though his best figures of 5 for 42 came against them ... Fernando's record includes one ODI for the Asia XI ...

THE FIGURES to 17.09.12   **ESPNcricinfo.com**

Batting & Fielding	M	Inns	NO	Runs	HS	Avge	S/R	100	50	4s	6s	Ct	St
Tests	40	47	14	249	39*	8.30	35.11	0	0	30	1	10	0
ODIs	147	61	35	239	20	9.19	60.96	0	0	19	2	27	0
T20Is	17	6	2	24	21	6.00	114.28	0	0	4	0	3	0
First-class	109	107	33	561	42	7.58	–	0	0	–	–	39	0

Bowling	M	Balls	Runs	Wkts	BB	Avge	RpO	S/R	5i	10m
Tests	40	6181	3784	100	5–42	37.84	3.67	61.81	3	0
ODIs	147	6507	5648	187	6–27	30.20	5.20	34.79	1	0
T20Is	17	366	457	18	3–19	25.38	7.49	20.33	0	0
First-class	109	14670	8846	291	6–29	30.39	3.61	50.41	6	0

STEVEN **FINN**

Full name	**Steven Thomas Finn**
Born	**April 4, 1989, Watford, Hertfordshire**
Teams	**Middlesex**
Style	**Right-hand bat, right-arm fast-medium bowler**
Test debut	**England v Bangladesh at Chittagong 2009-10**
ODI debut	**England v Australia at Brisbane 2010-11**
T20I debut	**England v West Indies at The Oval 2011**

THE PROFILE Steven Finn, who measures up at 6ft 7ins (201cm), is the latest beanpole fast bowler to carry England's hopes, and his impressive arrival sounded the death knell for the international career of the previous one, Steve Harmison. Finn pings the ball down from the clouds with a heady blend of pace and bounce, and can rattle the best. He was earmarked as an England prospect early on, and became Middlesex's youngest-ever player in 2005, breaking Fred Titmus's record. After he took 53 Championship wickets in 2009, Finn went with the England Lions to the UAE, when injures struck at the start of the Bangladesh tour early in 2010, Finn was parachuted in as cover. Barely 24 hours after arriving he did well in the warm-up game against Bangladesh A, and three days later made his Test debut, displaying good pace and bounce on a docile Chittagong surface. Back in England Finn took 14 wickets in a match for Middlesex, then claimed five-fors in both early-season Tests against Bangladesh, collecting the match award for his nine wickets at Lord's. He started the 2010-11 Ashes tour strongly – 6 for 125 at Brisbane – but looked a little tired after that and was eventually supplanted by Chris Tremlett and Tim Bresnan. Their successes meant that after taking 46 Test wickets in 2010 Finn played only once in 2011 – he took four wickets against Sri Lanka at Lord's to become the youngest Englishman to reach 50 – but he was back the following year, and used his local knowledge of the Lord's slope to take eight wickets in a close-fought Test against South Africa. He also featured more in the one-day side after successive four-fors against Pakistan on unhelpful surfaces in Abu Dhabi.

THE FACTS Finn took 9 for 37 (after 5 for 69 in the first innings) for Middlesex at Worcester in April 2010: his next two five-fors were in Tests against Bangladesh ... In 2011 Finn became the youngest bowler to reach 50 Test wickets for England, a record previously held by Ian Botham ... At 16 in 2005 Finn was the youngest player to appear in a first-class match for Middlesex, beating the record set by Fred Titmus in 1949 ...

THE FIGURES to 17.09.12   **ᴇsᴘп cricinfo.com**

Batting & Fielding	M	Inns	NO	Runs	HS	Avge	S/R	100	50	4s	6s	Ct	St
Tests	16	18	12	47	19	7.83	25.13	0	0	7	0	4	0
ODIs	25	9	6	77	35	25.66	104.05	0	0	9	2	4	0
T20Is	8	0	–	–	–	–	–	–	–	–	–	1	0
First-class	77	92	31	415	32	6.80	31.27	0	0	52	1	25	0

Bowling	M	Balls	Runs	Wkts	BB	Avge	RpO	S/R	5i	10m
Tests	16	3039	1858	66	6–125	28.15	3.66	46.04	3	0
ODIs	25	1330	1036	40	4–34	25.90	4.67	33.25	0	0
T20Is	8	168	199	12	3–22	16.58	7.50	14.00	0	0
First-class	77	13737	7855	285	9–37	27.56	3.43	48.20	7	1

DANIEL **FLYNN**

NEW ZEALAND

Full name	**Daniel Raymond Flynn**
Born	**April 16, 1985, Rotorua**
Teams	**Northern Districts**
Style	**Left-hand bat, occasional left-arm spinner**
Test debut	**England v New Zealand at Lord's 2008**
ODI debut	**New Zealand v England at Christchurch 2007-08**
T20I debut	**New Zealand v England at Christchurch 2007-08**

THE PROFILE The early days of Daniel Flynn's international career will be remembered for him walking off Old Trafford in May 2008 with fewer teeth than he started with, after being hit by James Anderson. Such an injury could have severely dented the confidence (as well as the gums) of a young batsman, but Flynn is made of sterner stuff. He made his first-class debut for Northern Districts soon after the 2003-04 Under-19 World Cup, in which he captained New Zealand. A stocky, powerful left-hander, he struck his maiden century in December 2005, but it wasn't until 2007-08 that he showed his true colours – particularly in one-dayers – and joined the national Twenty20 squad. He didn't get many opportunities at first, but made his Test debut at Lord's, defending coolly for 29 not out from 118 balls, in the second innings. Flynn then suffered that sickening blow in the mouth in the next game. However, he was fit enough to play in the final Test at Trent Bridge, and generally looked a readymade replacement for the just-retired Stephen Fleming (an altogether different type of left-hander). In 2008-09 Flynn just missed a maiden Test century, making 95 against West Indies at Dunedin, and added 67 against India at Hamilton. But he then lost his place after a run of low scores, and lost his central contract too for 2010-11. He kept his name in the frame with 162 in an unofficial Test in Zimbabwe in October 2010, and was restored to that contract list after a good home season included a career-best 241 against Otago. He was back in the black cap in 2012, getting several starts but still failing to nail the big score that would make his place secure.

THE FACTS Flynn made his maiden first-class hundred for Northern Districts v Otago in December 2005, then didn't make another one for almost two years ... He scored 241 for ND v Otago in March 2011, hitting nine sixes and 27 fours ... In one-day games in 2007-08 Flynn hit 143 (from 117 balls) v Wellington and 149 (with six sixes) v Canterbury ...

THE FIGURES *to 17.09.12*　　　　　　　　espncricinfo.com

Batting & Fielding	M	Inns	NO	Runs	HS	Avge	S/R	100	50	4s	6s	Ct	St
Tests	20	37	5	890	95	27.81	41.14	0	4	120	4	10	0
ODIs	20	17	2	228	35	15.20	63.33	0	0	23	2	4	0
T20Is	5	5	0	59	23	11.80	115.68	0	0	1	4	2	0
First-class	74	126	14	4124	241	36.82	52.01	11	15	–	–	31	0

Bowling	M	Balls	Runs	Wkts	BB	Avge	RpO	S/R	5i	10m
Tests	20	0	–	–	–	–	–	–	–	–
ODIs	20	24	25	0	–	–	6.25	–	0	0
T20Is	5	6	7	0	–	–	7.00	–	0	0
First-class	74	271	156	1	1–37	156.00	3.45	271.00	0	0

JAMES **FRANKLIN**

Full name	**James Edward Charles Franklin**
Born	**November 7, 1980, Wellington**
Teams	**Wellington, Mumbai Indians, Essex**
Style	**Left-hand bat, left-arm fast-medium bowler**
Test debut	**New Zealand v Pakistan at Auckland 2000-01**
ODI debut	**New Zealand v Zimbabwe at Taupo 2000-01**
T20I debut	**New Zealand v West Indies at Auckland 2005-06**

THE PROFILE James Franklin first represented New Zealand in 2000-01, when barely out of his teens, but made little impact at first. Back then he was a left-arm medium-pacer who swung the ball around, but he has worked on his batting and now has a double-century to his name. He was playing club cricket in Lancashire in 2004 when he was summoned for the third Test at Trent Bridge after Shane Bond was injured. Although New Zealand lost, Franklin took six wickets, five of them Test century-makers. In the one-dayers that followed he took 5 for 42 at Chester-le-Street as England were skittled for 101: not long afterwards he grabbed a Test hat-trick at Dhaka. In April 2006 he did his allrounder claims no harm with 122 – and a stand of 256 with Stephen Fleming – against South Africa at Cape Town. A stubborn knee injury, which eventually required surgery, kept him out for most of 2007-08 and the England tour that followed, but he was back for the Tests against India early in 2009, doing more with bat than ball (1 for 290 in 89 overs). Rather surprisingly, since he hadn't been in the one-day side since the 2007 World Cup, he did play in the World Twenty20 in England in 2009, in the middle of a successful season with Gloucestershire – but after that he fell out of favour and lost his central contract. After two injury-restricted seasons Franklin averaged 53 at home in 2011-12, and was slotted back into the national side as if he'd never been away – usually batting at No. 6 and bowling a bit. He slapped 60 in a Twenty20 international against Zimbabwe, and was consistent if unspectacular after that.

THE FACTS Franklin was the fourth of six men to take a hat-trick and score a century in Tests ... The only other New Zealander to take a Test hat-trick was Peter Petherick in 1976-77 ... Franklin made 219 for Wellington at Auckland in November 2008: in the next match (v Northern Districts) he scored 160 ... He took 7 for 14 as Derbyshire were bowled out for 44 on the first morning at Bristol in August 2010 – but Gloucestershire still lost the match ...

THE FIGURES to 17.09.12   **ESPNcricinfo.com**

Batting & Fielding	M	Inns	NO	Runs	HS	Avge	S/R	100	50	4s	6s	Ct	St
Tests	29	42	7	780	122*	22.28	38.16	1	2	80	5	12	0
ODIs	94	67	23	1036	98*	23.54	78.01	0	3	82	14	25	0
T20Is	24	19	6	296	60	22.76	118.40	0	1	14	17	9	0
First-class	145	223	32	6801	219	35.60	–	14	29	–	–	55	0

Bowling	M	Balls	Runs	Wkts	BB	Avge	RpO	S/R	5i	10m
Tests	29	4623	2705	80	6–119	33.81	3.51	57.78	3	0
ODIs	94	3485	2993	74	5–42	40.44	5.15	47.09	1	0
T20Is	24	228	283	12	3–23	23.58	7.44	19.00	0	0
First-class	145	21804	11452	431	7–14	26.57	3.15	50.58	14	1

GAUTAM **GAMBHIR**

INDIA

Full name	**Gautam Gambhir**
Born	**October 14, 1981, Delhi**
Teams	**Delhi, Kolkata Knight Riders**
Style	**Left-hand bat, occasional legspinner**
Test debut	**India v Australia at Mumbai 2004-05**
ODI debut	**India v Bangladesh at Dhaka 2002-03**
T20I debut	**India v Scotland at Durban 2006-07**

THE PROFILE Gautam Gambhir has set tongues wagging ever since he was a schoolboy. Compact footwork and high bat-speed meant defence was often replaced by the aerial route over point. He pasted successive double-centuries in 2002, then did well in the Caribbean with India A early in 2003, and joined the one-day squad when several seniors took a rest after the World Cup. He finally made the Test side late the following year, hitting 96 against South Africa in his second match and 139 against Bangladesh in his fifth. Leaner times followed, punctuated by cheap runs in Zimbabwe, and although he celebrated his one-day return after 30 months on the sidelines with 103 against Sri Lanka in April 2005, he struggled for big scores and soon found himself out again. After the disasters of the 2007 World Cup Gambhir was given another chance, and this time immediately looked the part. He made two one-day centuries in Australia early in 2008, and carried his good form into the inaugural IPL. He crashed 67, 104 and a superb 206 as Australia were beaten in October 2008, then – after a one-match ban for elbowing Shane Watson while running – helped ensure a series victory over England with 179 and 97 in the second Test. In ODIs he crashed 150 against Sri Lanka in Colombo in February 2009. Gambhir kept up this astonishing run of form with centuries in five successive Tests in 2009-10, although he had a quieter time after that. He was a star at the 2011 World Cup, never failing to reach double figures and taking India close to glory with 97 in the final, but he went off the boil in Tests in 2012, although he remained prolific in the 50-overs format, adding two more centuries against Sri Lanka.

THE FACTS Gambhir made 206 against Australia at Delhi in October 2008: VVS Laxman also scored a double-century, the first time Australia had ever conceded two in the same innings ... Gambhir scored centuries in five successive Test matches in 2009 and 2010: only Don Bradman (six) has ever done better ... He made 214 (for Delhi v Railways) and 218 (for the Board President's XI v Zimbabwe) in successive innings early in 2002 ...

THE FIGURES to 17.09.12   **espncricinfo.com**

Batting & Fielding	M	Inns	NO	Runs	HS	Avge	S/R	100	50	4s	6s	Ct	St
Tests	50	90	5	3770	206	44.35	52.18	9	19	471	7	36	0
ODIs	139	135	11	5077	150*	40.94	86.06	11	33	539	17	36	0
T20Is	28	27	2	755	75	30.20	122.56	0	7	89	9	6	0
First-class	135	231	21	10832	233*	51.58	–		32	48	–	–	85	0

Bowling	M	Balls	Runs	Wkts	BB	Avge	RpO	S/R	5i	10m
Tests	50	0	–	–	–	–	–	–	–	–
ODIs	135	6	13	0	–	–	13.00	–	0	0
T20Is	28	0	–	–	–	–	–	–	–	–
First-class	135	385	277	7	3–12	39.57	4.31	55.00	0	0

CHRIS **GAYLE**

Full name	**Christopher Henry Gayle**
Born	**September 21, 1979, Kingston, Jamaica**
Teams	**Jamaica, Royal Challengers Bangalore**
Style	**Left-hand bat, offspinner**
Test debut	**West Indies v Zimbabwe at Port-of-Spain 1999-2000**
ODI debut	**West Indies v India at Toronto 1999-2000**
T20I debut	**West Indies v New Zealand at Auckland 2005-06**

THE PROFILE   An attacking left-hander, Chris Gayle earned himself a black mark on his first tour when the new boys were felt to be insufficiently respectful of their elders. But a lack of respect, for opposition bowlers at least, has served him well since then. Tall and imposing, he loves to carve through the covers off either foot (without moving either of them much), and can take any bowling apart on his day: his 79-ball century at Cape Town in January 2004, after South Africa had made 532, was typical. He came unstuck against England shortly afterwards, when that lack of positive footwork was exposed – but men with little footwork often baffle experts, and in May 2005 he punched 317 against South Africa in Antigua. Gayle also bowls brisk non-turning offspin, which makes him a genuine one-day allrounder. He took over the captaincy in 2007, and immediately showed unexpected flair for the job. But it ended in tears: after several acrimonious disputes with the board, Gayle declined a central contract, preferring to keep his options open for lucrative Twenty20 offers. He was stripped of the captaincy, responded by scoring 333 against Sri Lanka in his next Test in December 2010, then – after battling injury in the World Cup – was dropped altogether after another public row with the board. Gayle stomped off to the IPL, and was the leading runscorer ... but was left out of the West Indian side as the standoff continued. It was finally resolved in mid-2012 – and Gayle roared back with a magnificent 150 against New Zealand in Antigua, in his first Test for 20 months.

THE FACTS   Gayle's 333 against South Africa in Antigua in May 2005 has been exceeded for West Indies only by Brian Lara (twice) and Garry Sobers ... The only others to have scored two Test triple-centuries are Lara, Don Bradman and Virender Sehwag ... Gayle hit the first century in Twenty20 internationals, 117 v South Africa at Johannesburg in September 2007 ... His record includes three ODIs for the World XI ...

THE FIGURES *to 17.09.12*   **ESPncricinfo.com**

Batting & Fielding	M	Inns	NO	Runs	HS	Avge	S/R	100	50	4s	6s	Ct	St
Tests	93	163	7	6603	333	42.32	59.47	14	34	961	82	87	0
ODIs	234	229	17	8360	153*	39.43	84.45	20	45	965	189	103	0
T20Is	23	23	2	757	117	36.04	143.91	1	7	67	43	6	0
First-class	168	298	22	12524	333	45.37	–	31	60	–	–	146	0

Bowling	M	Balls	Runs	Wkts	BB	Avge	RpO	S/R	5i	10m
Tests	93	6857	2995	72	5-34	41.59	2.62	95.23	2	0
ODIs	234	6936	5473	156	5-46	35.08	4.73	44.46	1	0
T20Is	23	209	254	12	2-15	21.16	7.29	17.41	0	0
First-class	168	12247	5066	131	5-34	38.67	2.48	93.48	2	0

MARTIN **GUPTILL**

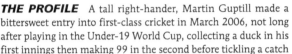

Full name	**Martin James Guptill**
Born	**September 30, 1986, Auckland**
Teams	**Auckland, Derbyshire**
Style	**Right-hand bat, occasional offspinner**
Test debut	**New Zealand v India at Hamilton 2008-09**
ODI debut	**New Zealand v West Indies at Auckland 2008-09**
ODI debut	**New Zealand v Australia at Sydney 2008-09**

THE PROFILE A tall right-hander, Martin Guptill made a bittersweet entry into first-class cricket in March 2006, not long after playing in the Under-19 World Cup, collecting a duck in his first innings then making 99 in the second before tickling a catch behind off his future Test team-mate Jesse Ryder. By 2007-08 Guptill was tickling the selectors, too: he topped the State Shield run-lists that season as Auckland reached the final. His rise continued with an A-team tour of India and, after a maiden first-class century at home, he received the national call for the one-day series against the touring West Indians early in 2009. He lit up his debut in familiar surroundings in Auckland, reaching three figures with a huge six off Chris Gayle and finishing with a superb unbeaten 122 – the second-highest score by anyone in their first ODI. He was dropped three times before he reached 30, but his running (not one of New Zealand's strengths) was notable. Indeed, Guptill's general speed – between wickets or in the outfield, from a high-stepping run – is particularly remarkable as he has only two toes on his left foot after a forklift accident when he was 13. He consolidated his place in 2009-10, although his stats were boosted by 91 in a one-dayer against Bangladesh, and a massive 189 against them in the Hamilton Test, where he shared a big stand with Brendon McCullum. Now a regular in all three formats, he had a reasonable World Cup in 2011 before widening his experience with a county stint for Derbyshire, during which he made a fine impression, not least with his sumptuous straight and cover-drives.

THE FACTS Guptill was the fifth batsman to score a century in his first one-day international, following Dennis Amiss, Desmond Haynes, Andy Flower and Saleem Elahi (Colin Ingram joined the list in October 2010) ... Guptill made 189 v Bangladesh at Hamilton in February 2010, sharing a sixth-wicket partnership of 339 with Brendon McCullum ... On his first-class debut, against Wellington in Auckland in March 2006, Guptill made 0 and 99 ...

THE FIGURES to 17.09.12   **ESPNcricinfo.com**

Batting & Fielding	M	Inns	NO	Runs	HS	Avge	S/R	100	50	4s	6s	Ct	St
Tests	26	49	1	1625	189	33.85	44.02	2	12	196	16	26	0
ODIs	65	63	6	2151	122*	37.73	80.62	2	17	210	42	24	0
T20Is	32	30	5	818	91*	32.72	124.88	0	4	71	35	14	0
First-class	69	125	8	4174	195*	35.67	48.72	7	24	562	40	65	0

Bowling	M	Balls	Runs	Wkts	BB	Avge	RpO	S/R	5i	10m
Tests	26	302	217	5	3–37	43.40	4.31	60.40	0	0
ODIs	65	67	55	2	2–7	27.50	4.92	33.50	0	0
T20Is	32	6	11	0	–	–	11.00	–	0	0
First-class	69	500	346	6	3–37	57.66	4.15	83.33	0	0

BRAD **HADDIN**

Full name	**Bradley James Haddin**
Born	**October 23, 1977, Cowra, New South Wales**
Teams	**New South Wales, Kolkata Knight Riders**
Style	**Right-hand bat, wicketkeeper**
Test debut	**Australia v West Indies at Kingston 2007-08**
ODI debut	**Australia v Zimbabwe at Hobart 2000-01**
T20I debut	**Australia v South Africa at Brisbane 2005-06**

THE PROFILE For years Brad Haddin held the most nerve-fraying position in Australian cricket – wicketkeeper-in-waiting, warming the seat whenever Adam Gilchrist needed a rest. Now Haddin is up there to be shot at himself. He became Australia's 400th Test cricketer in the West Indies early in 2008, and played through the series despite breaking a finger early on, which affected his batting. But he cemented his place with a blazing – almost Gilchristian – 169 against New Zealand at Adelaide in November, pulling and cutting strongly, and added another century in the first Ashes Test in 2009, before a valiant 80 in defeat at Lord's. After that, though, his fortunes waned: he broke another finger just before the start of the third Test, and had to surrender the gloves to Tim Paine for the one-dayers that followed. Surgery meant he missed the Champions Trophy in South Africa too, then an elbow-tendon problem forced him out of the internationals in England in 2010: Paine again showed himself to be a capable deputy. Haddin consolidated his position with some feisty displays in the 2010-11 Ashes defeat, including another century at Brisbane, but he was forced home from the West Indian tour in April 2012 by the illness of his young daughter – which allowed another rival, Matthew Wade, to stake an impressive claim. Haddin has long been a consistent scorer at domestic level, making 916 runs at 57.25 in 2004-05, leading NSW to a one-wicket Shield final victory over Queensland. He began his senior domestic career in 1997-98 with the Australian Capital Territory in their debut season in Australia's one-day competition.

THE FACTS Haddin took up a novel batting position behind the stumps for a free hit after a Shoaib Akhtar no-ball early in 2005: he reasoned that he had more time to sight the ball, and if it hit the stumps it would confuse the fielders (it did hit the stumps, and he managed a bye) ... At Edgbaston in 2005 Haddin rolled a ball near Glenn McGrath, who stepped on it, badly sprained his ankle, and missed the match, which England eventually won by two runs: in 2009 Haddin himself missed the Edgbaston Test when he broke a finger minutes before the start ...

THE FIGURES to 17.09.12   **ESPN**cricinfo.com

Batting & Fielding	M	Inns	NO	Runs	HS	Avge	S/R	100	50	4s	6s	Ct	St
Tests	43	71	8	2257	169	35.82	57.63	3	10	250	37	160	4
ODIs	93	87	7	2511	110	31.38	81.81	2	15	235	56	127	9
T20Is	25	23	4	342	47	18.00	110.32	0	0	26	10	12	4
First-class	145	238	29	8103	169	38.77	–	13	44	–	–	462	30

Bowling	M	Balls	Runs	Wkts	BB	Avge	RpO	S/R	5i	10m
Tests	43	0	–	–	–	–	–	–	–	–
ODIs	93	0	–	–	–	–	–	–	–	–
T20Is	25	0	–	–	–	–	–	–	–	–
First-class	145	0	–	–	–	–	–	–	–	–

ALEX **HALES**

Full name	**Alexander David Hales**
Born	**January 3, 1989, Hillingdon, Middlesex**
Teams	**Nottinghamshire**
Style	**Right-hand bat, right-arm medium-pace bowler**
Test debut	**No Tests yet**
ODI debut	**No ODIs yet**
T20I debut	**England v India at Manchester 2011**

THE PROFILE   Alex Hales is an aggressive top-order batsman whose performances in the shorter formats – he once pounded 150 not out in a 40-over game for Nottinghamshire – earned him a call-up to England's Twenty20 side at the end of the 2011 season. Hales is 6ft 5ins (196cm) tall, and likes to give the ball a hearty thump. But he's not just a one-day basher: he has overcome the tough batting conditions at Trent Bridge, comfortably passing 1000 runs in 2011 – despite missing a chunk of the season with a broken jaw – before falling just short in 2012, although he did hit 155 not out against eventual champions Warwickshire towards the end of the season. When he joined Nottinghamshire from the Lord's groundstaff in 2008, MCC's head coach Clive Radley said he was "a natural timer of a ball", and Hales showed that was true almost from the start, hitting 62 and 78 against Durham in one of his early games and completing his maiden first-class century – 136 against Hampshire – in his first match of 2010. In Twenty20 cricket for Notts in 2011 he biffed 544 runs at a strike-rate of 146, which led to that international call-up later in the season. He started with a debut duck against India, but clouted 62 in his second game, against West Indies. And when the West Indians returned the following year, Hales made 99 from 68 deliveries in front of his home crowd at Trent Bridge. In between he had toured Bangladesh and Sri Lanka with the England Lions in the winter. Sporting talent runs in Hales's genes: his grandfather Dennis once took tennis great Rod Laver to five sets in a Wimbledon qualifying match.

THE FACTS   Hales was the first man to be dismissed for 99 in a Twenty20 international, against West Indies at Trent Bridge in June 2012 ... He hit 150 not out – with eight sixes and 13 fours – in a 40-over match for Nottinghamshire v Worcestershire at Trent Bridge in August 2009 ... Hales made 184 for Notts v Somerset at Trent Bridge in July 2011 ... He has scored three double-centuries for Nottinghamshire's 2nd XI (two of them against Derbyshire) ...

THE FIGURES *to 17.09.12*

Batting & Fielding	M	Inns	NO	Runs	HS	Avge	S/R	100	50	4s	6s	Ct	St
Tests	0	0	–	–	–	–	–	–	–	–	–	–	–
ODIs	0	0	–	–	–	–	–	–	–	–	–	–	–
T20Is	7	7	2	196	99	39.20	122.50	0	2	16	6	3	0
First-class	51	86	5	3116	184	38.46	58.51	6	20	459	12	47	0

Bowling	M	Balls	Runs	Wkts	BB	Avge	RpO	S/R	5i	10m
Tests	0	0	–	–	–	–	–	–	–	–
ODIs	0	0	–	–	–	–	–	–	–	–
T20Is	7	0	–	–	–	–	–	–	–	–
First-class	51	281	167	3	2–63	55.66	3.56	93.66	0	0

HARBHAJAN SINGH

Full name	**Harbhajan Singh Plaha**
Born	**July 3, 1980, Jullundur, Punjab**
Teams	**Punjab, Mumbai Indians, Essex**
Style	**Right-hand bat, offspinner**
Test debut	**India v Australia at Bangalore 1997-98**
ODI debut	**India v New Zealand at Sharjah 1997-98**
T20I debut	**India v South Africa at Johannesburg 2006-07**

THE PROFILE Harbhajan Singh represents the spirit of the new Indian cricketer: arrogance and cockiness translate into self-belief and passion on the field. An offspinner with a windmilling, whiplash delivery, remodelled after questions about his action, he exercises great command over the ball, has the ability to vary his length and pace, and bowls a deadly doosra too – although his main wicket-taking ball is the one that climbs wickedly from a length. In March 2001 it proved too much for the previously all-conquering Australians, as Harbhajan collected 32 wickets in three Tests while none of his team-mates managed more than three. He has occasionally been bothered by injury, while in Pakistan early in 2006 he went for 0 for 355 in two Tests before bouncing back with five-fors in St Kitts and Jamaica. Harbhajan's rivalry with the Aussies – against whom he has taken 90 wickets in 16 Tests – boiled over in Sydney in January 2008 when he was charged with racially abusing Andrew Symonds. He was initially given a three-Test ban before the charge was reduced on appeal. Then in April Harbhajan slapped his Indian team-mate Sreesanth after an IPL game, which cost him an 11-match ban. He took 16 wickets in three Tests in New Zealand early in 2009, but although he took his 400th Test wicket in the West Indies in mid-2011, he looked jaded on the England tour that followed. Ravichandran Ashwin took his place and grabbed his chance – and now Harbhajan has to show that, at 32, he can come back and try to fulfil Muttiah Muralitharan's somewhat fanciful suggestion that Harbhajan was the man most likely to pass his own stratospheric wicket-tally of 800.

THE FACTS Harbhajan's match figures of 15 for 217 against Australia at Chennai in 2000-01 have been bettered for India only by Narendra Hirwani (16 for 136 in 1987-88, also at Chennai) ... Harbhajan took 32 wickets at 17.03 in that three-match series: his haul at Kolkata included India's first Test hat-trick ... He has taken 56 wickets at 22.60 in Tests against West Indies, but 25 at 52.04 v Pakistan ... His record includes two ODIs for the Asia XI ...

THE FIGURES to 17.09.12   **ESPNcricinfo.com**

Batting & Fielding	M	Inns	NO	Runs	HS	Avge	S/R	100	50	4s	6s	Ct	St
Tests	98	138	22	2164	115	18.65	65.39	2	9	271	40	42	0
ODIs	229	123	33	1190	49	13.22	80.51	0	0	89	34	69	0
T20Is	23	10	3	99	21	14.14	120.73	0	0	10	4	6	0
First-class	170	227	41	3678	115	19.77	–	2	13	–	–	87	0

Bowling	M	Balls	Runs	Wkts	BB	Avge	RpO	S/R	5i	10m
Tests	98	27651	13084	406	8–84	32.22	2.83	68.10	25	5
ODIs	229	12059	8651	259	5–31	33.40	4.30	46.55	3	0
T20Is	23	504	541	18	3–30	30.05	6.44	28.00	0	0
First-class	170	43099	20240	698	8–84	28.99	2.82	61.74	39	7

RYAN **HARRIS**

Full name	**Ryan James Harris**
Born	**October 11, 1979, Sydney**
Teams	**Queensland, Kings XI Punjab**
Style	**Right-hand bat, right-arm fast bowler**
Test debut	**Australia v New Zealand at Wellington 2009-10**
ODI debut	**Australia v South Africa at Hobart 2008-09**
T20I debut	**Australia v West Indies at Sydney 2009-10**

THE PROFILE Ryan Harris leapt onto the international stage in 2009-10, a season he initially feared would be a write-off after knee surgery: he narrowly avoided a second operation before benefiting from injuries to others. He remains susceptible to injury, and is generally mothballed for Tests – hence his new nickname "TMO" (Test Matches Only – a label originally coined for Terry Alderman). A stocky, skiddy bowler who is faster than he looks, Harris quickly became too good to ignore. He made a dream start to his international career: in only his second ODI, against Pakistan in January 2010, he collected five wickets, and did the same in the next game. All this led to a Test debut in New Zealand, and he did well during both matches there, taking nine wickets in terribly windy conditions at Wellington. Then he looked the best of the home bowlers in the 2010-11 Ashes disaster, taking 6 for 47 as Australia bounced back to win the second Test at Perth, and there was widespread disappointment when he limped out of the series during the next Test with an ankle injury. That kept him out of the World Cup, but he was back in Sri Lanka later in 2011, taking 11 wickets in the first two Tests before a hamstring niggle kept him out of the third. In 2012 his five wickets contributed to a win in Bridgetown, but he was rested for the next Test over fitness concerns. He is also a handy attacking batsman – an early limited-overs highlight was lofting a six over long-on when South Australia needed five to win against Queensland at Adelaide in December 2006. However, until his international debut at 29, he almost qualified as a journeyman. He was South Australia's top wicket-taker in 2007-08, and they might have tried harder to stop him moving to Queensland. He also played briefly for Sussex and Surrey.

THE FACTS Harris took five-fors in his second and third ODIs, a unique feat at the time (since bettered by Brian Vitori of Zimbabwe) ... Only Ajantha Mendis (48) had more wickets after 17 ODIs (Curtly Ambrose also had 41) ... Harris scored 94 for Surrey at Northampton in June 2009 ... He took 7 for 60 for Queensland v Tasmania at Brisbane in October 2011 ...

THE FIGURES *to 17.09.12*   **espncricinfo.com**

Batting & Fielding	M	Inns	NO	Runs	HS	Avge	S/R	100	50	4s	6s	Ct	St
Tests	12	18	6	212	68*	17.66	53.13	0	1	22	1	4	0
ODIs	21	13	7	48	21	8.00	100.00	0	0	3	1	6	0
T20Is	3	1	1	2	2*	–	200.00	0	0	0	0	0	0
First-class	57	90	14	1456	94	19.15	59.77	0	7	–	–	29	0

Bowling	M	Balls	Runs	Wkts	BB	Avge	RpO	S/R	5i	10m
Tests	12	2312	1111	47	6–47	23.63	2.88	49.19	2	0
ODIs	21	1031	832	44	5–19	18.90	4.84	23.43	3	0
T20Is	3	70	95	4	2–27	23.75	8.14	17.50	0	0
First-class	57	10808	5390	193	7–60	27.92	2.99	56.00	6	0

RANGANA **HERATH**

Full name	**Herath Mudiyanselage Rangana Keerthi Bandara Herath**
Born	**March 19, 1978, Kurunegala**
Teams	**Tamil Union, Basnahira**
Style	**Left-hand bat, left-arm orthodox spinner**
Test debut	**Sri Lanka v Australia at Galle 1999-2000**
ODI debut	**Sri Lanka v Zimbabwe at Harare 2003-04**
T20I debut	**Sri Lanka v Australia at Pallekele 2011**

THE PROFILE Slow left-armer Rangana Herath first came to prominence late in 1999, when his so-called mystery ball – *Wisden* called it "a wonderful delivery, bowled out of the front of his hand, which turned back into right-handers" – befuddled the touring Australians. He took four wickets on Test debut at Galle, including Steve Waugh and Ricky Ponting, but was soon unceremoniously dumped as other spinners were tried as foils for Muttiah Muralitharan. Herath's unprepossessing body shape – he's rather short with a hint of excess padding around the midriff – may have counted against him, but he continued to be a regular wicket-taker in domestic cricket. He took 17 wickets in four Tests in 2004, including seven in a rare Murali-less Sri Lankan victory over Pakistan at Faisalabad, flighting the ball well and making it grip and turn. However, he was soon left out again, seemingly for good. But the domestic wickets still kept coming and he was eventually recalled in 2008, although he might have returned to anonymity but for an injury which forced Murali out of the home series against Pakistan in July 2009. Herath took five wickets in each of the three Tests, then 11 in three in India that winter, but lost his place after an underwhelming bowling performance in Murali's final Test in July 2010, although he did manage a career-best with the bat. He looked unthreatening in England in 2011, but blossomed thereafter, revelling in the status of No. 1 spinner: 13 Tests in the year from August 2011 brought him 70 wickets, including a dozen – 6 for 74 and 6 for 97 – in the victory over England at Galle in March 2012, and six more in the first innings of the next Test.

THE FACTS Herath took 8 for 43 (11 for 72 in the match) for Moors v Police in Colombo in 2002–03 ... In January 2002 he took 8 for 47 (and caught one of the others) for Moors v Galle ... Herath took 72 wickets at 13.59 in Sri Lanka in 2000-01 ... He made 80 not out against India in Colombo in July 2010: he had never previously made more than 71 in first-class cricket, although he had reached 70 four times ...

THE FIGURES to 17.09.12   **ESPncricinfo.com**

Batting & Fielding	M	Inns	NO	Runs	HS	Avge	S/R	100	50	4s	6s	Ct	St
Tests	40	56	12	634	80*	14.40	49.60	0	1	69	5	8	0
ODIs	35	14	8	56	17*	9.33	71.79	0	0	1	2	8	0
T20Is	3	2	2	1	1*	–	100.00	0	0	0	0	0	0
First-class	205	292	68	3692	80*	16.48	–	0	12	–	–	88	0

Bowling	M	Balls	Runs	Wkts	BB	Avge	RpO	S/R	5i	10m
Tests	40	10481	4886	154	7–157	31.72	2.79	68.05	10	1
ODIs	35	1586	1161	26	3–28	44.65	4.39	61.00	0	0
T20Is	3	60	59	2	1–11	29.50	5.90	30.00	0	0
First-class	205	42083	19025	760	8–43	25.03	2.71	55.37	44	6

BEN **HILFENHAUS**

Full name	**Benjamin William Hilfenhaus**
Born	**March 15, 1983, Ulverstone, Tasmania**
Teams	**Tasmania, Chennai Super Kings**
Style	**Right-hand bat, right-arm fast-medium bowler**
Test debut	**Australia v South Africa at Johannesburg 2008-09**
ODI debut	**Australia v New Zealand at Hobart 2006-07**
T20I debut	**Australia v England at Sydney 2006-07**

THE PROFILE A few years ago Ben Hilfenhaus – Ricky Ponting's second cousin – was working on a building site, but now he has safely laid down his trowel. "Hilfy" soon established himself for Tasmania in 2005-06 – Man of the Match against Victoria in only his second game, ten wickets against NSW, then called up for Australia A after 39 wickets at 30.82 in his first season. In January 2007 he played a Twenty20 international and then his first ODI, on his home ground at Hobart, trapping Brendon McCullum in front in his second over. He had to wait until the South African trip early in 2009 to crack the Test side, but settled in fast, keeping the runs down. He was duly selected for the Ashes tour, but was not assured of a place, even when Brett Lee broke down. He finally got the vote for the first Test ahead of Stuart Clark and Doug Bollinger, and immediately looked at home, shaping the ball away and finding swing with the Duke ball more readily even than England's practised performers. Hilfenhaus finished the series with 22 wickets, and seemed set for a long run in the side ... but knee trouble kept him out for much of the home season that followed. Hilfenhaus returned for the Tests against Pakistan in England in July 2010, but looked jaded in the 2010-11 Ashes, taking only seven wickets at 59. He was dropped, but bounced back with 27 wickets in the four home Tests against India a year later, and by late 2012 seemed to be the new-ball bowler of choice in all three formats – good news for him (and Australia) with another tour of England looming.

THE FACTS Hilfenhaus was the leading wicket-taker on either side in the 2009 Ashes series, with 22 ... He took 7 for 58 (and 10 for 87 in the match) for Tasmania v New South Wales at Hobart in March 2006: in December 2006 he took 7 for 70 against South Australia at Hobart ... He took 5 for 14 as Queensland were bowled out for 62 at Brisbane in October 2008 ...

THE FIGURES *to 17.09.12*　　　　　　　　　　　　　　　　　　　　**espncricinfo.com**

Batting & Fielding	M	Inns	NO	Runs	HS	Avge	S/R	100	50	4s	6s	Ct	St
Tests	24	35	11	337	56*	14.04	54.35	0	1	44	5	7	0
ODIs	25	11	8	29	16	9.66	42.02	0	0	2	0	10	0
T20Is	7	3	1	2	2	1.00	20.00	0	0	0	0	0	0
First-class	78	107	30	955	56*	12.40	–	0	2	–	–	23	0

Bowling	M	Balls	Runs	Wkts	BB	Avge	RpO	S/R	5i	10m
Tests	24	5397	2579	92	5–75	28.03	2.86	58.66	2	0
ODIs	25	1216	1075	29	5–33	37.06	5.30	41.93	1	0
T20Is	7	156	161	9	2–15	17.88	6.19	17.33	0	0
First-class	78	17739	8889	309	7–58	28.76	3.00	57.40	11	1

PHILLIP **HUGHES**

Full name	**Phillip Joel Hughes**
Born	**November 30, 1988, Macksville, New South Wales**
Teams	**New South Wales, Worcestershire**
Style	**Left-hand bat**
Test debut	**Australia v South Africa at Johannesburg 2008-09**
ODI debut	**No ODIs yet**
T20I debut	**No T20Is yet**

THE PROFILE Phillip Hughes made an unconvincing start in Tests – a four-ball duck at the Wanderers after becoming Australia's youngest player since Craig McDermott 25 years previously – but he scored 75 in the second innings. But in the next Test he became the youngest to make two centuries in the same match, bringing up the first with two sixes. His 415 runs in the series were followed by centuries in each of three Championship matches for Middlesex, irritating England supporters angry he had been given the chance to fine-tune before the 2009 Ashes. As it happened it didn't do him much good, as he failed to shine in the first two Tests and was replaced by Shane Watson, a change made public by Hughes on Twitter before the official announcement, which provoked reactions ranging from rage to raucous laughter. His country-baked technique includes compulsive slicing through point and slashing to cover, as well as stepping away to provide room for tennis-style drives down the ground. He did make 86 not out at Wellington in March 2010 when Watson was injured – but then a dislocated shoulder, suffered while boxing, knocked Hughes himself out. After that he continued to score heavily in domestic cricket ... and continued to struggle in Tests. He was jettisoned after making only 97 runs in the first three Tests of the Ashes debacle, but restated his case in Sri Lanka later in 2011, with an important century in Colombo. However, four more Tests brought him only one score above 20 – 88 in a win in Johannesburg – and he lost his place again. He spent most of the 2012 season honing his technique with Worcestershire.

THE FACTS Hughes made 115 and 160 in only his second Test, against South Africa at Durban in March 2009: at 20 years 98 days he was the youngest to hit twin centuries in a Test, beating George Headley (20 years 271 days for West Indies v England in 1929-30) ... Hughes hit 198 for NSW v South Australia at Adelaide in November 2008 ... He played three Championship matches for Middlesex in 2009 – and scored centuries in each of them ...

THE FIGURES to 17.09.12   **ESPN**cricinfo.com

Batting & Fielding	M	Inns	NO	Runs	HS	Avge	S/R	100	50	4s	6s	Ct	St
Tests	17	32	1	1072	160	34.58	55.57	3	3	143	9	7	0
ODIs	0	0	–	–	–	–	–	–	–	–	–	–	–
T20Is	0	0	–	–	–	–	–	–	–	–	–	–	–
First-class	80	146	8	6259	198	45.35	58.55	19	32	870	32	47	0

Bowling	M	Balls	Runs	Wkts	BB	Avge	RpO	S/R	5i	10m
Tests	17	0	–	–	–	–	–	–	–	–
ODIs	0	0	–	–	–	–	–	–	–	–
T20Is	0	0	–	–	–	–	–	–	–	–
First-class	80	18	9	0	–	–	3.00	–	0	0

DAVID **HUSSEY**

AUSTRALIA

Full name	**David John Hussey**
Born	**July 15, 1977, Morley, Western Australia**
Teams	**Victoria, Kings XI Punjab**
Style	**Right-hand bat, occasional offspinner**
Test debut	**No Tests yet**
ODI debut	**Australia v West Indies at Basseterre 2007-08**
T20I debut	**Australia v India at Melbourne 2007-08**

THE PROFILE David Hussey copied his older brother Michael's talent for ridiculous scoring in English county cricket. And, like Michael, David was forced to pile up mountains of runs in Australia before convincing the national selectors. It took his first 1000-run home season before he was finally chosen for a tour (a one-day series in the Caribbean early in 2008) and earned his first national contract. Earlier that year he made his Twenty20 debut against India at the MCG. He made an ODI century against Scotland in 2009, and was in the squad for the 2011 World Cup, but had little chance to shine. Hussey had been one of the big surprises in the inaugural IPL auction in 2008, when Kolkata paid $625,000 for him – far more than his brother fetched. Despite his crash-and-bash style, he is desperate not to be pigeonholed as a Twenty20 player. His first-class record suggests it's a reasonable request: his average, in the mid-fifties, is even higher than his brother's. His hopes of a Test cap were strengthened in 2012 when chief selector John Inverarity nominated him as one of the next in line for a middle-order place – although, at 35, he would hardly be a long-term solution. Hussey was also a run-machine during his time with Nottinghamshire, with almost 6000 first-class runs at an average touching 65. An aggressive batsman with a strong bottom-hand technique, he hit a breathtaking 212 not out at nearly a run a ball in 2003-04, his first full season, as Victoria chased a record-breaking 455 for victory against NSW: Steve Waugh, the opposing captain, was impressed.

THE FACTS David Hussey hit 275 (27 fours, 14 sixes) for Nottinghamshire v Essex at Trent Bridge in May 2007 ... He reached 50 in only 19 balls – Australia's second-fastest ODI half-century – against West Indies in St Kitts in July 2008 ... Hussey fetched $625,000 at the inaugural IPL auction in February 2008, much more than his brother Michael ($350,000) and Australia's captain Ricky Ponting ($400,000) ...

THE FIGURES to 17.09.12   **ESPncricinfo.com**

Batting & Fielding	M	Inns	NO	Runs	HS	Avge	S/R	100	50	4s	6s	Ct	St
Tests	0	0	–	–	–	–	–	–	–	–	–	–	–
ODIs	64	56	5	1668	111	32.70	90.11	1	13	117	29	28	0
T20Is	38	35	3	756	88*	23.62	121.73	0	3	41	34	24	0
First-class	160	251	26	12339	275	54.84	70.90	41	55	–	–	216	0

Bowling	M	Balls	Runs	Wkts	BB	Avge	RpO	S/R	5i	10m
Tests	0	0	–	–	–	–	–	–	–	–
ODIs	64	772	674	18	4–21	37.44	5.23	42.88	0	0
T20Is	38	349	370	19	3–25	19.47	6.36	18.36	0	0
First-class	160	2644	1639	25	4–105	65.56	3.71	105.76	0	0

MICHAEL **HUSSEY**

Full name	**Michael Edward Killeen Hussey**
Born	**May 27, 1975, Morley, Western Australia**
Teams	**Western Australia, Chennai Super Kings**
Style	**Left-hand bat, occasional right-arm medium-pacer**
Test debut	**Australia v West Indies at Brisbane 2005-06**
ODI debut	**Australia v India at Perth 2003-04**
T20I debut	**Australia v New Zealand at Auckland 2004-05**

THE PROFILE   English fans couldn't understand why Australia's selectors took so long to recognise Michael Hussey's claims. Bradmanesque in county cricket, he was less prolific at home, and seemed destined to remain unfulfilled. Finally he got a chance after 15,313 first-class runs, a record for an Australian before wearing baggy green – and made an attractive century in his second Test, then a memorable 122 against South Africa at the MCG, when he and Glenn McGrath added 107 for the last wicket. The fairytale continued in the 2006-07 Ashes, although his one-day form did finally drop off a little. Hussey has a tidy, compact style: skilled off front foot and back, he is attractive to watch once set. He reinvented himself in one-day cricket as an innovative batsman with cool head and loose wrists, and supplanted Michael Bevan as the Aussies' one-day "finisher". A patchy 2009 Ashes series was redeemed by a fighting century (his first for 16 Tests) at The Oval, although that was tinged with regret as he was last out as the urn was surrendered again. But a superb century turned the Sydney Test against Pakistan on its head in January 2010; and in the World Twenty20 semi-final in the Caribbean later that year Hussey's astonishing 60 off 24 balls dragged Australia past Pakistan and into the final. In the 2010-11 Ashes he was often a lone beacon of excellence for Australia, scoring two centuries before running out of steam. After a couple of ducks the following season, he had a run of 11 innings in which he reached double figures – including 150 not out against India at Sydney in January 2012 – to show that, at 37, "Mr Cricket" wasn't finished yet.

THE FACTS   Hussey scored 229 runs in ODIs before he was dismissed, and averaged 100.22 after 32 matches ... He took only 166 days to reach 1000 Test runs, beating the 228-day record established by Andrew Strauss in 2005 ... Hussey's 331 not out v Somerset at Taunton in 2003 is the highest individual score for Northamptonshire ... He has captained Australia in four ODIs, and lost the lot ... Hussey averages 59.40 in Tests in Australia, but 41.37 overseas ...

THE FIGURES to 17.09.12   **espncricinfo.com**

Batting & Fielding	M	Inns	NO	Runs	HS	Avge	S/R	100	50	4s	6s	Ct	St
Tests	73	127	13	5708	195	50.07	49.20	16	28	638	33	73	0
ODIs	185	157	44	5442	109*	48.15	87.16	3	39	383	80	105	0
T20Is	32	25	8	566	60*	33.29	140.44	0	3	46	21	19	0
First-class	261	464	45	21853	331*	52.15	–	58	99	–	–	284	0

Bowling	M	Balls	Runs	Wkts	BB	Avge	RpO	S/R	5i	10m
Tests	73	510	240	7	1–0	34.28	2.82	72.85	0	0
ODIs	185	240	235	2	1–22	117.50	5.87	120.00	0	0
T20Is	32	6	5	0	–	–	5.00	–	0	0
First-class	261	1962	1019	27	3–34	37.74	3.11	72.66	0	0

IMRAN TAHIR

Full name **Mohammad Imran Tahir**
Born **March 27, 1979, Lahore, Pakistan**
Teams **Dolphins**
Style **Right-hand bat, legspinner**
Test debut **South Africa v Australia at Cape Town 2011-12**
ODI debut **South Africa v West Indies at Delhi 2010-11**
T20I debut **No T20Is yet**

THE PROFILE Legspinner Imran Tahir is the ultimate journeyman cricketer. Since starting his first-class career in his native Pakistan in 1996-97 he has played for almost 20 first-class teams, ranging from Sui Gas to Yorkshire. He has helped out four English counties – in 2011 he had his second spell with Hampshire – but he finally settled in South Africa, after marrying a local girl. He has a fine record, with well over 600 first-class wickets at an average around 25. Early on he played for Pakistan Under-19s, but after his marriage threw in his lot with South Africa. Match-winning spinners have always been scarce there, and the bouncy Tahir – who has all the variations, including a well-disguised googly – was soon being mentioned as a Test candidate. In fact he was selected for the Test squad – against England in January 2010 – before he was even eligible, which caused red faces all round. The situation was formalised after that, and he became a naturalised South African early in 2011. He had been picking up plenty of wickets on the domestic circuit for the Dolphins, his latest team, and was immediately chosen in the squad for the one-dayers against India. But the selectors kept him under wraps, and finally blooded him in the World Cup. He made up for lost time, taking four West Indian wickets in his first game, three in his second (against the Netherlands) and four more against England. He was hindered after that by a cracked thumb, but finished with 14 wickets at 10.71, a fine start. Tahir finally made his Test debut at 32 late in 2011, and performed respectably without quite showing that he was the attacking spin option that Graeme Smith had craved throughout his tenure as captain.

THE FACTS Imran Tahir took 8 for 76 for Redco Pakistan v Lahore Blues at Lahore in December 1999 ... He took 8 for 114 for Warwickshire (his fourth English county) against Durham at Edgbaston in May 2010 ... Tahir's first ODI was during the 2011 World Cup: he took 4 for 41 against West Indies ...

THE FIGURES *to 17.09.12* · **espncricinfo.com**

Batting & Fielding	M	Inns	NO	Runs	HS	Avge	S/R	100	50	4s	6s	Ct	St
Tests	10	11	4	78	29*	11.14	64.46	0	0	9	1	4	0
ODIs	5	2	2	1	1*	–	50.00	0	0	0	0	2	0
T20Is	0	0	–	–	–	–	–	–	–	–	–	–	–
First-class	153	189	43	2026	77*	13.87	–	0	3	–	–	69	0

Bowling	M	Balls	Runs	Wkts	BB	Avge	RpO	S/R	5i	10m
Tests	10	1929	1045	26	3–55	40.19	3.25	74.19	0	0
ODIs	5	237	150	14	4–38	10.71	3.79	16.92	0	0
T20Is	0	0	–	–	–	–	–	–	–	–
First-class	153	30492	16430	634	8–76	25.91	3.23	48.09	44	9

IMRUL KAYES

Full name	**Imrul Kayes**
Born	**February 2, 1987, Meherpur, Kushtia**
Teams	**Khulna**
Style	**Left-hand bat, occasional offspinner**
Test debut	**Bangladesh v South Africa at Bloemfontein 2008-09**
ODI debut	**Bangladesh v New Zealand at Chittagong 2008-09**
T20I debut	**Bangladesh v Pakistan at Gros Islet 2010**

THE PROFILE The elevation of left-hand opener Imrul Kayes to Bangladesh colours was hastened by the mass defections to the unauthorised Indian Cricket League late in 2008. With more than a dozen leading players suddenly unavailable, "Sagar" was called up after a fine home season in 2007-08, when he was the leading scorer for Khulna less than a year after making his first-class debut. His haul included two centuries in separate matches against Sylhet, and he finished the season with 600 runs. Kayes has a solid, compact technique, and likes to hit through the covers off the back foot, but he had the misfortune to make his Test debut against South Africa: he rarely looked settled against their high-quality pacemen, and managed only 25 runs in four attempts in the Tests; on his debut he was out twice in the space of about three hours on the second day. He fared a little better against Sri Lanka, then made 33 – and added a two-hour 24 in the second innings, in an opening stand of 82 with Tamim Iqbal – in Bangladesh's victory over a depleted West Indian side in St Vincent in July 2009. He showed he was coming to terms with the international game with an ODI hundred in New Zealand early in 2010, followed by a patient 75 during a record opening stand with Tamim in the Lord's Test. He had two important innings during Bangladesh's up-and-down 2011 World Cup campaign, making 60 in the upset win over England then 73 not out in a more routine victory over the Netherlands, then added 93 against Australia shortly after the tournament. But his Test record remains modest, and he lost his five-day place in 2012.

THE FACTS Imrul Kayes made 101 v New Zealand in an ODI in Christchurch in February 2010 ... At Lord's in 2010 he and Tamim Iqbal put on 185 – a new national Test record – for the first wicket ... Kayes's first two first-class hundreds were both scored for Khulna v Sylhet late in 2007 (121 at Fatullah and 138 at Khulna): in between he made 121 against them in a one-day game ...

THE FIGURES to 17.09.12   **ESPIN cricinfo.com**

Batting & Fielding	M	Inns	NO	Runs	HS	Avge	S/R	100	50	4s	6s	Ct	St
Tests	16	32	0	549	75	17.15	46.40	0	1	84	1	16	0
ODIs	48	48	1	1315	101	27.97	65.16	1	9	133	12	14	0
T20Is	4	4	0	24	22	6.00	64.86	0	0	3	1	0	0
First-class	41	78	1	2048	138	26.59	–	3	7	–	–	28	0

Bowling	M	Balls	Runs	Wkts	BB	Avge	RpO	S/R	5i	10m
Tests	16	12	8	0	–	–	4.00	–	0	0
ODIs	48	0	–	–	–	–	–	–	–	–
T20Is	4	0	–	–	–	–	–	–	–	–
First-class	41	47	27	0	–	–	3.44	–	0	0

COLIN **INGRAM**

SOUTH AFRICA

Full name	**Colin Alexander Ingram**
Born	**July 3, 1985, Port Elizabeth**
Teams	**Warriors**
Style	**Left-hand batsman, occasional legspinner**
Test debut	**No Tests yet**
ODI debut	**South Africa v Zimbabwe at Bloemfontein 2010-11**
T20I debut	**South Africa v Zimbabwe at Bloemfontein 2010-11**

THE PROFILE A blond, bruising left-hander who answers to the nickname "Bozie", Colin Ingram is among the brightest talents produced by the Eastern Cape in recent years. Happily for a region of South Africa that has often seen its budding stars bloom fully elsewhere, Ingram has remained true to his roots and stayed with the Warriors. He brings a bracing brand of aggression to the batting, and made an immediate impact to being elevated to the senior one-day side after a successful stint in the A team. In his first ODI, against Zimbabwe at Bloemfontein in October 2010, Ingram hit 124 from 126 balls, and in his fifth game he repeated the dose, this time against Pakistan in Abu Dhabi a fortnight later, making a round 100. Things calmed down a little after that, and for a while he lost his place to David Miller, but it was Ingram who made the 2011 World Cup squad (he played only once, scoring 46 against Ireland), and Ingram who was preferred for a national contract afterwards. He lost his place early in 2012, but remained in the frame with consistent runs for South Africa A. Some put his fluctuations in form down to being pushed up and down the order: he usually opens for the Warriors, and scored his two one-day hundreds for South Africa at No. 3. But Jacques Kallis is the immovable object there in the national side, and when Ingram moved down to No. 6 he looked less assured. Ingram, however, says: "I pride myself on being adaptable and flexible as a cricketer. When you are batting lower down the order, the situation dictates what you have to do, rather than when you are at No. 3 and you can just decide for yourself."

THE FACTS Ingram was the first South African – and only the sixth from any country – to score a century in his first one-day international, with 124 against Zimbabwe in October 2010 ... He scored 190 for Eastern Province v KwaZulu-Natal in Port Elizabeth in January 2009 ... Ingram made 78 from 50 balls in a Twenty20 international against India at Johannesburg in March 2012 ...

THE FIGURES *to 17.09.12*   **espn**cricinfo.com

Batting & Fielding	M	Inns	NO	Runs	HS	Avge	S/R	100	50	4s	6s	Ct	St
Tests	0	0	–	–	–	–	–	–	–	–	–	–	–
ODIs	15	13	2	388	124	35.27	90.02	2	0	36	6	4	0
T20Is	9	9	1	210	78	26.25	129.62	0	1	23	7	2	0
First-class	52	92	4	3021	190	34.32	–	6	12	–	–	30	0

Bowling	M	Balls	Runs	Wkts	BB	Avge	RpO	S/R	5i	10m
Tests	0	0	–	–	–	–	–	–	–	–
ODIs	15	0	–	–	–	–	–	–	–	–
T20Is	9	0	–	–	–	–	–	–	–	–
First-class	52	1771	1023	29	4–16	35.27	3.46	61.06	0	0

JAHURUL ISLAM

Full name	**Mohammad Jahurul Islam**
Born	**December 12, 1986, Rajshahi**
Teams	**Rajshahi**
Style	**Right-hand bat, occ. wicketkeeper and offspinner**
Test debut	**Bangladesh v England at Mirpur 2009-10**
ODI debut	**Bangladesh v Pakistan at Dambulla 2010**
T20I debut	**Bangladesh v Australia at Bridgetown 2010**

THE PROFILE A superb domestic season in 2009-10, during which he was the only man to pass 1000 runs, making 1008 at 63 with four centuries, propelled the tall, aggressive Jahurul Islam into national contention, and when Raqibul Hasan fell out with the selectors and announced a short-lived retirement just before the home Test series against England in March 2010, "Aumi" got the call. He made a duck in his first Test innings, courtesy of Graeme Swann, but took his revenge in the second, getting off the mark with a six off Swann over long-on, and adding another shortly afterwards to become only the second player (after his team-mate Shafiul Islam) to open his Test account with two sixes. Jahurul had long been earmarked for high honours: a product of the national academy, he made 78 on first-class debut in 2002-03, although he was into his fifth season before he finally cracked the three-figure barrier. In England in 2010 he hit 158 against Surrey, and did reasonably well in the first Test at Lord's (20 and 46) before two low scores in the second. He is also a handy stopgap wicketkeeper, and deputised in some of the one-dayers in Britain later in 2010 after Mushfiqur Rahim was injured. It didn't seem to affect his batting: at Bristol Jahurul made 40 during an important stand of 83 with Imrul Kayes, in a match Bangladesh ended up winning by five runs, their first-ever victory over England. He slipped down the pecking order after that, although he remained in the selectors' minds. He made 53 in a rare ODI victory over India at Mirpur during the Asia Cup in March 2012, and toured Europe's cricketing outposts (Scotland, Ireland and the Netherlands) later in the year.

THE FACTS Jahurul Islam's first two scoring shots in Test cricket were both sixes (against England in March 2010), equalling the feat of his team-mate Shafiul Islam earlier in the year ... Jahurul's 53 helped Bangladesh overhaul India's 289 in the Asia Cup in March 2012 ... He made 78 on first-class debut for Rajshahi v Sylhet at Fatullah in December 2002 ... Jahurul scored 158 against Surrey at The Oval in May 2010 ...

THE FIGURES to 17.09.12   **ᴇsᴘᴎcricinfo.com**

Batting & Fielding	M	Inns	NO	Runs	HS	Avge	S/R	100	50	4s	6s	Ct	St
Tests	3	6	0	114	46	19.00	40.71	0	0	13	2	3	0
ODIs	10	10	1	234	53	26.00	70.69	0	1	20	2	6	0
T20Is	2	2	0	20	18	10.00	142.85	0	0	1	1	2	0
First-class	77	142	12	4595	158	36.36	48.43	8	26	–	–	72	2

Bowling	M	Balls	Runs	Wkts	BB	Avge	RpO	S/R	5i	10m
Tests	3	0	–	–	–	–	–	–	–	–
ODIs	10	0	–	–	–	–	–	–	–	–
T20Is	2	0	–	–	–	–	–	–	–	–
First-class	77	18	10	1	1–0	10.00	3.33	18.00	0	0

KYLE **JARVIS**

Full name	**Kyle Malcolm Jarvis**
Born	**February 16, 1989, Harare**
Teams	**Mashonaland Eagles, Central Districts**
Style	**Right-hand bat, right-arm fast-medium bowler**
Test debut	**Zimbabwe v Bangladesh at Harare 2011**
ODI debut	**Zimbabwe v Kenya at Harare 2009-10**
T20I debut	**Zimbabwe v Pakistan at Harare 2011**

THE PROFILE Tall and muscular, Kyle Jarvis has the basic attribute of a good fast bowler – raw pace – and is beginning to tighten his control. The son of a former Test paceman, Malcolm Jarvis, Kyle was the chief strike bowler for Zimbabwe at the 2008 Under-19 World Cup (he also played rugby for the national under-19s). He was fast-tracked into the national side after the appointment as bowling coach of Heath Streak, who rated him highly. Jarvis was blooded in a home series against Kenya in October 2009 – less than a week after his first-class debut, also against the tourists – and made an impression with his pace, breaking the 90mph (144kph) barrier at times. Control was occasionally a problem, though, and his ten overs went for 76 against South Africa at Centurion in November 2009. Jarvis took 6 for 60 in his first Logan Cup match, and was included in the senior squad for the short tour of the West Indies early in 2010, only to pull out with stress fractures in the back. His international comeback coincided with Zimbabwe's own: Jarvis made his debut in the match in August 2011 which signalled his country's return after six years out of Test cricket. Jarvis looked the part, shaking up Bangladesh's batsmen with his speed and taking 4 for 61 in the second innings, wrapping up the last two wickets to secure a famous victory as Zimbabwe marked their return in some style. Things predictably got harder after that. Zimbabwe lost to Pakistan, and then narrowly to New Zealand despite Jarvis's 5 for 64 in the second innings. Then Zimbabwe were hammered in New Zealand early in 2012 – but Jarvis's pace and promise earned him a contract with NZ's Central Districts, for whom he took 31 wickets in six first-class games. He remains a beacon of hope for Zimbabwe's future.

THE FACTS Jarvis took 6 for 60 for Mashonaland Eagles v Mountaineers in November 2009, in only his second first-class match ... He took 5 for 23 and 5 for 30 for the Eagles v Southern Rocks at Harare in December 2011 ... Jarvis's father, Malcolm, played five Tests and 12 ODIs, and took the last wicket in Zimbabwe's surprise victory over England at the 1992 World Cup ...

THE FIGURES to 17.09.12

espncricinfo.com

Batting & Fielding	M	Inns	NO	Runs	HS	Avge	S/R	100	50	4s	6s	Ct	St
Tests	4	7	4	37	25*	12.33	26.24	0	0	5	0	0	0
ODIs	16	10	4	29	13	4.83	37.66	0	0	2	0	4	0
T20Is	6	2	0	0	0	0.00	0.00	0	0	0	0	0	0
First-class	20	25	11	167	35	11.92	38.04	0	0	17	1	3	0

Bowling	M	Balls	Runs	Wkts	BB	Avge	RpO	S/R	5i	10m
Tests	4	841	506	14	5–64	36.14	3.60	60.07	0	0
ODIs	16	767	804	18	3–36	44.66	6.28	42.61	0	0
T20Is	6	132	180	10	3–15	18.00	8.18	13.20	0	0
First-class	20	3404	1911	80	6–60	23.88	3.36	42.55	6	1

MAHELA **JAYAWARDENE**

Full name	**Denagamage Proboth Mahela de Silva Jayawardene**
Born	**May 27, 1977, Colombo**
Teams	**Sinhalese Sports Club, Wayamba, Delhi Daredevils**
Style	**Right-hand bat, right-arm medium-pacer**
Test debut	**Sri Lanka v India at Colombo 1997-98**
ODI debut	**Sri Lanka v Zimbabwe at Colombo 1997-98**
T20I debut	**Sri Lanka v England at Southampton 2006**

THE PROFILE A fine technician with an excellent temperament, Mahela Jayawardene's arrival heralded a new era for Sri Lanka's middle order. Perhaps mindful of his first Test, when he went in at 790 for 4, he soon developed an appetite for big scores. His 66 then, in the world-record 952 for 6 against India, was followed by a masterful 167 on a Galle minefield against New Zealand in only his fourth Test, and a marathon 242 against India in his seventh. However he lost form, hardly scored a run in the 2003 World Cup, and was briefly dropped. Jayawardene benefited from a settled spot at No. 4 after Aravinda de Silva retired: a good series against England was followed by more runs in 2004. He took over as captain in England in 2006, producing a stunning double of 61 and 119 to lead the rearguard that saved the Lord's Test. Later he put South Africa to the sword in Colombo, compiling a colossal 374 in a world-record stand of 624 with Kumar Sangakkara. In 2007 he inspired his side to the World Cup final with 548 runs at 60, including a century in the semi-final, then became Sri Lanka's leading Test runscorer during 2007-08, a period that included three successive centuries, one of them a double against England. He stepped down as captain early in 2009 to concentrate on his batting – not that leadership seemed to affect it much. He made a classy century in the 2011 World Cup final – in vain – and early the following year got the captaincy back, reluctantly, after Tillekeratne Dilshan was dumped. Jayawardene made a brilliant 180 against England in his first match back in charge, and added another century in the second Test. He's now passed 10,000 runs in both Tests and ODIs.

THE FACTS Jayawardene made 374 against South Africa in July 2006, the highest by a right-hander in Tests ... He took 77 Test catches off Muttiah Muralitharan, a record for a fielder-bowler combination ... Jayawardene has scored 2698 runs and ten centuries in Tests at the SSC in Colombo, a record for a single ground ... His record includes five ODIs for the Asia XI ...

THE FIGURES to 17.09.12   **ESPTn**cricinfo.com

Batting & Fielding	M	Inns	NO	Runs	HS	Avge	S/R	100	50	4s	6s	Ct	St
Tests	133	223	14	10540	374	50.43	51.65	31	42	1244	51	187	0
ODIs	382	358	35	10772	144	33.34	78.19	15	68	924	63	192	0
T20Is	37	37	5	981	100	30.65	138.95	1	6	110	23	11	0
First-class	217	349	23	16357	374	50.17	–	48	70	–	–	282	0

Bowling	M	Balls	Runs	Wkts	BB	Avge	RpO	S/R	5i	10m
Tests	133	553	297	6	2–32	49.50	3.22	92.16	0	0
ODIs	382	582	558	7	2–56	79.71	5.75	83.14	0	0
T20Is	37	6	8	0	–	–	8.00	–	0	0
First-class	217	2965	1616	52	5–72	31.07	3.27	57.01	1	0

PRASANNA **JAYAWARDENE**

Full name	**Hewasandatchige Asiri Prasanna Wishvanath Jayawardene**
Born	**October 9, 1979, Colombo**
Teams	**Bloomfield, Basnahira**
Style	**Right-hand bat, wicketkeeper**
Test debut	**Sri Lanka v Pakistan at Kandy 2000**
ODI debut	**Sri Lanka v Pakistan at Sharjah 2002–03**
T20I debut	**No T20Is yet**

THE PROFILE A neat, unflashy wicketkeeper rated by Kumar Sangakkara as the best in the world, Prasanna Jayawardene looked set for a long international career after touring England at 19, but became a back number after Sangakkara's own rocket-fuelled arrival in 2000. Waiting on the sidelines had already been a feature of Jayawardene's career: in his first Test, in June 2000, he was confined to the dressing-room, as rain washed out play on the last two days before Sri Lanka fielded. With the selectors worried about overburdening Sangakkara in Tests, Jayawardene was recalled in April 2004. Sangakkara soon got the gloves back then, but there was a sea-change two years later, after an England tour in which Jayawardene showed that his batting had improved. He was recalled for South Africa's visit in July 2006, and this time the decision to lighten Sangakkara's load paid off spectacularly: he hammered 287 in a world-record stand of 642 with Mahela Jayawardene (no relation) in the first Test. Prasanna finally seemed to have booked in for a long run behind the stumps – at least in Tests, with Sangakkara continuing in one-dayers – and cemented his place in June 2007 with a Test ton of his own, against Bangladesh. A finger injury kept him out briefly in 2009, but he was back for the New Zealand Tests in August, and later that year shared a Test-record stand of 351 with Mahela against India at Ahmedabad. He made another century at Cardiff in May 2011, but bagged a pair against Australia soon afterwards. Injuries impinged later, although he kept the challenge of Dinesh Chandimal at bay for a while with 120 against Pakistan in Abu Dhabi in October 2011.

THE FACTS Prasanna Jayawardene made 154 not out v India at Ahmedabad in November 2009: he and Mahela Jayawardene (275) put on 351 for the sixth wicket, beating the old Test record of 346 by Don Bradman and Jack Fingleton in 1936-37 ... He took seven catches in an innings for Sebastianites v Sinhalese in Colombo in January 2000... All Jayawardene's ODIs have been in the UAE (in Sharjah in 2003 and Abu Dhabi in 2007) ...

THE FIGURES to 17.09.12   **ᴇsᴘɴcricinfo.com**

Batting & Fielding	M	Inns	NO	Runs	HS	Avge	S/R	100	50	4s	6s	Ct	St
Tests	48	66	10	1770	154*	31.60	50.11	4	4	184	14	93	27
ODIs	6	5	0	27	20	5.40	61.36	0	0	3	0	4	1
T20Is	0	0	–	–	–	–	–	–	–	–	–	–	–
First-class	213	326	38	8443	229*	29.31	–	14	35	–	–	478	95

Bowling	M	Balls	Runs	Wkts	BB	Avge	RpO	S/R	5i	10m
Tests	48	0	–	–	–	–	–	–	–	–
ODIs	6	0	–	–	–	–	–	–	–	–
T20Is	0	0	–	–	–	–	–	–	–	–
First-class	213	18	9	0	–	–	3.00	–	0	0

MITCHELL **JOHNSON**

Full name	**Mitchell Guy Johnson**
Born	**November 2, 1981, Townsville, Queensland**
Teams	**Western Australia**
Style	**Left-hand bat, left-hand fast-medium bowler**
Test debut	**Australia v Sri Lanka at Brisbane 2007-08**
ODI debut	**Australia v New Zealand at Christchurch 2005-06**
T20I debut	**Australia v Zimbabwe at Cape Town 2007-08**

THE PROFILE He's quick, he's tall, he's talented ... but most of all, Mitchell Johnson is a left-armer, and only two others before him (Alan Davidson and Bruce Reid) took 100 Test wickets for Australia. Dennis Lillee spotted him at 17, and called him a "once-in-a-generation bowler". In December 2005 Johnson was supersubbed into the final one-dayer in New Zealand. However, the following season was a sobering one. Johnson, who runs up as if carrying a crate of milk bottles in his left hand, started by reducing India to 35 for 5 in a one-dayer in Kuala Lumpur, but narrowly missed out to the steadier Stuart Clark for the 2006-07 Ashes, then sat out the World Cup. Test rewards finally came in 2007-08, when he grabbed 16 wickets against India and ten in the West Indies. Next season Johnson was superb against South Africa both home and away, adding a wicked in-ducker to his repertoire and claiming 33 wickets in six Tests (and also hammering a maiden century), but then he struggled in England, spraying the ball around from an arm seemingly lower than usual. He did take 5 for 69 in the innings victory at Headingley, but overall he was a disappointment given the advance hype. The start of 2010 was similarly up-and-down – ten wickets against New Zealand at Hamilton, but only 11 in five other matches, and it was the same story at the end of the year in the Ashes: dropped for the second Test, matchwinner in the third with nine wickets and a handy 62, then down to earth again. Injuries then kept him out for a while in 2012, but he said they probably stopped him from retiring – which would have been much too soon for a bowler who, on his day, can turn a match in a trice.

THE FACTS Johnson took 8 for 61 – the best bowling figures in Tests by any left-arm fast bowler – against South Africa at Perth in 2008-09 ... He was the world's leading Test wicket-taker in 2009, with 63 ... Johnson took 6 for 51 (and 10 for 106 in the match) for Queensland v Victoria in the Pura Cup final at Brisbane in March 2006 ... He reached his maiden Test (and first-class) century against South Africa at Cape Town in March 2009 with a six ...

THE FIGURES to 17.09.12   **espncricinfo.com**

Batting & Fielding	M	Inns	NO	Runs	HS	Avge	S/R	100	50	4s	6s	Ct	St
Tests	47	69	10	1287	123*	21.81	59.94	1	6	158	23	13	0
ODIs	112	64	23	720	73*	17.56	96.12	0	2	57	18	25	0
T20Is	28	16	6	106	28*	10.60	117.77	0	0	8	3	4	0
First-class	83	116	22	2122	123*	22.57	–	2	10	–	–	20	0

Bowling	M	Balls	Runs	Wkts	BB	Avge	RpO	S/R	5i	10m
Tests	47	10672	5946	190	8–61	31.29	3.34	56.16	7	2
ODIs	112	5492	4441	174	6–31	25.52	4.85	31.56	3	0
T20Is	28	608	724	36	3–15	20.11	7.14	16.88	0	0
First-class	83	16698	9567	310	8–61	30.86	3.39	53.86	12	3

JUNAID KHAN

Full name	**Mohammad Junaid Khan**
Born	**December 24, 1989, Matra, NW Frontier Province**
Teams	**Abbottabad**
Style	**Right-hand bat, left-arm fast-medium bowler**
Test debut	**Pakistan v Zimbabwe at Bulawayo 2011**
ODI debut	**Pakistan v West Indies at Gros Islet 2010-11**
T20I debut	**Pakistan v West Indies at Gros Islet 2010-11**

THE PROFILE Junaid Khan had an unenviable task as the left-arm fast bowler called up in 2011 to replace the banned Mohammad Aamer. Junaid bowls at a good pace – the upper 80s mph according to the man himself – and moves the ball around when conditions are right. He was called up for Pakistan's 2011 World Cup squad as a late replacement, but didn't actually get a game. His debut had to wait until the West Indian tour that followed, and he made a slow start – only three wickets in six internationals, one of them a Twenty20 game. Junaid did grab six cheap scalps in two subsequent matches in Ireland, which was enough to keep him in the squad for the Zimbabwe tour that followed (in between he had a promising stint in limited-overs cricket for Lancashire). He made his Test debut at Bulawayo in September 2011, but although he kept things quiet in the first innings he took only one wicket, and was generally overshadowed by his fellow debutant Aizaz Cheema. Things improved after that, though, with 5 for 38 against Sri Lanka in Abu Dhabi, and when Pakistan toured Sri Lanka in mid-2012 he added further five-fors in Colombo and Pallekele. Junaid is from the Khyber-Pakhtunkhwa (formerly North West Frontier) province, and plays at home for Abbottabad, who are among the weaker sides on Pakistan's domestic circuit. But he still managed to catch the selectors' eye, taking 75 wickets at a fraction under 24 apiece in first-class cricket in 2009-10 (Tanvir Ahmed, now a rival for a Test place, led the way with 97).

THE FACTS Junaid Khan took 7 for 46 (13 for 77 in the match) for Abbottabad at Peshawar in November 2007 ... He had figures of 4-0-4-5 as Khan Research Laboratories bowled Customs out for 79 – the last nine wickets went down for 13 – in a first-class match at Mirpur in February 2009 ... Junaid's first three Test five-fors all came against Sri Lanka ... He played for Lancashire in 2011 ...

THE FIGURES *to 17.09.12*   **ESPncricinfo.com**

Batting & Fielding	M	Inns	NO	Runs	HS	Avge	S/R	100	50	4s	6s	Ct	St
Tests	8	8	3	19	8	3.80	34.54	0	0	2	0	1	0
ODIs	13	3	2	2	1*	2.00	22.22	0	0	0	0	3	0
T20Is	3	1	1	3	3*	–	75.00	0	0	0	0	0	0
First-class	45	59	19	481	71	12.02	–	0	2	–	–	7	0

Bowling	M	Balls	Runs	Wkts	BB	Avge	RpO	S/R	5i	10m
Tests	8	1497	721	27	5–38	26.70	2.88	55.44	3	0
ODIs	13	554	468	17	4–12	27.52	5.06	32.58	0	0
T20Is	3	60	80	2	2–23	40.00	8.00	30.00	0	0
First-class	45	8943	4483	199	7–46	22.52	3.00	44.93	16	3

JUNAID SIDDIQUE

Full name	**Mohammad Junaid Siddique**
Born	**October 30, 1987, Rajshahi**
Teams	**Rajshahi**
Style	**Left-hand bat, occasional offspinner**
Test debut	**Bangladesh v New Zealand at Dunedin 2007-08**
ODI debut	**Bangladesh v New Zealand at Auckland 2007-08**
T20I debut	**Bangladesh v Pakistan at Cape Town 2007-08**

THE PROFILE   Left-hander Junaid Siddique made a sensational start in Test cricket, when he and fellow debutant Tamim Iqbal flayed New Zealand's bowlers in an opening stand of 161 to light up the inaugural Test at Dunedin's University Oval at the start of 2008. *Wisden* said they began "with an entrancing display of classical strokes, their timing perfect as the ball was distributed around the short boundaries". Sadly, this fine start came to nothing: the other batsmen made only 83 between them, and Bangladesh lost yet again. "Imrose" also made a stylish 74 against South Africa at Mirpur – no-one else made more than 24 – and added 71 on his Twenty20 international debut. However, the faster bowlers noticed a compulsion to get onto the front foot – bred on slow, low pitches in Bangladesh – and Junaid began to cop a lot of short stuff. But he persevered, making 78 in victory over a depleted West Indian side in St Vincent in July 2009, while his ODI performances improved: after an anaemic start (62 runs in eight innings), he hit 85 against New Zealand in November 2008, then scored consistently against admittedly modest attacks in the West Indies and Zimbabwe. He settled in at No. 3, and made his first Test century against England at Chittagong in March 2010, before adding a maiden one-day international hundred against Ireland a few months later. Typically, though, Bangladesh lost both matches. After an up-and-down 2011, during which he struggled at the World Cup, Junaid was dropped for a while – but kept his name on the selectors' radar with a career-best 161 for Rajshahi against Dhaka at Sylhet in December 2011.

THE FACTS   Junaid Siddique scored 74 on his Test debut at Dunedin in January 2008, putting on 161 for the first wicket with Tamim Iqbal, who was also winning his first cap: it was the highest opening stand between debutants in Tests since Billy Ibadulla and Abdul Kadir put on 249 for Pakistan v Australia at Karachi in 1964-65 ... Junaid hit 71 off 49 balls in his first Twenty20 international, against Pakistan at Cape Town in September 2007 ...

THE FIGURES to 17.09.12   **ESPN**cricinfo.com

Batting & Fielding	M	Inns	NO	Runs	HS	Avge	S/R	100	50	4s	6s	Ct	St
Tests	18	35	0	942	106	26.91	41.22	1	7	121	1	11	0
ODIs	54	53	1	1196	100	23.00	68.22	1	6	118	7	23	0
T20Is	7	7	0	159	71	22.71	147.22	0	1	16	7	1	0
First-class	53	96	1	2598	161	27.34	–	3	15	–	–	41	0

Bowling	M	Balls	Runs	Wkts	BB	Avge	RpO	S/R	5i	10m
Tests	18	18	11	0	–	–	3.66	–	0	0
ODIs	54	12	13	0	–	–	6.50	–	0	0
T20Is	7	0	–	–	–	–	–	–	–	–
First-class	53	203	127	1	1–30	127.00	3.75	203.00	0	0

JACQUES **KALLIS**

SOUTH AFRICA

Full name	**Jacques Henry Kallis**
Born	**October 16, 1975, Pinelands, Cape Town**
Teams	**Warriors, Kolkata Knight Riders**
Style	**Right-hand bat, right-arm fast-medium bowler**
Test debut	**South Africa v England at Durban 1995-96**
ODI debut	**South Africa v England at Cape Town 1995-96**
T20I debut	**South Africa v New Zealand at Johannesburg 2005-06**

THE PROFILE In an era of fast scoring and high-octane entertainment, Jacques Kallis is a throwback – an astonishingly effective one – to a more sedate age, when your wicket was to be guarded with your life. He blossomed after a quiet start into arguably the world's leading batsman, with the adhesive qualities of a Cape Point limpet. In 2005, he was the ICC's first Test Player of the Year, but his batting is not for the romantic: a Kallis century (of which there have now been 60 in international cricket) tends to see ruthless efficiency taking precedence over derring-do, and he has never quite dispelled the notion that he is a selfish batsman, something the Aussies played on during the 2007 World Cup. His team-mates, though, vouch for the fact that he bats the way he does precisely because he puts his team first and his personal ambitions some way behind. He had a purple patch at the turn of 2010-11, scoring five Test centuries – including a long-awaited maiden 200 – inside two months. He started 2012 with another double-century – 224 against Sri Lanka at Cape Town – and almost bagged another (182 not out) against England at The Oval in July. Kallis has sailed to the top of South Africa's batting charts, and is a fine bowler too, capable of swinging the ball sharply at a surprising pace. Strong, with powerful shoulders and a deep chest, Kallis has the capacity to play a wide array of attacking strokes, and has a good Twenty20 record. He has a batting average in the mid-fifties to go with more than 550 international wickets all told. He's a fine slip fielder too.

THE FACTS Kallis and Shaun Pollock were the first South Africans to play 100 Tests, reaching the mark, appropriately enough, at Centurion in April 2006 ... Kallis averages 169.75 in Tests against Zimbabwe, and scored 388 runs against them in two Tests in 2001-02 without being dismissed ... Including his next innings he batted for a record 1241 minutes in Tests without getting out ... Kallis's record includes one Test and three ODIs for the World XI, and two ODIs for the Africa XI ...

THE FIGURES to 17.09.12   **ESPNcricinfo.com**

Batting & Fielding	M	Inns	NO	Runs	HS	Avge	S/R	100	50	4s	6s	Ct	St
Tests	155	262	40	12641	224	56.94	45.79	43	55	1409	92	187	0
ODIs	321	307	53	11498	139	45.26	72.97	17	85	903	136	125	0
T20Is	20	20	4	642	73	40.12	122.28	0	5	54	19	7	0
First-class	246	403	57	19047	224	55.04	–	60	94	–	–	251	0

Bowling	M	Balls	Runs	Wkts	BB	Avge	RpO	S/R	5i	10m
Tests	155	19344	9137	280	6–54	32.63	2.83	69.08	5	0
ODIs	321	10636	8558	270	5–30	31.69	4.82	39.39	2	0
T20Is	20	210	260	5	2–20	52.00	7.42	42.00	0	0
First-class	246	28145	13134	415	6–54	31.64	2.79	67.81	8	0

KAMRAN AKMAL

Full name	**Kamran Akmal**
Born	**January 13, 1982, Lahore, Punjab**
Teams	**Lahore, National Bank**
Style	**Right-hand bat, wicketkeeper**
Test debut	**Pakistan v Zimbabwe at Harare 2002-03**
ODI debut	**Pakistan v Zimbabwe at Bulawayo 2002-03**
T20I debut	**Pakistan v England at Bristol 2006**

THE PROFILE Kamran Akmal made his first-class debut at 15 as a useful wicketkeeper and a hard-hitting batsman. He has had good times since – and bad ones, as his keeping fell away, leading to several costly errors, none more so than in an iron-gloved performance that cost Pakistan victory at Sydney in January 2010: Akmal dropped four catches, most of them sitters, failed with the bat too, and later had to fend off accusations of match-fixing. After that he was briefly dropped, and although he returned his form since has been fitful, and he was replaced again after the 2011 World Cup by his brother Adnan (another brother, Umar, has also kept wicket for Pakistan). But Kamran is a survivor, and returned after 18 months for the limited-overs matches against Australia in the UAE late in 2012. It all started so promisingly: by October 2004 he was Pakistan's first-choice keeper, and the following year hit five international centuries. Three of them came while opening in one-dayers, and two in Tests, one to save the match against India at Mohali, and a blistering 154 in the emphatic series-sealing win over England at Lahore. However, a nightmare series in England in 2006 set him back again. Since then he has rarely regained his best touch with bat or gloves: he did make an important 119 against India in the Kolkata Test in November 2007, but continued fumbles behind the stumps eventually cost him an automatic place. There were still some highlights, though: Akmal started 2009 with an unbeaten 158 in a Test against Sri Lanka and a century against Australia, and also played his part in winning the World Twenty20 in England in June 2010.

THE FACTS Kamran Akmal scored five international hundreds in December 2005 and January 2006, including 154 in the Lahore Test against England, when he shared a sixth-wicket stand of 269 with Mohammad Yousuf ... Akmal has scored more Test hundreds than any other Pakistan wicketkeeper: Moin Khan made four and Imtiaz Ahmed three ... His brothers Umar and Adnan Akmal have both also played – and kept wicket – for Pakistan ...

THE FIGURES to 17.09.12   ESPncricinfo.com

Batting & Fielding	M	Inns	NO	Runs	HS	Avge	S/R	100	50	4s	6s	Ct	St
Tests	53	92	6	2648	158*	30.79	63.10	6	12	372	14	184	22
ODIs	140	122	14	2930	124	27.12	84.07	5	9	341	31	137	27
T20Is	41	36	5	778	73	25.09	125.68	0	5	76	26	19	28
First-class	174	272	29	8244	268	33.92	–	17	39	–	–	592	48

Bowling	M	Balls	Runs	Wkts	BB	Avge	RpO	S/R	5i	10m
Tests	53	0	–	–	–	–	–	–	–	–
ODIs	140	0	–	–	–	–	–	–	–	–
T20Is	41	0	–	–	–	–	–	–	–	–
First-class	174	0	–	–	–	–	–	–	–	–

ZAHEER **KHAN**

Full name	**Zaheer Khan**
Born	**October 7, 1978, Shrirampur, Maharashtra**
Teams	**Mumbai, Royal Challengers Bangalore**
Style	**Right-hand bat, left-arm fast-medium bowler**
Test debut	**India v Bangladesh at Dhaka 2000-01**
ODI debut	**India v Kenya at Nairobi 2000-01**
T20I debut	**India v South Africa at Johannesburg 2006-07**

THE PROFILE Like Waqar Younis before him, Zaheer Khan yorked his way into the cricket world's consciousness: his performances at the Champions Trophy in September 2000 announced the arrival of an all-too-rare star in the Indian fast-bowling firmament. Zaheer can move the ball both ways off the pitch and swing the old ball at a decent pace. After initial struggles, he came of age in the West Indies in 2002, when he led the attack with great heart. His subsequent displays in England and New Zealand – and some eye-catching moments at the 2003 World Cup – established him at the forefront of the new pace generation, but a hamstring injury relegated him to bit-part performer as India enjoyed some of their finest moments away in Australia and Pakistan. In a bid to jump the queue of left-arm hopefuls, Zaheer put in the hard yards for Worcestershire in 2006. It worked: Zaheer reclaimed his Test place, survived the fallout from the World Cup, and led the way in England in 2007, where his nine wickets at Trent Bridge clinched the match and the series: he was one of *Wisden*'s Cricketers of the Year. After an ankle injury he led the attack in the 2011 World Cup success – but his early exit from the England tour that followed, after a hamstring problem in the first Test, visibly deflated India, who subsided to a 4-0 whitewash. He returned for the Australian tour that followed and, carefully managed, made it to the World Twenty20 in Sri Lanka in September 2012, by which time he was close to 300 wickets in both the other two formats.

THE FACTS Zaheer Khan's 75 against Bangladesh at Dhaka in December 2004 was the highest Test score by a No. 11 at the time: he dominated a last-wicket stand of 133 with Sachin Tendulkar ... He took 9 for 138 (including a spell of 9 for 28) for Worcestershire v Essex at Chelmsford in June 2006, but a last-wicket stand of 97 cost him the chance of taking all ten wickets ... Zaheer averages 17.46 with the ball in ODIs against Zimbabwe, but 46.42 against Australia ... His record includes six ODIs for the Asia XI ...

THE FIGURES to 17.09.12   ESPNcricinfo.com

Batting & Fielding	M	Inns	NO	Runs	HS	Avge	S/R	100	50	4s	6s	Ct	St
Tests	85	115	23	1121	75	12.18	51.37	0	3	127	24	18	0
ODIs	200	101	35	792	34*	12.20	73.46	0	0	69	24	43	0
T20Is	13	4	2	13	9	6.50	130.00	0	0	0	1	2	0
First-class	152	199	39	2196	75	13.72	–	0	4	–	–	42	0

Bowling	M	Balls	Runs	Wkts	BB	Avge	RpO	S/R	5i	10m
Tests	85	17081	9332	291	7–87	32.06	3.27	58.69	10	1
ODIs	200	10097	8301	282	5–42	29.43	4.93	35.80	1	0
T20Is	13	274	354	14	4–19	25.28	7.75	19.57	0	0
First-class	152	30941	17060	617	9–138	27.64	3.30	50.14	32	8

CRAIG **KIESWETTER**

Full name	**Craig Kieswetter**
Born	**November 28, 1987, Johannesburg, South Africa**
Teams	**Somerset**
Style	**Right-hand bat, wicketkeeper**
Test debut	**No Tests yet**
ODI debut	**England v Bangladesh at Mirpur 2009-10**
T20I debut	**England v West Indies at Providence 2009-10**

THE PROFILE Craig Kieswetter's attractive, uncomplicated front-foot technique pushed him close to an England place even before he'd finished his qualification period, after choosing his adopted country ahead of his native South Africa (despite a late plea from Graeme Smith). The day after he was qualified, he hit 81 for the Lions against the full England side in Abu Dhabi. He spanked a classy century in only his third one-day international, in Bangladesh, then gave England a series of rapid starts in the World Twenty20 in the West Indies, crowning his campaign with 63 – and the match award – as the final was won. And then it all started to go wrong. Kieswetter, who had scored 1242 first-class runs in 2009, managed less than 500 in 2010. He did make more than 500 in one-dayers for the second year running – but at almost half his 2009 average, and duly lost his England place. The problem seemed to be twofold: bowlers had got wise to his strengths, and avoided them more; so, in a bid to combat the lack of drivable balls, Kieswetter moved his stance outside leg and was therefore exposing his stumps. By the end of 2010 he had moved back across, and looked better for it: the first-class average was back above 40 the following year, and reached 50 in 2012, which included a hundred for the Lions against Australia A. By then he was restored as a one-day regular, after Matt Prior was preferred for the 2011 World Cup, and smacked a 32-ball 50 against South Africa in a Twenty20 game in September 2012. He first came to prominence at Millfield School, and made his Somerset first-team debut in April 2007, scoring 69 not out off 58 balls and taking a catch his coach described as "world class".

THE FACTS Kieswetter made 107 in only his third ODI, against Bangladesh at Chittagong in March 2010 ... Kieswetter made 164 for Somerset v Nottinghamshire at Trent Bridge in July 2011 ... He scored 150 not out against Warwickshire at Taunton in April 2009, and next day hit 138 not out against them in a 50-over game ...

THE FIGURES *to 17.09.12* **ESPMcricinfo.com**

Batting & Fielding	M	Inns	NO	Runs	HS	Avge	S/R	100	50	4s	6s	Ct	St
Tests	0	0	–	–	–	–	–	–	–	–	–	–	–
ODIs	43	37	4	1012	107	30.66	91.08	1	5	102	30	51	12
T20Is	21	21	1	487	63	24.35	115.13	0	3	43	21	15	2
First-class	89	131	19	4613	164	41.18	–	10	230	–	–	251	5

Bowling	M	Balls	Runs	Wkts	BB	Avge	RpO	S/R	5i	10m
Tests	0	0	–	–	–	–	–	–	–	–
ODIs	43	0	–	–	–	–	–	–	–	–
T20Is	21	0	–	–	–	–	–	–	–	–
First-class	89	18	3	2	2–3	1.50	1.00	9.00	0	0

VIRAT **KOHLI**

Full name	**Virat Kohli**
Born	**November 5, 1988, Delhi**
Teams	**Delhi, Royal Challengers Bangalore**
Style	**Right-hand bat, occasional medium-pacer**
Test debut	**India v West Indies at Kingston 2011**
ODI debut	**India v Sri Lanka at Dambulla 2008**
T20I debut	**India v Zimbabwe at Harare 2010**

THE PROFILE An attacking player with a cool head and the hint of a swagger that suggests he knows he's pretty good, Virat Kohli has been making big scores from a young age. He made three double-centuries for Delhi's Under-17s, then captained India to victory in the Under-19 World Cup in 2008. By then he had already made his Ranji Trophy debut, making 90 (after Delhi had been 14 for 4) against Karnataka in his fourth match. The upward curve continued with a maiden century against Rajasthan, and a superb 169 against Karnataka. He was consistent in one-day cricket without making big scores – that came later – and was called up for a series in Sri Lanka in August 2008. He wasn't expected to play, but injuries gave him a chance: he reached double figures in all five innings, with 54 in the fourth game. Another good domestic season followed – 613 runs at 55, with a career-best 197 against Pakistan's national champions – then he improved his IPL form after a disappointing first campaign. Kohli enjoyed a dream run in ODIs in 2009-10: successive innings against Sri Lanka and Bangladesh produced 54, 107, 9, 91, 71 not out and 102 not out. He couldn't quite keep that up, but it did cement his place in the side. He kicked off the 2011 World Cup with a hundred against Bangladesh, and later contributed 35 as the final was won. After a slow start in Tests Kohli blossomed in 2012, making hundreds against Australia and New Zealand – but it was in the 50-overs game that he really caught the eye, turning into a prolific scorer – and an accomplished "finisher". One purple patch included five centuries in eight innings, including a rollicking 183 against Pakistan in the Asia Cup in Dhaka.

THE FACTS Kohli scored 197 for Delhi against Pakistan's champions Sui Northern Gas in the Mohammad Nissar Trophy match at Delhi in September 2008 ... He made 183 against Pakistan at Dhaka in the Asia Cup in March 2012, during a run of four centuries in five ODI innings (and 66 in the other one) ... Kohli took a wicket with his first delivery in Twenty20 internationals (Kevin Pietersen stumped off a wide) at Old Trafford in August 2011 ...

THE FIGURES *to 17.09.12* ▄▄▄cricinfo.com

Batting & Fielding	M	Inns	NO	Runs	HS	Avge	S/R	100	50	4s	6s	Ct	St
Tests	10	18	1	703	116	41.35	49.78	2	5	79	4	14	0
ODIs	90	87	12	3886	183	51.81	86.43	13	21	366	20	49	0
T20Is	11	9	1	278	70	34.75	134.29	0	2	37	4	4	0
First-class	40	62	8	2834	197	52.48	55.62	9	13	377	17	41	0

Bowling	M	Balls	Runs	Wkts	BB	Avge	RpO	S/R	5i	10m
Tests	10	66	35	0	–	–	3.18	–	0	0
ODIs	90	292	276	2	1–20	138.00	5.67	146.00	0	0
T20Is	11	82	97	2	1–13	41.00	7.09	41.00	0	0
First-class	40	534	289	3	1–19	96.33	3.24	178.00	0	0

NUWAN **KULASEKARA**

Full name	**Kulasekara Mudiyanselage Dinesh Nuwan Kulasekara**
Born	**July 22, 1982, Nittambuwa**
Teams	**Colts, Basnahira, Chennai Super Kings**
Style	**Right-hand bat, right-arm fast-medium bowler**
Test debut	**Sri Lanka v New Zealand at Napier 2004-05**
ODI debut	**Sri Lanka v England at Dambulla 2003-04**
T20I debut	**Sri Lanka v Pakistan at King City 2008-09**

THE PROFILE Nuwan Kulasekara has a bustling run-up and a whippy open-chested action, and moves the ball off the seam at around 80mph. He can also maintain a tight line and length, and, after adding a yard or two of pace, suddenly emerged as a formidable bowler, especially in one-day internationals. He did so well in 2008 (33 wickets at 20.87 in 21 matches) that by March 2009 he was proudly sitting on top of the ICC's world one-day rankings for bowlers. He maintained that form throughout 2009, and also began to look the part in Tests, too: he grabbed four wickets in each innings as Pakistan lost in Colombo in August, and ending that series with 17 victims. After that, though, the old worries about his supposed lack of pace returned, and he has been in and out of the side ever since, although he did play six matches in the 2011 World Cup, including the final. After that, nine ODIs against England and Australia produced only three wickets, but he was back in one-day favour by 2012 – and in June took five wickets against Pakistan in his first Test for 19 months. Shortly after that, though, he was sidelined by an untimely groin injury. Kulasekara's initial mark on Test cricket was with the bat: at Lord's in May 2006 he hung on for more than three hours for 64, helping Chaminda Vaas ensure that Sri Lanka managed a draw after following on 359 behind. Kulasekara also made an instant impression in his first one-dayer, taking 2 for 19 in nine overs as England subsided for 88 at Dambulla in November 2003. That came soon after a fine first season, in which he took 61 wickets at 21.06 for Colts. He started as a softball enthusiast before turning to cricket, first with Negegoda CC and then with Galle.

THE FACTS Playing for North Central Province at Dambulla in March 2005, Kulasekara dismissed all of Central Province's top six, finishing with 6 for 71 ... He took 7 for 27 for Colts v Bloomfield in January 2008 ... In March 2009 Kulasekara was top of the ICC world rankings for ODI bowlers ... He made 95 for Galle v Nondescripts in Colombo in October 2003: he and Primal Buddika doubled the score from 174 for 6 ...

THE FIGURES to 17.09.12   **espncricinfo.com**

Batting & Fielding	M	Inns	NO	Runs	HS	Avge	S/R	100	50	4s	6s	Ct	St
Tests	15	20	1	295	64	15.52	44.29	0	1	39	4	5	0
ODIs	123	81	27	880	73	16.29	77.73	0	2	60	21	31	0
T20Is	17	12	3	62	19*	6.88	98.41	0	0	2	2	6	0
First-class	77	101	21	1467	95	18.33	–	0	4	–	–	27	0

Bowling	M	Balls	Runs	Wkts	BB	Avge	RpO	S/R	5i	10m
Tests	15	2350	1170	34	4–21	34.41	2.98	69.11	0	0
ODIs	123	5754	4454	132	4–40	33.74	4.64	43.59	0	0
T20Is	17	371	479	18	3–4	26.61	7.74	20.61	0	0
First-class	77	10866	5793	251	7–27	23.07	3.19	43.29	9	1

PRAVEEN **KUMAR**

INDIA

Full name	**Praveenkumar Sakat Singh**
Born	**October 2, 1986, Meerut, Uttar Pradesh**
Teams	**Uttar Pradesh, Kings XI Punjab**
Style	**Right-hand bat, right-arm fast-medium bowler**
Test debut	**India v West Indies at Kingston 2011**
ODI debut	**India v Pakistan at Jaipur 2007-08**
T20I debut	**India v Australia at Melbourne 2007-08**

THE PROFILE A medium-pacer accustomed to plugging away on unresponsive Indian wickets, Praveen Kumar can also double up as a carefree hitter down the order. He shone on debut in November 2005, with nine wickets against Haryana, and was a key performer – 41 wickets and 368 runs – as Uttar Pradesh won the Ranji Trophy in his first season. He followed that with 49 wickets the following term, and earned an A-team place for a one-day series in mid-2007 in Kenya, where he excelled with both bat and ball. Another strong Ranji season – including 8 for 68 in vain in the final against Delhi – sent him to Australia for the one-day series early in 2008, and he returned with reputation enhanced after ten wickets in his four games, including a matchwinning 4 for 46 in the second (and conclusive) final at Brisbane: he dismissed Adam Gilchrist and Ricky Ponting for single figures in both finals. After that Kumar did well in the inaugural IPL, then produced another matchwinning four-wicket effort against Pakistan in a one-dayer in Bangladesh. His progress stalled a little after that – only 18 first-class wickets at 37 in 2008-09 – and he sat out the World Twenty20 in the Caribbean in 2010 with a side strain. He also missed the 2011 World Cup with an elbow injury but, not previously seen as a Test prospect, he was a lone star as India suffered a 4-0 whitewash in England later in the year, manfully undertaking long spells – and moving the ball around artfully – after Zaheer Khan limped out of the series. But then Kumar himself was injured – a fractured rib followed an ankle problem – and he found it hard to regain his place in 2012.

THE FACTS Kumar took 8 for 68 for Uttar Pradesh v Delhi in the Ranji Trophy final at Mumbai in January 2008 ... He took 5 for 93 (and 4 for 55 in the second innings) on his first-class debut for UP v Haryana at Kanpur in November 2005 ... Kumar took an IPL hat-trick for Bangalore against Rajasthan in March 2010 ... He scored 78 and 57, and also took 5 for 73 and 5 for 87, for UP v Andhra at Anantapur in January 2006 ...

THE FIGURES *to 17.09.12*   **ESPncricinfo.com**

Batting & Fielding	M	Inns	NO	Runs	HS	Avge	S/R	100	50	4s	6s	Ct	St
Tests	6	10	0	149	40	14.90	93.71	0	0	21	5	2	0
ODIs	68	33	12	292	54*	13.90	88.21	0	1	25	7	11	0
T20Is	10	3	0	7	6	2.33	43.75	0	0	0	0	1	0
First-class	45	72	4	1607	98	23.63	76.05	0	8	172	56	8	0

Bowling	M	Balls	Runs	Wkts	BB	Avge	RpO	S/R	5i	10m
Tests	6	1611	697	27	5–106	25.81	2.59	59.66	1	0
ODIs	68	3242	2774	77	4–31	36.02	5.13	42.10	0	0
T20Is	10	156	193	8	2–14	24.12	7.42	19.50	0	0
First-class	45	10257	4738	201	8–68	23.57	2.76	57.22	14	1

NATHAN **LYON**

Full name	**Nathan Michael Lyon**
Born	**November 20, 1987, Young, New South Wales**
Teams	**South Australia**
Style	**Right-hand bat, offspinner**
Test debut	**Australia v Sri Lanka at Galle 2011**
ODI debut	**Australia v Sri Lanka at Adelaide 2011-12**
T20I debut	**No T20Is yet**

THE PROFILE As rags-to-riches stories go, it's right up there: Nathan Lyon is a groundsman at Adelaide Oval, bowls a bit in the nets when he can, gets noticed by the coach, plays for the state and does reasonably well, then, in a time of an Australia-wide drought of quality spin, is called up for the tour of Sri Lanka in 2011. If that doesn't sound implausible enough, Lyon then goes even further – a first-ball wicket, and figures of 5 for 34. The dream debut of the lanky Lyon started when he replaced his fellow newcomer, Trent Copeland, who had earlier taken a wicket with his second ball. Lyon went one better, sending down a venomous offbreak which Kumar Sangakkara – a veteran of almost 100 Tests and more than 8000 runs – could only edge low to Michael Clarke at slip. Unlike some, Lyon built on that early success, polishing off the tail to finish with five wickets. Things got harder after that – just one tailender in the second innings, and two wickets in the next Test – but Lyon looked level-headed enough to know that he was, as Australia's wicketkeeper Brad Haddin put it, still "work in progress" as a bowler. The first Test was, after all, just the sixth match of a first-class career which had begun only seven months earlier. After a quiet time consolidating his position at home in 2011-12, Lyon did well in the Caribbean, following an important 40 not out from No. 11 in victory at Bridgetown with 5 for 68 in the next Test at Port-of-Spain. His repertoire increased, with a sneaky legbreak tossed in occasionally, along with better use of the width of the crease. Lyon's early cricket was for the Australian Capital Territory in Canberra, where he worked as a groundsman before he got the job in Adelaide.

THE FACTS Lyon was the third Australian (after Tom Horan in 1882-83 and Arthur Coningham in 1894-95) to take a wicket with his first ball in a Test, dismissing Kumar Sangakkara of Sri Lanka at Galle in September 2011 ... Lyon finished with 5 for 34, still his best figures in first-class cricket (this was only his sixth match) ...

THE FIGURES to 17.09.12

cricinfo.com

Batting & Fielding	M	Inns	NO	Runs	HS	Avge	S/R	100	50	4s	6s	Ct	St
Tests	13	17	9	117	40*	14.62	42.54	0	0	13	0	4	0
ODIs	2	2	1	4	4*	4.00	66.66	0	0	0	0	1	0
T20Is	0	0	–	–	–	–	–	–	–	–	–	–	–
First-class	24	32	12	260	40*	13.00	40.37	0	0	31	0	6	0

Bowling	M	Balls	Runs	Wkts	BB	Avge	RpO	S/R	5i	10m
Tests	13	2417	1169	42	5–34	27.83	2.90	57.54	2	0
ODIs	2	96	77	1	1–4	77.00	4.81	96.00	0	0
T20Is	0	0	–	–	–	–	–	–	–	–
First-class	24	4926	2540	71	5–34	35.77	3.09	69.38	2	0

BRENDON **McCULLUM**

Full name	**Brendon Barrie McCullum**
Born	**September 27, 1981, Dunedin, Otago**
Teams	**Otago, Kolkata Knight Riders**
Style	**Right-hand bat, wicketkeeper**
Test debut	**New Zealand v South Africa at Hamilton 2003-04**
ODI debut	**New Zealand v Australia at Sydney 2001-02**
T20I debut	**New Zealand v Australia at Auckland 2004-05**

NEW ZEALAND

THE PROFILE Brendon McCullum stepped up to the national side as a wicketkeeper-batsman after an outstanding career in youth cricket, where he often dominated opposition attacks. Not surprisingly he found it hard to replicate that at the highest level at first, although there were occasional fireworks in domestic cricket. But he finally made his mark in England in 2004, with an entertaining 96 at Lord's. He collected his maiden century in Bangladesh that October, and added another hundred in a victory over Zimbabwe in August 2005, and hammered 86 as New Zealand overhauled Australia's 346 at Hamilton in February 2007 with one wicket to spare. But he really made his mark in April 2008, at the opening night of the inaugural IPL, by smacking 158 not out from 73 balls for Kolkata Knight Riders. There were signs he was having trouble tempering his natural attacking instincts in the longer game, but in the summer of 2008 he lit up Lord's again with 97, before walloping ten sixes in 166 in a one-day mismatch against Ireland. McCullum showed he could still hack it in Tests with 84 and 115 against India in March 2009 and 185 against Bangladesh a year later. After regular back niggles, he announced that he would no longer keep wicket in Tests, and in only his second match unencumbered by the gloves applied himself for 543 minutes to score 225 against India at Hyderabad in November 2010. The runs continued to flow, although similar big scores proved elusive: in the year from September 2011 he passed fifty 11 times but only once (in an ODI against Zimbabwe) reached three figures. He did slam 91 from 55 balls at Chennai in September 2012 as New Zealand rounded off an otherwise disappointing tour of India with a T20 victory.

THE FACTS McCullum made 185, the highest score by a New Zealand wicketkeeper in Tests, against Bangladesh at Hamilton in February 2010 ... He was the first man to score 1000 runs in Twenty20 internationals ... McCullum hit 166, and shared an opening stand of 274 with James Marshall, in an ODI against Ireland at Aberdeen in July 2008 ... His brother Nathan has also played for New Zealand ...

THE FIGURES to 17.09.12

ESPNcricinfo.com

Batting & Fielding	M	Inns	NO	Runs	HS	Avge	S/R	100	50	4s	6s	Ct	St
Tests	68	118	7	3978	225	35.83	60.19	6	23	479	45	172	11
ODIs	203	175	25	4554	166	30.36	89.55	4	22	410	130	231	15
T20Is	48	48	8	1443	116*	36.07	132.75	1	9	139	57	30	7
First-class	114	200	11	6687	225	35.38	–	11	38	–	–	279	19

Bowling	M	Balls	Runs	Wkts	BB	Avge	RpO	S/R	5i	10m
Tests	68	36	18	0	–	–	3.00	–	0	0
ODIs	203	–	–	–	–	–	–	–	–	–
T20Is	48	–	–	–	–	–	–	–	–	–
First-class	114	36	18	0	–	–	3.00	–	0	0

NATHAN **McCULLUM**

Full name	**Nathan Leslie McCullum**
Born	**September 1, 1980, Dunedin, Otago**
Teams	**Otago**
Style	**Right-hand bat, offspinner**
Test debut	**No Tests yet**
ODI debut	**New Zealand v Sri Lanka at Colombo 2009**
T20I debut	**New Zealand v South Africa at Durban 2007-08**

THE PROFILE The older brother of Brendon McCullum, Nathan is an offspinning allrounder from Otago who played a few matches in the IPL in 2011. Less lavishly gifted than his brother, this McCullum had to work patiently at his game to earn his national colours. He was in the 30-man preliminary squad for the Champions Trophy in 2006 but didn't make the cut, and had to wait until the inaugural World Twenty20 in South Africa in September 2007 for the chance to appear alongside Brendon in New Zealand colours. He scored a single in his only match and didn't bowl – and promptly disappeared back into domestic cricket for nearly 18 months. He was back for the next World Twenty20, in England in 2009, and this time added more to the cause, particularly with some tight bowling and taut fielding. Three 50-overs outings produced fewer runs and even fewer wickets, but McCullum was back for the third edition of the World Twenty20 in the West Indies in 2010, where he turned the match against Sri Lanka with a four and a six in the last over, after earlier taking a wicket and three catches: for once he overshadowed his brother, who failed to score. He then took 3 for 16 in his four overs against Zimbabwe to ensure New Zealand reached the second phase. McCullum took eight wickets on helpful pitches at the 2011 World Cup, and made a half-century against Australia. The following year he made 50, then took 2 for 40, as West Indies were demolished in St Kitts. Limited-overs cricket is his forte: he has only one century and a couple of five-fors in a first-class career spanning more than a decade. In his younger days, he was also a useful footballer.

THE FACTS McCullum took 6 for 90 for New Zealand A v India A at Chennai in September 2008 ... He scored 106 not out for Otago v Northern Districts at Hamilton in March 2008 ... He has played Twenty20 matches in India (for Pune Warriors), England (Lancashire) and Australia (Sydney Sixers) ... McCullum's brother Brendon has also played for New Zealand, while their father Stu represented Otago ...

THE FIGURES to 17.09.12   ESPNcricinfo.com

Batting & Fielding	M	Inns	NO	Runs	HS	Avge	S/R	100	50	4s	6s	Ct	St
Tests	0	0	–	–	–	–	–	–	–	–	–	–	–
ODIs	36	31	3	588	65	21.00	82.35	0	4	37	15	14	0
T20Is	34	20	8	188	36*	15.66	103.29	0	0	10	5	14	0
First-class	56	86	7	1988	106*	25.16	–	1	12	–	–	63	0

Bowling	M	Balls	Runs	Wkts	BB	Avge	RpO	S/R	5i	10m
Tests	0	0	–	–	–	–	–	–	–	–
ODIs	36	1443	1173	26	3–24	45.11	4.87	55.50	0	0
T20Is	34	548	597	36	4–16	16.58	6.53	15.22	0	0
First-class	56	10172	4801	113	6–90	42.48	2.83	90.01	2	0

RYAN **McLAREN**

SOUTH AFRICA

Full name	**Ryan McLaren**
Born	**February 9, 1983, Kimberley**
Teams	**Knights**
Style	**Left-hand bat, right-arm fast-medium bowler**
Test debut	**South Africa v England at Johannesburg 2009-10**
ODI debut	**South Africa v Zimbabwe at Benoni 2009-2010**
T20I debut	**South Africa v England at Johannesburg 2009-2010**

THE PROFILE   Ryan McLaren made an eye-catching start to his first-class career: his first four seasons produced more than 1000 forthright runs, and over 100 wickets with some aggressive seam bowling. But an international call-up seemed far off, with Shaun Pollock and Jacques Kallis entrenched in the South African side. Like several of his compatriots McLaren opted for county cricket as a Kolpak player, and soon became a key performer for Kent, taking a hat-trick as they won the Twenty20 Cup final in 2007. After signing a three-year contract before another impressive county season in 2008 McLaren was named in South Africa's one-day squad that October – but Kent refused to release him, and he was forced to return to Canterbury. At the end of 2009, though, they did let him go – and South Africa lost no time in blooding him. McLaren kept things tight against Zimbabwe and England, then injuries to others led to a first Test cap on a fast-bowler-friendly pitch at Johannesburg, where the England series was emphatically squared: his contribution was a handy 33 not out and the wicket of England's first-innings top-scorer Paul Collingwood. McLaren is accurate and bowls at a nagging pace, factors which helped him pick up 5 for 19 in a Twenty20 international in the West Indies in May 2010. He has done little with the bat on the international stage, though, which may be why he was dropped and missed the 2011 World Cup, but he remains marketable in the Twenty20 game, as contracts with Punjab and Middlesex showed. He lost his central contract despite a good allround season at home in 2011-12 – but was recalled for the one-day leg of South Africa's triumphant tour of England in 2012.

THE FACTS   McLaren took a hat-trick for Kent v Gloucestershire in the English Twenty20 Cup final at Edgbaston in August 2007 ... He made 140 for Eagles v Warriors at Bloemfontein in March 2006 ... McLaren took 5 for 19 in a T20 international against West Indies in May 2010 ... He took 8 for 38 for Eagles v Cape Cobras at Stellenbosch in February 2007 ... His father, uncle and cousin all played for Griqualand West ...

THE FIGURES *to 17.09.12*   **ESPNcricinfo.com**

Batting & Fielding	M	Inns	NO	Runs	HS	Avge	S/R	100	50	4s	6s	Ct	St
Tests	1	1	1	33	33*	–	58.92	0	0	5	0	0	0
ODIs	13	9	2	38	12	5.42	62.29	0	0	4	0	5	0
T20Is	5	3	3	8	6*	–	88.88	0	0	0	0	1	0
First-class	99	146	27	3699	140	31.08	–	3	19	–	–	48	0

Bowling	M	Balls	Runs	Wkts	BB	Avge	RpO	S/R	5i	10m
Tests	1	78	43	1	1–30	43.00	3.30	78.00	0	0
ODIs	13	528	449	9	3–51	49.88	5.10	58.66	0	0
T20Is	5	119	144	9	5–19	16.00	7.26	13.22	1	0
First-class	99	15862	7966	317	8–38	25.12	3.01	50.03	12	1

MAHMUDULLAH

Full name	**Mohammad Mahmudullah**
Born	**February 4, 1986, Mymensingh**
Teams	**Dhaka**
Style	**Right-hand bat, offspinner**
Test debut	**Bangladesh v West Indies at Kingstown 2009**
ODI debut	**Bangladesh v Sri Lanka at Colombo 2007**
T20I debut	**Bangladesh v Kenya at Nairobi 2007-08**

THE PROFILE An offspinning allrounder who is also an assured close-in fielder, Mahmudullah was something of a surprise selection for Bangladesh's chastening tour of Sri Lanka in mid-2007 (all three Tests were lost by an innings, and all three ODIs ended in defeat too). He made his international debut in the second one-dayer, scoring 36 and picking up two wickets in his five overs. As a bowler he does turn the ball, and can also keep the runs down. Mahmudullah spent the summer of 2005 on the groundstaff at Lord's: MCC's head coach, Clive Radley, remembered him delivering "from quite wide of the crease – he spun it a lot and bowled a good doosra". Bangladesh have a lot of slow left-armers, but not many offspinners made a mark before "Riyad" – although so far he has been needed more for his batting, which improved as he got to grips with international cricket. He was stranded on 96 not out against India at Mirpur early in 2010, but made sure of his maiden century in the next Test, with 115 against New Zealand, before making assured fifties in both home Tests against England. Mahmudullah's bowling, after a good start against a depleted West Indian side in July 2009 – 12 wickets in his first two Tests – has proved less incisive, but he looks set to remain a fixture in the side for some time. He came to prominence after a superb domestic season in 2008-09, when 710 runs at 54.61 earned him a place on that West Indian tour. He anchored Bangladesh's upset victory over England in the 2011 World Cup, and is quietly maturing into a fine player.

THE FACTS Mahmudullah took 5 for 51 (and 8 for 110 in the match) on his Test debut, against West Indies in St Vincent in July 2009 ... His first four first-class centuries all came within a month at the end of 2008, including 152 for Dhaka at Khulna ... After being stranded on 96 against India at Mirpur in January 2010, Mahmudullah completed his maiden Test century in his next game, against New Zealand at Hamilton ...

THE FIGURES *to 17.09.12*   **espncricinfo.com**

Batting & Fielding	M	Inns	NO	Runs	HS	Avge	S/R	100	50	4s	6s	Ct	St
Tests	12	24	2	664	115	30.18	56.60	1	4	93	4	10	0
ODIs	80	68	22	1427	68*	31.02	69.84	0	6	100	13	20	0
T20Is	18	17	0	166	41	9.76	85.12	0	0	12	4	7	0
First-class	55	100	11	3020	152	33.93	–	5	14	–	–	51	0

Bowling	M	Balls	Runs	Wkts	BB	Avge	RpO	S/R	5i	10m
Tests	12	1721	973	24	5–51	40.54	3.39	71.70	1	0
ODIs	80	2365	2027	44	3–4	46.06	5.14	53.75	0	0
T20Is	18	199	226	7	2–28	32.28	6.81	28.42	0	0
First-class	55	4984	2640	73	5–51	36.16	3.17	68.27	1	0

LASITH **MALINGA**

SRI LANKA

Full name	**Separamadu Lasith Malinga Swarnajith**
Born	**August 28, 1983, Galle**
Teams	**Nondescripts, Basnahira, Mumbai Indians**
Style	**Right-hand bat, right-arm fast bowler**
Test debut	**Sri Lanka v Australia at Darwin 2004**
ODI debut	**Sri Lanka v United Arab Emirates at Dambulla 2004**
T20I debut	**Sri Lanka v England at Southampton 2006**

THE PROFILE A rare Sri Lankan cricketer from the south, Lasith Malinga - whose exotic hairstyles make him stand out on and off the park – played hardly any proper cricket until he was 17, preferring the softball version in the coconut groves of Rathgama, a village near Galle. But once he was unearthed, he took eight wickets in his first-class debut, and hardly looked back. He bowls with a distinctive explosive round-arm action, and generates genuine pace, often disconcerting batsmen who struggle to pick up the ball's trajectory. "Slinga" Malinga was a surprise selection for the 2004 tour of Australia, and started with 6 for 90 in a warm-up game. That led to a first Test cap, and he acquitted himself well, with six wickets in his first match and four in the second: he added nine against New Zealand at Napier in April 2005, when the opposing batsmen complained his action meant the ball often got lost in the umpires' clothing. He was originally thought too erratic for one-dayers, but buried that reputation with 13 wickets in the 5–0 whitewash of England in 2006. The following year he scalped 18 during the World Cup, including four in four balls against South Africa. After that he became a fixture in limited-overs matches, where his toe-crushing yorkers proved difficult to get away. He officially retired from the five-day game in 2011, ostensibly to spare his body wear and tear, although the lure of lucrative Twenty20 contracts might have helped make up his mind. Malinga remained a stunning limited-overs force, picking up two more ODI hat-tricks, including another in the World Cup, and reached 200 wickets late in 2012.

THE FACTS Malinga is the only bowler to take four wickets in four balls in international cricket, against South Africa at Providence during the 2007 World Cup ... He has taken two further ODI hat-tricks, against Kenya in the 2011 World Cup and Australia in August 2011 ... Malinga took 6 for 17 as Galle bowled out the Police for 51 in Colombo in November 2003 ... He played for Kent in 2007 ...

THE FIGURES to 17.09.12   **ESPN cricinfo.com**

Batting & Fielding	M	Inns	NO	Runs	HS	Avge	S/R	100	50	4s	6s	Ct	St
Tests	30	37	13	275	64	11.45	44.42	0	1	36	6	7	0
ODIs	127	63	19	371	56	8.43	78.93	0	1	28	16	17	0
T20Is	33	14	7	64	27	9.14	95.52	0	0	3	3	13	0
First-class	83	100	41	584	64	9.89	40.58	0	1	–	–	23	0

Bowling	M	Balls	Runs	Wkts	BB	Avge	RpO	S/R	5i	10m
Tests	30	5209	3349	101	5–50	33.15	3.85	51.57	3	0
ODIs	127	6247	5315	200	6–38	26.57	5.10	31.23	5	0
T20Is	33	675	818	40	3–12	20.45	7.27	16.87	0	0
First-class	83	11867	7751	255	6–17	30.39	3.91	46.53	7	0

SHAUN **MARSH**

Full name **Shaun Edward Marsh**
Born **July 9, 1983, Narrogin, Western Australia**
Teams **Western Australia, Glamorgan, Kings XI Punjab**
Style **Left-hand bat, occasional left-arm spinner**
Test debut **Australia v Sri Lanka at Galle 2011**
ODI debut **Australia v West Indies at Kingstown 2007-08**
T20I debut **Australia v West Indies at Bridgetown 2008**

AUSTRALIA

THE PROFILE As a child Shaun Marsh spent a lot of time in the Australian set-up travelling with his father Geoff, the former Test opener. That grounding and a backyard net helped him develop into one of Australia's finest young batsmen. It also gave him a taste of what to expect when he joined the one-day side in the Caribbean in 2008. That came after a fine domestic season: he was also the surprise hit of the inaugural IPL. More gifted than his father – "He's got a few more shots than me," Geoff once admitted – Shaun is a left-hander who reached his maiden first-class hundred in 2003 with successive sixes over midwicket off Mark Waugh. The second century had to wait until 2004-05 as Marsh struggled with concentration, the finest trait of his father's batting. In 2008-09 he had successive scores of 79 and 78 against South Africa, but tore a hamstring while fielding against New Zealand, and later hurt his leg again, which kept him out of the World Twenty20 in England in June 2009. He returned with a century in India then, after a back injury, made a classy 59 (and took two superb boundary-riding catches) as Australia ended the one-day series against England in July 2010 with a victory at Lord's. He finally got a Test chance in Sri Lanka in 2011, with Ricky Ponting on paternity leave. Watched by his dad, Marsh grabbed the opportunity greedily, making a superb 141 and adding 81 in the next Test. When Ponting returned, Marsh stayed at No. 3 ... but not for long. He endured a horror run against India at home at the start of 2012 – just 17 runs in six innings, with three ducks – and was sent back to Shield cricket. "He just has to keep working hard and put some runs on the board," siad Michael Clarke.

THE FACTS Marsh was the 19th Australian to score a century on Test debut, five years after he hit 81 in his first ODI ... Marsh made 166 not out for Western Australia v Queensland at Perth in November 2007 ... His father Geoff won 50 Test caps (they are only the second father-son combination to play Tests for Australia), and his younger brother Mitchell played his first limited-overs internationals in October 2011 ...

THE FIGURES *to 17.09.12*

espncricinfo.com

Batting & Fielding	M	Inns	NO	Runs	HS	Avge	S/R	100	50	4s	6s	Ct	St
Tests	7	11	0	301	141	27.36	41.00	1	1	36	0	4	0
ODIs	36	36	1	1274	112	36.40	75.65	2	8	117	13	8	0
T20Is	8	8	0	108	29	13.50	105.88	0	0	8	5	1	0
First-class	73	132	16	4284	166*	36.93	46.41	7	24	–	–	60	0

Bowling	M	Balls	Runs	Wkts	BB	Avge	RpO	S/R	5i	10m
Tests	7	0	–	–	–	–	–	–	–	–
ODIs	36	0	–	–	–	–	–	–	–	–
T20Is	8	0	–	–	–	–	–	–	–	–
First-class	73	174	131	2	2–20	65.50	4.51	87.00	0	0

CHRIS **MARTIN**

Full name	**Christopher Stewart Martin**
Born	**December 10, 1974, Christchurch, Canterbury**
Teams	**Auckland**
Style	**Right-hand bat, right-arm fast-medium bowler**
Test debut	**New Zealand v South Africa at Bloemfontein 2000-01**
ODI debut	**New Zealand v Zimbabwe at Taupo 2000-01**
T20I debut	**New Zealand v Kenya at Durban 2007-08**

THE PROFILE Chris Martin is an angular fast-medium bowler who receives almost as much attention for his inept batting as for his nagging bowling, which has produced more than 200 Test wickets, including 11 as New Zealand whipped South Africa at Auckland in March 2004. Seven more scalps followed in the next game. It was all the more remarkable as they were his first Tests in almost two years: he had been overlooked since Pakistan piled up 643 at Lahore in May 2002 (Martin 1 for 108). He got his original chance after a crop of injuries, but did not disgrace himself in the first portion of his Test career, taking 34 wickets at 34 in 11 Tests, including six as Pakistan were crushed by an innings at Hamilton in 2000-01. Since his return he has largely maintained that average, happy to bowl long spells *à la* Ewen Chatfield – he took 5 for 152 at Brisbane in November 2004, after a surprisingly unproductive England tour. Back in England in 2008, he again failed to make much impression in the Tests (four wickets at 58.75), but returned to form at home with 14 wickets against India, including seven in a high-scoring draw at Wellington. In 2012 he improved his Test-best with 6 for 26 as Zimbabwe were blitzed at Napier. But whatever Martin does with the ball he is likely to be remembered more for his clueless batting: 35 of his 51 Test dismissals have been for ducks, he finally reached double figures against Bangladesh in his 36th match (a Test record) in January 2008, and has bagged seven pairs (no-one else has more than four). Mind you, he did once manage 25 for Canterbury, helping Chris Harris put on 75.

THE FACTS Very few players approach Martin's negative ratio of Test runs to wickets: two that do are England's Bill Bowes (28 runs, 68 wickets) and David Larter (15, 37) ... Martin is the only man to have bagged seven pairs in Tests ... He finally reached 100 Test runs in his 87th innings: the previous record was 40, by India's Bhagwat Chandrasekhar ... Only Richard Hadlee (431) and Daniel Vittori (359) have taken more wickets in Tests for New Zealand ...

THE FIGURES to 17.09.12   **ESPN**cricinfo.com

Batting & Fielding	M	Inns	NO	Runs	HS	Avge	S/R	100	50	4s	6s	Ct	St
Tests	70	102	51	123	12*	2.41	20.09	0	0	15	0	14	0
ODIs	20	7	2	8	3	1.60	29.62	0	0	0	0	7	0
T20Is	6	1	1	5	5*	–	83.33	0	0	0	0	1	0
First-class	185	233	112	471	25	3.89	–	0	0	–	–	33	0

Bowling	M	Balls	Runs	Wkts	BB	Avge	RpO	S/R	5i	10m
Tests	70	13910	7815	230	6–26	33.97	3.37	60.47	10	1
ODIs	20	948	804	18	3–62	44.66	5.08	52.66	0	0
T20Is	6	138	193	7	2–14	27.57	8.39	19.71	0	0
First-class	185	35540	18282	579	6–54	31.57	3.08	61.38	23	1

HAMILTON **MASAKADZA**

ZIMBABWE

Full name	**Hamilton Masakadza**
Born	**August 9, 1983, Harare**
Teams	**Mountaineers**
Style	**Right-hand bat, right-arm medium-pacer**
Test debut	**Zimbabwe v West Indies at Harare 2001**
ODI debut	**Zimbabwe v South Africa at Bulawayo 2001-02**
T20I debut	**Zimbabwe v Bangladesh at Khulna 2006-07**

THE PROFILE Hamilton Masakadza was still a schoolboy when he set the record – since beaten by Bangladesh's Mohammad Ashraful – as the youngest man to score a century on Test debut. Against West Indies in July 2001, he made a composed 119 from No. 3 – driving well, and showing few signs of nerves in the nineties. A year later, though, he put his cricket career on hold while at university in South Africa. Masakadza's return to the team brought mixed results at first, but he was the best batsman, technically, on the tour of South Africa early in 2005, showing an application lacking in his team-mates. Masakadza's form in one-day cricket – admittedly largely against lesser teams like Bangladesh and Kenya – has steadily improved: 2009 was a bumper year, bringing him more than 1000 runs in ODIs at an average of 43.48 and a strike-rate of 88. It included two towering scores of more than 150, both against Kenya in October. Late the following year, though, he went through a lean patch, and was rather surprisingly left out of the 2011 World Cup. But Masakadza was soon back, and helped set up Zimbabwe's victory in their comeback Test, against Bangladesh at Harare in August, with a five-hour 104, a second Test century more than ten years after his first. He remained in the runs during an otherwise disappointing tour of New Zealand early in 2012, making 53 and 62 in the two Twenty20 internationals, then had a triumphant time in the home T20 series against Bangladesh and South African XIs in June, making four fifties and a 36 in his five visits to the crease.

THE FACTS Masakadza was only the second Zimbabwean, after Dave Houghton in 1992-93, to make a century on Test debut: he made 119 against West Indies in July 2001, when 11 days short of his 18th birthday ... His second Test hundred came more than ten years later, against Bangladesh in August 2011 ... Masakadza is the only man ever to make two scores above 150 in the same ODI series – 156 and 178 not out v Kenya in October 2009 ... His brother Shingirai, a fast bowler, made his Test debut for Zimbabwe in 2012 ...

THE FIGURES to 17.09.12

ESPП cricinfo.com

Batting & Fielding	M	Inns	NO	Runs	HS	Avge	S/R	100	50	4s	6s	Ct	St
Tests	19	38	1	954	119	25.78	41.87	2	3	121	5	8	0
ODIs	115	115	4	3006	178*	27.08	73.19	3	18	298	38	50	0
T20Is	20	20	0	559	79	27.95	120.99	0	5	47	20	7	0
First-class	99	172	9	6622	208*	40.62	–	16	31	–	–	73	0

Bowling	M	Balls	Runs	Wkts	BB	Avge	RpO	S/R	5i	10m
Tests	19	360	117	5	1–9	23.40	1.95	72.00	0	0
ODIs	115	1148	1034	29	3–39	35.65	5.40	39.58	0	0
T20Is	20	42	71	1	1–9	71.00	10.14	42.00	0	0
First-class	99	3074	1361	47	4–11	28.95	2.65	65.40	0	0

ZIMBABWE

SHINGI **MASAKADZA**

Full name	**Shingirai Winston Masakadza**
Born	**September 4, 1986, Harare**
Teams	**Mountaineers**
Style	**Right-hand bat, right-arm fast-medium bowler**
Test debut	**Zimbabwe v New Zealand at Napier 2011-12**
ODI debut	**Zimbabwe v West Indies at Providence 2009-10**
T20I debut	**Zimbabwe v West Indies at Port-of-Spain 2009-10**

THE PROFILE Shingi Masakadza, an honest fast-medium seamer who opens the bowling for the Mountaineers franchise, has a lot to live up to – his older brother Hamilton was the first black African to hit a Test century (and, for a short time, the youngest to do so on debut). Born in Harare's Highfield township, Shingi first learned the game at Mbizi Primary School, and eventually joined the prominent Takashinga club. He made his first-class debut in 2007-08, and caused a stir with 21 wickets in four Logan Cup matches at the remarkable average of 11.95. He remained a consistent wicket-taker in first-class cricket, picking up 24 in 2008-09 and 40 the following season, which earned him a call-up to the national side for the tour of the West Indies early in 2010. His first over in international cricket was despatched for 14, but he bounced back well, grabbing three quick wickets late on to seal a tense two-run victory in the first one-day international in Guyana. He was out of the side for a while, but was on the fringe when Zimbabwe returned to Test cricket late in 2011: he duly made his Test debut in New Zealand early the following year. Zimbabwe won't want to remember that match – they were bowled out twice on the third day, for 51 and 143. Before that Masakadza had a rough baptism with the ball too, collecting the wicket of Martin Guptill but going for 102 in his 23 overs. He did run Kane Williamson out, though. Masakadza is a handy lower-order batsman, and has a first-class century to his name. He was a promising footballer before opting for cricket.

THE FACTS Shingi Masakadza took 6 for 54 for Mountaineers v Mid West Rhinos at Kwekwe in January 2010 (his brother Hamilton, who also played for Zimbabwe, scored 155 in the same game) ... Shingi equalled his best figures with 6 for 54 (9 for 75 in the match) against Mashonaland Eagles at Harare in January 2012 ... He hit 100 not out, from 79 balls, against Southern Rocks at Mutare in January 2010 ...

THE FIGURES to 17.09.12   ᴇꜱᴘᴨcricinfo.com

Batting & Fielding	M	Inns	NO	Runs	HS	Avge	S/R	100	50	4s	6s	Ct	St
Tests	1	2	1	24	21	24.00	54.54	0	0	3	0	0	0
ODIs	9	6	2	115	45*	28.75	100.87	0	0	12	5	6	0
T20Is	4	3	0	9	8	3.00	81.81	0	0	1	0	1	0
First-class	39	57	12	817	100*	18.15	51.19	1	2	99	13	16	0

Bowling	M	Balls	Runs	Wkts	BB	Avge	RpO	S/R	5i	10m
Tests	1	138	102	1	1–102	102.00	4.43	138.00	0	0
ODIs	9	415	524	16	4–46	32.75	7.57	25.93	0	0
T20Is	4	57	101	2	2–39	50.50	10.63	28.50	0	0
First-class	39	6495	3368	156	6–54	21.58	3.11	41.63	7	0

MASHRAFE MORTAZA

Full name	**Mashrafe bin Mortaza**
Born	**October 5, 1983, Norail, Jessore, Khulna**
Teams	**Khulna**
Style	**Right-hand bat, right-arm fast-medium bowler**
Test debut	**Bangladesh v Zimbabwe at Dhaka 2001-02**
ODI debut	**Bangladesh v Zimbabwe at Chittagong 2001-02**
T20I debut	**Bangladesh v Zimbabwe at Khulna 2006-07**

THE PROFILE Mashrafe Mortaza has long been the standard-bearer for Bangladesh's pacemen, although injuries have bedevilled him: he hurt his right knee after only 6.3 overs in the first Test in West Indies in July 2009, and had to undergo an operation (on both knees, in fact). This was doubly disappointing as it was his first match as captain, and it ended in only Bangladesh's second Test victory – their first overseas. He returned for the mid-season one-dayers in Britain in 2010, leading Bangladesh to their first win over England, but injured the knee again in a domestic game at the end of the year. He was not thought ready for the 2011 World Cup, and although he played two ODIs against Australia shortly afterwards – and took five wickets – his long-suffering right knee then went under the knife again. Mashrafe won his first Test cap in 2001-02, in what was also his first-class debut. However, he was back among the wickets when Bangladesh toured Europe in mid-2012. "Koushik" has proved adept at reining in his attacking instincts to concentrate on line and length. He did well in the second Test against England in 2003-04, taking 4 for 60 in the first innings to keep Bangladesh in touch, but then twisted his knee, which kept him out of Tests for over a year. Mashrafe's 4 for 38 in the 2007 World Cup set up the famous defeat of India, and he remains the only fast bowler to take 100 ODI wickets for Bangladesh. He is not a complete mug with the bat: he has a first-class century to his name, and over 20% of his ODI runs have come in sixes.

THE FACTS Mashrafe Mortaza was the first Bangladeshi to make his first-class debut in a Test match: only three others have done this since 1899 ... Mashrafe started the famous ODI victory over Australia at Cardiff in 2005 by dismissing Adam Gilchrist for 0 ... His 6 for 26 v Kenya in Nairobi in August 2006 remain Bangladesh's best bowling figures in ODIs ... Only Mike Hendrick of England has claimed more Test wickets (87) without ever taking a five-for ... Mashrafe's record includes two ODIs for the Asia XI ...

THE FIGURES to 17.09.12   **ESPN**cricinfo.com

Batting & Fielding	M	Inns	NO	Runs	HS	Avge	S/R	100	50	4s	6s	Ct	St
Tests	36	67	5	797	79	12.85	67.20	0	3	95	22	9	0
ODIs	124	94	16	1196	51*	15.33	86.85	0	1	97	40	38	0
T20Is	18	15	4	191	36	17.36	133.56	0	0	6	14	3	0
First-class	51	91	7	1341	132*	15.96	–	1	5	–	–	21	0

Bowling	M	Balls	Runs	Wkts	BB	Avge	RpO	S/R	5i	10m
Tests	36	5990	3239	78	4–60	41.52	3.24	76.79	0	0
ODIs	124	6225	4837	157	6–26	30.80	4.66	39.64	1	0
T20Is	18	405	556	18	4–19	30.88	8.23	22.50	0	0
First-class	51	8391	4371	123	4–27	35.53	3.12	68.21	0	0

ANGELO **MATHEWS**

SRI LANKA

Full name **Angelo Davis Mathews**
Born **June 2, 1987, Colombo**
Teams **Colts, Basnahira, Pune Warriors**
Style **Right-hand bat, right-arm fast-medium bowler**
Test debut **Sri Lanka v Pakistan at Galle 2009**
ODI debut **Sri Lanka v Zimbabwe at Harare 2008-09**
T20I debut **Sri Lanka v Australia at Nottingham 2009**

THE PROFILE Angelo Mathews is capable of batting anywhere in the top order, and is also a handy medium-pacer in limited-overs games. He made a quiet start in first-class cricket in 2006-07, but made big strides the following season, scoring 696 runs at 58 and also making two hundreds for the A team in South Africa. He scored 52 not out in his third ODI, in Bangladesh in January 2009, and shortly after that hammered 270 in a domestic match. Later that year he helped Sri Lanka to the World Twenty20 final in England, notably with three West Indian wickets at The Oval, which effectively settled the semi in the first over. There was also handy batting (35 not out in the final) and frenetic fielding, especially a gymnastic juggling effort – leaping around on and behind the boundary – the legality of which MCC had to confirm. Mathews came into the side as an allrounder, but in Tests batting is his forte, an impression sharpened by his 99 – he cried when he was narrowly run out – against India in Mumbai in December 2009. After a consistent time the following year more heartache followed in 2011: a late six in the semi helped ensure Sri Lanka reached the World Cup final, but Mathews already knew he wouldn't be playing in that, as he had injured his leg. That kept him out of the IPL and the England tour, but he was back for the home series against Australia, reaching that elusive century in the third Test, after another near-miss (trying for a six when 95) in the first one at Galle. But his next ten Tests in 2011 and 2012 produced a highest score of just 63 – not the output expected of the man touted as Sri Lanka's next captain.

THE FACTS Mathews was run out for 99 against India in Mumbai in December 2009 ... He made 270 for Basnahira North v Kandurata in Colombo in February 2009 ... Mathews took 6 for 20 in an ODI against India in Colombo in September 2009 ... In the World Twenty20 in England in 2009 his shirt had "Mathew" on the back before he added the final "s" with a marker pen ...

THE FIGURES *to 17.09.12*   **ESPNcricinfo.com**

Batting & Fielding	M	Inns	NO	Runs	HS	Avge	S/R	100	50	4s	6s	Ct	St
Tests	26	41	8	1283	105*	38.87	48.26	1	8	147	11	12	0
ODIs	81	66	18	1642	80*	34.20	83.43	0	11	111	21	20	0
T20Is	28	23	8	363	58	24.20	113.08	0	1	23	10	9	0
First-class	58	90	15	3620	270	48.26	50.97	9	17	396	34	35	0

Bowling	M	Balls	Runs	Wkts	BB	Avge	RpO	S/R	5i	10m
Tests	26	1188	622	9	1–13	69.11	3.14	132.00	0	0
ODIs	81	2242	1721	48	6–20	35.85	4.60	46.70	1	0
T20Is	28	337	386	17	3–16	22.70	6.87	19.82	0	0
First-class	58	3701	1772	39	5–47	45.43	2.87	94.89	1	0

TINO **MAWOYO**

Full name	**Tinotenda Mbiri Kanayi Mawoyo**
Born	**January 8, 1986, Umtali (now Mutare)**
Teams	**Mountaineers**
Style	**Right-hand bat, occasional medium-pacer**
Test debut	**Zimbabwe v Bangladesh at Harare 2011**
ODI debut	**Zimbabwe v Bangladesh at Dhaka 2006-07**
T20I debut	**No T20Is yet**

THE PROFILE A top-order batsman, Tino Mawoyo had already played first-class cricket when he captained Zimbabwe at the Under-19 World Cup in 2004. To start with his appearances were limited by educational commitments, but he turned out enough to emphasise his class, and played for the A team against Bangladesh in 2006. He made his full ODI debut later that year, also in Bangladesh. Mawoyo appeared to be set for a more permanent place when he was appointed captain of Zimbabwe A, but he was subsequently reduced to the ranks, after some supposedly inappropriate behaviour while the team was in a training camp. Nevertheless, he remained one of Zimbabwe's most talented young batsmen, and when Easterns completed the domestic double in 2006-07, Mawoyo was their leading runscorer in the first-class Logan Cup. By 2009-10 he was heading the run-charts in the national one-day competition too, but then experienced wildly varied emotions as the 2011 World Cup approached. Initially left out, he was called up when Sean Ervine withdrew – then had to pull out himself shortly before the tournament after injuring a stomach muscle. The disappointment forced a rethink: Mawoyo lost weight, and elbowed his way into the side for Zimbabwe's comeback Tests later in the year. He shared opening stands of 102 and 69 with Vusi Sibanda in the first Test, against Bangladesh at Harare, and carried his bat for 163 in the second, resisting Pakistan's bowlers for well over ten hours. He made 52 in the next Test, as Zimbabwe lost narrowly to New Zealand, but fared less well as they were walloped in the return Test at Napier. He then reminded the selectors of his one-day capabilities with 66 against Sri Lanka and 52 v South Africa in an A-team one-day series in Harare in July 2012.

THE FACTS Mawoyo carried his bat for 163 in only his second Test, against Pakistan at Bulawayo in September 2011: he was only the third opener to do this for Zimbabwe, after Mark Dekker and Grant Flower, also against Pakistan ... Mawoyo scored 208 not out for Mountaineers against New Zealand A in a non-first-class game in October 2010 ...

THE FIGURES to 17.09.12

ESPncricinfo.com

Batting & Fielding	M	Inns	NO	Runs	HS	Avge	S/R	100	50	4s	6s	Ct	St
Tests	4	8	1	314	163*	44.85	36.46	1	1	39	0	3	0
ODIs	3	3	0	33	14	11.00	44.59	0	0	3	0	1	0
T20Is	0	0	–	–	–	–	–	–	–	–	–	–	–
First-class	79	138	9	3680	163*	28.52	43.22	3	20	–	–	54	0

Bowling	M	Balls	Runs	Wkts	BB	Avge	RpO	S/R	5i	10m
Tests	4	0	–	–	–	–	–	–	–	–
ODIs	3	0	–	–	–	–	–	–	–	–
T20Is	0	0	–	–	–	–	–	–	–	–
First-class	79	72	44	2	1–0	22.00	3.66	36.00	0	0

AJANTHA **MENDIS**

Full name	**Balapuwaduge Ajantha Winslo Mendis**
Born	**March 11, 1985, Moratuwa**
Teams	**Army, Wayamba**
Style	**Right-hand bat, right-arm off- and legspinner**
Test debut	**Sri Lanka v India at Colombo 2008**
ODI debut	**Sri Lanka v West Indies at Port-of-Spain 2007-08**
T20I debut	**Sri Lanka v Zimbabwe at King City 2008-09**

THE PROFILE Those batsmen who thought one Sri Lankan mystery spinner was enough found more on their plate during 2008, when Ajantha Mendis stepped up to join Muttiah Muralitharan in the national side. Mendis sends down a mesmerising mixture of offbreaks, legbreaks, top-spinners, googlies and flippers, plus his very own "carrom ball" – one flicked out using a finger under the ball, in the style of the old Australians Jack Iverson and John Gleeson. Mendis was a prolific wicket-taker in 2007-08 for the Army (he received not one but two promotions following his meteoric rise) and was called up for the West Indian tour early in 2008 after taking 46 wickets in six matches. After doing well there he ran rings round the Indians – the supposed masters of spin – in the Asia Cup, rather ruining the final with 6 for 13. In his first Test series – against India again – he took 26 wickets at 18.38 in three home Tests, and even achieved the rare feat of outperforming Murali (21 wickets at 22.23). Soon, though, batsmen began to spot how to work out Mendis's variations. Some tight spells were instrumental in Sri Lanka reaching the World Twenty20 final in England, but shortly after that he lost his place in the Test side. He remained effective in one-dayers, and it was a surprise when, after keeping things tight in the 2011 World Cup, he was left out of the side for the final. Test success continued to be elusive, but it was a different story in the shorter stuff: he took 6 for 16 in a Twenty20 game against Australia in August 2011. A back injury kept him out for most of 2012, but he was included in the team for the World Twenty20 after doing well in the inaugural Sri Lanka Premier League in August.

THE FACTS Mendis claimed 26 wickets in his first Test series, against India in 2008, the most by anyone in a debut series of three Tests, beating Alec Bedser's 24 for England v India in 1946 ... Mendis took 6 for 16, the best figures in Twenty20 internationals, against Australia at Pallekele in August 2011 ... He took 6 for 13 in the Asia Cup final against India at Karachi in July 2008, and 7 for 37 for Army v Lankan CC at Panagoda in February 2008 ...

THE FIGURES to 17.09.12   **ᴇsᴘ₦cricinfo.com**

Batting & Fielding	M	Inns	NO	Runs	HS	Avge	S/R	100	50	4s	6s	Ct	St
Tests	16	17	6	164	78	14.90	43.50	0	1	19	1	2	0
ODIs	59	27	13	109	15*	7.78	63.00	0	0	8	0	8	0
T20Is	21	6	4	7	4*	3.50	46.66	0	0	1	0	2	0
First-class	45	58	6	688	78	13.23	58.05	0	1	74	6	12	0

Bowling	M	Balls	Runs	Wkts	BB	Avge	RpO	S/R	5i	10m
Tests	16	3993	2014	62	6–117	32.48	3.02	64.40	3	1
ODIs	59	2756	1992	96	6–13	20.75	4.33	28.70	3	0
T20Is	21	474	445	40	6–16	11.12	5.63	11.85	1	0
First-class	45	9400	4684	213	7–37	21.99	2.98	44.13	12	2

KEEGAN **METH**

Full name	**Keegan Orry Meth**
Born	**February 8, 1988, Bulawayo**
Teams	**Matabeleland Tuskers**
Style	**Right-hand bat, right-arm fast-medium bowler**
Test debut	**No Tests yet**
ODI debut	**Zimbabwe v Kenya at Bulawayo 2005-06**
T20I debut	**Zimbabwe v New Zealand at Auckland 2011-12**

THE PROFILE An allrounder who takes the new ball for Matabeleland Tuskers and bats in the lower middle order, Keegan Meth's bowling is his stronger suit and, although he is not truly fast, he does have the invaluable ability to move the ball both ways through the air. His made his international debut when just 18, in the wake of the messy dispute that cost Zimbabwe several senior players in 2004-05: when he played his first ODI he had never appeared in a senior first-class or one-day game at home. It was obvious that his elevation had come too early, and he was soon discarded: he remained on the fringes for a while, and broadened his experience by playing club cricket in Ireland. Meth blossomed in the revamped franchise system, leading the Tuskers' attack with increasing proficiency. In 2010-11 he was a key factor in their Logan Cup triumph, collecting 54 wickets at 13.31, and almost singlehandedly securing victory over the Mountaineers in the final with 13 for 109. That led to a call for the pre-World Cup tour of Bangladesh, but he struggled in the unfamiliar conditions and was passed over for the Cup itself. He was back later in 2011, in the squad for Zimbabwe's comeback Test against Bangladesh (although he didn't play in the end), and featured in the last one-dayer, which ended painfully when he was smashed in the mouth by a straight drive after earlier dismissing Imrul Kayes and Shakib Al Hasan. Meth was confident the accident wouldn't affect him long-term ... and was quite proud that the video of it was viewed around 200,000 times on YouTube. He did return for the New Zealand tour early in 2012, seemingly none the worse for wear.

THE FACTS Meth took 6 for 40 and 7 for 69 as Matabeleland Tuskers beat Mountaineers in the 2010-11 Logan Cup final ... He lost four teeth (and subsequently more than a stone in weight, as he was unable to eat) after being hit in the mouth during an ODI against Bangladesh in August 2011 ... Meth's mother Yvonne confirms that his first name is spelt like the former England football captain's (not "Keagan" as sometimes shown) ...

THE FIGURES to 17.09.12   **ESPn** cricinfo.com

Batting & Fielding	M	Inns	NO	Runs	HS	Avge	S/R	100	50	4s	6s	Ct	St
Tests	0	0	–	–	–	–	–	–	–	–	–	–	–
ODIs	11	8	0	106	53	13.25	57.92	0	1	10	1	1	0
T20Is	2	1	1	6	6*	–	100.00	0	0	0	0	1	0
First-class	25	34	1	828	94	25.87	60.52	0	5	96	11	11	0

Bowling	M	Balls	Runs	Wkts	BB	Avge	RpO	S/R	5i	10m
Tests	0	0	–	–	–	–	–	–	–	–
ODIs	11	406	419	6	2–52	69.83	6.19	67.66	0	0
T20Is	2	42	64	0	–	–	9.14	–	0	0
First-class	25	4047	1721	102	7–42	16.87	2.55	39.67	7	1

DAVID **MILLER**

SOUTH AFRICA

Full name	**David Andrew Miller**
Born	**June 10, 1989, Pietermaritzburg**
Teams	**Dolphins, Yorkshire, Kings XI Punjab**
Style	**Left-hand bat, occasional offspinner**
Test debut	**No Tests yet**
ODI debut	**South Africa v West Indies at North Sound 2010**
T20I debut	**South Africa v West Indies at North Sound 2010**

THE PROFILE An explosive left-hander, David Miller was called up to the full South African limited-overs sides at 20 in the wake of the national team's disappointing performance at the World Twenty20 in the Caribbean in 2010. His first assignment was back in the West Indies – and he did as well as could have been expected, smashing his sixth ball in international cricket (from Sulieman Benn) into the stands on the way to 33 in the first Twenty20 match. He made a similarly brisk start in one-day internationals, calmly swinging the pacy Ravi Rampaul over square leg for six more during another cameo. Miller joined the South African Academy in mid-2009, and then caught the eye during a successful domestic season, in which he was the Dolphins' leading scorer in both 50- and 20-overs cricket. A rapid unbeaten 90 from 52 balls against the Lions in a Pro20 match at Potchefstroom in February 2010 ensured his selection for a triangular A-team tournament in Bangladesh, and it was while he was there that Miller received the call from the national selectors: "We are looking to strengthen our power-hitting in the middle order," explained chairman Andrew Hudson, the former Test opener. But Miller's form fell away in 2010-11, with four successive single-figure scores in ODIs against Pakistan and India: others moved ahead in the queue and Miller missed the 2011 World Cup. He was back for the one-dayers against Australia later in the year, making 59 at Port Elizabeth, but was then overtaken again. He played for Yorkshire in 2012, after a Twenty20 stint with Durham the previous year.

THE FACTS Miller hit four sixes en route to his maiden first-class century, 108 not out for Dolphins v Eagles at Kimberley in December 2009 ... He raised his highest score to 149 against the Lions at Durban in April 2011 ... Miller also made a century in 55 balls in a 50-over match for South Africa A v Bangladesh A at Mirpur in April 2010 ...

THE FIGURES to 17.09.12   espncricinfo.com

Batting & Fielding	M	Inns	NO	Runs	HS	Avge	S/R	100	50	4s	6s	Ct	St
Tests	0	0	–	–	–	–	–	–	–	–	–	–	–
ODIs	16	13	4	267	59	29.66	111.71	0	2	18	8	4	0
T20Is	8	8	3	153	36*	30.60	123.38	0	0	13	5	5	0
First-class	35	56	5	1466	149	28.74	54.64	2	6	205	24	34	0

Bowling	M	Balls	Runs	Wkts	BB	Avge	RpO	S/R	5i	10m
Tests	0	0	–	–	–	–	–	–	–	–
ODIs	16	0	–	–	–	–	–	–	–	–
T20Is	8	0	–	–	–	–	–	–	–	–
First-class	35	26	23	0	–	–	5.30	–	0	0

100

KYLE **MILLS**

Full name **Kyle David Mills**
Born **March 15, 1979, Auckland**
Teams **Auckland**
Style **Right-hand bat, right-arm fast-medium bowler**
Test debut **New Zealand v England at Nottingham 2004**
ODI debut **New Zealand v Pakistan at Sharjah 2000-01**
T20I debut **New Zealand v Australia at Auckland 2004-05**

NEW ZEALAND

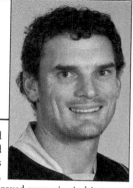

THE PROFILE   Injuries at inopportune times have hampered Kyle Mills. They delayed his arrival as an international player, and impinged again in 2009-10, when knee and shoulder problems shortened his season and kept him out of the IPL: he did, however, make it to the World Twenty20 in the West Indies, although he proved expensive in his two matches there. A genuine swing bowler of lively pace, Mills yo-yoed in and out of the team after the 2003 World Cup, but he did enough to tour England in 2004, and made his Test debut in the third match at Trent Bridge. But he suffered a side strain there, and missed the one-day series. That was a shame, as one-day cricket is really his forte: he played throughout 2005-06, chipping in with wickets in almost every game, even if his once-promising batting had diminished to the point that he managed double figures only once in 16 matches. A feisty temper remains, though: he was fined after an on-field incident in the 2011 World Cup ... and he was only the 12th man at the time. Then, early in 2012, he slammed the small boundaries on many New Zealand grounds, although he did admit: "I'm a bowler so I'm going to be a little bit biased." Ankle surgery, then knee trouble – which necessitated another op – sidelined him early in 2007, but after missing that year's World Cup, Mills bounced back, following up 5 for 25 in a one-dayer in South Africa with a Test-best 4 for 16 against England at Hamilton in March 2008. He lost his Test spot after some anaemic performances the following season, but remained a one-day force, starting the Chappell-Hadlee Series in Australia in February 2009 by taking the match award after claiming four prime scalps.

THE FACTS   Mills's only first-class hundred came from No. 9 at Wellington in 2000-01, helping Auckland recover from 109 for 7 ... His 5 for 25 at Durban in November 2007 remain NZ's best one-day figures v South Africa ... Mills achieved the only ten-wicket haul of his career, and in the process reached 100 first-class wickets, for Auckland v Canterbury in December 2004 ... Only Daniel Vettori has taken more wickets in ODIs for New Zealand ...

THE FIGURES to 17.09.12

ESPncricinfo.com

Batting & Fielding	M	Inns	NO	Runs	HS	Avge	S/R	100	50	4s	6s	Ct	St
Tests	19	30	5	289	57	11.56	38.58	0	1	37	3	4	0
ODIs	139	86	28	869	54	14.98	79.21	0	2	64	31	34	0
T20Is	29	16	5	127	33*	11.54	115.45	0	0	9	5	7	0
First-class	71	102	25	2083	117*	27.05	–	1	13	–	–	23	0

Bowling	M	Balls	Runs	Wkts	BB	Avge	RpO	S/R	5i	10m
Tests	19	2902	1453	44	4–16	33.02	3.00	65.95	0	0
ODIs	139	6814	5328	205	5–25	25.99	4.69	33.23	1	0
T20Is	29	640	895	31	3–37	28.87	8.39	20.64	0	0
First-class	71	11331	5522	186	5–33	29.68	2.92	60.91	3	1

MISBAH-UL-HAQ

Full name	**Misbah-ul-Haq Khan Niazi**
Born	**May 28, 1974, Mianwali, Punjab**
Teams	**Faisalabad, Sui Northern Gas**
Style	**Right-hand bat, occasional legspinner**
Test debut	**Pakistan v New Zealand at Auckland 2000-01**
ODI debut	**Pakistan v New Zealand at Lahore 2001-02**
T20I debut	**Pakistan v Bangladesh at Nairobi 2007-08**

THE PROFILE An orthodox right-hander with a tight technique, Misbah-ul-Haq caught the eye in a one-day tournament in Nairobi in 2002, making 50 in the final against Australia. But then his form slumped: his highest score in three Tests against Australia was 17. Pakistan's abysmal 2003 World Cup gave him another chance, but he did little of note. Misbah remained a consistent domestic performer, making 951 runs at 50 in 2004-05, 882 the following season, and capping that with 1108 at 61 in 2006-07, but it was nonetheless a shock when he was called up for the inaugural World Twenty20 in South Africa late in 2007. But he was a surprise hit there, and added 464 runs in three Tests against India, including two important centuries. Suddenly, in his mid-thirties but with a first-class average which remains above 50, he was an automatic choice. He played his part in winning the World Twenty20 in 2009, but then had a poor time in Australia, and wasn't required for the tour of England in 2010. That ended in turmoil, with three players banned for spot-fixing ... and from the ruins strode Misbah, suddenly the Test captain. He celebrated with six successive fifties then, after a decent World Cup, made a hundred in the West Indies in May 2011. Hardly a long-term solution – he's 39 in 2013 – Misbah turned out to be an inspired choice as a stopgap. Series victories came against Zimbabwe, Sri Lanka and Bangladesh, before a satisfying 3-0 clean sweep against top-ranked England in the UAE early in 2012. A setback followed later in the year in Sri Lanka, although Pakistan drew both Tests in which Misbah played, after losing the first one when he was banned for earlier over-rate sluggishness.

THE FACTS Misbah-ul-Haq has made six first-class double-centuries, the highest 284 for Sui Northern Gas v Lahore Shalimar in October 2009 ... He also made 208 not out (in a total of 723 for 4) for Punjab v Baluchistan at Sialkot in March 2008 ... He scored 161 and 133, both not out, in successive Tests against India in 2007-08 ... Misbah hit 87 not out, Pakistan's highest score in Twenty20 internationals, against Bangladesh in April 2008 ...

THE FIGURES *to 17.09.12*   **ESPncricinfo.com**

Batting & Fielding	M	Inns	NO	Runs	HS	Avge	S/R	100	50	4s	6s	Ct	St
Tests	36	61	11	2284	161*	45.68	41.15	3	17	247	24	35	0
ODIs	106	95	24	2995	93*	42.18	74.15	0	20	205	39	52	0
T20Is	39	34	13	788	87*	37.52	110.20	0	3	45	26	14	0
First-class	173	280	35	12533	284	51.15	–	33	66	–	–	170	0

Bowling	M	Balls	Runs	Wkts	BB	Avge	RpO	S/R	5i	10m
Tests	36	0	–	–	–	–	–	–	–	–
ODIs	106	24	30	0	–	–	7.50	–	0	0
T20Is	39	0	–	–	–	–	–	–	–	–
First-class	173	318	242	3	1–2	80.66	4.56	106.00	0	0

ABHIMANYU **MITHUN**

INDIA

Full name	**Abhimanyu Mithun**
Born	**October 25, 1989, Bangalore**
Teams	**Karnataka, Royal Challengers Bangalore**
Style	**Right-hand bat, right-arm fast-medium bowler**
Test debut	**India v Sri Lanka at Galle 2010**
ODI debut	**India v South Africa at Ahmedabad 2009-10**
T20I debut	**No T20Is yet**

THE PROFILE Abhimanyu Mithun spent his early years striving for success in athletics – he was a fine discus thrower – and didn't bowl with a leather ball until he was 17. But three years later, after a remarkably successful debut season in 2009-10, he had forced his way into the national squad. Mithun's build, honed in his father's Bangalore gym, is perfect for a fast bowler: he's 6ft 2ins (188cm) tall, and uses his height to good effect for his favourite weapon, the bouncer. Mithun was snapped up by the Bangalore Royal Challengers before the second IPL in 2009 and, although he didn't do much in his only outing then, he certainly made people sit up when he finally made his Ranji Trophy debut in November: 11 Uttar Pradesh wickets, including a second-innings hat-trick. He made batsmen hop about, and finished with 52 wickets at 23.26 as Karnataka reached the Ranji final for the first time in 12 years. Mithun sat out the home Tests against South Africa, but did play in one of the ensuing one-dayers, although he proved expensive. Still, he went to Sri Lanka in July, and this time played in all three Tests, starting with the early wicket of Tillekeratne Dilshan. After four wickets in the first Test, he managed only two in the other two, but did reveal unexpected tenacity with the bat, playing long defensive knocks in each Test. After that, though, he was overtaken by others and played little in 2011, although he was a late replacement for the disappointing tours of England and Australia. In 2012 he was again called up as a replacement, when Zaheer Khan tweaked his shoulder in Sri Lanka, but again Mithun failed to get a game: he faces an important home season in 2012-13.

THE FACTS Mithun took 6 for 86 and 5 for 95 – including a hat-trick – on his first-class debut for Karnataka v Uttar Pradesh at Meerut in November 2009 ... He took 6 for 71 for Karnataka v Mumbai in the Ranji Trophy final at Mysore in January 2010 ... Mithun's first Test, at Galle in July 2010, was only his 12th first-class match ...

THE FIGURES to 17.09.12   **ESPN** cricinfo.com

Batting & Fielding	M	Inns	NO	Runs	HS	Avge	S/R	100	50	4s	6s	Ct	St
Tests	4	5	0	120	46	24.00	48.19	0	0	16	0	0	0
ODIs	5	3	0	51	24	17.00	92.72	0	0	2	4	1	0
T20Is	0	0	–	–	–	–	–	–	–	–	–	–	–
First-class	29	34	7	512	63*	18.96	57.33	0	1	63	10	5	0

Bowling	M	Balls	Runs	Wkts	BB	Avge	RpO	S/R	5i	10m
Tests	4	720	456	9	4–105	50.66	3.80	80.00	0	0
ODIs	5	80	203	3	2–32	67.66	6.76	60.00	0	0
T20Is	0	0	–	–	–	–	–	–	–	–
First-class	29	5441	3157	107	6–71	29.50	3.48	50.85	4	1

MOHAMMAD ASHRAFUL

Full name **Mohammad Ashraful**
Born **July 7, 1984, Dhaka**
Teams **Dhaka**
Style **Right-hand bat, legspinner**
Test debut **Bangladesh v Sri Lanka at Colombo 2001-02**
ODI debut **Bangladesh v Zimbabwe at Bulawayo 2000-01**
T20I debut **Bangladesh v Kenya at Nairobi 2007-08**

THE PROFILE In September 2001, Mohammad Ashraful enlivened a terrible mismatch in Colombo by becoming the youngest man – or boy – to make a Test century. Just 17, he broke the long-standing record set by Mushtaq Mohammad of Pakistan in 1960-61. Bangladesh still crashed to heavy defeat, but "Matin" was unbowed, repeatedly dancing down to hit Muttiah Muralitharan and his fellow spinners back over their heads. Inevitably, such a heady early achievement proved hard to live up to, and Ashraful remains the problem child of Bangladesh cricket – fitfully brilliant, but maddeningly inconsistent. He was dropped for England's first visit in October 2003, and returned a better player, but no less flamboyant, producing a glorious unbeaten 158 in defeat against India. Still not 21 when Bangladesh toured England for the first time in 2005, Ashraful confirmed his talent at Cardiff, when his well-paced century set up a stunning one-day victory over Australia. He continued to fire spasmodically: his 87 helped defeat South Africa in the 2007 World Cup, but that was surrounded by more low scores. When Habibul Bashar stood down as captain in May 2007 Ashraful took over – but he looked careworn by the time he was replaced after a dismal World Twenty20 campaign in England in 2009. He celebrated his return to the ranks with a couple of fifties against West Indies and a fine hundred against Zimbabwe, but again indifferent form cost him his place. And again the selectors came back to him, and again Ashraful remained inconsistent. A back number in the 2011 World Cup, he was controversially recalled for the first Test against Pakistan in December 2011, but made 1 and 0 and was promptly dumped once again.

THE FACTS Only 11 players have made their Test debuts when younger than Ashraful: three of them are from Bangladesh ... He scored 263, putting on 420 with Marshall Ayub, for Dhaka v Chittagong in November 2006 ... Ashraful averages 42.88 in Tests v India, but only 9.12 v England ... His Test batting average is easily the lowest for anyone with five or more centuries: Grant Flower (29.54) is next ... Ashraful's record includes two ODIs for the Asia XI ...

THE FIGURES to 17.09.12   **ESPN**cricinfo.com

Batting & Fielding	M	Inns	NO	Runs	HS	Avge	S/R	100	50	4s	6s	Ct	St
Tests	57	111	4	2419	158*	22.60	46.68	5	8	302	21	24	0
ODIs	171	164	13	3397	109	22.49	70.12	3	20	344	29	35	0
T20Is	20	20	0	372	65	18.60	126.10	0	2	38	9	4	0
First-class	118	221	5	5629	263	28.28	–		14	23	–	–	56	0

Bowling	M	Balls	Runs	Wkts	BB	Avge	RpO	S/R	5i	10m
Tests	57	1615	1208	20	2–42	60.40	4.48	80.75	0	0
ODIs	171	697	661	18	3–26	36.72	5.69	38.72	0	0
T20Is	20	138	210	8	3–42	26.25	9.13	17.25	0	0
First-class	118	8102	4869	132	7–99	36.88	3.60	61.37	5	0

MOHAMMAD HAFEEZ

PAKISTAN

Full name	**Mohammad Hafeez**
Born	**October 17, 1980, Sargodha, Punjab**
Teams	**Faisalabad, Sui Northern Gas**
Style	**Right-hand bat, offspinner**
Test debut	**Pakistan v Bangladesh at Karachi 2003**
ODI debut	**Pakistan v Zimbabwe at Sharjah 2002-03**
T20I debut	**Pakistan v England at Bristol 2006**

THE PROFILE For years Mohammad Hafeez – stylish opener, handy offspinner, brilliant fielder – was in and out of the Pakistan side. But finally he put together the sort of run that ensured he couldn't be dropped, and in 2012 took over as Twenty20 captain, suitable perhaps for someone with the nickname "Professor". His first chance followed the 2003 World Cup, after Pakistan's poor showing led to a clearout. Hafeez made 50 on debut and 102 in his second Test, against Bangladesh, but then struggled against South Africa – just 33 runs in five one-day innings – and was briefly dropped, then lost his place again early in 2005. He was not originally chosen for the 2006 England tour, but 180 against Australia A in Darwin in July, while Pakistan struggled to find an opening combination worth the name in England, led to a surprise call-up for the final Test at The Oval, and he made a tidy 95 before the ball-tampering row overshadowed everything. Another century followed against West Indies, but then he was left out for more than two years before a surprise recall for the World Twenty20 in the Caribbean and the one-day portion of the England tour later in 2010; a maiden ODI hundred followed in New Zealand early in 2011. After a consistent World Cup he was a star in the Caribbean – another one-day hundred and a surprise bowling hit, dismissing Devon Smith in six successive innings, often taking the new ball so he could get at the opener quickly. Hafeez confirmed his arrival with his first Test century for five years, against Zimbabwe in September 2011, and the following July added a seven-hour 196 against Sri Lanka in Colombo.

THE FACTS Mohammad Hafeez scored 50 in his first Test, against Bangladesh in August 2003, and added 102 not out in his second, a week later … He is the only man to open the batting and bowling in the same Test, ODI and T20I … Hafeez scored 196 against Sri Lanka in Colombo in June 2012 … He took 8 for 57 (10 for 87 in the match) for Faisalabad v Quetta in December 2004 …

THE FIGURES *to 17.09.12*   **ESPNcricinfo.com**

Batting & Fielding	M	Inns	NO	Runs	HS	Avge	S/R	100	50	4s	6s	Ct	St
Tests	29	56	5	1959	196	38.41	53.93	5	8	245	12	18	0
ODIs	107	107	4	2795	139*	27.13	68.15	4	14	308	26	34	0
T20Is	34	32	0	647	71	20.21	112.52	0	2	78	12	13	0
First-class	155	264	11	8834	196	34.91	–	19	42	–	–	135	0

Bowling	M	Balls	Runs	Wkts	BB	Avge	RpO	S/R	5i	10m
Tests	29	2498	1015	29	4–31	35.00	2.43	86.13	0	0
ODIs	107	4343	2925	89	3–17	32.86	4.04	48.79	0	0
T20Is	34	542	620	27	4–10	22.96	6.86	20.07	0	0
First-class	155	11751	5248	188	8–57	27.91	2.67	62.50	6	2

MOHAMMAD SAMI

Full name **Mohammad Sami**
Born **February 24, 1981, Karachi**
Teams **Karachi, Sind**
Style **Right-hand bat, right-arm fast-medium bowler**
Test debut **Pakistan v New Zealand at Auckland 2000-01**
ODI debut **Pakistan v Sri Lanka at Sharjah 2000-01**
T20I debut **Pakistan v Bangladesh at St Lucia 2010**

THE PROFILE Fast bowler Mohammad Sami is a great survivor: a Test player in his teens, he returned in 2012 after 18 months in the wilderness, and played for Pakistan in all three international formats during the year. He had kept his name in the frame with consistent performances in domestic cricket, but despite a Test hat-trick his overall stats are remarkably modest – no-one who has taken more than 45 Test wickets has done so at a higher average. Still, in June 2012 Sami went to Sri Lanka and took 3 for 16 in a Twenty20 international, and 3 for 19 in an ODI four days later ... but then looked unthreatening in taking 1 for 92 in the Test at Pallekele. Sami had shouldered his way into the Test side more than a decade earlier, claiming eight wickets on debut against New Zealand in March 2001. Then, in only his third match, he took a hat-trick, prising out the last three Sri Lankans in the Asian Test Championship final: he has a one-day hat-trick too. But after that the story has been a fitful one. There have been some impressive performances – particularly against India early in 2005, in the Kolkata Test and some of the ODIs. Mostly, however, he has been surprisingly ineffective, and prone to leaking runs. Nobody is sure where the problem lies: he's fit, he's athletic, he generates surprising pace from a shortish run-up, he does outswing, reverse-swing and yorkers, he has been given licence to attack with the new ball ... but still that Test average is comfortably over 50. Some say it's a confidence thing, but few players – especially bowlers – have been given so many chances.

THE FACTS Mohammad Sami took a hat-trick against Sri Lanka in the Asian Test Championship final at Lahore in March 2002 ... He also took a hat-trick in an ODI against West Indies at Sharjah the previous month: neither one involved a fielder, as all the victims were bowled or lbw ... Sami's 5 for 36 on debut, against New Zealand at Auckland in March 2001, remain his best figures in Tests ... He took 8 for 64 for Kent v Nottinghamshire at Maidstone in 2003 ...

THE FIGURES to 17.09.12   **ESPN**cricinfo.com

Batting & Fielding	M	Inns	NO	Runs	HS	Avge	S/R	100	50	4s	6s	Ct	St
Tests	36	56	14	487	49	11.59	30.78	0	0	53	4	7	0
ODIs	85	46	19	314	46	11.62	64.08	0	0	16	10	19	0
T20Is	5	2	2	9	5*	–	75.00	0	0	0	0	2	0
First-class	131	180	43	2208	61*	16.11	–	0	2	–	–	65	0

Bowling	M	Balls	Runs	Wkts	BB	Avge	RpO	S/R	5i	10m
Tests	36	7499	4483	85	5–36	52.74	3.58	88.22	2	0
ODIs	85	4188	3451	121	5–10	28.52	4.94	34.61	1	0
T20Is	5	96	146	10	3–16	14.60	9.12	9.60	0	0
First-class	131	23289	13112	448	8–39	29.26	3.37	51.98	24	4

EOIN **MORGAN**

Full name	**Eoin Joseph Gerard Morgan**
Born	**September 10, 1986, Dublin, Ireland**
Teams	**Middlesex**
Style	**Left-hand bat, occasional right-arm medium-pacer**
Test debut	**England v Bangladesh at Lord's 2010**
ODI debut	**Ireland v Scotland at Ayr 2006**
T20I debut	**England v Netherlands at Lord's 2009**

THE PROFILE Eoin Morgan is an impish batsman capable of inventive and audacious strokeplay, and he's a natural "finisher", a role England struggled to fill for a decade. A compact left-hander, he gained initial recognition with Ireland, playing 23 one-day internationals for them, although he was disappointing at the 2007 World Cup. He had joined his fellow Dubliner, Ed Joyce, at Middlesex in 2006, and two years later helped them win the Twenty20 Cup. In 2009 he was called up by England. After a quiet start in which his fielding was probably more impressive than his batting, Morgan did well as England won the World Twenty20 in the West Indies early in 2010 then, although not widely viewed as a five-day player, he was a surprise inclusion for the first Test of the home summer, against Bangladesh: he confidently collected his first boundary with a reverse-sweep. He added a gutsy 130 to set up victory over Pakistan in the first Test at Trent Bridge, and finished the season with a fine century to seal a 3-2 victory in a fractious one-day series. With a middle-order spot up for grabs in 2011, Morgan claimed it with 193 for the Lions against Sri Lanka, and he cemented it with three gritty seventies before making 104 against India at Edgbaston ... all this despite adding a curious low squat in the stance. Morgan lost his Test place after struggling against Pakistan's spinners in the UAE early in 2012 – only 82 runs in six innings – but remained a one-day fixture.

THE FACTS Morgan is the only player ever to be out (run out, too!) for 99 in his first ODI, against Scotland in August 2006 ... His first 23 ODIs were for Ireland: he made 744 runs at 35.42 for them, including 115 against Canada in Nairobi in February 2007 ... Morgan scored 209 not out – the first double-century for Ireland – against the UAE in Abu Dhabi in February 2007 ... Morgan was the third Irish-born player to score a Test century, after Fred Fane for England in 1905-06 and Australia's Tom Horan (1881-82) ...

THE FIGURES to 17.09.12   ᴇsᴘɴcricinfo.com

Batting & Fielding	M	Inns	NO	Runs	HS	Avge	S/R	100	50	4s	6s	Ct	St
Tests	16	24	1	700	130	30.43	54.72	2	3	77	6	11	0
ODIs	86	81	17	2605	115	40.70	85.04	4	17	226	49	34	0
T20Is	25	25	8	618	85*	36.35	132.90	0	3	62	18	15	0
First-class	76	123	14	3763	209*	34.52	51.31	9	18	–	–	61	1

Bowling	M	Balls	Runs	Wkts	BB	Avge	RpO	S/R	5i	10m
Tests	16	0	–	–	–	–	–	–	–	–
ODIs	86	0	–	–	–	–	–	–	–	–
T20Is	25	0	–	–	–	–	–	–	–	–
First-class	76	97	83	2	2–24	41.50	5.13	48.50	0	0

ALBIE **MORKEL**

SOUTH AFRICA

Full name	**Johannes Albertus Morkel**
Born	**June 10, 1981, Vereeniging, Transvaal**
Teams	**Titans, Somerset, Chennai Super Kings**
Style	**Left-hand bat, right-arm fast-medium bowler**
Test debut	**South Africa v Australia at Cape Town 2008-09**
ODI debut	**South Africa v New Zealand at Wellington 2003-04**
T20I debut	**South Africa v New Zealand at Johannesburg 2005-06**

THE PROFILE Albie Morkel, a fast-medium bowler and big-hitting left-handed batsman, was lumbered with the tag of the "new Lance Klusener", and was touted early on by Ray Jennings (his provincial coach, and a former national coach too) as a potential world-class allrounder. It never quite happened, although he does average over 40 in first-class cricket, and scored a half-century in his only Test (he was included after his brother Morne lost form). But the 20-over game seemed to be tailor-made for Albie's style of play. His huge sixes were a feature of the inaugural World Twenty20 late in 2007, but by 2009-10 the expectation of more rope-clearing every time he came in seemed to be affecting his performances. He eventually lost his one-day place, and rather surprisingly missed the 2011 World Cup. Morkel responded by being named Titans' player of the season, and was recalled when Marchant de Lange broke down in England in 2012 (Morkel was on hand, playing for Somerset). For Easterns (now the Titans) against the touring West Indians at Benoni in 2003-04 Albie defied food poisoning to score a century – putting on 141 for the ninth wicket with his brother – and also took five wickets in the match. He was picked for the senior tour of New Zealand shortly after that, and performed solidly, if unspectacularly, for a while until the selectors looked elsewhere. Morkel was back for the Afro-Asia Cup in June 2007. In the second match, at Chennai, Albie and Morne opened the bowling together for the African XI, the first instance of brothers sharing the new ball in an ODI since Kenya's Martin and Tony Suji did so during the 1999 World Cup.

THE FACTS Morkel made 204 not out, putting on 264 with Justin Kemp, as Titans drew with Western Province Boland in March 2005 after following on ... He took 6 for 36 for Easterns v Griqualand West in December 1999 ... Morkel's brother Morne has also played for South Africa, while another brother, Malan, represented SA Schools ... His record includes two ODIs for the Africa XI, in one of which he opened the bowling with Morne ...

THE FIGURES *to 17.09.12*   **ᴇѕᴘⁿcricinfo.com**

Batting & Fielding	M	Inns	NO	Runs	HS	Avge	S/R	100	50	4s	6s	Ct	St
Tests	1	1	0	58	58	58.00	81.69	0	1	10	1	0	0
ODIs	58	43	10	782	97	23.69	100.25	0	2	71	25	15	0
T20Is	38	30	9	502	43	23.90	142.20	0	0	28	33	15	0
First-class	75	111	21	4046	204*	44.95	–	8	23	–	–	32	0

Bowling	M	Balls	Runs	Wkts	BB	Avge	RpO	S/R	5i	10m
Tests	1	192	132	1	1–44	132.00	4.12	192.00	0	0
ODIs	58	2073	1899	50	4–29	37.98	5.49	41.46	0	0
T20Is	38	509	674	20	2–12	33.70	7.94	25.45	0	0
First-class	75	11493	5977	203	6–36	29.44	3.12	56.61	5	0

MORNE **MORKEL**

Full name	**Morne Morkel**
Born	**October 6, 1984, Vereeniging, Transvaal**
Teams	**Titans, Delhi Daredevils**
Style	**Left-hand bat, right-arm fast bowler**
Test debut	**South Africa v India at Durban 2006-07**
ODI debut	**Africa XI v Asia XI at Bangalore 2007**
T20I debut	**South Africa v West Indies at Johannesburg 2007-08**

THE PROFILE Morne Morkel, the taller, faster brother of Easterns allrounder Albie, has been a hot property ever since his first-class debut in 2003-04, when he and Albie put on 141 against the West Indians at Benoni. An out-and-out fast bowler, Morne excelled with 20 wickets at 18.20 apiece in 2004-05, and impressed Allan Donald: "He gets serious bounce, and he's got really great pace – genuine pace." Morkel used that to shake up the Indians for the Rest of South Africa in December 2006, bowling Sehwag with his first ball and adding Laxman, Tendulkar and Dhoni as the tourists lurched to 69 for 5. That got him into the national frame, and he played in the second Test when Dale Steyn was ruled out, although three wickets and some handy runs in a crushing victory weren't enough to keep him in when Steyn was fit again. A stress fracture temporarily halted the rapid rise, but he returned in England in 2008, without ever quite being at his best as South Africa won the Test series. Early the following year Morne had the unusual experience of being replaced in the Test side by his brother, but later cemented his place with seven wickets in a crushing victory over England at Johannesburg, and six more in another comfortable win over West Indies at Port-of-Spain later in 2010. After that he took 15 in three matches against India at the turn of 2010-11, but he was less effective on subcontinental pitches at the World Cup. Back on juicier tracks, though, he again proved a handful, taking 6 for 23 against New Zealand at Wellington in March 2012, then 11 wickets as South Africa won again in England to claim top spot in the Test rankings.

THE FACTS Morkel took 6 for 43 and 6 for 48 for Titans v Eagles at Bloemfontein in March 2009, a week after being dropped from the Test side ... He took 6 for 23 v New Zealand at Wellington in March 2012 ... Morkel's first three ODIs were for the Africa XI: in one he opened the bowling with his brother Albie, the first instance of siblings sharing the new ball in an ODI since Kenya's Martin and Tony Suji during the 1999 World Cup ...

THE FIGURES to 17.09.12   **ESP∩cricinfo.com**

Batting & Fielding	M	Inns	NO	Runs	HS	Avge	S/R	100	50	4s	6s	Ct	St
Tests	42	50	7	618	40	14.37	49.12	0	0	93	2	12	0
ODIs	58	21	7	124	25	8.85	75.15	0	0	13	2	17	0
T20Is	24	2	1	2	1*	2.00	40.00	0	0	0	0	3	0
First-class	78	96	13	1326	82*	15.97	49.36	0	4	–	–	32	0

Bowling	M	Balls	Runs	Wkts	BB	Avge	RpO	S/R	5i	10m
Tests	42	8330	4554	150	6–23	30.36	3.28	55.53	5	0
ODIs	58	2844	2309	99	5–38	23.32	4.87	28.72	1	0
T20Is	24	521	587	34	4–17	17.26	6.76	15.32	0	0
First-class	78	14315	7830	284	6–23	27.57	3.28	50.40	12	2

MUSHFIQUR RAHIM

Full name   **Mohammad Mushfiqur Rahim**
Born   **September 1, 1988, Bogra**
Teams   **Rajshahi**
Style   **Right-hand bat, wicketkeeper**
Test debut   **Bangladesh v England at Lord's 2005**
ODI debut   **Bangladesh v Zimbabwe at Harare 2006**
T20I debut   **Bangladesh v Zimbabwe at Khulna 2006-07**

THE PROFILE   A wild-card inclusion for Bangladesh's maiden tour of England in 2005, the diminutive Mushfiqur Rahim was just 16 when he was selected for that daunting trip. He was principally chosen as understudy to long-serving wicketkeeper Khaled Mashud, but he had also shown signs of promise with the bat (a century in an A-team Test in Zimbabwe, and 88 against England Under-19s). He showed more evidence of grit with the full team, with a maiden first-class half-century to soften the pain of defeat against Sussex, followed by a hundred at Northampton. That earned him a call-up – as a batsman – to become the youngest player to appear in a Test at Lord's: Mushfiqur was one of only three players to reach double figures in a disappointing first innings. Two years later he supplanted Mashud for the 2007 World Cup, anchoring the win over India with 56 not out, and soon established himself as the first-choice keeper. He is now one of Bangladesh's most consistent batsmen, and their captain too: he just missed a one-day hundred against Zimbabwe in August 2009, but made sure in Tests with 101 against India at Chittagong in January 2010, Bangladesh's fastest hundred in Tests at the time. There was a near-miss against England at home (95, again at Chittagong), although he was less prolific in England later the same year. After a modest 2011 World Cup with the bat, Mushfiqur bounced back with 126 runs for once out in three one-dayers against Australia, then made a 99-ball hundred in an ODI in Zimbabwe – although it was not enough to prevent another defeat on that embarrassing tour, after which he replaced Shakib Al Hasan as captain. The results remained disappointing, but Mushfiqur's batting kept getting better.

THE FACTS   Mushfiqur Rahim's hundred for Bangladesh v Northants in 2005 made him the youngest century-maker in English first-class cricket: he was 16 years 261 days old, 211 days younger than Sachin Tendulkar in 1990 ... Mushfiqur was stumped for 98 in an ODI in Zimbabwe in August 2009, but made amends with 101 against them two years later ... He had played two Tests before he appeared in a first-class match at home ...

THE FIGURES *to 17.09.12*   **ESPncricinfo.com**

Batting & Fielding	M	Inns	NO	Runs	HS	Avge	S/R	100	50	4s	6s	Ct	St
Tests	28	55	4	1480	101	29.01	44.29	1	9	196	9	41	9
ODIs	108	99	18	2047	101	25.27	66.59	1	10	151	24	75	31
T20Is	23	21	6	222	41*	14.80	104.71	0	0	9	9	10	14
First-class	53	97	11	2546	115*	29.60	–	3	16	–	–	89	14

Bowling	M	Balls	Runs	Wkts	BB	Avge	RpO	S/R	5i	10m
Tests	28	0	–	–	–	–	–	–	–	–
ODIs	108	0	–	–	–	–	–	–	–	–
T20Is	23	0	–	–	–	–	–	–	–	–
First-class	53	0	–	–	–	–	–	–	–	–

WEST INDIES

SUNIL **NARINE**

Full name	**Sunil Philip Narine**
Born	**May 26, 1988, Trinidad**
Teams	**Trinidad & Tobago, Kolkata Knight Riders**
Style	**Left-hand bat, right-arm offspinner**
Test debut	**West Indies v England at Birmingham 2012**
ODI debut	**West Indies v India at Ahmedabad 2011-12**
T20I debut	**West Indies v Australia at Gros Islet 2011-12**

THE PROFILE Few cricketers have had as meteoric a rise as Sunil Narine, an unorthodox offspinner from Trinidad. Virtually unknown outside his native island, he bamboozled several distinguished batsmen during the Champions League T20 in India in October 2011, taking ten wickets with his mixture of offbreaks and hard-to-fathom "knuckle" balls, and was snapped up by Kolkata at the IPL auction the following spring for $700,000. He went on to be the player of the tournament as his side won their first IPL title. Narine took 24 wickets (more than anyone else except Morne Morkel) at an unmatched average of 13.50 and – arguably more importantly – went for less than five and a half runs per over. Just before this he had taken 31 wickets in three first-class games, then befuddled the Australians in the limited-overs portion of their tour of the Caribbean – they were highly relieved when Narine, without a West Indian contract at the time, toddled off to the IPL and missed the Tests. He was hurried back for the end of the 2012 England tour, and although rain ruined his Test debut there, he soon proved his worth with 32 wickets in the nine internationals of New Zealand's visit, including eight in a thumping Test victory on Antigua's usually batsman-friendly pitch in July: "In our conditions," pronounced his captain Darren Sammy, "he is unplayable." Narine originally came to notice by taking all ten wickets in a trial game, which led to his inclusion in the T&T squad early in 2009. Doubts were raised about his action a couple of years later, but remedial work with biomechanical experts in Australia, who made him go more side-on, seemed to do the trick.

THE FACTS Narine took only three wickets in his first three first-class matches for Trinidad, but then in February 2012 collected 5 for 22 and 8 for 17 against Combined Campuses & Colleges in Bridgetown, 5 for 78 and 3 for 54 v Barbados, and 5 for 49 and 5 for 78 v Windward Islands ... His next match (his seventh) was his Test debut ... In the home ODIs against Australia early in 2012 Narine bowled 20 balls to Matthew Wade, and dismissed him three times ...

THE FIGURES to 17.09.12   ESPNcricinfo.com

Batting & Fielding	M	Inns	NO	Runs	HS	Avge	S/R	100	50	4s	6s	Ct	St
Tests	3	3	0	16	11	5.33	40.00	0	0	2	0	1	0
ODIs	15	10	2	76	27*	9.50	71.02	0	0	9	1	3	0
T20Is	5	1	0	2	2	2.00	50.00	0	0	0	0	0	0
First-class	9	13	4	165	40*	18.33	–	0	0	–	–	7	0

Bowling	M	Balls	Runs	Wkts	BB	Avge	RpO	S/R	5i	10m
Tests	3	828	378	12	5–132	31.50	2.73	69.00	1	0
ODIs	15	863	527	28	5–27	18.82	3.66	30.82	1	0
T20Is	5	120	128	7	4–12	18.28	6.40	17.14	0	0
First-class	9	1927	782	46	8–17	17.00	2.43	41.89	6	2

NAZIMUDDIN

Full name	**Mohammad Nazimuddin Ahmed**
Born	**October 1, 1985, Chittagong**
Teams	**Chittagong**
Style	**Right-hand bat, occasional medium-pacer**
Test debut	**Bangladesh v Pakistan at Chittagong 2011-12**
ODI debut	**Bangladesh v South Africa at Mirpur 2007-08**
T20I debut	**Bangladesh v Kenya at Nairobi 2007-08**

THE PROFILE It was a long route to Test cricket for Nazimuddin, a diminutive but well-organised opener from Chittagong. He made his first-class debut at 16: asked to open, he managed only 12 and 9 – but had made a century before he turned 18. During 2004-05 he followed a seven-hour 204 against Sylhet with 103 (in five hours) and 82 in the final of the national four-day championship (but couldn't prevent Dhaka from winning the title), and toured England with Bangladesh A later in 2005. After a couple of years when big scores proved elusive he did well against England A early in 2007 – successive innings of 108, 58 and 42 in the one-day series – and was called up for the inaugural World Twenty20 in South Africa later in the year. Despite some adhesive innings in first-class cricket, Nazimuddin had developed a reputation as a big hitter, which helped his cause in the shorter formats, and he duly clobbered 81 from 50 balls against Pakistan in only his second 20-over game, although he was less impressive in the World Twenty20 itself. Soon afterwards he joined the unauthorised Indian Cricket League: initially he was banned for ten years, although this was rescinded in 2010. Nazimuddin was soon back in the domestic runs, and finally made his Test debut against Pakistan in December 2011, producing doughty innings of 31 and 78 to delay defeat. Bangladesh badly need a reliable foil for Tamim Iqbal at the top of the order, and Nazimuddin is currently seen as the man most likely to succeed there in Tests – but he had a quiet time in the Asia Cup in March 2012 (only 57 runs from four innings) and missed the one-day tour of Europe later in the year.

THE FACTS Nazimuddin hit 81 – Bangladesh's highest score in Twenty20 internationals – in only his second such match, against Pakistan in Nairobi in September 2007 ... He scored 205 and 136 for Chittagong in successive matches against Dhaka in February 2010, and also made 204 against Sylhet in February 2005 ... Nazimuddin scored 108 for Bangladesh A v England A at Bogra in March 2007 ...

THE FIGURES to 17.09.12   **ESPNcricinfo.com**

Batting & Fielding	M	Inns	NO	Runs	HS	Avge	S/R	100	50	4s	6s	Ct	St
Tests	2	4	0	121	78	30.25	38.65	0	1	16	2	1	0
ODIs	11	11	0	147	47	13.36	62.02	0	0	18	2	1	0
T20Is	7	7	0	178	81	25.42	112.65	0	1	13	10	0	0
First-class	83	146	10	5256	205	38.64	49.54	11	30	–	–	33	0

Bowling	M	Balls	Runs	Wkts	BB	Avge	RpO	S/R	5i	10m
Tests	2	0	–	–	–	–	–	–	–	–
ODIs	11	0	–	–	–	–	–	–	–	–
T20Is	7	0	–	–	–	–	–	–	–	–
First-class	83	180	118	2	1–9	59.00	3.93	90.00	0	0

NAZMUL HOSSAIN

Full name	**Mohammad Nazmul Hossain**
Born	**October 5, 1987, Hobigonj**
Teams	**Sylhet**
Style	**Right-hand bat, right-arm fast-medium bowler**
Test debut	**Bangladesh v India at Chittagong 2004-05**
ODI debut	**Bangladesh v South Africa at Edgbaston 2004**
T20I debut	**Bangladesh v West Indies at Basseterre 2009**

THE PROFILE Nazmul Hossain is a hard-working fast bowler with a delivery style not unlike that of Makhaya Ntini, although he is not as quick. He did well at the Under-19 World Cup early in 2004, and was given a premature Test debut later that year, when he was called up to make what was also his first-class debut against India. Only 17, he did well enough, claiming the wickets of Gautam Gambhir (for 139) and Harbhajan Singh. After that Nazmul was seen as more of a one-day specialist – although his style of bowling might have been useful on the early-season pitches the Bangladeshis encountered in England in 2010. He spent 30 months out of the side, but returned in August 2008 a cannier bowler. Early in 2009 his 3 for 30 in the tri-series final in Mirpur gave Sri Lanka a severe case of the jitters: chasing a modest 153, they were 6 for 5 after Nazmul's initial burst, but regrouped to win by two wickets. Nazmul sticks to an off-stump line, with the natural angle taking the ball in. But the dangerous one is the delivery which straightens or just moves a shade away – batsmen don't expect that from a bowler with his kind of action. He is also a fine fielder. He missed the 2011 World Cup, but later that year played another Test – exactly seven years after his first – and dismissed Mohammad Hafeez of Pakistan with his first ball back (it was a long-winded two in two, actually, as he'd struck with the last delivery of his 2004 debut).

THE FACTS Nazmul Hossain was the second Bangladeshi (after Mashrafe Mortaza in 2001-02) to make his first-class debut in a Test match: only three others have done this since 1899 – Graham Vivian of New Zealand (1964-65), Zimbabwe's Ujesh Ranchod (1992-93) and Yasir Ali of Pakistan (2003-04) ... He was 17 years 73 days old at the time of his debut (the fifth-youngest for Bangladesh) ... Nazmul took 5 for 30 for Sylhet at Rajshahi in March 2006 ... His father, an army man, was a Bangladesh football international ...

THE FIGURES to 17.09.12

ESPNcricinfo.com

Batting & Fielding	M	Inns	NO	Runs	HS	Avge	S/R	100	50	4s	6s	Ct	St
Tests	2	4	2	16	8*	8.00	76.19	0	0	2	1	0	0
ODIs	38	21	13	35	6*	4.37	27.34	0	0	0	0	6	0
T20Is	4	2	2	3	3*	–	20.00	0	0	0	0	0	0
First-class	33	53	13	411	49	10.27	36.21	0	0	–	–	16	0

Bowling	M	Balls	Runs	Wkts	BB	Avge	RpO	S/R	5i	10m
Tests	2	329	194	5	2–61	38.80	3.53	65.80	0	0
ODIs	38	1649	1386	44	4–40	31.50	5.04	37.47	0	0
T20Is	4	42	67	1	1–15	67.00	9.57	42.00	0	0
First-class	33	4417	2098	71	5–30	29.54	2.84	62.21	2	0

INDIA

PRAGYAN **OJHA**

Full name	**Pragyan Prayash Ojha**
Born	**September 5, 1986, Bhubaneshwar**
Teams	**Hyderabad, Mumbai Indians**
Style	**Left-hand bat, left-arm orthodox spinner**
Test debut	**India v Sri Lanka at Kanpur 2009-10**
ODI debut	**India v Bangladesh at Karachi 2008**
T20I debut	**India v Bangladesh at Nottingham 2009**

THE PROFILE A left-arm spinner of teasing flight and pleasing loop, Pragyan Ojha made a stunning start in first-class cricket: for Hyderabad in the Ranji Trophy semi-final in March 2005, he took the first five wickets to fall in eventual champions Railways' first innings, starting with the Test allrounder Sanjay Bangar. Ojha showed his control in the inaugural IPL in 2008: he finished with 11 wickets, then took 21 – four more than anyone else – in 2010. He also made an immediate impact in his first ODI, in the Asia Cup in June 2008, with three outfield catches and an absolute ripper which foxed Bangladesh's Raqibul Hasan. Ojha started the 2009 World Twenty20 in England well, taking a wicket with his first ball and finishing with 4 for 21 against Bangladesh, but was omitted later in the tournament, then missed out on the one-day Compaq Cup in Sri Lanka in September as the selectors tried out legspinner Amit Mishra as Harbhajan Singh's partner. But Ojha did win his first Test cap late in 2009, taking a catch off his first ball in the field, and although his strike-rate was unspectacular he claimed 21 wickets in his first six matches, with seven – including danger men Sangakkara and Jayawardene in both innings – as India squared the series in Sri Lanka in August 2010. By 2012 he was forming a potent spin partnership with Ravichandran Ashwin – they claimed 73 wickets between them in their first five Tests together – with Ojha taking six-fors against West Indies at Delhi and Mumbai, and adding 5 for 99 as New Zealand went down fighting in Bangalore in September 2012.

THE FACTS Ojha took a wicket (Bangladesh's Shakib Al Hasan) with his first ball in Twenty20 internationals, at Trent Bridge in June 2009, and finished with 4 for 21 ... On his first-class debut, against Railways at Delhi in March 2005, Ojha took the first five wickets to fall, finishing with 5 for 55 ... Ojha was the leading wicket-taker in the third IPL, with 21 ... He took 7 for 114 for Hyderabad v Rajasthan in December 2006: the previous week he took 6 for 84 against Maharashtra ...

THE FIGURES to 17.09.12   **espncricinfo.com**

Batting & Fielding	M	Inns	NO	Runs	HS	Avge	S/R	100	50	4s	6s	Ct	St
Tests	16	17	12	74	18*	14.80	19.78	0	0	5	0	6	0
ODIs	18	10	8	46	16*	23.00	41.07	0	0	3	0	7	0
T20Is	6	1	1	10	10*	–	166.66	0	0	0	1	1	0
First-class	61	77	31	464	35	10.08	30.36	0	0	48	0	22	0

Bowling	M	Balls	Runs	Wkts	BB	Avge	RpO	S/R	5i	10m
Tests	16	5192	2387	75	6–47	31.82	2.75	69.22	3	0
ODIs	18	876	652	21	4–38	31.04	4.46	41.71	0	0
T20Is	6	126	132	10	4–21	13.20	6.28	12.60	0	0
First-class	61	15213	7199	269	7–114	26.76	2.83	56.55	16	1

GRAHAM **ONIONS**

Full name	**Graham Onions**
Born	**September 9, 1982, Gateshead**
Teams	**Durham**
Style	**Right-hand bat, right-arm fast-medium bowler**
Test debut	**England v West Indies at Lord's 2009**
ODI debut	**England v Australia at Chester-le-Street 2009**
T20I debut	**No T20Is yet**

THE PROFILE A brisk seam bowler, with a name that is a headline-writer's dream (especially when Durham's keeper Phil Mustard does the catching), Graham Onions first took the eye in 2006, with 54 wickets. He maintained an impressive workload for Durham, and didn't just take wickets on helpful surfaces at Chester-le-Street. The following two seasons were more of a struggle – Ottis Gibson sometimes kept him out of the county side in 2007, then he had injury problems – but Onions began 2009 in rare form, and made the early-season Tests against West Indies. He started in fairytale fashion, mopping up the tail with four wickets in seven balls to finish with 5 for 38 at Lord's, bowling at a lively pace and swinging the ball away. He played in three of the Ashes Tests without quite recapturing this form, although he did enliven the second morning at Edgbaston by striking with the first two balls of the day. Although he was left out for the final Test he was at The Oval as the Ashes were recaptured, then returned to Durham as they retained the Championship. After that he picked up 11 wickets in three Tests in South Africa – although he will be better remembered for his obstinate batting, twice surviving the last over to stave off defeats. But he also picked up a stress fracture in the back, which ruled him out of the whole of 2010. Onions returned to form and fitness the following year, taking 53 first-class wickets, and he played one Test in 2012, although more noteworthy was what happened when he was left out of the final XI for the Lord's Test against South Africa in August. Onions drove to Nottingham, missed his lunch, and went out and took 9 for 67 for Durham. And he ran the tenth one out, for good measure.

THE FACTS Onions took 9 for 67 for Durham v Nottinghamshire at Trent Bridge in 2012: he ran the other man out with a direct hit ... At Edgbaston in July 2009 Onions took wickets with the first two balls of the second day's play against Australia: this is believed to have happened only once before in Test history, when Australia's "Chuck" Fleetwood-Smith did it against England at Melbourne in 1936-37 ...

THE FIGURES to 17.09.12   **ESPNcricinfo.com**

Batting & Fielding	M	Inns	NO	Runs	HS	Avge	S/R	100	50	4s	6s	Ct	St
Tests	9	10	7	30	17*	10.00	30.92	0	0	4	0	0	0
ODIs	4	1	0	1	1	1.00	50.00	0	0	0	0	1	0
T20Is	0	0	–	–	–	–	–	–	–	–	–	–	–
First-class	98	128	44	1085	41	12.91	52.95	0	0	–	–	22	0

Bowling	M	Balls	Runs	Wkts	BB	Avge	RpO	S/R	5i	10m
Tests	9	1606	957	32	5–38	29.90	3.57	50.18	1	0
ODIs	4	204	185	4	2–58	46.25	5.44	51.00	0	0
T20Is	0	0	–	–	–	–	–	–	–	–
First-class	98	16572	9553	359	9–67	26.61	3.45	46.16	16	3

JACOB **ORAM**

Full name	**Jacob David Philip Oram**
Born	**July 28, 1978, Palmerston North, Manawatu**
Teams	**Central Districts**
Style	**Left-hand bat, right-arm fast-medium bowler**
Test debut	**New Zealand v India at Wellington 2002-03**
ODI debut	**New Zealand v Zimbabwe at Wellington 2000-01**
T20I debut	**New Zealand v South Africa at Johannesburg 2005-06**

THE PROFILE It's hard to miss Jacob Oram, and not just because of his height of 6ft 6ins (198cm). He is agile in the field, especially at gully, and complements that with solid fast-medium bowling and aggressive batting. Foot problems cost him a season at a vital stage, but he came back strongly in 2002-03 to seal a regular international place. He narrowly missed a century against Pakistan in the Wellington Boxing Day Test of 2003, but made up for that by carving 119 not out against South Africa, then 90 in the second Test, which earned him an England tour in 2004. By then his bowling was starting to lose its sting, and he went down with back trouble shortly after pounding 126 against Australia at Brisbane in November 2004. After nearly 18 months out Oram showed what New Zealand's middle order had been missing, coming in at 38 for 4 at Centurion and making 133, his highest Test score. He missed the start of the 2006-07 Australian one-day series with a hamstring injury, but bucked the team up with some stirring performances when he did get there, including a 71-ball century – NZ's fastest, and his first in ODIs – against Australia at Perth. Oram continued to be a regular member of all New Zealand's sides until 2009, when he retired from Tests to preserve himself for limited-overs games ... and a lucrative IPL contract. He played an important part in New Zealand's run to the semi-final of the 2011 World Cup, collecting 12 wickets, four of them in the shock quarter-final victory over South Africa. He remained an integral member of the limited-overs team, although he did little with the bat in 2012.

THE FACTS Oram averages 62.00 in Tests against Australia, 52.50 v South Africa – and 10.25 v India ... With the ball in ODIs he averages 23.05 v South Africa, but 74.72 v Australia ... Oram took a hat-trick in a Twenty20 international against Sri Lanka in Colombo in 2009 ... He scored his maiden century in only his fourth first-class match, for Central Districts v Canterbury at Christchurch in 1998-99, and his 155 remains his highest score ...

THE FIGURES to 17.09.12   **ESPNcricinfo.com**

Batting & Fielding	M	Inns	NO	Runs	HS	Avge	S/R	100	50	4s	6s	Ct	St
Tests	33	59	10	1780	133	36.32	50.38	5	6	209	21	15	0
ODIs	159	115	15	2432	101*	24.32	86.67	1	13	182	81	49	0
T20Is	31	26	6	441	66*	22.05	143.18	0	2	34	22	11	0
First-class	85	136	18	3992	155	33.83	–	8	18	–	–	36	0

Bowling	M	Balls	Runs	Wkts	BB	Avge	RpO	S/R	5i	10m
Tests	33	4964	1983	60	4–41	33.05	2.39	82.73	0	0
ODIs	159	6869	5004	173	5–26	28.92	4.37	39.70	2	0
T20Is	31	465	669	14	3–33	47.78	8.63	33.21	0	0
First-class	85	10670	4158	155	6–45	26.82	2.33	68.83	3	0

TIM **PAINE**

Full name	**Timothy David Paine**
Born	**December 8, 1984, Hobart, Tasmania**
Teams	**Tasmania**
Style	**Right-hand bat, wicketkeeper**
Test debut	**Australia v Pakistan at Lord's 2010**
ODI debut	**Australia v Scotland at Edinburgh 2009**
T20I debut	**Australia v England at Manchester 2009**

THE PROFILE A talented top-order batsman and wicket-keeper, Tasmania's Tim Paine was earmarked as next in line behind Brad Haddin when he joined the squad for the one-dayers that followed the Ashes Tests in England in 2009. In the event Paine ended up playing throughout, as Haddin had to have surgery on the finger he broke before the Edgbaston Test. And he did not disappoint, pulling off a couple of quicksilver stumpings to go with some forthright batting from the top of the order, the highlight a fine century at Trent Bridge which included several whips off the pads – stork-like, with the back foot in the air – which fizzed down to fine leg. When Haddin had elbow-tendon trouble in 2010, Paine deputised again, playing his first two Tests against Pakistan in England. There were 11 catches in those two matches, and a fine leg-side stumping to dismiss Salman Butt for 92 at Lord's. But he sat on the bench throughout the 2011 World Cup, then later in the year broke a finger just as Haddin was going through a rough patch with the bat. Soon after this Paine broke the same finger in pre-season practice for Tasmania, and in all he was out for more than a year before returning for Australia A in England in 2012. By then, though, Matthew Wade had stated his own claim to the gloves, and Paine faced another battle. Paine's initial call-up came soon after a strong showing for Australia A, including a six-studded 134 against Pakistan A in July 2009. He had made headlines early on in his career, too, extending his maiden first-class century against Western Australia at Perth to 215 in only his fifth match in October 2006.

THE FACTS Paine made 215 (his only first-class century) for Tasmania v Western Australia at Perth in October 2006 ... He scored 111 against England in an ODI at Trent Bridge in September 2009 ... Paine captained Australia at the Under-19 World Cup in Bangladesh in 2003-04, and signed his first contract with Tasmania when he was 16 ...

THE FIGURES to 17.09.12

ESPNcricinfo.com

Batting & Fielding	M	Inns	NO	Runs	HS	Avge	S/R	100	50	4s	6s	Ct	St
Tests	4	8	0	287	92	35.87	43.09	0	2	35	0	16	1
ODIs	26	26	1	737	111	29.48	68.87	1	5	86	5	35	4
T20Is	5	3	0	22	21	7.33	122.22	0	0	2	1	4	0
First-class	50	90	7	2637	215	31.77	44.61	1	19	290	8	143	8

Bowling	M	Balls	Runs	Wkts	BB	Avge	RpO	S/R	5i	10m
Tests	4	0	–	–	–	–	–	–	–	–
ODIs	26	0	–	–	–	–	–	–	–	–
T20Is	5	0	–	–	–	–	–	–	–	–
First-class	50	6	3	0	–	–	3.00	–	0	0

MONTY **PANESAR**

Full name	**Mudhsuden Singh Panesar**
Born	**April 25, 1982, Luton, Bedfordshire**
Teams	**Sussex**
Style	**Left-hand bat, slow left-arm orthodox spinner**
Test debut	**England v India at Nagpur 2005-06**
ODI debut	**England v Australia at Melbourne 2006-07**
T20I debut	**England v Australia at Sydney 2006-07**

THE PROFILE Monty Panesar made himself a cult hero to English crowds enchanted by his enthusiastic celebrations and endearingly erratic fielding. That, and equally amateurish batting, had threatened to hold him back, but when Ashley Giles was ruled out of the 2005-06 Indian tour Panesar received a late summons. He's a throwback to an earlier slow left-armer, Bishan Bedi, who also twirled away for Northants in a patka, teasing and tempting with flight and guile, although Panesar gives it more of a rip. Panesar's arrival was delayed while he finished university, but in 2005 he took 46 Championship wickets at 21.54. He made his Test debut at Nagpur that winter, picking up Sachin Tendulkar as his first wicket. At home in 2006 he delivered the ball of the season to bowl Younis Khan and set up victory at Leeds; next summer he claimed 31 wickets in seven home Tests, and remained the crowd's favourite as Montymania showed no sign of abating. But, lacking variety, he struggled in Sri Lanka at the end of 2007, and laboured a little in England too, while his antics and frequent appealing rubbed some up the wrong way. By the start of 2009 he had lost his place as England's No. 1 spinner to Graeme Swann (ironically, since Panesar's arrival had hastened Swann's departure from Northants), and his only contribution to the Ashes series was an unlikely match-saving display with the bat in the first Test. Panesar became a back number after that and lost his England contract, but a move to Sussex paid off: he passed 50 wickets for them in both 2010 and 2011, and in between made a second Ashes tour, although he didn't play in the Tests. Early in 2012 he took Test five-fors against Pakistan in Abu Dhabi and Dubai, but returned to the bench when only one spinner (Swann) was required after that.

THE FACTS Panesar took 7 for 60 (13 for 137 in the match) for Sussex v Somerset at Taunton in August 2012 ... He was the first Sikh to play Test cricket for anyone other than India ... Panesar took 6 for 37 for England v New Zealand at Old Trafford in 2008 ... He averages 25.00 in Tests against West Indies – but 53.57 v India ...

THE FIGURES to 17.09.12   **ESPncricinfo.com**

Batting & Fielding	M	Inns	NO	Runs	HS	Avge	S/R	100	50	4s	6s	Ct	St
Tests	42	57	19	208	26	5.47	31.27	0	0	22	1	9	0
ODIs	26	8	3	26	13	5.20	28.57	0	0	2	0	3	0
T20Is	1	1	0	1	1	1.00	50.00	0	0	0	0	0	0
First-class	170	214	68	1263	46*	8.65	33.94	0	0	–	–	35	0

Bowling	M	Balls	Runs	Wkts	BB	Avge	RpO	S/R	5i	10m
Tests	42	10170	4734	142	6–37	33.33	2.79	71.61	10	1
ODIs	26	1308	980	24	3–25	40.83	4.49	54.50	0	0
T20Is	1	24	40	2	2–40	20.00	10.00	12.00	0	0
First-class	170	38497	17491	577	7–60	30.31	2.72	66.71	30	4

THARANGA **PARANAVITANA**

Full name	**Nishad Tharanga Paranavitana**
Born	**April 15, 1982, Kegalle**
Teams	**Sinhalese Sports Club, Kandurata**
Style	**Left-hand bat, offspinner**
Test debut	**Sri Lanka v Pakistan at Karachi 2008-09**
ODI debut	**No ODIs yet**
T20I debut	**No T20Is yet**

THE PROFILE Tharanga Paranavitana is a tall left-hand opener who scored consistently on the domestic scene before a stellar 2007-08 season established him as a real Test prospect. Paranavitana was the leading runscorer in the top tier of the Premier League with 893, and his 236 against Colombo in the last match helped Sinhalese Sports Club clinch the title. That was his third century of the summer (and the second double of his career), and he added another in the regional competition for Kandurata to finish the first-class season with 1059 runs at 81. All that – and 159 against South Africa A – meant he had to be given a Test chance, and he eventually won his first cap at Karachi early in 2009. The disappointment of a first-ball duck was followed by a chest wound in the terrorist attack on the Sri Lankan team bus in Lahore. Thankfully, Paranavitana was back to full fitness in time for the return series in Sri Lanka, and made his mark with 72 and 49 in a narrow victory at Galle, and 73 in the final Test in Colombo. Leaner times followed against New Zealand, and he was also fined for claiming a catch which replays showed had clearly bounced in front of him. But in July 2010 Paranavitana made a maiden Test century against India at Galle – Murali's last match – and added another in the next game. Back at Galle there was a near-miss (95) against West Indies, then a couple of classy fifties in England in 2011. However, by September 2012 he had gone 18 Tests without a century, and faced competition for his place. In Tests he ambles along at a strike rate well below 50, the main reason why he is yet to feature in Sri Lanka's limited-overs teams.

THE FACTS Paranavitana scored 236 (and 80 not out) for Sinhalese Sports Club v Colombo CC in March 2008 ... He made 232 not out for Sinhalese v Tamil Union in February 2007, and early in 2012 scored 216 against Tamil Union and 223 v Bloomfield ... Paranavitana started his Test career (against Pakistan at Karachi in February 2009) with a first-ball duck against Bangladesh in June 2007 ...

THE FIGURES to 17.09.12   **ESFN**cricinfo.com

Batting & Fielding	M	Inns	NO	Runs	HS	Avge	S/R	100	50	4s	6s	Ct	St
Tests	30	56	4	1721	111	33.09	42.03	2	11	200	4	24	0
ODIs	0	0	–	–	–	–	–	–	–	–	–	–	–
T20Is	0	0	–	–	–	–	–	–	–	–	–	–	–
First-class	143	237	21	9327	236	43.18	51.51	24	40	–	–	142	0

Bowling	M	Balls	Runs	Wkts	BB	Avge	RpO	S/R	5i	10m
Tests	30	102	86	1	1–26	86.00	5.05	102.00	0	0
ODIs	0	0	–	–	–	–	–	–	–	–
T20Is	0	0	–	–	–	–	–	–	–	–
First-class	143	2177	1082	30	4–39	36.06	2.98	72.56	0	0

WAYNE **PARNELL**

Full name	**Wayne Dillon Parnell**
Born	**July 30, 1989, Port Elizabeth, Cape Province**
Teams	**Warriors, Pune Warriors**
Style	**Left-hand bat, left-arm fast-medium bowler**
Test debut	**South Africa v England at Johannesburg 2009-10**
ODI debut	**South Africa v Australia at Perth 2008-09**
T20I debut	**South Africa v Australia at Brisbane 2008-09**

THE PROFILE   Tall, slim, and waspishly fast, left-armer Wayne Parnell can also bat well, and exhibited strong leadership qualities during a glittering junior career. In the Under-19 World Cup in Malaysia in 2008 he led by example, taking 18 wickets and scoring useful middle-order runs to steer South Africa into the final, where they lost to India. The national selectors were already on alert, and Parnell was drafted for the one-day series in Australia early in 2009. He played only one ODI there, proving a little expensive in a victory over Australia at the WACA, but began to make his presence felt in the return series back home, taking 4 for 25 as the Aussies were rolled for 131 at Centurion. He was rewarded by becoming the youngest South African to be awarded a national contract. Then, after warming up with some useful spells for Kent, Parnell was one of the stars of the World Twenty20 in England in 2009, derailing England (3 for 16) and West Indies (4 for 13) inside 48 hours. He bowled with pace and accuracy during the powerplays and the final overs, at an economy rate of less than six an over, qualities which earned him a big-money IPL contract for 2010 – only for a groin injury, picked up in practice, to stop him appearing. It took him a long time to recover, mentally as well as physically: he played only once in the 2011 World Cup, but a decent IPL season for Pune helped. Reports of a failed drugs test marred his 2012 IPL season, but Parnell did well for South Africa A later in the year, and regained his one-day place at the end of the triumphant tour of England.

THE FACTS   In the quarter-final of the Under-19 World Cup in Kuala Lumpur in 2008 Parnell top-scored with 57 from No. 7, then took 6 for 8 as Bangladesh were bowled out for 41 ... He scored 90 for Kent v Glamorgan at Canterbury in May 2009, putting on 151 for the seventh wicket with James Tredwell ... Parnell took 7 for 56 for South Africa A v Ireland at Wicklow in August 2012 ...

THE FIGURES to 17.09.12   **ESPNcricinfo.com**

Batting & Fielding	M	Inns	NO	Runs	HS	Avge	S/R	100	50	4s	6s	Ct	St
Tests	3	2	0	34	22	17.00	35.41	0	0	6	0	1	0
ODIs	27	13	3	182	49	18.20	74.89	0	0	13	3	2	0
T20Is	16	4	2	69	29*	34.50	138.00	0	0	7	3	1	0
First-class	40	51	4	1079	90	22.95	52.27	0	5	130	10	14	0

Bowling	M	Balls	Runs	Wkts	BB	Avge	RpO	S/R	5i	10m
Tests	3	306	227	5	2–17	45.40	4.45	61.20	0	0
ODIs	27	950	945	31	5–48	30.48	5.96	30.64	2	0
T20Is	16	245	287	14	4–13	20.50	7.02	17.50	0	0
First-class	40	6240	3648	106	7–56	34.41	3.50	58.86	2	0

JEETAN **PATEL**

Full name	**Jeetan Shashi Patel**
Born	**May 7, 1980, Wellington**
Teams	**Wellington, Warwickshire**
Style	**Right-hand bat, offspinner**
Test debut	**New Zealand v South Africa at Cape Town 2005-06**
ODI debut	**New Zealand v Zimbabwe at Harare 2005-06**
T20I debut	**New Zealand v South Africa at Johannesburg 2005-06**

THE PROFILE The son of Indian parents, but born and brought up in Wellington's eastern suburbs, offspinner Jeetan Patel was fast-tracked into New Zealand's one-day side after being identified as the type of slow bowler who could be effective at the death. He usually keeps the runs down, while his batting, initially underwhelming, has improved: he more than doubled his highest score during his first county stint with Warwickshire in 2009, biffing 120 from No. 10 against Yorkshire. Patel first played for Wellington in 1999-2000, bowling 59 overs and taking 5 for 145 against Auckland on debut. Three middling seasons followed, and he seemed to be heading nowhere, with an average in the mid-forties. But then he took 6 for 32 against Otago in 2004-05, propelling Wellington into the final against Auckland, which they lost. Suddenly good judges were noting his ability to make the ball loop and drift, not unlike a right-handed Daniel Vettori. Patel toured Zimbabwe in August 2005, and became a one-day regular for a while (although his last ODIs were in 2009). Highlights included 2 for 23 from ten overs to throttle Sri Lanka at Wellington, and three wickets at Christchurch to subdue West Indies. All this led to a first Test cap against South Africa in April 2006: he wheeled down 42 overs and took three good wickets. Patel was often been used as a foil to Vettori on spinning tracks, winkling out six West Indians at Napier in December 2008 and six Sri Lankans in Colombo the following August. After that, though, he fell out of favour – before, given another chance late in 2012 when Vettori was injured, he claimed seven wickets in two Tests in India.

THE FACTS Patel was Man of the Match for his 2 for 23 in ten overs against Sri Lanka at Wellington in 2005-06 after being supersubbed into the game ... He also won the match award in his first T20 international, after taking 3 for 20 ... Patel made 120 for Warwickshire v Yorkshire at Edgbaston in May 2009, sharing a county-record ninth-wicket stand of 233 with Jonathan Trott ... He took 7 for 75 for Warwickshire v Somerset in July 2012 ...

THE FIGURES to 17.09.12

ESPNcricinfo.com

Batting & Fielding	M	Inns	NO	Runs	HS	Avge	S/R	100	50	4s	6s	Ct	St
Tests	15	22	4	226	27*	12.55	46.79	0	0	23	1	8	0
ODIs	39	13	7	88	34	14.66	58.66	0	0	5	2	12	0
T20Is	11	4	1	9	5	3.00	64.28	0	0	1	0	4	0
First-class	128	158	43	2317	120	20.14	–	1	10	–	–	47	0

Bowling	M	Balls	Runs	Wkts	BB	Avge	RpO	S/R	5i	10m
Tests	15	4004	2182	47	5–110	46.42	3.26	85.19	1	0
ODIs	39	1804	1513	42	3–11	36.02	5.03	42.95	0	0
T20Is	11	199	269	16	3–20	16.81	8.11	12.43	0	0
First-class	127	24815	12210	319	7–75	38.27	2.95	77.78	12	1

MUNAF **PATEL**

INDIA

Full name	**Munaf Musa Patel**
Born	**July 12, 1983, Ikhar, Gujarat**
Teams	**Baroda, Mumbai Indians**
Style	**Right-hand bat, right-arm fast-medium bowler**
Test debut	**India v England at Mohali 2005-06**
ODI debut	**India v England at Goa 2005-06**
T20I debut	**India v South Africa at Durban 2010-11**

THE PROFILE Few fast men generated as much hype before bowling a ball in first-class cricket as Munaf Patel, from the little town of Ikhar in Gujarat, early in 2003. Kiran More spotted him: soon Patel was being hailed as the fastest bowler in India, although initially he spent more time recovering from injuries than actually playing. He's strongly built, though not overly tall, and bustles up to the crease before releasing in a windmill-whirl of hands. He has a well-directed yorker, and can reverse-swing the ball. In March 2006 he finally received a call from the selectors – now chaired by his old pal More – after taking ten wickets in a match against the England tourists. He finished his first Test with seven more, and struck consistently in the West Indies later in 2006. But then things got harder. He tweaked an ankle in South Africa, and was criticised when it bothered him in the final Test, but was fit in time for the 2007 World Cup. Then it was a back injury, and Patel returned to the Chennai academy – which he calls his "second home" – to remodel his action. He played his first Test for 16 months in New Zealand in March 2009, taking five wickets in a comfortable victory at Hamilton, although his bowling after that was unspectacular, and lacked the fiery speed that earned him those early rave reviews. These days Patel is little more than medium-pace, although he controls the ball well and played his part as the 2011 World Cup was won – he took 11 wickets and was rarely collared. After that, though, Patel had a quiet time in the 2012 IPL – apart from an argument with a batsman that earned him a fine – and lost his national place: he will probably need others to lose form to get it back.

THE FACTS Patel's match figures of 7 for 97 were the best on Test debut by an Indian fast bowler, beating Mohammad Nissar's 6 for 135 against England at Lord's in 1932 (Abid Ali, more of a medium-pacer, took 7 for 116 on debut against Australia in 1967-68) ... Patel claimed 6 for 50 for Maharashtra v Railways at Delhi in January 2006 ... He took 5 for 59 and 5 for 32 for the Board President's XI against the England tourists in February 2006 ...

THE FIGURES to 17.09.12   **ESPncricinfo.com**

Batting & Fielding	M	Inns	NO	Runs	HS	Avge	S/R	100	50	4s	6s	Ct	St
Tests	13	14	6	60	15*	7.50	42.25	0	0	8	1	6	0
ODIs	70	27	16	74	15	6.72	66.07	0	0	7	1	11	0
T20Is	3	1	0	0	0	0.00	0.00	0	0	0	0	0	0
First-class	54	62	21	617	78	15.04	69.24	0	1	–	–	13	0

Bowling	M	Balls	Runs	Wkts	BB	Avge	RpO	S/R	5i	10m
Tests	13	2658	1349	35	4–25	38.54	3.04	75.94	0	0
ODIs	70	3154	2603	86	4–29	30.26	4.95	36.67	0	0
T20Is	3	60	86	4	2–25	21.50	8.60	15.00	0	0
First-class	54	9839	4661	192	6–50	24.27	2.84	51.24	7	1

SAMIT **PATEL**

Full name	**Samit Rohit Patel**
Born	**November 30, 1984, Leicester**
Teams	**Nottinghamshire**
Style	**Right-hand bat, slow left-arm orthodox spinner**
Test debut	**England v Sri Lanka at Galle 2011-12**
ODI debut	**England v Scotland at Edinburgh 2008**
T20I debut	**England v Sri Lanka at Bristol 2011**

THE PROFILE Samit Patel was long considered a player of great promise, but struggled to produce the goods consistently at first-team level. He has also faced a battle with fitness, which led to him being publicly humiliated before the 2011 World Cup: "All we were saying was 'Get into reasonable shape'. It didn't have to be perfect," said England's coach Andy Flower in announcing Patel's demotion from the preliminary squad. It seemed to do the trick: he worked hard in the gym, slimmed down, and got his place back, although his early returns weren't spectacular. He made a couple of Test appearances in Sri Lanka early in 2012, but his bowling proved unpenetrative and he returned to one-day action. Patel is a hard-hitting middle-order batsman and a capable slow left-armer who delivers leg-stump darts à la Sanath Jayasuriya. He made his debut for Nottinghamshire's 2nd XI in 1999, when only 14. In 2006, he finally began to show signs of realising his potential, hammering 156 not out, with eight sixes, against Middlesex at Lord's – he hurtled from 100 to 150 in just 17 balls. Some of his most eye-catching performances have come in Twenty20 cricket, including a double-wicket maiden against Derbyshire in 2006, but it was in the 50-over game that he first attracted the interest of the selectors. Patel was called up for the late-season one-day internationals against South Africa in 2008. Replacing his Nottinghamshire team-mate Graeme Swann, he kept the runs down in his first couple of matches, then struck a brisk 31 at The Oval before ruining South Africa's reply with 5 for 41. Suddenly a left-field pick was looking like an inspired one ... but then those fitness concerns intruded.

THE FACTS Patel took 7 for 68 (11 for 111 in the match) for Nottinghamshire v Hampshire at Southampton in July 2011 ... In his fourth ODI he took 5 for 41 against South Africa at The Oval in August 2008 ... He made 176 for Nottinghamshire v Gloucestershire at Bristol in April 2007 ... Patel hit 173, his maiden first-class century, in his fifth match, against Durham UCCE at Durham in April 2006 ...

THE FIGURES to 17.09.12

ESPη cricinfo.com

Batting & Fielding	M	Inns	NO	Runs	HS	Avge	S/R	100	50	4s	6s	Ct	St
Tests	2	3	0	40	29	13.33	33.89	0	0	1	0	0	0
ODIs	31	18	5	407	70*	31.30	89.64	0	1	28	10	7	0
T20Is	11	8	1	81	25*	11.57	97.59	0	0	6	2	0	0
First-class	107	168	13	6076	176	39.20	62.77	13	35	–	–	60	0

Bowling	M	Balls	Runs	Wkts	BB	Avge	RpO	S/R	5i	10m
Tests	2	354	122	3	2–36	40.66	2.06	118.00	0	0
ODIs	31	1055	960	23	5–41	41.73	5.45	45.86	1	0
T20Is	11	174	213	5	2–22	42.60	7.34	34.80	0	0
First-class	107	11408	5840	151	7–68	38.67	3.07	75.54	3	1

IRFAN **PATHAN**

Full name	**Irfan Khan Pathan**
Born	**October 27, 1984, Baroda, Gujarat**
Teams	**Baroda, Delhi Daredevils**
Style	**Left-hand bat, left-arm fast-medium bowler**
Test debut	**India v Australia at Adelaide 2003-04**
ODI debut	**India v Australia at Melbourne 2003-04**
T20I debut	**India v South Africa at Johannesburg 2006-07**

INDIA

THE PROFILE Irfan Pathan was initially rated the most talented swing and seam bowler to emerge from India since Kapil Dev, and was soon being thought of as a possible successor for Kapil in the allround department too. He was strikingly composed in his Test debut at 19. A potent left-armer's outswinger helped him to a hat-trick in the first over of the Karachi Test in January 2006, and he could reverse it too, although his pace has reduced in recent years. When batting, he was regularly pushed up the order, sometimes even opening in one-dayers. At No. 3 he produced a spectacular 83 against Sri Lanka, and he often bailed India out in Tests as well, with 93 and 82 against Sri Lanka late in 2005, and 90 as India piled up 603 at Faisalabad early in 2006. After that he struggled with shoulder trouble, but returned to the one-day side in 2007, then celebrated his first Test for 19 months – against Pakistan in December – by clubbing his first century, reaching it with his fourth six. Early in 2008 he played two important innings and took five wickets as Australia were beaten at Perth, but after that other left-arm pacemen shoved him down the queue a little as his pace dropped. After the World Twenty20 in England in 2009 Pathan disappeared from the national scene, seemingly for good – but popped up in the one-day team again in 2012, taking 4 for 32 against Sri Lanka in the Asia Cup in March, and 5 for 61 against them at Pallekele later in the year. A Test return looks unlikely, but since remarkably he's still only 28 there's time for that too.

THE FACTS Pathan was the first bowler to take a hat-trick in the first over of a Test match, when he dismissed Salman Butt, Younis Khan and Mohammad Yousuf at Karachi in January 2006: from 0 for 3, Pakistan recovered to win by 341 runs ... Pathan took 12 for 126 in the match against Zimbabwe at Harare in September 2005 ... He is one of only six players to have scored a century and taken a hat-trick in Tests ... His half-brother Yusuf Pathan has also played for India ...

THE FIGURES to 17.09.12

ᴇꜱᴘⁿcricinfo.com

Batting & Fielding	M	Inns	NO	Runs	HS	Avge	S/R	100	50	4s	6s	Ct	St
Tests	29	40	5	1105	102	31.57	53.22	1	6	131	18	8	0
ODIs	120	87	21	1544	83	23.39	79.54	0	5	142	37	21	0
T20Is	19	12	7	133	33*	26.60	125.47	0	0	6	6	2	0
First-class	92	126	24	3098	111*	30.37	–	2	18	–	–	26	0

Bowling	M	Balls	Runs	Wkts	BB	Avge	RpO	S/R	5i	10m
Tests	29	5884	3226	100	7–59	32.26	3.28	58.84	7	2
ODIs	120	5855	5143	173	5–27	29.72	5.27	33.84	2	0
T20Is	19	378	497	23	3–16	21.60	7.88	16.43	0	0
First-class	92	17231	9126	322	7–35	28.34	3.17	53.51	17	3

JAMES **PATTINSON**

Full name	**James Lee Pattinson**
Born	**May 3, 1990, Melbourne**
Teams	**Victoria**
Style	**Left-hand bat, right-arm fast-medium bowler**
Test debut	**Australia v New Zealand at Brisbane 2011-12**
ODI debut	**Australia v Bangladesh at Mirpur 2010-11**
T20I debut	**Australia v South Africa at Cape Town 2011-12**

AUSTRALIA

THE PROFILE A strong fast bowler who hits the bat hard, James Pattinson will be one of Australia's players to watch over the next few years – or so the selectors thought when they surprised him with a national contract in 2011. He made a dream start in Test cricket, demolishing New Zealand at Brisbane in December with 5 for 27, and adding 5 for 51 in the next Test at Hobart. After four Tests he had 25 wickets, but a back injury led to an early return home from the West Indies in mid-2012. Pattinson had first caught the eye in one-day cricket: in December 2009 he swung the ball impressively against New South Wales at the SCG, finishing with 6 for 48, the best figures by a Victorian in a domestic one-day game, breaking Graeme Watson's 40-year-old record. Pattinson had already represented Australia's Under-19s, and soon afterwards joined the academy and also played for Australia A. He is the younger brother of Nottinghamshire's Darren Pattinson – with whom he competes for a spot in the Victoria side – who played one Test for England in 2008. Unlike Darren, who was born in Grimsby, James popped out in Melbourne after the family emigrated, so his only passport is an Australian one. James honed his skills against his brother, who is ten years older, in the back yard of their Melbourne home: both of them played for the Dandenong club in the eastern suburbs.

THE FACTS Pattinson took 6 for 48 – the only six wickets to fall – for Victoria v New South Wales in a one-day game at Sydney in December 2009 ... He took 5 for 27 (reducing New Zealand to 28 for 5) on his Test debut at Brisbane in December 2011 ... His brother Darren played one match for England in 2008: they were the first brothers to play Test cricket for different countries since the 19th century ...

THE FIGURES to 17.09.12   **ESPNcricinfO.com**

Batting & Fielding	M	Inns	NO	Runs	HS	Avge	S/R	100	50	4s	6s	Ct	St
Tests	5	6	2	120	37*	30.00	34.88	0	0	16	0	0	0
ODIs	11	6	3	36	13	12.00	57.14	0	0	2	0	2	0
T20Is	4	2	2	5	5*	–	166.66	0	0	1	0	3	0
First-class	14	18	3	212	37*	14.13	32.76	0	0	24	0	5	0

Bowling	M	Balls	Runs	Wkts	BB	Avge	RpO	S/R	5i	10m
Tests	5	881	493	26	5–27	18.96	3.35	33.88	2	0
ODIs	11	553	468	15	4–51	31.20	5.07	36.86	0	0
T20Is	4	78	104	3	2–17	34.66	8.00	26.00	0	0
First-class	14	2710	1396	58	5–27	24.06	3.09	46.72	2	0

THISARA **PERERA**

Full name	**Narangoda Liyanaarachchilage Thisara Chirantha Perera**
Born	**April 3, 1989, Colombo**
Teams	**Colts, Wayamba, Mumbai Indians**
Style	**Left-hand bat, right-arm fast-medium bowler**
Test debut	**Sri Lanka v England at Cardiff 2011**
ODI debut	**Sri Lanka v India at Kolkata 2009-10**
T20I debut	**Sri Lanka v Zimbabwe at Providence 2009-10**

THE PROFILE A big-hitting left-hander who also bowls at a lively pace, Thisara Perera was originally primarily seen as a bowler, taking the new ball for the national under-19 side. He played in the Under-19 World Cup in 2008, and received his first senior call late the following year, replacing the injured Angelo Mathews on tour in India. Perera made his ODI debut there, hammering 31 from just 14 balls at the death. He proved less successful with the ball – none for 66 from nine overs as Gautam Gambhir and Virat Kohli gambolled to centuries. Two matches later he was at it again, slamming 36 from 15 balls to set up another victory, one which improved his bank balance as it led to an IPL contract. Perera's batting didn't fire in his early ODIs, but his bowling did: 5 for 28 as India were skittled for 103 at Dambulla in August 2010, and not long afterwards he bounced in combatively at Melbourne for another five-for, his victims including Michael Clarke and Brad Haddin. After being a fringe performer at the 2011 World Cup – he played only four matches, but that did include the final, in which he slammed 22 from nine balls and took one expensive wicket – Perera made his Test debut at Cardiff in 2011. He made 25 in the first innings and 20 in the second ... but that was the top score as Sri Lanka crashed to 82 all out and a defeat that had looked impossible when the last day began. He hasn't done much in Tests yet, beyond 75 against Pakistan at Pallekele in July 2012, but has started to make his mark in the shorter formats, especially with the ball.

THE FACTS Perera took 5 for 28 as India were bowled out for 103 at Dambulla in August 2010, and 5 for 46 v Australia at Melbourne six weeks later ... He took 6 for 44 v Pakistan at Pallekele in June 2012 ... Perera scored 113 not out, with eight sixes, for Colts v Moors in December 2009, then took a career-best 5 for 69 when Moors batted ...

THE FIGURES *to 17.09.12*   **cricinfo.com**

Batting & Fielding	M	Inns	NO	Runs	HS	Avge	S/R	100	50	4s	6s	Ct	St
Tests	6	10	0	203	75	20.30	73.02	0	1	21	4	1	0
ODIs	44	34	6	476	69*	17.00	112.26	0	1	36	15	19	0
T20Is	13	11	4	116	32*	16.57	138.09	0	0	7	7	5	0
First-class	23	38	6	1050	113*	32.81	85.99	1	6	95	41	11	0

Bowling	M	Balls	Runs	Wkts	BB	Avge	RpO	S/R	5i	10m
Tests	6	954	653	11	4–63	59.36	4.10	86.72	0	0
ODIs	44	1799	1624	67	6–44	24.23	5.41	26.85	3	0
T20Is	13	214	272	9	2–19	30.22	7.62	23.77	0	0
First-class	23	2729	1726	42	5–69	41.09	3.79	64.97	1	0

ALVIRO **PETERSEN**

Full name	**Alviro Nathan Petersen**
Born	**November 25, 1980, Port Elizabeth**
Teams	**Lions, Essex**
Style	**Right-hand bat, occasional medium-pacer**
Test debut	**South Africa v India at Kolkata 2009-10**
ODI debut	**South Africa v Zimbabwe at East London 2006-07**
T20I debut	**South Africa v West Indies at North Sound 2009-10**

THE PROFILE Alviro Petersen grew up in the suburbs of Cape Town, honing his skills at the Gelvandale club, which also produced Ashwell Prince. A century in only his second first-class match kick-started his career in 2001-02, and he was soon playing for South Africa A: but the next step eluded him until 2006, when he hit 80 against Zimbabwe in his second one-day international. However, opportunities at the top of the order were few, and by mid-2008 Petersen had played only three more one-dayers. But then it all changed: in 2008-09 he hit a record 1376 first-class runs, including six centuries, two in the Lions' final game against the Titans. With Gibbs out of favour, Petersen was given another chance in the one-day team, and capitalised with half-centuries in each of his three innings against England. That got him on the plane to India, and he finally made his Test debut at 29 at Kolkata in February 2010. He opened, with his old pal Prince sliding down the order, and made a round 100, pulling and hooking well. It was a particularly sweet moment for Petersen's father, Isaac, who had driven journalists around Cape Town for years and rarely missed an opportunity to remind them of his son's abilities. However, eight further Tests produced only three fifties, and Petersen agreed a return to Glamorgan (who he captained in 2011) as a Kolpak player. But a surprise Test recall in January 2012, after a year, resulted in a century against Sri Lanka – and a change of mind. He added 156 against New Zealand then, after a duck in the run-fest at The Oval, Petersen made 182 in nearly nine hours against England at Headingley in August.

THE FACTS At Kolkata in February 2010 Petersen became only the third batsman to score a century on Test debut for South Africa, following Andrew Hudson (in 1991-92) and Jacques Rudolph (2002-03) ... Petersen made 152 for North West v Northerns at Potchefstroom in February 2009 ... He scored 129 and 105 not out for Lions v Titans at Johannesburg in April 2009, and finished the season with 1376 runs, a South African record ...

THE FIGURES *to 17.09.12*   **ESFil cricinfo.com**

Batting & Fielding	M	Inns	NO	Runs	HS	Avge	S/R	100	50	4s	6s	Ct	St
Tests	16	30	2	1187	182	42.39	51.34	4	3	142	8	9	0
ODIs	17	15	1	437	80	31.21	83.23	0	4	44	3	3	0
T20Is	2	2	0	14	8	7.00	73.68	0	0	1	0	1	0
First-class	146	261	14	9774	210	39.57	–	29	39	–	–	112	0

Bowling	M	Balls	Runs	Wkts	BB	Avge	RpO	S/R	5i	10m
Tests	16	72	36	1	1–2	36.00	3.00	72.00	0	0
ODIs	17	6	7	0	–	–	7.00	–	0	0
T20Is	2	0	–	–	–	–	–	–	–	–
First-class	146	1076	556	11	2–7	50.54	3.10	97.81	0	0

VERNON **PHILANDER**

Full name	**Vernon Darryl Philander**
Born	**June 24, 1985, Bellville**
Teams	**Cape Cobras, Somerset**
Style	**Right-hand bat, right-arm fast-medium bowler**
Test debut	**South Africa v Australia at Cape Town 2011-12**
ODI debut	**South Africa v Ireland at Belfast 2007**
T20I debut	**South Africa v West Indies at Johannesburg 2007-08**

THE PROFILE   The possessor of one of international cricket's more remarkable surnames (Brian Johnston would have loved it, and his initials), the muscular Vernon Philander is a powerful allrounder – mainly a bowler who swings the ball at a decent pace, but also a handy batsman whose two forthright innings did much to swing the 2012 Lord's Test South Africa's way. After a good domestic season for the Cape Cobras, Philander received his first international call-up for the mid-2007 tour of Ireland (a team he had been lined up to play for before a shin stress fracture). In his first match – on his 22nd birthday – he took 4 for 12 to make sure the Irish did not approach South Africa's modest total in a rain-hit game. Philander played a few Twenty20 internationals, and had an unspectacular stint with Middlesex, before apparently fading out of the picture. It seemed that his face didn't fit ... but he was still a force in domestic cricket, following 56 wickets at less than 13 apiece in 2009-10 with 35 at 16 next season, and eventually the selectors brought him back, to face Australia in the criminally short two-Test series late in 2011. Philander made hay, and hasn't stopped harvesting since: he marked his debut with 5 for 15 as Australia were rolled for 47 at Cape Town, collected another five-for in the next Test, then ten in victory over Sri Lanka at Centurion. Philander sprinted to 50 wickets in just seven Tests: only one man has ever done it quicker. And the success continued in England, where he took 5 for 30 to quell English resistance at Lord's, as South Africa cemented their rise to the No. 1 Test ranking.

THE FACTS   Philander reached 50 wickets in only his seventh Test: only Charles Turner, the 19th-century Australian, got there quicker (six) ... Philander's current strike-rate of 33.19 balls per wicket is unapproached by anyone at Test level ... He scored 168 for Western Province v Griqualand West at Kimberley in November 2004, in only his fourth first-class match ... He took 7 for 61 for Cape Cobras v Knights at Cape Town in February 2012 ...

THE FIGURES *to 17.09.12*   **ESPN**cricinfo.com

Batting & Fielding	M	Inns	NO	Runs	HS	Avge	S/R	100	50	4s	6s	Ct	St
Tests	10	11	0	211	61	19.18	46.06	0	1	25	1	3	0
ODIs	8	6	3	75	23	25.00	85.22	0	0	7	0	2	0
T20Is	7	4	0	14	6	3.50	50.00	0	0	0	0	1	0
First-class	87	116	15	2559	168	25.33	47.48	2	7	–	–	23	0

Bowling	M	Balls	Runs	Wkts	BB	Avge	RpO	S/R	5i	10m
Tests	10	2091	1006	63	6–44	15.96	2.88	33.19	7	2
ODIs	8	311	248	7	4–12	35.42	4.78	44.42	0	0
T20Is	7	83	114	4	2–23	28.50	8.24	20.75	0	0
First-class	87	15533	6760	349	7–61	19.36	2.61	44.50	18	2

KEVIN **PIETERSEN**

Full name	**Kevin Peter Pietersen**
Born	**June 27, 1980, Pietermaritzburg, Natal, South Africa**
Teams	**Surrey**
Style	**Right-hand bat, offspinner**
Test debut	**England v Australia at Lord's 2005**
ODI debut	**England v Zimbabwe at Harare 2004-05**
T20I debut	**England v Australia at Southampton 2005**

THE PROFILE Expansive with bat and explosive with bombast, Kevin Pietersen is not one for the quiet life. Bold-minded and big-hitting, he first ruffled feathers by quitting South Africa – he was disenchanted with the race-quota system – in favour of England, his eligibility coming courtesy of an English mother. As soon as he was eligible, he was chosen for a one-day series in Zimbabwe, where he averaged 104. Then, in South Africa, he hammered a robust century in the second match, undeterred by hostile crowds. Test cricket was next. In 2005 he replaced Graham Thorpe, against Australia, at Lord's ... and coolly blasted a brace of fifties. Then, with the Ashes at stake, he hit 158 on the final day at The Oval: "KP" had arrived. The runs kept coming: 158 at Adelaide and 226 against West Indies at Headingley sandwiched two tons in the 2007 World Cup. Late the following year he succeeded Michael Vaughan as captain, starting with a hundred as South Africa were beaten in the Oval Test, then inspiring a one-day landslide. But his captaincy ended in tears after a fallout with the coach, then his form dipped as he battled an Achilles problem. But just as people were beginning to wonder, Pietersen hammered 227 at Adelaide in December 2010 then hit another double-century against India at Lord's and 175 at The Oval to emphasise that he wasn't going anywhere just yet. Things went pear-shaped, though, in 2012: not long after announcing his retirement from one-day cricket, Pietersen was dropped – despite just having stroked a superb 149 – from the final Test of the summer, after it emerged that he had been texting the South Africans with derogatory remarks about Andrew Strauss. Much humble pie had to be eaten before he was welcomed back into the England dressing-room.

THE FACTS Pietersen reached 100 against South Africa at East London in February 2005 in 69 balls, the fastest for England in ODIs ... He averages 64.60 in ODIs v South Africa – but 14.80 v Bangladesh ... Pietersen was out for 158 three times in Tests before going on to 226 against West Indies in May 2007 ... His record includes two ODIs for the World XI ...

THE FIGURES *to 17.09.12*

ᴇsʀⁿ cricinfo.com

Batting & Fielding	M	Inns	NO	Runs	HS	Avge	S/R	100	50	4s	6s	Ct	St
Tests	88	157	8	7076	227	49.48	63.26	21	27	857	68	53	0
ODIs	127	116	16	4184	130	41.84	86.76	9	23	398	73	39	0
T20Is	36	36	5	1176	79	37.93	141.51	0	7	119	32	14	0
First-class	191	313	21	14545	254*	49.81	–	45	61	–	–	139	0

Bowling	M	Balls	Runs	Wkts	BB	Avge	RpO	S/R	5i	10m
Tests	88	1239	844	9	3–52	93.77	4.08	137.66	0	0
ODIs	127	400	370	7	2–22	52.85	5.55	57.14	0	0
T20Is	36	30	53	1	1–27	53.00	10.60	30.00	0	0
First-class	191	6271	3657	71	4–31	51.50	3.49	88.32	0	0

KIERON **POLLARD**

Full name	**Kieron Adrian Pollard**
Born	**May 12, 1987, Cacariqua, Trinidad**
Teams	**Trinidad, Mumbai Indians**
Style	**Right-hand bat, right-arm medium-pacer**
Test debut	**No Tests yet**
ODI debut	**West Indies v South Africa at St George's 2006-07**
T20I debut	**West Indies v Australia at Bridgetown 2008**

THE PROFILE Kieron Pollard shot to prominence in 2006-07 when still only 19, with his muscular batting doing much to take Trinidad & Tobago to the final of the inaugural Stanford 20/20 competition: in the semi-final, against Nevis, he clobbered 83 in only 38 balls, and then grabbed a couple of wickets with his medium-pacers. That won him a first-class start against Barbados: he got off the mark with a six, and added six more on his way to 117. Another hundred, and six more sixes, followed in his third match, and in between he hit 87 off 58 balls – seven sixes this time – in a one-dayer against Guyana. That was followed by inclusion in West Indies' squad for the 2007 World Cup. The cometary rise almost inevitably tailed off a little: he finished his first Carib Beer season with 420 runs at 42, and played only once in the World Cup itself. Pollard spent some time on the sidelines after that, but his big-hitting potential earned him megabucks contracts in the IPL, and in England and Australia (he thumped 52 off 22 balls against Victoria early in 2010). But while his bank balance rocketed, international success proved elusive: Pollard's first 50 limited-overs internationals featured only one half-century, and although he added three more in the first half of 2011, two of them came against Netherlands and Ireland in the World Cup. He continued to consolidate at one-day level, making a maiden century – with ten sixes – against India at Chennai in December 2011. He added another (only eight sixes this time) against Australia in St Vincent in March 2012, but there was still no sign of a Test cap.

THE FACTS Pollard made 126 on his first-class debut, for Trinidad & Tobago v Barbados in January 2007: he hit 11 fours and seven sixes, one of which got him off the mark ... In his second match he hit 69 in 31 balls, with six sixes, and in his third 117 from 87 balls with 11 fours and six more sixes ... In a Twenty20 match for Somerset in 2010 Pollard failed by just a couple of inches to become only the second person ever to hit a ball over the Lord's pavilion ...

THE FIGURES to 17.09.12   **ESPN**cricinfo.com

Batting & Fielding	M	Inns	NO	Runs	HS	Avge	S/R	100	50	4s	6s	Ct	St
Tests	0	0	–	–	–	–	–	–	–	–	–	–	–
ODIs	43	39	1	826	94	21.73	102.22	0	4	55	36	19	0
T20Is	20	17	2	190	38	12.66	124.18	0	0	17	8	11	0
First-class	21	34	1	1247	174	37.78	–	3	5	–	–	32	0

Bowling	M	Balls	Runs	Wkts	BB	Avge	RpO	S/R	5i	10m
Tests	0	0	–	–	–	–	–	–	–	–
ODIs	43	1289	1126	35	3–27	32.17	5.24	36.82	0	0
T20Is	20	258	360	11	2–22	32.72	8.37	23.45	0	0
First-class	21	643	349	7	2–29	49.85	3.25	91.85	0	0

RICKY **PONTING**

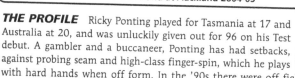

AUSTRALIA

Full name **Ricky Thomas Ponting**
Born **December 19, 1974, Launceston, Tasmania**
Teams **Tasmania**
Style **Right-hand bat, right-arm medium-pace bowler**
Test debut **Australia v Sri Lanka at Perth 1995-96**
ODI debut **Australia v South Africa at Wellington 1994-95**
T20I debut **Australia v New Zealand at Auckland 2004-05**

THE PROFILE Ricky Ponting played for Tasmania at 17 and Australia at 20, and was unluckily given out for 96 on his Test debut. A gambler and a buccaneer, Ponting has had setbacks, against probing seam and high-class finger-spin, which he plays with hard hands when off form. In the '90s there were off-field indiscretions, but his growing maturity was acknowledged when he succeeded Steve Waugh as one-day captain in 2002. It was a seamless transition: Ponting led the 2003 World Cup campaign from the front, clouting a coruscating century in the final, and took over in Tests too when Waugh finally stepped down early in 2004. But things changed the following year. A humiliating one-day defeat by Bangladesh was followed by the loss of the Ashes, after a fabulous series. The loss of the urn hurt, and the pain lingered. Ponting bounced back by winning 11 of 12 Tests in 2005-06, which was just a warm-up for the following season's Ashes rematch. He led that off with 196 at Brisbane, and remained tight-lipped until the 5-0 whitewash was sealed. He retained the World Cup in 2007, and sailed past 25,000 international runs during 2010, but Ashes defeats in 2009 and 2010-11 reopened those old wounds far enough to have Ponting dreaming of a possible return to England in 2013. But he won't be captain, having passed the reins to Michael Clarke after Australia's early elimination from the 2011 World Cup: Ponting returned to the ranks, and kept hold of his place by following 134 against India at Sydney in January 2012 with 221 at Adelaide. Soon after that, though, he was elbowed out of the one-day side.

THE FACTS Ponting uniquely scored two hundreds in his 100th Test, against South Africa at Sydney in January 2006 ... His 242 against India at Adelaide in 2003-04 is the highest in a losing cause in a Test (in the next game he made 257, and they won) ... When he was 8, Ponting's grandmother gave him a T-shirt that read "Under this shirt is a Test player" ... His record includes one ODI for the World XI ...

THE FIGURES to 17.09.12   **ESPNcricinfo.com**

Batting & Fielding	M	Inns	NO	Runs	HS	Avge	S/R	100	50	4s	6s	Ct	St
Tests	165	282	29	13346	257	52.75	58.76	41	62	1503	73	194	0
ODIs	375	365	39	13704	164	42.03	80.39	30	82	1231	162	160	0
T20Is	17	16	2	401	98*	28.64	132.78	0	2	41	11	8	0
First-class	273	467	56	22714	257	55.26	–	77	101	–	–	289	0

Bowling	M	Balls	Runs	Wkts	BB	Avge	RpO	S/R	5i	10m
Tests	165	575	273	5	1–0	54.60	2.84	115.00	0	0
ODIs	375	150	104	3	1–12	34.66	4.16	50.00	0	0
T20Is	17	–	–	–	–	–	–	–	–	–
First-class	273	1470	799	14	2–10	57.07	3.26	105.00	0	0

KIERAN **POWELL**

Full name	**Kieran Omar Akeem Powell**
Born	**March 6, 1990, Nevis**
Teams	**Leeward Islands**
Style	**Left-hand bat**
Test debut	**West Indies v India at Roseau 2011**
ODI debut	**West Indies v Bangladesh at Basseterre 2009**
T20I debut	**No T20Is yet**

THE PROFILE A powerful opener, Kieran Powell started playing cricket when he was eight – initially alongside his brother Alan, who followed him into Nevis's youth teams. But Kieran trained on, and made the West Indian Under-19 squad. His first taste of big cricket came in the Stanford 20/20 competition in 2006, and two years later he scored at a healthy clip in the Under-19 World Cup. Powell was drafted into the makeshift squad that took on Bangladesh – and lost – in mid-2009, when the senior players withdrew in a contracts dispute. Powell made his one-day debut at home in St Kitts ... and was lbw to the first ball of the match. Not long afterwards the dispute was finally settled, and the seniors returned – but Powell kept his name in the frame with a century against England Lions early in 2011, and made his Test debut against India that July ... but failed again with 3 and 4. But then he came up against Bangladesh, hit 72 in a Test at Mirpur, and added 81 against India shortly afterwards. Powell, like several of his team-mates, struggled in England in the first part of the 2012 summer, but looked a different prospect back home, especially once Chris Gayle was restored to the top of the order. Powell made his maiden century in the first Test against New Zealand in July, helping Gayle add 254 for the first wicket. "There was a time I used to go in and look to play all the shots and see how many I could get," said Powell, whose innings lasted six hours. All that has changed now. I'm more settled and aware of my role."

THE FACTS Powell was only the sixth Test cricketer from Nevis, following Elquemedo Willett, Derick Parry, Keith Arthurton, Stuart Williams and the late Runako Morton ... Powell made 131 for Leeward Islands v England Lions at Basseterre in February 2011, and 139 for West Indies A v India A in St Lucia in June 2012 ... Powell and Chris Gayle put on 254 against New Zealand in Antigua in July 2012, West Indies' fourth-highest opening stand in Tests ...

THE FIGURES to 17.09.12   ESPNcricinfo.com

Batting & Fielding	M	Inns	NO	Runs	HS	Avge	S/R	100	50	4s	6s	Ct	St
Tests	11	21	0	535	134	25.47	45.72	1	2	73	1	5	0
ODIs	8	8	0	72	25	9.00	64.86	0	0	10	1	1	0
T20Is	0	0	–	–	–	–	–	–	–	–	–	–	–
First-class	42	73	4	2425	139	35.14	–	4	12	–	–	19	0

Bowling	M	Balls	Runs	Wkts	BB	Avge	RpO	S/R	5i	10m
Tests	11	0	–	–	–	–	–	–	–	–
ODIs	8	0	–	–	–	–	–	–	–	–
T20Is	0	0	–	–	–	–	–	–	–	–
First-class	42	43	34	0	–	–	4.74	–	0	0

NUWAN **PRADEEP**

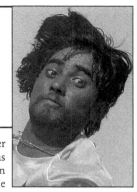

Full name	**Aththachchi Nuwan Pradeep Roshan Fernando**
Born	**October 19, 1986, Negombo**
Teams	**Bloomfield, Basnahira**
Style	**Right-hand bat, right-arm fast-medium bowler**
Test debut	**Sri Lanka v Pakistan at Abu Dhabi 2011-12**
ODI debut	**Sri Lanka v India at Colombo 2012**
T20I debut	**No T20Is yet**

THE PROFILE Nuwan Pradeep didn't play with a proper cricket ball until he was 20 – but less than three years later he was in the Test squad. He won a pace contest at a soft-ball event in 2007, and was sent straight to Sri Lanka's Cricket's academy. He follows in the local tradition of unconventional bowlers: like Lasith Malinga, he has a slinging action, and has troubled many in domestic cricket with his speed, generated from a long run-up. "He's got raw pace, beautiful rhythm and consistency," says the national bowling coach Champaka Ramanayake. Pradeep's early international career, though, was stymied by injury. In May 2011 he took 4 for 29 against the England Lions at Derby, and looked set to feature in the Tests ... but was forced home with knee trouble. Then, at the end of the year, he had sent down just ten balls in a warm-up game in South Africa when he tore a hamstring, and was out for another three months. He had made his Test debut in Abu Dhabi a couple of months previously, but went wicketless as Pakistan amassed 511 for 6. When Pakistan toured Sri Lanka in mid-2012 Pradeep won two more caps, but managed only one wicket (the debutant Mohammad Ayub at Galle) and was promptly dropped again, nursing an embarrassing bowling average. An injury to Nuwan Kulasekara meant he was recalled for his first one-day internationals against India shortly afterwards: although he proved a little expensive he did produce a jaffa to castle Rohit Sharma at Pallekele. Pradeep is no batsman – perhaps a legacy of his late start – and may have to improve before he can become a regular in the national team.

THE FACTS After three Tests Pradeep's bowling average was 690 times higher than his batting one, an unprecedented figure ... He took 5 for 36 for Bloomfield against Ragama in December 2008 ... He was signed by Bangalore Royal Challengers for the 2011 IPL, but didn't actually play ...

THE FIGURES *to 17.09.12*   **ESPNcricinfo.com**

Batting & Fielding	M	Inns	NO	Runs	HS	Avge	S/R	100	50	4s	6s	Ct	St
Tests	3	4	0	2	1	0.50	13.33	0	0	0	0	0	0
ODIs	2	1	1	0	0*	–	–	0	0	0	0	0	0
T20Is	0	0	–	–	–	–	–	–	–	–	–	–	–
First-class	40	50	19	104	16	3.35	39.84	0	0	13	3	17	0

Bowling	M	Balls	Runs	Wkts	BB	Avge	RpO	S/R	5i	10m
Tests	3	504	345	1	1-56	345.00	4.10	504.00	0	0
ODIs	2	108	115	3	2-63	38.33	6.38	36.00	0	0
T20Is	0	0	–	–	–	–	–	–	–	–
First-class	40	3748	2525	65	5-36	38.84	4.04	57.66	1	0

RAYMOND **PRICE**

Full name	**Raymond William Price**
Born	**June 12, 1976, Salisbury (now Harare)**
Teams	**Mashonaland Eagles**
Style	**Right-hand bat, slow left-arm orthodox spinner**
Test debut	**Zimbabwe v Sri Lanka at Harare 1999-2000**
ODI debut	**Zimbabwe v India at Colombo 2002-03**
T20I debut	**Zimbabwe v Sri Lanka at King City 2008-09**

THE PROFILE   A slow left-armer who takes wickets with guile and aggression, rather than massive spin, Ray Price has the tenacity and self-belief to compete against the best. He took seven wickets in only his second Test, against Bangladesh at Harare in April 2001, and generally did well in his early matches, picking up consecutive five-fors against South Africa and India in 2001-02 and 6 for 121 in Australia's first innings at Sydney in October 2003. He almost bowled Zimbabwe to a remarkable victory in the first Test against West Indies in November that year (6 for 73 and 4 for 88), but was denied by the obdurate pair of Ridley Jacobs and Fidel Edwards. He collected nine more wickets in the second match to cap a superb year – 33 wickets in just five Tests. But just as he had established himself, Price was part of the "rebellion" which cost Zimbabwe several senior players in 2004-05. He joined Worcestershire, doing well at first and inspiring suggestions that he might qualify for England. But he rejected the offer of a new contract for 2008, and rejoined the national team. Since then he has been successful and parsimonious in one-day cricket, rising to second in the ICC world bowling rankings in 2009: two years later he was a calm presence in Zimbabwe's Test return, wheeling down 50.1 overs (for 2 for 69) in the first innings of their second Test back, against Pakistan at Bulawayo in September 2011. He remains an experienced elder statesman in a largely young team – although there were signs in 2012 that his powers might be declining a little, as his economy-rate began to creep up. Price suffers from partial deafness, caused by the after-effects of meningitis as a youngster.

THE FACTS   Price took 8 for 35 (12 for 79 in the match) for Midlands against the CFX Academy at Kwekwe in April 2002: later that year he took 8 for 78 against Matabeleland at Bulawayo ... When Matthew Hayden broke the Test record with 380 at Perth in October 2003, Price's figures were 0 for 187: in the next Test, at Sydney, he took 6 for 121 ... His uncle, Nick Price, won three major golf championships, including the British Open in 1994 ...

THE FIGURES to 17.09.12   **ESPNcricinfo.com**

Batting & Fielding	M	Inns	NO	Runs	HS	Avge	S/R	100	50	4s	6s	Ct	St
Tests	21	36	7	242	36	8.34	30.36	0	0	39	0	4	0
ODIs	102	59	17	406	46	9.66	57.91	0	0	31	5	17	0
T20Is	15	8	3	8	3	1.60	36.36	0	0	0	0	3	0
First-class	113	178	32	2422	117*	16.58	–	1	11	–	–	57	0

Bowling	M	Balls	Runs	Wkts	BB	Avge	RpO	S/R	5i	10m
Tests	21	6027	2838	79	6–73	35.92	2.82	76.29	5	1
ODIs	102	5374	3575	100	4–22	35.75	3.99	53.74	0	0
T20Is	15	351	359	13	2–6	27.61	6.13	27.00	0	0
First-class	113	27003	11796	404	8–35	29.19	2.62	66.83	20	3

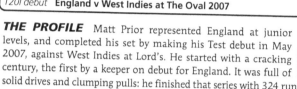

MATT **PRIOR**

Full name	**Matthew James Prior**
Born	**February 26, 1982, Johannesburg, South Africa**
Teams	**Sussex**
Style	**Right-hand bat, wicketkeeper**
Test debut	**England v West Indies at Lord's 2007**
ODI debut	**England v Zimbabwe at Bulawayo 2004-05**
T20I debut	**England v West Indies at The Oval 2007**

THE PROFILE   Matt Prior represented England at junior levels, and completed his set by making his Test debut in May 2007, against West Indies at Lord's. He started with a cracking century, the first by a keeper on debut for England. It was full of solid drives and clumping pulls: he finished that series with 324 runs – but there were already rumbles about his wicketkeeping technique, which didn't seem to matter while England were winning. But then India arrived, and Prior's fumbles were magnified as the series slipped away: he dropped Tendulkar and Laxman as India ran up 664 at The Oval. The runs dried up, too, and suddenly Prior's talkativeness behind the stumps, and his footwork, were called into question. He went back to Hove and sharpened up his technique, and was ready when his replacement (and former Sussex team-mate) Tim Ambrose faltered himself during 2008: Prior returned for the one-dayers against South Africa, and pouched six catches (one of them a one-handed flying stunner) at Trent Bridge. By 2009 he looked even more the part – and even more like his mentor, Alec Stewart – in the Ashes victory. More runs followed in 2010, including an important century to swell the lead over Pakistan at Trent Bridge: Prior was entrenched as England's Test keeper, and emphasised that with an Ashes century at Sydney in January 2011, two more tons in the home English summer that followed, and consistent runs after a slowish start in 2012. The only downside was that he lost his one-day place again after the World Cup. Prior was born in South Africa, but moved to England at 11: he says he lost his accent within a week.

THE FACTS   Prior was the 17th man to score a century on Test debut for England: he was the fifth to score a century on debut at Lord's, after Australia's Harry Graham, John Hampshire and Andrew Strauss of England, and India's Sourav Ganguly ... Prior equalled the ODI wicketkeeping record with six catches against South Africa at Nottingham in August 2008 ... He made 201 not out for Sussex v Loughborough University at Hove in May 2004 ...

THE FIGURES to 17.09.12   **ESPN** cricinfo.com

Batting & Fielding	M	Inns	NO	Runs	HS	Avge	S/R	100	50	4s	6s	Ct	St
Tests	58	87	15	3568	131*	42.61	64.82	6	22	343	12	167	12
ODIs	68	62	9	1282	87	24.18	76.76	0	3	141	6	71	8
T20Is	10	8	2	127	32	21.16	127.00	0	0	11	5	6	3
First-class	213	324	37	11502	201*	40.07	67.71	26	66	–	–	536	39

Bowling	M	Balls	Runs	Wkts	BB	Avge	RpO	S/R	5i	10m
Tests	58	0	–	–	–	–	–	–	–	–
ODIs	68	0	–	–	–	–	–	–	–	–
T20Is	10	0	–	–	–	–	–	–	–	–
First-class	213	0	–	–	–	–	–	–	–	–

CHETESHWAR **PUJARA**

Full name	**Cheteshwar Arvind Pujara**
Born	**January 25, 1988, Rajkot, Gujarat**
Teams	**Saurashtra, Royal Challengers Bangalore**
Style	**Right-hand bat, occasional legspinner**
Test debut	**India v Australia at Bangalore 2010-11**
ODI debut	**No ODIs yet**
T20I debut	**No T20Is yet**

THE PROFILE   After years of prolific runscoring at domestic level, Cheteshwar Pujara finally got an opportunity in a Test match, against Australia in October 2010. He made it count, coming in at No. 3 instead of Rahul Dravid and making an excellent 72 in a tricky run-chase. Pujara's game-plan is simple, and he plays within his limitations. His technique is classical: upright at the crease and confident on both sides of the wicket. The son of a former Ranji Trophy player, Pujara was a mighty achiever at age-group cricket: in 2006 he had been the leading scorer at the Under-19 World Cup, and before that had made a triple-century for Saurashtra's Under-14s and 211 in an Under-19 Test against England. The runs just kept stacking up: 907 in first-class cricket in 2007-08, and more than 1000 the following season. In 2008-09 he had a purple patch Don Bradman would have been hard-pushed to match: two triple-centuries for Saurashtra's Under-22s were followed by one in first-class cricket too, all in the space of little more than a month. The figures couldn't be ignored, and after a double-century while captaining the A team in England Pujara finally got the Test call. He started well, but following two failures in South Africa he injured his knee during IPL4. It needed an operation, and he was out of international action for more than a year. He returned as captain of India A, scoring 50 and 96 not out in the "Test" at Bridgetown in June 2012, and then made a triumphant return to the full Test side, with 159 against New Zealand at Hyderabad in August, an innings notable for his ability to put the bad balls away. *The Times of India* had previously likened him to Dravid, with added power: "He is like the Wall, but packs a wallop too."

THE FACTS   Pujara scored 386 and 309 in successive matches for Saurashtra Under-22s in October 2008 ... Next month he made 302 not out in Saurashtra's Ranji Trophy match against Orissa at Rajkot, sharing a stand of 520 with Ravindra Jadeja ... Pujara made his first triple-century shortly before his 13th birthday, for Saurashtra's Under-14s in January 2001 ... Eight of his 15 first-class hundreds have been scores of 150 or more ...

THE FIGURES *to 17.09.12*   **espncricinfo.com**

Batting & Fielding	M	Inns	NO	Runs	HS	Avge	S/R	100	50	4s	6s	Ct	St
Tests	5	8	0	323	159	40.37	50.94	1	1	39	1	6	0
ODIs	0	0	–	–	–	–	–	–	–	–	–	–	–
T20Is	0	0	–	–	–	–	–	–	–	–	–	–	–
First-class	66	107	17	4855	302*	53.94	–	15	21	–	–	40	0

Bowling	M	Balls	Runs	Wkts	BB	Avge	RpO	S/R	5i	10m
Tests	5	0	–	–	–	–	–	–	–	–
ODIs	0	0	–	–	–	–	–	–	–	–
T20Is	0	0	–	–	–	–	–	–	–	–
First-class	66	153	83	5	2–4	16.60	3.25	30.60	0	0

SURESH **RAINA**

Full name **Suresh Kumar Raina**
Born **November 27, 1986, Ghaziabad, Uttar Pradesh**
Teams **Uttar Pradesh, Chennai Super Kings**
Style **Left-hand bat, occasional offspinner**
Test debut **India v Sri Lanka at Colombo 2010**
ODI debut **India v Sri Lanka at Dambulla 2005**
T20I debut **India v South Africa at Johannesburg 2006-07**

THE PROFILE In April 2005 Suresh Raina strolled in to bat in the domestic one-day final, spanked nine fours and a six in 48 from 33 balls as Uttar Pradesh tied with Tamil Nadu and shared the title, then left to catch the flight home for his school exams. The following season his 620 runs helped UP win the Ranji Trophy for the first time. Electric fielding added zing to India's one-day side, but eventually the runs dried up, and he was dropped early in 2007 after 16 innings without a half-century. A powerful left-hander, he was back a year later and hit two centuries in the Asia Cup in June 2008, against Hong Kong and Bangladesh, then made 53 and 76 in Sri Lanka as India fought back to win the one-day series there. In New Zealand at the start of 2009 he slammed 61 not out from 43 balls in a Twenty20 international then 66 from 39 in a one-dayer, but was underwhelming in the World Twenty20 in England in June. Test cricket seemed to have passed him by, but after a record 98 ODIs he finally made his debut in Sri Lanka the following month, and made up for lost time with a fine 120, adding 62 and 41 not out in the next match. He joined the 2011 World Cup party late, playing only the last four matches – but that included the joyous final, in which he didn't need to bat. After that, though, Raina had a tough time in the Tests in England, his ponderous technique against the short stuff being exposed. That cost him his five-day place for a while, but he remained a reliable one-day performer throughout 2012 – and cracked a first-class double-century to show that he could still knuckle down in the long game too.

THE FACTS Raina played a record 98 ODIs before his first Test in July 2010 – then promptly became the 12th Indian to score a century on debut ... He captained India in an ODI before he played in a Test ... Raina made 204 not out for Uttar Pradesh v Punjab in November 2011, and 203 for UP v Orrissa in November 2007 ... Raina made 520 runs in the third IPL in 2010, a number exceeded only by Sachin Tendulkar and Jacques Kallis ...

THE FIGURES *to 17.09.12*   ESPncricinfo.com

Batting & Fielding	M	Inns	NO	Runs	HS	Avge	S/R	100	50	4s	6s	Ct	St
Tests	17	29	2	768	120	28.44	53.29	1	7	100	4	22	0
ODIs	151	131	27	3699	116*	35.56	93.66	3	24	312	80	63	0
T20Is	27	24	4	653	101	32.90	137.94	1	3	56	28	9	0
First-class	73	121	7	4832	204*	42.38	59.87	9	33	–	–	83	0

Bowling	M	Balls	Runs	Wkts	BB	Avge	RpO	S/R	5i	10m
Tests	17	921	532	13	2–1	40.92	3.46	70.84	0	0
ODIs	151	1003	853	16	2–17	53.31	5.10	62.68	0	0
T20Is	27	84	129	5	2–49	25.80	9.21	16.80	0	0
First-class	73	2157	1104	26	3–31	42.46	3.07	82.96	0	0

DENESH **RAMDIN**

Full name	**Denesh Ramdin**
Born	**March 13, 1985, Couva, Trinidad**
Teams	**Trinidad & Tobago**
Style	**Right-hand bat, wicketkeeper**
Test debut	**West Indies v Sri Lanka at Colombo 2005**
ODI debut	**West Indies v India at Dambulla 2005**
T20I debut	**West Indies v New Zealand at Auckland 2005-06**

THE PROFILE Originally a fast bowler who kept wicket when he had finished with the ball, at 13 Denesh Ramdin decided to concentrate on keeping. He led both the Trinidad and West Indies Under-19 sides before in 2005, still only 19 and with Ridley Jacobs retired, Ramdin went to Sri Lanka as the first-choice keeper. He impressed everyone with his work behind and in front of the stumps, and continued to do so in Australia later in 2005, especially with a plucky 71 at Hobart, where he shared a fine partnership of 182 with his fellow Trinidadian Dwayne Bravo. Carlton Baugh was preferred for some of the home one-dayers early in 2006, and it was a surprise when Ramdin returned for the Tests against India. But he justified his selection with some neat keeping on pitches on which the ball often died before it reached him, and a gritty unbeaten 62 that nearly brought victory in the deciding fourth Test in Jamaica. But the runs dried up after that, and his keeping went off a little too: but early in 2009 he cashed in on a Bridgetown featherbed to make a seven-hour 166 against England. Another fallow period followed, and the selectors went back to Baugh (then, when he was injured just before the 2011 World Cup, to Devon Thomas). But when Baugh also failed to provide enough runs, Ramdin returned for the 2012 tour of England – and silenced his critics with an unbeaten century at Edgbaston. Those critics had included Viv Richards, and Ramdin pointedly unfurled a message telling Sir Viv what he thought. He copped a fine for that – but he had got his Test place back for a while.

THE FACTS Ramdin's 166 against England at Bridgetown in 2008-09 was the second-highest score by a West Indian wicketkeeper in a Test, after Clyde Walcott's 168 not out at Lord's in 1950 ... Ramdin also made 166 not out for Trinidad and Tobago v Barbados in January 2010 ... He played in the West Indies side that won the Under-15 World Challenge in 2000, beating Pakistan in the Lord's final; four years later he captained in the Under-19 World Cup, when WI lost the final at Dhaka – to Pakistan ...

THE FIGURES *to 17.09.12* 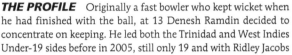 **ᴇsᴘɴcricinfo.com**

Batting & Fielding	M	Inns	NO	Runs	HS	Avge	S/R	100	50	4s	6s	Ct	St
Tests	47	80	9	1663	166	23.42	48.09	2	8	219	2	135	3
ODIs	94	71	16	1105	96	20.09	75.68	0	3	90	3	125	6
T20Is	26	18	5	229	44	17.61	115.65	0	0	28	2	21	5
First-class	102	167	23	4403	166*	30.57	–	10	19	–	–	270	24

Bowling	M	Balls	Runs	Wkts	BB	Avge	RpO	S/R	5i	10m
Tests	47	0	–	–	–	–	–	–	–	–
ODIs	94	0	–	–	–	–	–	–	–	–
T20Is	26	0	–	–	–	–	–	–	–	–
First-class	102	0	–	–	–	–	–	–	–	–

RAVI **RAMPAUL**

Full name	**Ravindranath Rampaul**
Born	**October 15, 1984, Preysal, Trinidad**
Teams	**Trinidad & Tobago**
Style	**Left-hand bat, right-arm fast-medium bowler**
Test debut	**West Indies v Australia at Brisbane 2009-10**
ODI debut	**West Indies v Zimbabwe at Bulawayo 2003-04**
T20I debut	**West Indies v England at The Oval 2007**

THE PROFILE Ravi Rampaul is tall and well-built, but his career has been hamstrung by injuries and ill-luck. He made his Trinidad debut in 2002, and 18 wickets in six matches the following season – and an aggressive approach – propelled him to the verge of full international selection. Just 19, he made his ODI debut late in 2003: he was rarely collared, but hardly ran through sides either – in 14 matches he took nine wickets, only once managing more than one, a statistic that was echoed when his Test career eventually started. Nonetheless he was retained for the 2004 England tour, and played three more ODIs before he broke down and returned home ahead of the Tests. Sidelined by shin splints, Rampaul did not play another first-class match until 2006-07, taking 7 for 51 as T&T beat Barbados in the Carib Beer final. That won him another England tour but, restricted by a groin tear, he again missed the Tests, before helping to turn the one-day series around with 4 for 41 in the pivotal second match at Edgbaston. Rampaul finally made his Test debut in Australia late in 2009 – he'd been around so long it was a surprise he was still only 25 – but although he worked up a fair head of steam, success proved elusive at first. He took only four wickets in his first five Tests, but his strike-rate improved with 21 wickets in five further matches against Pakistan and India in mid-2011, and although the big hauls continued to elude him he continued to threaten, and by late 2012 had an enviable Test economy-rate too.

THE FACTS Rampaul scored 86 not out against India at Visakhapatnam in December 2011, the highest score by a No. 10 batsman in any ODI ... He took 7 for 51 as Trinidad & Tobago beat Barbados in the final of the Carib Beer Challenge at Pointe-à-Pierre in February 2007 ... In the World Under-15 Challenge in 2000, Rampaul took 7 for 11 against the Netherlands ... He played for Ireland in the Friends Provident Trophy in 2008 ...

THE FIGURES to 17.09.12   **ESPN**cricinfo.com

Batting & Fielding	M	Inns	NO	Runs	HS	Avge	S/R	100	50	4s	6s	Ct	St
Tests	17	30	8	330	40*	15.00	53.92	0	0	40	10	3	0
ODIs	70	31	7	314	86*	13.08	79.89	0	1	29	11	10	0
T20Is	12	4	3	11	8	11.00	61.11	0	0	0	0	0	0
First-class	58	85	14	963	64*	13.56	–	0	2	–	–	18	0

Bowling	M	Balls	Runs	Wkts	BB	Avge	RpO	S/R	5i	10m
Tests	17	3182	1555	44	4–48	35.34	2.93	72.31	0	0
ODIs	70	2989	2524	83	5–51	30.40	5.06	36.01	1	0
T20Is	12	275	408	16	3–17	25.50	8.90	17.18	0	0
First-class	58	9219	5123	168	7–51	30.49	3.33	54.87	6	1

SURAJ **RANDIV**

Full name	**Hewa Kaluhalamullage Suraj Randiv Kaluhalamulla**
Born	**January 30, 1985, Matara**
Teams	**Bloomfield, Kandurata**
Style	**Right-hand bat, offspinner**
Test debut	**Sri Lanka v India at Colombo 2010**
ODI debut	**Sri Lanka v India at Nagpur 2009-10**
T20I debut	**Sri Lanka v Zimbabwe at Providence 2009-10**

THE PROFILE Suraj Randiv – who changed his name from Mohamed Marshuk Mohamed Suraj in 2009, after converting to Buddhism – had the unenviable task of replacing Muttiah Muralitharan as Sri Lanka's offspinner. A consistent domestic performer, Randiv made his Test debut in July 2010 in the match immediately following Murali's retirement, and matched his predecessor's appetite for hard work by toiling through 73 overs in the first innings, taking 2 for 222. On a more sporting pitch for the third Test, at Colombo's Sara Oval, Randiv claimed nine wickets, including all five to fall in the second innings as India successfully chased 257. After that, though, he faded a little: he was not in the original 2011 World Cup squad, although he was summoned very late as a replacement and controversially played in the final. He had a quiet time in England in 2011, apart from 5 for 42 in the ODI at Old Trafford, and has rarely featured in the one-day side since. But in Tests he has formed a useful spin partnership with left-armer Rangana Herath: Randiv took six wickets (to Herath's 12) as England were beaten at Galle in March 2012, and seven when Pakistan succumbed there three months later. Randiv actually started as a fast bowler, but switched to offspin at school. He is a tidy bowler – and a better batsman than Murali, with a first-class century as nightwatchman to his name – but doesn't possess the variety of his illustrious predecessor. He took 55 first-class wickets at 15.05 in domestic cricket in 2005-06, including the first of his two nine-wicket hauls, and after a couple of quieter seasons returned to top form with 43 in 2008-09 and 67 (at 20.85) the following season.

THE FACTS Randiv took 2 for 222 in his first Test innings, the most runs ever conceded by a debutant ... He claimed 9 for 62 for Sinhalese SC v Colombo CC in February 2006 ... Randiv took 9 for 109 (the other wicket was a run-out) for Bloomfield v Army in October 2009: earlier in the match he had scored his maiden century ...

THE FIGURES to 17.09.12   **ESFIFicricinfo.com**

Batting & Fielding	M	Inns	NO	Runs	HS	Avge	S/R	100	50	4s	6s	Ct	St
Tests	10	14	1	99	18	7.61	30.00	0	0	12	0	1	0
ODIs	28	15	1	239	56	17.07	71.55	0	1	24	1	6	0
T20Is	7	2	0	8	6	4.00	133.33	0	0	1	0	0	0
First-class	88	122	22	1867	112	18.67	52.06	1	6	–	–	59	0

Bowling	M	Balls	Runs	Wkts	BB	Avge	RpO	S/R	5i	10m
Tests	10	2659	1383	38	5–82	36.39	3.12	69.97	1	0
ODIs	28	1269	1008	33	5–42	30.54	4.76	38.45	1	0
T20Is	7	126	139	7	3–20	19.85	6.61	18.00	0	0
First-class	88	17585	10039	390	9–62	25.74	3.42	45.08	26	8

KEMAR **ROACH**

WEST INDIES

Full name	**Kemar Andre Jamal Roach**
Born	**June 30, 1988, St Lucy, Barbados**
Teams	**Barbados**
Style	**Right-hand bat, right-arm fast-medium bowler**
Test debut	**West Indies v Bangladesh at Kingstown 2009**
ODI debut	**West Indies v Bermuda at King City 2008**
T20I debut	**West Indies v Australia at Bridgetown 2008**

THE PROFILE   A genuinely fast bowler with a free-flowing action, Kemar Roach was only 19, and had played only four first-class matches, when he was called into the squad for the third Test against Australia at Bridgetown in June 2008. Roach didn't actually play, but he was included for the Twenty20 international shortly afterwards, and took two of the three wickets to fall, dismissing both Australian openers after starting with a nervous beamer. The following year he was one of West Indies' few successes after the senior players withdrew from the series against Bangladesh, taking 13 wickets in the two Tests. Floyd Reifer, his captain then, observed: "He does a lot, especially with the old ball, getting it to move in and out." Roach hit trouble during the ODIs, when he let loose two beamers and was taken off and fined, but he still took ten wickets. When the seniors returned Roach retained his place, winning admirers in Australia in 2009-10 for his hostile pace. He unsettled Ricky Ponting, dismissing him in each of the three Tests, and also smashed him on the elbow at Perth, forcing him to retire hurt. But in 2011, after a World Cup hat-trick against the Netherlands, he struggled at home, eventually losing his place. But he bounced back in 2012, with 19 wickets in the three home Tests against Australia, including ten in the second one at Port-of-Spain. Later in the year he took 12 more as New Zealand lost both their Tests in the Caribbean.

THE FACTS   Roach took 6 for 48 against Bangladesh at St George's in July 2009, and followed that with 5 for 44 in the first ODI at Roseau ... Roach took a hat-trick – West Indies' first in the World Cup, and only their second in all ODIs – against the Netherlands at Delhi in February 2011 ... He took 7 for 23 (five bowled and two lbw) for Barbados v Combined Colleges and Campuses in Nevis in January 2010 ...

THE FIGURES to 17.09.12

ᴇsᴘɴ cricinfo.com

Batting & Fielding	M	Inns	NO	Runs	HS	Avge	S/R	100	50	4s	6s	Ct	St
Tests	21	35	7	291	41	10.39	34.31	0	0	31	1	6	0
ODIs	41	25	13	138	24*	11.50	48.59	0	0	11	1	7	0
T20Is	10	1	1	3	3*	–	150.00	0	0	0	0	1	0
First-class	50	71	13	591	52*	10.18	–	0	1	–	–	19	0

Bowling	M	Balls	Runs	Wkts	BB	Avge	RpO	S/R	5i	10m
Tests	21	4183	2271	82	6–48	27.69	3.25	57.01	5	1
ODIs	41	2089	1714	67	6–27	25.58	4.92	31.17	2	0
T20Is	10	210	248	9	2–25	27.55	7.08	23.33	0	0
First-class	50	8278	4786	166	7–23	28.83	3.46	49.86	8	1

JOE **ROOT**

ENGLAND

Full name	**Joseph Edward Root**
Born	**December 30, 1990, Sheffield**
Teams	**Yorkshire**
Style	**Right-hand bat, offspinner**
Test debut	**No Tests yet**
ODI debut	**No ODIs yet**
T20I debut	**No T20Is yet**

THE PROFILE Joe Root, a calm, collected opener, has already drawn comparisons with two of Yorkshire's finest: his patience and stubbornness at the crease had Geoffrey Boycott gushing that he reminded him of himself, while Root is a product of the Sheffield Collegiate club, which also nurtured Michael Vaughan. And there are similarities between Root's batting style and Vaughan's, particularly when it comes to driving off the front foot. Root first made his mark with the England Under-19s in Bangladesh, winning the man of the series award, shortly before the 2010 Youth World Cup. He started with Yorkshire later that year, and narrowly missed a thousand runs in his first season, although he was chosen for the England Lions. In 2011 he was one of the few bright spots in a miserable season for relegated Yorkshire: Root made 937 runs in the Championship (only Jonny Bairstow had more), and extended his maiden century – against Sussex at Scarborough – to 160. By now he was being spoken of as a future England opener, and did his cause no harm with a century for the Lions against the West Indian tourists in May 2012, soon followed by successive innings of 125 and 222 not out for Yorkshire. Darren Gough watched the double-century, against Hampshire at Southampton, and enthused: "What a knock – I was at the Rose Bowl for the first day and we didn't see a ball bowled, so to score so many runs in such green, damp conditions was unbelievable. That's the type of innings that can get you on an England tour." And Root's tour chances, already high, were enhanced when Andrew Strauss announced his retirement at the end of the 2012 season.

THE FACTS Root made three centuries in four first-class innings in 2012 – 115 not out for England Lions v West Indians, 125 for Yorkshire v Northamptonshire and 222 not out v Hampshire ... He was the Cricket Writers' Club's young player of the year in 2012 ... Root scored 160 for Yorkshire v Sussex at Scarborough in August 2011 ...

THE FIGURES *to 17.09.12* ██▀▀ cricinfo.com

Batting & Fielding	M	Inns	NO	Runs	HS	Avge	S/R	100	50	4s	6s	Ct	St
Tests	0	0	–	–	–	–	–	–	–	–	–	–	–
ODIs	0	0	–	–	–	–	–	–	–	–	–	–	–
T20Is	0	0	–	–	–	–	–	–	–	–	–	–	–
First-class	36	61	8	2015	222*	38.01	51.14	4	8	256	4	19	0

Bowling	M	Balls	Runs	Wkts	BB	Avge	RpO	S/R	5i	10m
Tests	0	0	–	–	–	–	–	–	–	–
ODIs	0	0	–	–	–	–	–	–	–	–
T20Is	0	0	–	–	–	–	–	–	–	–
First-class	36	897	510	8	3–33	63.75	3.41	112.12	0	0

RILEE **ROSSOUW**

Full name	**Rilee Roscoe Rossouw**
Born	**October 9, 1989, Bloemfontein**
Teams	**Knights**
Style	**Left-hand bat, occasional offspinner**
Test debut	**No Tests yet**
ODI debut	**No ODIs yet**
T20I debut	**No T20Is yet**

THE PROFILE Rilee Rossouw, a free-flowing left-hander from Free State, was long tipped for stardom. After playing for SA Schools he made his first-class debut just after his 18th birthday, scoring 83 against Easterns. The following summer, Rossouw finished as the Eagles' leading runscorer, with 765. And he rounded off the following season in amazing style, with 319 against the Titans at Centurion, where he shared a record stand of 480 with another highly rated left-hander, Dean Elgar. At 322 minutes it was the fastest triple-century in a domestic match in South Africa (Denis Compton made a faster one for MCC in a tour game in 1948-49), and he came within six of Barry Richards's South African record for runs in one day by a batsman. After that he was a marked man, playing for the national A team in Bangladesh and Sri Lanka. Almost inevitably, his form slipped a little in 2010-11 – 426 runs at less than 30 – but he was recalled to the A team as an injury replacement for a one-day triangular series in Zimbabwe in July 2011, and scored 52 against Australia and 92 against the hosts. A senior spot remained elusive – not helped by another consistent but unspectacular domestic season in 2011-12 – but it seems unlikely that the international arrival of a man described by one onlooker as "better than Jacques Kallis at the same age" will be long delayed. Boeta Dippenaar, a Knights team-mate and a former Test centurymaker himself, has no doubts: "I am prepared to bet my mortgage on it that he will have a long, successful career for South Africa."

THE FACTS Rossouw scored 319 for Eagles v Titans at Centurion in March 2010, all on the first day: it was the second-highest number of runs scored in a day by a South African batsman after Barry Richards (325 in 1970-71) ... During that innings Rossouw shared a South African-record stand of 480 for the second wicket with Dean Elgar ... Rossouw made 131 v Warriors in November 2008, which helped Eagles clinch the domestic one-day title ...

THE FIGURES to 17.09.12   **ESPN** cricinfo.com

Batting & Fielding	M	Inns	NO	Runs	HS	Avge	S/R	100	50	4s	6s	Ct	St
Tests	0	0	–	–	–	–	–	–	–	–	–	–	–
ODIs	0	0	–	–	–	–	–	–	–	–	–	–	–
T20Is	0	0	–	–	–	–	–	–	–	–	–	–	–
First-class	48	85	2	3562	319	42.91	61.32	11	14	524	25	55	0

Bowling	M	Balls	Runs	Wkts	BB	Avge	RpO	S/R	5i	10m
Tests	0	0	–	–	–	–	–	–	–	–
ODIs	0	0	–	–	–	–	–	–	–	–
T20Is	0	0	–	–	–	–	–	–	–	–
First-class	48	6	10	1	1–10	10.00	10.00	6.00	0	0

RUBEL HOSSAIN

Full name	Mohammad Rubel Hossain
Born	January 1, 1990, Bagerhat
Teams	Chittagong
Style	Right-hand bat, right-arm fast-medium bowler
Test debut	Bangladesh v West Indies at Kingstown 2009
ODI debut	Bangladesh v Sri Lanka at Mirpur 2008-09
T20I debut	Bangladesh v South Africa at Johannesburg 2008-09

THE PROFILE A right-arm fast bowler with a slingy action not unlike Lasith Malinga's, Rubel Hossain began by playing tape-ball cricket in his home town of Bagerhat (in Khulna), before he was discovered during a national search for fast bowlers after getting the highest reading on the speed-gun. He made his first-class debut in October 2007 against a Khulna side including his hero Mashrafe Mortaza – not that that stopped him letting Mashrafe have a few bouncers. He played in the Under-19 World Cup early in 2008, and later that year made the full national squad. In his first ODI, a rain-affected game against Sri Lanka at Mirpur in January 2009, he helped set up a rare Bangladesh victory with 4 for 33. He toured the Caribbean later in the year, playing in both Tests as Bangladesh pulled off a clean sweep against a depleted West Indian side. Once again he made a decent start: his three wickets – Ryan Austin, Omar Phillips and Nikita Miller – were, like himself, making their Test debut. But Rubel didn't strike again in the Tests, and went for a few in the subsequent one-dayers: he was left out for a while, then returned to take five expensive wickets in a Test against New Zealand early in 2010, before looking the pick of the pacemen in the home-and-away series against England. After a subdued World Cup – only five wickets on largely spin-friendly pitches – he showed his worth with 11 victims in five one-dayers in Zimbabwe later in 2011. However, just one wicket in three Tests after that meant his average remained worryingly high: then he was sidelined by an injured shoulder, that needed surgery in mid-2012. Rubel's love of speed also runs to a fascination with motor-bikes.

THE FACTS Rubel Hossain took 5 for 60 for Chittagong at Sylhet in December 2008 ... He took 4 for 33 on his ODI debut as Bangladesh beat Sri Lanka at Mirpur in January 2009 ... Rubel took 5 for 166 (in 29 overs) against New Zealand at Hamilton in February 2010 ... He took 4 for 19 against the Netherlands and 5 for 16 against Scotland on successive days in warm-up games for the World Twenty20 in England in May 2009 ...

THE FIGURES to 17.09.12   **ESP∩cricinfo.com**

Batting & Fielding	M	Inns	NO	Runs	HS	Avge	S/R	100	50	4s	6s	Ct	St
Tests	12	21	11	84	17	8.40	33.87	0	0	11	0	5	0
ODIs	37	19	11	38	15*	4.75	53.52	0	0	5	0	7	0
T20Is	5	2	2	8	8*	–	80.00	0	0	1	0	1	0
First-class	24	37	14	124	17	5.39	–	0	0	–	–	9	0

Bowling	M	Balls	Runs	Wkts	BB	Avge	RpO	S/R	5i	10m
Tests	12	2022	1415	17	5–166	83.23	4.19	118.94	1	0
ODIs	37	1723	1573	48	4–25	32.77	5.47	35.89	0	0
T20Is	5	98	142	3	1–13	47.33	8.69	32.66	0	0
First-class	24	3658	2524	41	5–60	61.56	4.13	89.21	2	0

JACQUES **RUDOLPH**

Full name	**Jacobus Andries Rudolph**
Born	**May 4, 1981, Springs, Transvaal**
Teams	**Titans, Surrey**
Style	**Left-hand bat, occasional legspinner**
Test debut	**South Africa v Bangladesh at Chittagong 2002-03**
ODI debut	**South Africa v India at Dhaka 2002-03**
T20I debut	**South Africa v Australia at Brisbane 2005-06**

SOUTH AFRICA

THE PROFILE Jacques Rudolph's debut double-century – and a record-breaking 429-run stand with Boeta Dippenaar – against Bangladesh in April 2003 came 18 months after he had forced his way into the squad through sheer weight of runs. Twice before he had been expecting to win his first cap, and twice politics intervened. At Centurion in November 2001 the Indians were in dispute with the ICC, who ruled the match unofficial. Then two months later he was named to face Australia at Sydney, but South Africa's board president vetoed his selection, saying there were not enough "players of colour" in the side. But once he finally got in Rudolph became a fixture for three years. An undemonstrative left-hander, he has neat footwork and balance, and favours the cover-drive. His long unbeaten 102 – a classic seven-hour rearguard – saved the Perth Test in December 2005. That was his fifth Test century, but his highest score in five more matches against the Aussies was only 41. After an indifferent run – not helped by a shoulder operation – he was left out for the 2007 World Cup, and threw in his lot with Yorkshire as a Kolpak player. He scored heavily there, and matured as a person, before returning home after the 2010 season for another crack at international cricket. He captained the A team in a triangular series in Zimbabwe in June 2011, and reached 90 three times in his five innings. Still only 30, Rudolph returned to the Test side – after more than five years – against Australia in November 2011. He made a century against New Zealand at Dunedin early the following year, but was otherwise underwhelming in a strong middle order.

THE FACTS Rudolph was the fifth man to score a double-century on Test debut, with 222 not out v Bangladesh at Chittagong in April 2003: he put on 429 for the third wicket with Boeta Dippenaar ... He scored 228 not out for Yorkshire v Durham in April 2010 ... Occasional legspinner Rudolph took a wicket with his second ball in Tests, dismissing Nasser Hussain for 42 at Headingley in 2003 ... His record includes two ODIs for the Africa XI ...

THE FIGURES to 17.09.12

ESPNcricinfo.com

Batting & Fielding	M	Inns	NO	Runs	HS	Avge	S/R	100	50	4s	6s	Ct	St
Tests	46	79	9	2548	222*	36.40	44.07	6	11	356	7	29	0
ODIs	45	39	6	1174	81	35.57	68.05	0	7	109	5	11	0
T20Is	1	1	1	6	6*	–	85.71	0	0	0	0	0	0
First-class	225	383	25	16096	228*	44.96	–	46	73	–	–	204	0

Bowling	M	Balls	Runs	Wkts	BB	Avge	RpO	S/R	5i	10m
Tests	46	664	432	4	1–1	108.00	3.90	166.00	0	0
ODIs	45	24	26	0	–	–	6.50	–	0	0
T20Is	1	0	–	–	–	–	–	–	–	–
First-class	225	4523	2572	58	5–80	44.34	3.41	77.98	3	0

ANDRE **RUSSELL**

Full name	**Andre Dwayne Russell**
Born	**April 29, 1988, Jamaica**
Teams	**Jamaica, Delhi Daredevils**
Style	**Right-hand bat, right-arm fast-medium bowler**
Test debut	**West Indies v Sri Lanka at Galle 2010-11**
ODI debut	**West Indies v Ireland at Mohali 2010-11**
T20I debut	**West Indies v Pakistan at Gros Islet 2010-11**

THE PROFILE A bowler with a bit of nip and a big-hitting batsman, Andre Russell has showed signs of maturing into an international-class allrounder, something West Indies are badly in need of as question-marks persist over the futures of Dwayne Bravo and Chris Gayle. Russell made his international debut against England during the 2011 World Cup. First he dismissed Matt Prior in his second over and Andrew Strauss in his third, finishing with 4 for 49; then, with West Indies struggling to keep up the chase, Russell spanked 49 from 46 balls from No. 8, and only when he and Ramnaresh Sarwan were out in successive overs could England breathe again. Two matches later, though, Russell was left out of the quarter-final against Pakistan, to general surprise. He was back for the home one-dayers that followed, and although he did little against Pakistan and was dropped, on his return he enlivened the third match of the India series by hammering 92 not out after entering at 96 for 7. "This was my biggest innings as it came on a big stage," said Russell, who cheerfully admits that he remains a bowling allrounder: "Bowling is my first choice. I bowl first in the nets and then have a hit. I want to have that balance and enjoy the success." Russell does have two first-class centuries to his name: the first was against Ireland, and included no fewer than ten sixes, nine of them as he sailed past three figures in just 62 balls. Russell played in the 2012 IPL, and later did well in the home one-dayers against New Zealand in July. He looks like one for the future, although his similarity in style to the current West Indies captain Darren Sammy might limit his opportunities in the short term.

THE FACTS Russell hit 92 not out against India in Antigua in June 2011, the highest score by a No. 9 in any ODI ... He reached his maiden first-class century, against Ireland at Spanish Town in April 2010, in just 62 balls, with nine sixes and seven fours ... He hit 128 for West Indies A v Bangladesh A in November 2011 ... Russell's first two first-class five-fors came in successive matches for West Indies A v India A in England in June 2010 ...

THE FIGURES to 17.09.12   **espncricinfo.com**

Batting & Fielding	M	Inns	NO	Runs	HS	Avge	S/R	100	50	4s	6s	Ct	St
Tests	1	1	0	2	2	2.00	22.22	0	0	0	0	1	0
ODIs	27	21	5	586	92*	36.62	123.62	0	3	53	28	7	0
T20Is	5	4	1	23	12*	7.66	79.31	0	0	2	0	0	0
First-class	16	23	1	565	128	25.68	–	2	0	–	–	6	0

Bowling	M	Balls	Runs	Wkts	BB	Avge	RpO	S/R	5i	10m
Tests	1	138	104	1	1–73	104.00	4.52	138.00	0	0
ODIs	27	1127	1031	37	4–35	27.86	5.48	30.45	0	0
T20Is	5	72	106	1	1–14	106.00	8.83	72.00	0	0
First-class	16	1924	1044	50	5–36	20.88	3.25	38.48	3	0

JESSE **RYDER**

Full name	**Jesse Daniel Ryder**
Born	**August 6, 1984, Masterton, Wellington**
Teams	**Wellington, Pune Warriors**
Style	**Left-hand bat, right-arm medium-pacer**
Test debut	**New Zealand v Bangladesh at Chittagong 2008-09**
ODI debut	**New Zealand v England at Wellington 2007-08**
T20I debut	**New Zealand v England at Auckland 2007-08**

THE PROFILE Jesse Ryder had a troubled childhood, and latterly battled with his weight and demons of his own: just after establishing himself in the one-day side early in 2008, he injured tendons in his hand when he smashed a window in a bar at 5.30am after a tight series victory over England. He missed the Tests, and the England tour which followed. Then, early in 2012, he lost his central contract and withdrew from international cricket, vowing to return "when the time was right". But Ryder, who can also bowl useful gentle seamers, is seriously talented, and it seems certain that the time will soon come. The NZ board had already forgiven him for snubbing their A team (he briefly threatened to try to qualify for England), and gave him several more chances despite continued concerns about his drinking. Ryder gives the ball a good thump: he biffed 79 not out in the second game of that 2008 series against England, going run for run with Brendon McCullum in a rollicking opening stand of 165 which won the Hamilton encounter with half the overs unused. He finally made his Test debut in Bangladesh in November 2008, collecting 91 in his second match then three successive fifties against West Indies at home. A maiden Test century followed against India at Hamilton, then he went one better in the second Test at Napier with a superb 201, setting up a massive total of 619 after entering at 23 for 3. Muscle strains mucked up the World Twenty20 in England in 2009, and the following home season, but he was back for the next World Twenty20 in the West Indies early in 2010, and the following year starred with 83 in the shock World Cup quarter-final victory over South Africa.

THE FACTS Ryder scored 236 for Wellington v Central Districts at Palmerston North in March 2005 ... When he scored 201 against India at Napier in March 2009 it was the second time "J. Ryder" had made 201 in a Test – Jack of Australia made 201 not out against England at Adelaide in 1924-25 ... Ryder played two one-day games for Ireland in 2007 before being dumped after missing the plane to the next match ...

THE FIGURES *to 17.09.12*   ᴇsᴘᴨcricinfo.com

Batting & Fielding	M	Inns	NO	Runs	HS	Avge	S/R	100	50	4s	6s	Ct	St
Tests	18	33	2	1269	201	40.93	55.19	3	6	146	6	12	0
ODIs	39	33	1	1100	107	34.37	89.72	2	6	115	31	14	0
T20Is	20	19	1	412	62	22.88	122.98	0	3	42	16	5	0
First-class	63	104	6	4257	236	43.43	–	10	21	–	–	53	0

Bowling	M	Balls	Runs	Wkts	BB	Avge	RpO	S/R	5i	10m
Tests	18	492	280	5	2–7	56.00	3.41	98.40	0	0
ODIs	39	383	399	11	3–29	36.27	6.25	34.81	0	0
T20Is	20	60	68	2	1–2	34.00	6.80	30.00	0	0
First-class	63	2903	1362	46	4–23	29.60	2.81	63.10	0	0

SAEED AJMAL

Full name	**Saeed Ajmal**
Born	**October 14, 1977, Faisalabad, Punjab**
Teams	**Faisalabad, Zarai Taraqiati Bank**
Style	**Right-hand bat, offspinner**
Test debut	**Pakistan v Sri Lanka at Galle 2009**
ODI debut	**Pakistan v India at Karachi 2008**
T20I debut	**Pakistan v Australia at Dubai 2009**

THE PROFILE Offspinner Saeed Ajmal had been a first-class cricketer for more than ten years when the selectors finally called. Given Pakistan's usual propensity for plucking teenagers from obscurity, he must have thought, at 30, that his chance had gone. However, another impressive domestic season – 38 wickets in 2007-08, plus some decent one-day performances, after 62 wickets at 24.29 the previous term – earned him a place at the Asia Cup in Pakistan in mid-2008. He started with 1 for 47 against India, then strangled Bangladesh with two late strikes in his second match. Ajmal is very much a modern offspinner, tossing in a handy doosra to complement his stock offbreak. He received a jolting setback when his action was reported early in 2009 – he was also fined after he complained about being complained about – but tests found any elbow flexion was within the permitted 15-degree limit. He showed his delight by performing with guile and maturity as Pakistan swept to the World Twenty20 title in England in June, taking 12 wickets (only Umar Gul, with 13, took more) and often bottling up the middle overs. Then he embarked on Test cricket, with 14 wickets in three Tests in Sri Lanka, and two years later claimed 17 in two matches in the West Indies, although doubts about his action resurfaced (an occasional pause in delivery, to fox the batsman, keeps the doubters interested). Ajmal really came into his own in Tests in 2011-12, following 18 wickets against Sri Lanka in the UAE with nine in two games in Bangladesh, before orchestrating top-ranked England's embarrassing whitewash with 24 scalps in three Tests, including ten (seven of then lbw) in the first in Dubai. Later in 2012 he was a hit in Sri Lanka, too.

THE FACTS Saeed Ajmal took 7 for 55 (with five lbws) for Pakistan v England in Dubai in January 2012 ... He had unique match figures of 11 for 111 in a Test against West Indies in May 2011 ... Ajmal claimed 7 for 220 in 63 overs in only his second first-class match, for Faisalabad v Karachi Whites in November 1996 ... He was only the third bowler (after Clarrie Grimmett and Dilip Doshi) to take 100 wickets after making his Test debut when over 30 ...

THE FIGURES *to 17.09.12*

Batting & Fielding	M	Inns	NO	Runs	HS	Avge	S/R	100	50	4s	6s	Ct	St
Tests	23	32	9	250	50	10.86	40.51	0	1	23	2	8	0
ODIs	71	42	18	211	33	8.79	58.61	0	0	14	0	12	0
T20Is	42	15	9	58	21*	9.66	109.43	0	0	5	1	6	0
First-class	110	146	45	1222	53	12.09	–	0	3	–	–	36	0

Bowling	M	Balls	Runs	Wkts	BB	Avge	RpO	S/R	5i	10m
Tests	23	7481	3306	122	7–55	27.09	2.65	61.31	6	2
ODIs	71	3668	2537	109	5–43	23.27	4.14	33.65	0	0
T20Is	42	924	929	60	4–19	15.48	6.03	15.40	0	0
First-class	110	24428	11124	410	7–55	27.13	2.73	59.58	25	3

THILAN **SAMARAWEERA**

Full name	**Thilan Thusara Samaraweera**
Born	**September 22, 1976, Colombo**
Teams	**Sinhalese Sports Club, Wayamba**
Style	**Right-hand bat, offspinner**
Test debut	**Sri Lanka v India at Colombo 2001-02**
ODI debut	**Sri Lanka v India at Sharjah 1998-99**
T20I debut	**No T20Is yet**

THE PROFILE Early in 2009, cricket seemed insignificant for Thilan Samaraweera as he lay in hospital, the most badly injured of the Sri Lankan players subjected to terrorist attack in Pakistan. A bullet was lodged in his left thigh, and a distinguished career hung in the balance – all the more galling as he was in the form of his life, having scored 231 in the first Test at Karachi and 214 in the ongoing one at Lahore. Mercifully, he was soon back to his best, scoring 159 and 143 in successive Tests against New Zealand at home in August before settling a few scores with his first one-day international century, after long being branded too slow for the limited-overs side. In all he made 1234 runs in 11 Tests in 2009 at 72.58, and did well the following year too, although a modest run cost him his place late in 2011. At 35, it looked like the end of the road – but, after initially being omitted from the tour of South Africa, Samaraweera made centuries at Durban and Cape Town in January 2012 to reclaim his Test spot. An adhesive, well-organised right-hander, he started out as an offspinner, seemingly destined to play the odd Test in the shadow of Muttiah Muralitharan. Realising he was on a hiding to nothing there, Samaraweera reinvented himself as a specialist batsman, starting with a century on Test debut against India in August 2001. The retirement of Aravinda de Silva helped him secure a middle-order place, where his patient approach makes him a valuable foil for his more flamboyant colleagues. His steady offspin is rarely used now, although he has a reputation as a partnership-breaker.

THE FACTS Samaraweera was the third Sri Lankan, after Brendon Kuruppu and Romesh Kaluwitharana, to score a century on Test debut, against India in August 2001 ... Five of his Test centuries have come at the Sinhalese Sports Club, his home ground in Colombo, where he averages 77.43 ... He averages 75.00 in Tests against New Zealand, but 28.23 against Australia ... Samaraweera's brother Dulip played seven Tests for Sri Lanka in the early 1990s ...

THE FIGURES to 17.09.12   **ESP∩cricinfo.com**

Batting & Fielding	M	Inns	NO	Runs	HS	Avge	S/R	100	50	4s	6s	Ct	St
Tests	76	123	20	5283	231	51.29	47.28	14	29	619	7	44	0
ODIs	53	42	11	862	105*	27.80	69.29	2	0	76	0	17	0
T20Is	0	0	–	–	–	–	–	–	–	–	–	–	–
First-class	247	352	65	14156	231	49.32	–	38	70	–	–	190	0

Bowling	M	Balls	Runs	Wkts	BB	Avge	RpO	S/R	5i	10m
Tests	76	1327	689	15	4–49	45.93	3.11	88.46	0	0
ODIs	53	702	542	11	3–34	49.27	4.63	63.81	0	0
T20Is	0	0	–	–	–	–	–	–	–	–
First-class	247	17961	8366	357	6–55	23.43	2.79	50.31	15	2

DARREN **SAMMY**

WEST INDIES

Full name	**Darren Julius Garvey Sammy**
Born	**December 20, 1983, Micoud, St Lucia**
Teams	**Windward Islands**
Style	**Right-hand bat, right-arm medium-pacer**
Test debut	**West Indies v England at Manchester 2007**
ODI debut	**West Indies v New Zealand at Southampton 2004**
T20I debut	**West Indies v England at The Oval 2007**

THE PROFILE Darren Sammy was the surprise choice as captain when the West Indian board decided to dump Chris Gayle, a hard act to follow – especially for someone who was not a regular in the side before his elevation. Sammy did as well as could be expected during the 2011 World Cup, and probably better than that shortly afterwards, squaring a home series with Pakistan (Sammy took 5 for 29 as the tourists slid to defeat in Guyana) then holding India to two draws, although victory in a low-scoring first Test at Kingston ultimately gave the visitors the series. Later in 2011 West Indies won in Bangladesh, and competed well with the Aussies at home early the following year, before predictably coming unstuck in early-season England. But although Sammy leads with a smile, fields like a panther, and has improved his always attacking batting – he smacked a maiden Test century at Trent Bridge in 2012 – he remains under pressure, as several ex-players have questioned his right to a place in the side on grounds of ability. And although his bowling is supposed to be his strongest suit, it's a painful truth that his nagging medium-pace is not quite good enough – or quick enough – to make him a genuine third seamer at Test level: this despite a stunning debut, at Old Trafford in 2007, when he wobbled the ball around and finished up with seven wickets, three of them in one over. Sammy was the first Test cricketer from St Lucia, and is also thought to be Test cricket's only Seventh Day Adventist. He was first called up to the West Indian squad for the Champions Trophy in England in 2004.

THE FACTS Sammy took 7 for 66 in his first Test, against England at Old Trafford in 2007: only Alf Valentine, with 8 for 104 against England at Old Trafford in 1950, has returned better figures on a Test debut for West Indies ... Sammy made 121 for Windward Islands v Barbados at Bridgetown in March 2009 ... He took 5 for 26 in a Twenty20 international against Zimbabwe at Port-of-Spain in February 2010 ...

THE FIGURES *to 17.09.12*   **ESPncricinfo.com**

Batting & Fielding	M	Inns	NO	Runs	HS	Avge	S/R	100	50	4s	6s	Ct	St
Tests	29	49	1	1066	106	22.20	67.94	1	3	122	26	46	0
ODIs	82	64	18	978	84	21.26	104.15	0	3	70	45	42	0
T20Is	29	22	5	184	30	10.82	112.88	0	0	10	8	14	0
First-class	85	140	8	3269	121	24.76	–		2	20	–	–	116	0

Bowling	M	Balls	Runs	Wkts	BB	Avge	RpO	S/R	5i	10m
Tests	29	5152	2419	71	7–66	34.07	2.81	72.56	4	0
ODIs	82	3419	2618	58	4–26	45.13	4.59	58.94	0	0
T20Is	29	502	542	31	5–26	17.48	6.47	16.19	1	0
First-class	85	12423	5620	196	7–66	28.67	2.71	63.38	10	0

MARLON **SAMUELS**

Full name	**Marlon Nathaniel Samuels**
Born	**January 5, 1981, Kingston, Jamaica**
Teams	**Jamaica, Pune Warriors**
Style	**Right-hand bat, offspinner**
Test debut	**West Indies v Australia at Adelaide 2000-01**
ODI debut	**West Indies v Sri Lanka at Nairobi 2000-01**
T20I debut	**West Indies v England at The Oval 2007**

THE PROFILE Marlon Samuels returned to international cricket in 2011 not long after completing a two-year ban for alleged involvement with bookmakers. He protested his innocence, but served his time. At his best Samuels is a classy right-hander, whose composed start in Tests prompted comparisons with Viv Richards, and his return bolstered West Indies' suspect middle order – he made 57 in his first Test back, against Pakistan in St Kitts in May 2011, and 78 not out in his next one, against India. The rehabilitation continued with a defiant century at Trent Bridge in 2012 – in all he made 386 runs in the three Tests, at an average of 96.50 – and 123 and 52 at home in Kingston in August 2012, in a match that coincided with the 50th anniversary of Jamaican independence. His start was exceptional: he flew to Australia for the third Test of the 2000-01 series, only 19 and with just one first-class match under his belt, but showed a beautifully balanced technique, standing still at the crease and moving smoothly into his strokes off either foot. A combination of over-confidence and arrogance almost got him sent home from India late in 2002, after he defied a team curfew – but he survived, and responded with a disciplined maiden Test century at Kolkata (it was his first one in first-class cricket too). He also excelled in South Africa in 2007-08, making 94 and 40 in the first Test, 51 in the second, and 105 in the third – but that inopportune ban stopped him in his tracks shortly afterwards. Samuels also bowls flattish offspin, having rethought his action after being reported to the ICC on suspicion of throwing.

THE FACTS Samuels scored 257 and then took 5 for 87 – both career-bests – for the West Indians v Queensland in Brisbane in October 2005 ... He scored his maiden first-class century in a Test – 104 v India at Kolkata in October 2002: he was the fifth West Indian to do this, following Clifford Roach, Clairmonte Depeiaza, Gerry Alexander and Bernard Julien ... His brother Robert Samuels, older by ten years, played six Tests and eight ODIs as a left-hand opener, and scored 125 against New Zealand in his second Test ...

THE FIGURES *to 17.09.12*   **ESPncricinfo.com**

Batting & Fielding	M	Inns	NO	Runs	HS	Avge	S/R	100	50	4s	6s	Ct	St
Tests	42	75	6	2413	123	34.97	47.54	4	17	328	16	19	0
ODIs	137	127	20	3285	108*	30.70	74.74	3	22	324	57	39	0
T20Is	15	14	2	269	58	22.41	128.09	0	2	18	14	4	0
First-class	90	153	11	5658	257	39.84	–	11	32	–	–	58	0

Bowling	M	Balls	Runs	Wkts	BB	Avge	RpO	S/R	5i	10m
Tests	42	2883	1611	24	3–74	67.12	3.35	120.12	0	0
ODIs	137	4009	3176	74	3–25	42.91	4.75	54.17	0	0
T20Is	15	160	219	10	1–24	21.90	8.21	16.00	0	0
First-class	90	5923	3075	54	5–87	56.94	3.11	109.69	1	0

KUMAR **SANGAKKARA**

SRI LANKA

Full name	**Kumar Chokshanada Sangakkara**
Born	**October 27, 1977, Matale**
Teams	**Nondescripts, Kandurata, Deccan Chargers**
Style	**Left-hand bat, wicketkeeper**
Test debut	**Sri Lanka v South Africa at Galle 2000**
ODI debut	**Sri Lanka v Pakistan at Galle 2000**
T20I debut	**Sri Lanka v England at Southampton 2006**

THE PROFILE Within months of his debut at 22, Kumar Sangakkara was one of Sri Lanka's most influential players: a talented left-hand strokemaker, a slick wicketkeeper, and a sharp-eyed strategist with an even sharper tongue. From the start his effortless batting oozed class: he possesses the grace of David Gower, but the attitude of an Aussie. At the outset he was happier on the back foot, but he is now as comfortable driving through the covers as cutting behind point. He was briefly relieved of keeping duties after the 2003 World Cup: he made more runs, but soon got the gloves back. The extra burden had no obvious effect: he made 185 against Pakistan in March 2006. But there was a change of thinking after that, and Prasanna Jayawardene was given the gloves in Tests. Sangakkara responded with seven hundreds, three of them doubles, in his next nine Tests, including 287 as he and Mahela Jayawardene put on a world-record 624 against South Africa, successive double-centuries against Bangladesh, and a magnificent 192 against Australia at Hobart in November 2007. An astute thinker, he took over as captain early in 2009, and reached the final of the World Twenty20 in England. His batting seemed unaffected: he made five hundreds in his first ten Tests in charge, including three in successive matches against India in 2009 and 2010. Sangakkara relinquished the captaincy after defeat in the World Cup final, but stayed on as a player to complete 100 Tests later in 2011. He remained in prime form, scoring 199 not out and 192 in successive home Tests against Pakistan in June 2012, although he was slowed down for a while after that by a broken finger.

THE FACTS Sangakkara scored 287, and put on a record 624 with Mahela Jayawardene against South Africa in Colombo in July 2006 ... He has now scored eight Test double-centuries, behind only Don Bradman (12) and Brian Lara (9) ... Sangakkara averages 69.63 in Tests when not the designated wicketkeeper, but 40.48 when lumbered with the gloves ... His record includes three ODIs for the World XI and four for the Asia XI ...

THE FIGURES *to 17.09.12*   **ESPNcricinfo.com**

Batting & Fielding	M	Inns	NO	Runs	HS	Avge	S/R	100	50	4s	6s	Ct	St
Tests	111	189	15	9872	287	56.73	54.16	30	39	1227	33	168	20
ODIs	333	312	32	10842	138*	38.72	75.68	14	73	1038	56	328	81
T20Is	35	34	4	910	78	30.33	119.89	0	6	92	15	17	11
First-class	199	322	26	14461	287	48.85	–	39	63	–	–	329	33

Bowling	M	Balls	Runs	Wkts	BB	Avge	RpO	S/R	5i	10m
Tests	111	78	42	0	–	–	3.23	–	0	0
ODIs	333	0	–	–	–	–	–	–	–	–
T20Is	35	0	–	–	–	–	–	–	–	–
First-class	199	204	112	1	1–13	112.00	3.29	204.00	0	0

VIRENDER **SEHWAG**

Full name	**Virender Sehwag**
Born	**October 20, 1978, Delhi**
Teams	**Delhi, Delhi Daredevils**
Style	**Right-hand bat, offspinner**
Test debut	**India v South Africa at Bloemfontein 2001-02**
ODI debut	**India v Pakistan at Mohali 1998-99**
T20I debut	**India v South Africa at Johannesburg 2006-07**

THE PROFILE Soon after his 2001 Test-debut century Virender Sehwag was being compared to Sachin Tendulkar. It is half-true: Sehwag is also short and square, and plays the straight drive, back-foot punch and whip off the hips identically – but he leaves even Sachin standing when it comes to audacity. He also bowls effective, loopy offspin. Opening in England in 2002, Sehwag proved an instant hit, and many pivotal innings followed, including India's first triple-century (brought up, characteristically, with a six), in Pakistan early in 2004. His fitness levels dropped for a while, and he struggled in ODIs – but continued to sparkle in Tests, making 254 at Lahore in January 2006. In St Lucia he came excruciatingly close (99 not out) to a century before lunch on the first day, a feat no Indian has yet managed. Dropped after the disastrous 2007 World Cup, Sehwag practised hard, lost a stone, and the following March bounced back with another triple-century, against South Africa. Later that year he carried his bat for 201 at Galle, and overall scored 1462 Test runs in 2008, at a strike-rate (85.84) unprecedented for an opener. Sehwag started the 2011 World Cup with 175 against Bangladesh, although his desire to start every innings with a boundary saw productivity drop off after that. A shoulder injury bothered him for a while, and he had a relatively quiet time after returning ... apart from a big explosion against West Indies in December 2011. People had long been wondering how many Sehwag might score if he batted through an ODI innings – and at Indore they found out: he carved 219 from 149 balls, with 25 fours and seven sixes (and was still out before the end, in the 47th over).

THE FACTS Sehwag has made India's three highest Test scores (319, 309 and 293) ... He made 105 on his Test debut, v South Africa in November 2001 ... Sehwag carried his bat for 201 v Sri Lanka at Galle in mid-2008 ... He hit 219, the highest score in ODIs, v West Indies at Indove in December 2011 ... His record includes a Test and three ODIs for the World XI, and seven ODIs for the Asia XI ...

THE FIGURES to 17.09.12   **ESF** cricinfo.com

Batting & Fielding	M	Inns	NO	Runs	HS	Avge	S/R	100	50	4s	6s	Ct	St
Tests	98	170	6	8306	319	50.64	82.17	22	32	1198	89	80	0
ODIs	249	243	9	8235	219	35.20	104.60	15	38	1128	136	91	0
T20Is	16	15	0	340	68	22.66	152.46	0	2	37	15	1	0
First-class	162	271	10	12811	319	49.08	–	36	50	–	–	139	0

Bowling	M	Balls	Runs	Wkts	BB	Avge	RpO	S/R	5i	10m
Tests	98	3725	1893	40	5-104	47.32	3.04	93.12	1	0
ODIs	249	4392	3853	96	4-6	40.13	5.26	45.75	0	0
T20Is	16	6	20	0	–	–	20.00	–	0	0
First-class	162	8464	4393	105	5-104	41.83	3.11	80.60	1	0

BANGLADESH

SHAFIUL ISLAM

Full name	**Shafiul Islam**
Born	**October 6, 1989, Bogra**
Teams	**Rajshahi**
Style	**Right-hand bat, right-arm fast-medium bowler**
Test debut	**Bangladesh v India at Chittagong 2009-10**
ODI debut	**Bangladesh v Sri Lanka at Dhaka 2009-10**
T20I debut	**Bangladesh v New Zealand at Hamilton 2009-10**

THE PROFILE   An enthusiastic medium-pacer, Shafiul Islam's early marks in international cricket, oddly enough, came with bat in hand. Against India in January 2010 his first two scoring shots were big sixes smeared off the legspin of Amit Mishra (his next runs came when he was dropped on the boundary): Shafiul was the first to do this in Tests, although his team-mate Jahurul Islam followed suit against England at Mirpur two months later. During that match, "Suhas" again starred with the bat, making a forthright 53 (from 51 balls, with 11 fours) from No. 10 in a partnership of 74 with Naeem Islam as the total reached 419. Then, in the 2011 World Cup, Shafiul biffed a seemingly nerveless 24 not out in the ninth-wicket stand of 58 with Mahmudullah that spirited Bangladesh to an unlikely victory over England. This partly made up for an uninspiring tournament with the ball. Still, it is as a bowler that Shafiul is likely to make his mark long term. In 2008-09, his first full season, he took 23 wickets at 22.30 on Bangladesh's usually benign pitches, and received a national call-up after several senior bowlers were injured. He made his one-day debut in the Asia Cup at the start of 2010, and started promisingly – but he proved expensive later on, going for 95 in ten overs against Pakistan (with Shahid Afridi in full flow) in June 2010 and 97 off nine against England a month later. Injuries disrupted his 2011-12 season: a foot problem kept him out during West Indies' visit, then he injured his side during the Asia Cup. But Shafiul was restored when fit, despite modest returns, and was boosted by chief selector Akram Khan describing him as "one of our first-choice pace bowlers".

THE FACTS   Shafiul Islam's first two scoring shots in Test cricket were sixes, off Amit Mishra in two innings at Chittagong in January 2010: he was the first to achieve this in Tests (his team-mate Jahurul Islam soon emulated him) ... Shafiul took 4 for 21 against Ireland during the 2011 World Cup, while his best first-class figures of 4 for 38 came for Rajshahi at Khulna in November 2008 ...

THE FIGURES to 17.09.12   ** espncricinfo.com**

Batting & Fielding	M	Inns	NO	Runs	HS	Avge	S/R	100	50	4s	6s	Ct	St
Tests	6	12	1	149	53	13.54	60.08	0	1	24	2	1	0
ODIs	45	24	7	103	24*	6.05	56.28	0	0	11	2	8	0
T20Is	6	4	1	18	16	6.00	75.00	0	0	1	1	1	0
First-class	20	31	7	314	53	13.08	61.44	0	1	43	7	6	0

Bowling	M	Balls	Runs	Wkts	BB	Avge	RpO	S/R	5i	10m
Tests	6	996	569	8	3–86	71.12	3.42	124.50	0	0
ODIs	45	1875	1834	51	4–21	35.96	5.86	36.76	0	0
T20Is	6	120	131	5	2–19	26.20	6.55	24.00	0	0
First-class	20	3031	1543	42	4–38	36.73	3.05	72.16	0	0

SHAHADAT HOSSAIN

Full name	**Kazi Shahadat Hossain**
Born	**August 7, 1986, Narayanganj, Dhaka**
Teams	**Dhaka**
Style	**Right-hand bat, right-arm fast-medium bowler**
Test debut	**Bangladesh v England at Lord's 2005**
ODI debut	**Bangladesh v Kenya at Bogra 2005-06**
T20I debut	**Bangladesh v Zimbabwe at Khulna 2006-07**

THE PROFILE Shahadat Hossain was discovered at a talent-spotting camp, and whisked away to the Institute of Sports for refinement. "Rajib" has all the necessary attributes for a genuine fast bowler: he is tall and strong, and doesn't put unnecessary pressure on his body, with a slightly open-chested delivery position after a smooth run-up. He is naturally aggressive, and has raw pace. But his Test debut at Lord's in 2005 was a chastening experience, as his 12 overs disappeared for 101. He was just 18 then: after that he did well against Sri Lanka, taking four wickets in an innings twice before going one better in Bogra's inaugural Test in March 2006. Early in 2008 his 6 for 27 at Mirpur gave Bangladesh a rare first-innings lead over South Africa – and an even rarer (if illusory) sniff of victory. In one-day internationals, despite a hat-trick against Zimbabwe, he has been in and out of the side: he played only once in the 2007 World Cup (and was hit around in the sobering defeat by Ireland), and has since generally been viewed as too expensive and erratic for limited-overs games, an impression he failed to dispel during the Asia Cup in March 2012. In Tests, however, he played his part as Bangladesh won an overseas series for the first time, in the Caribbean in mid-2009, and in May 2010 he erased some of the memories of that painful Test debut with 5 for 98 at Lord's, although England still won comfortably in the end. Shahadat was set back by injury after that, and missed the 2011 World Cup – although 5 for 82 for Dhaka against Rajshahi (all but one of his victims a Test player) shortly afterwards suggested he was returning to his best, and indeed he was soon restored to the Test side, although wickets proved elusive.

THE FACTS Shahadat Hossain's 6 for 27 against South Africa at Mirpur in February 2008 are the best figures by a Bangladesh fast bowler in Tests ... He took Bangladesh's first ODI hat-trick, against Zimbabwe at Harare in August 2006 ... Shahadat averages 26.75 with the ball in Tests against India, and 27.86 v South Africa – but 258.00 v Australia ... He took only two wickets – both against Kenya – in his first six ODIs ...

THE FIGURES to 17.09.12   **ESPNcricinfo.com**

Batting & Fielding	M	Inns	NO	Runs	HS	Avge	S/R	100	50	4s	6s	Ct	St
Tests	33	62	17	459	40	10.20	45.80	0	0	63	4	8	0
ODIs	50	27	17	79	16*	7.90	52.31	0	0	7	1	5	0
T20Is	5	5	3	8	4*	4.00	66.66	0	0	0	0	0	0
First-class	61	103	30	863	40	11.82	–	0	0	–	–	14	0

Bowling	M	Balls	Runs	Wkts	BB	Avge	RpO	S/R	5i	10m
Tests	33	4832	3386	68	6–27	49.79	4.20	71.05	4	0
ODIs	50	2138	2072	46	3–34	45.04	5.81	46.47	0	0
T20Is	5	96	144	4	2–22	36.00	9.00	24.00	0	0
First-class	61	8877	5970	147	6–27	40.61	4.03	60.38	8	0

SHAHID AFRIDI

PAKISTAN

Full name	**Sahibzada Mohammad Shahid Khan Afridi**
Born	**March 1, 1980, Khyber Agency**
Teams	**Karachi, Habib Bank**
Style	**Right-hand bat, legspinner**
Test debut	**Pakistan v Australia at Karachi 1998-99**
ODI debut	**Pakistan v Kenya at Nairobi 1996-97**
T20I debut	**Pakistan v England at Bristol 2006**

THE PROFILE A flamboyant allrounder introduced to international cricket as a 16-year-old legspinner, Shahid Afridi astonished everyone except himself by pinch-hitting the fastest one-day hundred in his maiden innings. He's a compulsive shotmaker, and although initially that was too often his undoing, he eventually blossomed. A violent century against India in April 2005 (the only faster one in ODIs was Afridi's own) came soon after he walloped 58 in 34 balls to square the Test series at Bangalore. Then came a Test ton against West Indies, important runs against England, and mayhem against India on some flat tracks early in 2006. A typical Afridi assault is laced with lofted drives and short-arm jabs over midwicket. He's at his best when forcing straight, and at his weakest pushing just outside off. With the ball he can get turn as well as lazy drift, but variety is the key: a vicious faster ball and an offbreak too. After a poor run, Afridi roared back to form in the World Twenty20 in England in 2009, and made a ferocious 51 as Pakistan bossed the final at Lord's. He had retired from Tests in 2006 but returned as captain four years later, only to quit dramatically after two irresponsible shots in a big defeat by Australia at Lord's. His slogging powers seemed to be waning, but his bowling remained a potent one-day weapon, as he showed with 21 wickets in the 2011 World Cup. Not long after that, though, Afridi fell out with the board and was dumped as one-day captain. He immediately retired again ... but was soon back, although his performances – in the first half of 2012 at least – were fairly subdued: he had more success with ball than bat.

THE FACTS In his second match (he hadn't batted in the first) Shahid Afridi hit the fastest hundred in ODIs, from only 37 balls, against Sri Lanka in October 1996 ... Afridi has the highest strike-rate – 113.78 runs per 100 balls – of anyone with more than 40 innings in ODIs ... Afridi has hit more sixes in ODIs than anyone else ... Afridi's record includes three ODIs for the Asia XI and two for the World XI ...

THE FIGURES to 17.09.12   **ESPncricinfo.com**

Batting & Fielding	M	Inns	NO	Runs	HS	Avge	S/R	100	50	4s	6s	Ct	St
Tests	27	48	1	1716	156	36.51	86.97	5	8	220	52	10	0
ODIs	349	323	20	7075	124	23.34	113.78	6	33	648	298	112	0
T20Is	50	48	4	801	54*	18.20	142.52	0	4	64	31	14	0
First-class	111	183	4	5631	164	31.45	–	12	30	–	–	75	0

Bowling	M	Balls	Runs	Wkts	BB	Avge	RpO	S/R	5i	10m
Tests	27	3194	1709	48	5–52	35.60	3.21	66.54	1	0
ODIs	349	15276	11727	348	6–38	33.69	4.60	43.89	5	0
T20Is	50	1121	1141	58	4–11	19.67	6.10	19.32	0	0
First-class	111	13493	7023	258	6–101	27.22	3.12	52.29	8	0

SHAHRIAR NAFEES

Full name	**Shahriar Nafees Ahmed**
Born	**January 25, 1986, Dhaka**
Teams	**Barisal**
Style	**Left-hand bat**
Test debut	**Bangladesh v Sri Lanka at Colombo 2005-06**
ODI debut	**Bangladesh v England at Nottingham 2005**
T20I debut	**Bangladesh v Zimbabwe at Khulna 2006-07**

THE PROFILE A talented left-hand opener, Shahriar Nafees went on Bangladesh's maiden tour of England in 2005, aged 19 and with just five first-class matches behind him. He hadn't fared too badly in those, making 350 runs at 35. That England trip was a case of watching and learning, but "Abir" did get an opportunity in the one-day series, and made 75 in the last game, against Australia. A Test debut followed in Sri Lanka, and Shahriar made 51 in his second match. Then, in April 2006, he exploded in sensational fashion against the might of Australia, stroking his way to a brilliant hundred, his maiden first-class ton as well as his first in Tests, at Fatullah. His stunning 138, with 19 fours, set up a scarcely believable first-day total of 355 for 5 as the Aussies reeled, and a brisk 79 in the second Test showed this was no flash in the pan. There were also three one-day hundreds against Zimbabwe, and one against Bermuda, but he found life harder against the big boys, being dropped after six innings in the 2007 World Cup produced only 31 runs and a top score of 12. After that Shahriar seemed to have been lost to international cricket, copping a ten-year ban after signing up for the unauthorised Indian Cricket League, but he was the first to be welcomed back after an amnesty. He had another quiet World Cup in 2011, but then spanked 56 and 60 against his old friends Australia. After this he slipped out of the limited-overs teams, but 97 against Pakistan at Mirpur in December 2011 emphasised his Test credentials.

THE FACTS Shahriar Nafees's 138 against Australia at Fatullah in 2005-06 was his maiden century in first-class cricket: his previous-highest score was 97, for the Board President's XI v the Zimbabwean tourists in January 2005 ... Shahriar hit four of Bangladesh's first seven ODI hundreds ... He averages 55.50 in ODIs against Zimbabwe, with three centuries, but only 5.50 v India (and 0 v Canada) ... Shahriar captained Bangladesh Under-19s in a one-day game against England, skippered by Alastair Cook, in 2004 ... His brother, Iftekhar Nayem, has also played first-class cricket ...

THE FIGURES to 17.09.12   **ESPN cricinfo.com**

Batting & Fielding	M	Inns	NO	Runs	HS	Avge	S/R	100	50	4s	6s	Ct	St
Tests	21	42	0	1126	138	26.80	54.58	1	7	165	1	17	0
ODIs	75	75	5	2201	123*	31.44	69.49	4	13	277	7	13	0
T20Is	1	1	0	25	25	25.00	147.05	0	0	3	1	1	0
First-class	54	105	3	3320	138	32.54	58.62	5	22	–	–	33	0

Bowling	M	Balls	Runs	Wkts	BB	Avge	RpO	S/R	5i	10m
Tests	21	0	–	–	–	–	–	–	–	–
ODIs	75	0	–	–	–	–	–	–	–	–
T20Is	1	0	–	–	–	–	–	–	–	–
First-class	54	72	50	0	–	–	4.16	–	0	0

SHAKIB AL HASAN

Full name	**Shakib Al Hasan**
Born	**March 24, 1987, Magura, Jessore**
Teams	**Khulna, Kolkata Knight Riders**
Style	**Left-hand bat, slow left-arm orthodox spinner**
Test debut	**Bangladesh v India at Chittagong 2006-07**
ODI debut	**Bangladesh v Zimbabwe at Harare 2006**
T20I debut	**Bangladesh v Zimbabwe at Khulna 2006-07**

THE PROFILE   A stylish left-hand batsman and flattish left-arm spinner, Shakib Al Hasan was earmarked for great things after starring for the Under-19s. His full debut duly arrived in August 2006: he took a wicket then strolled in at No. 4 to make 30 not out in the matchwinning partnership. From the start Shakib proved remarkably consistent, being dismissed in single figures only once in 18 one-dayers leading up to the 2007 World Cup. The heady start continued in the Caribbean with a half-century in the famous win over India, and another against England. After that came the inevitable dip – 17 runs in three innings in Sri Lanka – but he soon returned to form. He sealed Bangladesh's 2-0 triumph against West Indies in July 2009, finishing just short of a maiden Test ton in Grenada: by then he had taken over from the injured Mashrafe Mortaza as captain. Shakib's spin bowling – always effective and economical in ODIs – blossomed almost overnight in Tests. After only three wickets in his first six matches, he took 7 for 36 against New Zealand in October 2008, and rubber-stamped his arrival as an international-class allrounder with 13 wickets in those two Tests in the West Indies. He also sailed past 100 one-day wickets in mid-2010, just before becoming the first Bangladeshi to play county cricket. By 2011 Shakib seemed entrenched as captain, his own successes contrasting with his team's often woeful performances. However, after a disheartening tour of Zimbabwe, Shakib was sacked as skipper, despite doing well himself with bat and ball. It didn't affect his performances, and he briefly sat atop the ICC's rankings for Test allrounders after scoring 144 – and taking seven wickets – against Pakistan in December 2011.

THE FACTS   Shakib Al Hasan took 7 for 36, Bangladesh's best Test bowling figures, against New Zealand at Chittagong in October 2008 ... He made 144 against Pakistan at Mirpur in December 2011, and a round 100 v New Zealand in February 2010 – and additionally has scored 96 in Tests three times ... Shakib hit 134 not out v Canada in Antigua in February 2007 ... He averages 59.66 with the bat in Tests against New Zealand – but 15.12 v South Africa ...

THE FIGURES to 17.09.12   **espncricinfo.com**

Batting & Fielding	M	Inns	NO	Runs	HS	Avge	S/R	100	50	4s	6s	Ct	St
Tests	26	49	2	1630	144	34.68	58.42	2	9	210	6	9	0
ODIs	126	121	19	3635	134*	35.63	78.07	5	25	319	25	35	0
T20Is	22	22	0	328	57	14.90	113.10	0	1	31	5	6	0
First-class	60	110	9	3496	144	34.61	–	5	19	–	–	30	0

Bowling	M	Balls	Runs	Wkts	BB	Avge	RpO	S/R	5i	10m
Tests	26	6381	3011	96	7–36	31.36	2.83	66.46	9	0
ODIs	126	6452	4617	160	4–16	28.85	4.29	40.32	0	0
T20Is	22	486	550	27	4–34	20.37	6.79	18.00	0	0
First-class	60	12234	5626	192	7–32	29.30	2.75	63.71	14	0

ISHANT **SHARMA**

INDIA

Full name	**Ishant Sharma**
Born	**September 2, 1988, Delhi**
Teams	**Delhi, Deccan Chargers**
Style	**Right-hand bat, right-arm fast-medium bowler**
Test debut	**India v Bangladesh at Dhaka 2006-07**
ODI debut	**India v South Africa at Belfast 2007**
T20I debut	**India v Australia at Melbourne 2007-08**

THE PROFILE Tall fast bowlers have always been a much-prized rarity in India. Their earliest Tests featured Mohammad Nissar, a few years ago Abey Kuruvilla shone briefly ... and now there's Ishant Sharma, a lofty 6ft 4ins (193cm). He's regularly above 80mph, with a sharp and deceptive bouncer, delivered from a high arm action. After starting the game seriously at 14, he was playing one-dayers for Delhi only three years later in 2005-06. The following season he took 4 for 65 from 34 overs on first-class debut, and finished his first term with 29 wickets at 20.10. Early in 2007 he was on the verge of reinforcing the national team in South Africa – flights had been booked and visa arrangements made – but in the end he was left to concentrate on domestic cricket and a youth tour. However, when Munaf Patel was injured again in Bangladesh in May, Sharma finally did get on the plane, and took a wicket in a landslide victory at Dhaka. In Australia at the end of 2007 he looked the real deal, especially in the Perth Test, where he dismissed Ricky Ponting during a sensational spell, and again in the one-dayers as India ambushed the hosts to snaffle the series. In 2011 he took 22 wickets in three Tests in the Caribbean, including ten at Bridgetown, but then blew hot and cold in England – listless in the first innings at Lord's, magnificent in the second – before missing the one-day series with an ankle injury. That eventually needed an operation – in March 2012 – which kept him out of the IPL and most of India's internationals for the rest of the year. "I am feeling strong and good again," he announced to general delight in June.

THE FACTS Ishant Sharma took 7 for 24 (11 for 51 in the match) for Delhi v Orissa at Delhi in November 2008 ... Almost half his ODI wickets (30 out of 64) have been Sri Lankans ... His bowling average in ODIs against Australia is 25.13, but 66.33 against West Indies ... In 2006-07, his first season of first-class cricket, Sharma took 29 wickets at 20.10 for Delhi, then made his Test debut in only his seventh match ...

THE FIGURES to 17.09.12   **ᴇsᴘⁿcricinfo.com**

Batting & Fielding	M	Inns	NO	Runs	HS	Avge	S/R	100	50	4s	6s	Ct	St
Tests	45	67	25	432	31*	10.28	29.32	0	0	48	0	11	0
ODIs	47	16	6	47	13	4.70	34.05	0	0	4	0	12	0
T20Is	11	2	2	8	5*	–	100.00	0	0	1	0	2	0
First-class	67	88	36	497	31*	9.55	29.35	0	0	56	0	17	0

Bowling	M	Balls	Runs	Wkts	BB	Avge	RpO	S/R	5i	10m
Tests	45	8835	5037	133	6–55	37.87	3.42	66.42	3	1
ODIs	47	2153	2056	64	4–38	32.12	5.72	33.64	0	0
T20Is	11	206	291	6	2–34	48.50	8.47	34.33	0	0
First-class	67	12970	7063	217	7–24	32.54	3.26	59.76	5	2

ROHIT **SHARMA**

Full name	**Rohit Gurunathan Sharma**
Born	**April 30, 1987, Bansod, Nagpur, Maharashtra**
Teams	**Mumbai, Mumbai Indians**
Style	**Right-hand bat, offspinner**
Test debut	**No Tests yet**
ODI debut	**India v Ireland at Belfast 2007**
T20I debut	**India v England at Durban 2007-08**

INDIA

THE PROFILE Rohit Sharma made a great start to his first-class career, making 205 against Gujarat in only his fourth match for Mumbai. Earlier in 2006 he had made his first-class debut for India A, and also exuded class in the Under-19 World Cup. Sharma is an adaptable batsman, strong off the back foot, equally happy as accumulator or aggressor. He finished 2006-07 with 600 runs at 40, plus 356 in one-dayers and a 49-ball Twenty20 century against Gujarat, which earned him a national call as the dust settled on India's disastrous World Cup campaign. He had a couple of useful innings in the inaugural World Twenty20 in South Africa later in 2007. Then, during the second season of the IPL in 2009, Sharma's Deccan Chargers entered the last over against Kolkata needing 21 to win – and he hit 26, including a six off the final ball, off Bangladesh's Mashrafe Mortaza. A few matches previously Sharma's seldom-seen offspin had claimed an unlikely hat-trick to derail the Mumbai Indians. In 2009-10 he followed a triple-century for Mumbai with successive one-day hundreds against Zimbabwe and Sri Lanka. He would have had that elusive Test cap, too, except he twisted his ankle during the warm-up before the first match against South Africa at Nagpur in February 2010. The following year he was the unlucky batsman to miss out on World Cup selection, but returned in the Caribbean shortly afterwards and passed 50 in three of his five innings. He remained a one-day fixture – at least until a horror run in Sri Lanka late in 2012, when he made only 13 runs in five innings despite looking, according to Gautam Gambhir, "our best batsman in the nets".

THE FACTS Rohit Sharma extended his maiden first-class century to 205, for Mumbai v Gujarat in December 2006... He scored 309 not out for Mumbai v Gujarat in December 2009: in his next innings he was out for a duck ... Sharma took a hat-trick (and four wickets in five balls) as Deccan Chargers beat Mumbai Indians in the IPL at Centurion in May 2009 ... He hit 101 not out, off only 45 balls, against Gujarat in a Twenty20 match in April 2007 ...

THE FIGURES to 17.09.12   **ESPN**cricinfo.com

Batting & Fielding	M	Inns	NO	Runs	HS	Avge	S/R	100	50	4s	6s	Ct	St
Tests	0	0	–	–	–	–	–	–	–	–	–	–	–
ODIs	85	80	16	1974	114	30.84	78.20	2	12	137	23	31	0
T20Is	27	21	7	419	79*	29.92	126.96	0	4	33	18	11	0
First-class	49	73	8	3893	309*	59.89	–	12	17	–	–	36	0

Bowling	M	Balls	Runs	Wkts	BB	Avge	RpO	S/R	5i	10m
Tests	0	0	–	–	–	–	–	–	–	–
ODIs	85	527	450	8	2–27	56.25	5.12	65.87	0	0
T20Is	27	50	78	1	1–22	78.00	9.36	50.00	0	0
First-class	49	1368	716	19	4–41	37.68	3.14	72.00	0	0

SHANE **SHILLINGFORD**

Full name	**Shane Shillingford**
Born	**February 22, 1983, Dominica**
Teams	**Windward Islands**
Style	**Right-hand bat, offspinner**
Test debut	**West Indies v South Africa at Port-of-Spain 2010**
ODI debut	**No ODIs yet**
T20I debut	**No T20Is yet**

THE PROFILE Offspinner Shane Shillingford certainly experienced the highs and lows of international cricket in 2012. Recalled for his first Tests for 18 months after whispers about his bowling action, Shillingford warmed up with four wickets against Australia in Port-of-Spain then, at home in Dominica, claimed ten wickets in the match – enough to earn him a diplomatic passport from the island's government as their ambassador for sport. But it didn't earn him a permanent place: he sat out the very next Test, in supposedly seam-friendly conditions at Lord's a couple of weeks later. Restored at Trent Bridge, Shillingford took only one wicket, and was dropped again, replaced by the new wonder boy Sunil Narine, who may well stand in the way of further opportunities. Shillingford had started with a bang back in January 2001, taking 7 for 66 on his first-class debut, for Windward Islands against Jamaica at Kingston. It was always going to be difficult to live up to such a start, and his career received what might have been a terminal setback later the same month when he was called for throwing by Steve Bucknor. But the new rules which permitted a 15-degree elbow-bend quietened the talk about his action, and Shillingford returned with 31 wickets in 2007-08, and went even better the following season with 56 at 19.05. The selectors could ignore him no longer, and in 2010 he became only the fifth Dominican to play Test cricket. Two of his predecessors share his surname, but they are not related: "Shillingford is a very common name in Dominica," says the veteran West Indian journalist Tony Cozier. "The original Mr Shillingford must have been quite a man."

THE FACTS Shillingford took 7 for 66 on his first-class debut, for the Windward Islands v Jamaica at Kingston in January 2001 ... He took 6 for 119 (and 4 for 100) against Australia at Roseau in April 2010: he was the first West Indian spinner to take ten in a Test since Lance Gibbs in 1966 ... He was the fifth Dominican to play a Test for West Indies, after Grayson and Irvine Shillingford (no relations), Norbert Phillip and Adam Sanford ...

THE FIGURES to 17.09.12   **espn**cricinfo.com

Batting & Fielding	M	Inns	NO	Runs	HS	Avge	S/R	100	50	4s	6s	Ct	St
Tests	8	12	2	116	31*	11.60	42.96	0	0	16	2	4	0
ODIs	0	0	–	–	–	–	–	–	–	–	–	–	–
T20Is	0	0	–	–	–	–	–	–	–	–	–	–	–
First-class	74	121	21	1341	63	13.41	–	0	4	–	–	42	0

Bowling	M	Balls	Runs	Wkts	BB	Avge	RpO	S/R	5i	10m
Tests	8	2580	1299	29	6–119	44.79	3.02	88.96	1	1
ODIs	0	0	–	–	–	–	–	–	–	–
T20Is	0	0	–	–	–	–	–	–	–	–
First-class	74	16927	7488	290	8–33	25.82	2.65	58.36	14	3

VUSI **SIBANDA**

Full name **Vusimuzi Sibanda**
Born **October 10, 1983, Highfields, Harare**
Teams **Mid West Rhinos**
Style **Right-hand bat, occasional medium-pacer**
Test debut **Zimbabwe v West Indies at Harare 2003-04**
ODI debut **Zimbabwe v West Indies at Bulawayo 2003-04**
T20I debut **Zimbabwe v Australia at Cape Town 2007-08**

THE PROFILE Like Tatenda Taibu, Hamilton Masakadza and Stuart Matsikenyeri, Vusi Sibanda comes from the Harare black township of Highfield. An opening batsman, Sibanda was one of a clutch of young players promoted to the national team before they were ready, as the dispute that cost Zimbabwe several senior players rumbled on. He was retained despite modest returns, his continued selection down almost entirely to outstanding potential rather than actual performance. Sibanda has always been a superb timer of the ball, predominantly off the front foot, but was slow to learn how to build a big innings. He made 78 and 116 against Bermuda in the tri-series in Trinidad in May 2006, but he continued to struggle against top-class opposition – and fought a similar long battle to get used to contact lenses. It all came right in 2009-10, when he kicked off a record-breaking domestic season with four centuries in two matches, and went on to score nine in all, a world record. He played only twice in the 2011 World Cup, making 61 against Kenya, but hit form when Bangladesh came calling in August for a tour that included Zimbabwe's first Test for six years. Sibanda started that in style, stroking an elegant 78, and continued his good form in the one-day series, hitting 96 and 67 in the first two matches. Innings of 45 and 93 followed in the home Tests against Pakistan and New Zealand, but he missed the NZ tour early in 2012 after missing some domestic games while playing club cricket in Australia. But, finally recognised as a class act, Sibanda was restored for the unofficial Twenty20 series in June 2012, in which Zimbabwe upset a strong South African side in the final at Harare.

THE FACTS Sibanda hit nine centuries in Zimbabwe in 2009-10, the most by any batsman in an overseas season, breaking the record of Don Bradman (eight in Australia in 1947-48); the run included four centuries in two successive matches, and seven in nine innings overall ... The sequence began with 209 (and 116 not out) for Zimbabwe v Kenya at Kwekwe in October 2009, and included a career-best 215 for Mid West Rhinos v Mountaineers ...

THE FIGURES *to 17.09.12*   **ESPncricinfo.com**

Batting & Fielding	M	Inns	NO	Runs	HS	Avge	S/R	100	50	4s	6s	Ct	St
Tests	6	12	0	320	93	26.66	53.60	0	2	43	3	4	0
ODIs	98	97	2	2274	116	23.93	62.54	1	17	253	24	34	0
T20Is	5	5	0	74	29	14.80	104.22	0	0	12	1	1	0
First-class	92	170	7	5254	215	32.23	–	14	21	–	–	96	0

Bowling	M	Balls	Runs	Wkts	BB	Avge	RpO	S/R	5i	10m
Tests	6	0	–	–	–	–	–	–	–	–
ODIs	98	141	149	2	1–12	74.50	6.34	70.50	0	0
T20Is	5	0	–	–	–	–	–	–	–	–
First-class	92	1869	1207	22	4–30	54.86	3.87	84.95	0	0

PETER SIDDLE

AUSTRALIA

Full name	**Peter Matthew Siddle**
Born	**November 25, 1984, Traralgon, Victoria**
Teams	**Victoria**
Style	**Right-hand bat, right-arm fast bowler**
Test debut	**Australia v India at Mohali 2008-09**
ODI debut	**Australia v New Zealand at Brisbane 2008-09**
T20I debut	**Australia v New Zealand at Sydney 2008-09**

THE PROFILE Peter Siddle was long considered one of the most dangerous fast bowlers in Australia – but also one of the most fragile. A shoulder reconstruction sidelined him for most of 2006-07, then he dislocated the joint at the start of the following season, and aggravated it again later on. He still finished 2007-08 with 33 wickets in just five matches. He emerged from reconstructive surgery fitter than ever, and was a surprise inclusion for the Indian tour in October 2008. His first Test wicket was the plum one of Sachin Tendulkar. The burly Siddle has echoes of two illustrious predecessors: the run-up is reminiscent of Craig McDermott's, while the bustling delivery reminds some of Merv Hughes – and he has a touch of the old Hughes banter, too. In England in 2009 he fought off the challenges of other pacemen to play throughout the series, moving the ball at pace and finishing up with 20 wickets. That included a decisive first-day spell of 5 for 21 to put England on the ropes at Headingley, where Australia won easily. He looked to have booked a spot – but then a stress fracture ruled him out for most of 2010. He returned for the Ashes, and started with a sensational first-day hat-trick on the way to 6 for 54, although he took only eight more wickets in that depressing series. Back trouble intruded again in 2012, sending him home early from a West Indian tour and preventing a planned stint with Essex. Siddle grew up in Morwell in rural Victoria, and was a promising competitive wood-chopper before concentrating on cricket at 14. "I thought if I was going to play competitive sport I should give it away because I didn't want to chop any toes off!"

THE FACTS Siddle took a Test hat-trick – on his birthday – on the first day of the 2010-11 Ashes series at Brisbane: he finished with a Test-best 6 for 54 ... Siddle took 5 for 21 v England at Headingley in 2009 ... He took 9 for 167 in the match in the Pura Cup final against New South Wales at Sydney in March 2008, although Victoria still lost ...

THE FIGURES to 17.09.12   **ESPN** cricinfo.com

Batting & Fielding	M	Inns	NO	Runs	HS	Avge	S/R	100	50	4s	6s	Ct	St
Tests	32	45	8	587	43	15.86	50.69	0	0	65	2	14	0
ODIs	17	4	2	21	9*	10.50	116.66	0	0	1	0	1	0
T20Is	2	1	1	1	1*	–	100.00	0	0	0	0	1	0
First-class	62	84	16	1097	45*	16.13	48.09	0	0	120	4	29	0

Bowling	M	Balls	Runs	Wkts	BB	Avge	RpO	S/R	5i	10m
Tests	32	6706	3425	117	6–54	29.27	3.06	57.31	5	0
ODIs	17	751	581	15	3–55	38.73	4.64	50.06	0	0
T20Is	2	48	58	3	2–24	19.33	7.25	16.00	0	0
First-class	62	12118	6165	234	6–43	26.34	3.05	51.78	12	0

LENDL **SIMMONS**

Full name	**Lendl Mark Platter Simmons**
Born	**January 25, 1985, Port-of-Spain, Trinidad**
Teams	**Trinidad & Tobago**
Style	**Right-hand bat, occasional medium-pacer**
Test debut	**West Indies v England at Port-of-Spain 2008-09**
ODI debut	**West Indies v Pakistan at Faisalabad 2006-07**
T20I debut	**West Indies v England at The Oval 2007**

THE PROFILE Lendl Simmons, the nephew of the former Test opener Phil, made a steady rise through the junior ranks, playing in the Under-19 World Cups of 2002 and 2004. An opener, and a fine fielder who can keep wicket, Simmons – named after the top 1980s tennis player Ivan Lendl – made his first-class debut six weeks after his 17th birthday. After passing 500 runs in the previous two domestic seasons, he toured England with West Indies A in 2006. He stepped up to the full one-day side in Pakistan later that year, collecting a duck in his first match but a mature 70 in his second. He struggled after that – only 42 runs in four innings – but retained his place for the 2007 World Cup, although he made only one appearance in that. A massive 282 against the England tourists early in 2009 finally earned him a Test place, but he failed to set the world alight. Later he hammered 77 off 50 balls against South Africa in the World Twenty20 in England (he had earlier taken four wickets against Sri Lanka), but was then surprisingly dropped again. After nearly two years on the sidelines (save for a forgettable one-day series in Australia early in 2010), Simmons regained his place when new coach Ottis Gibson shuffled the pack after the 2011 World Cup. He has done well in limited-overs matches since: seven fifties in 12 games against Pakistan and India in mid-2011 were followed by 122, his first century, in Bangladesh in October. Simmons added 80 in the next match, and 78 against India shortly afterwards – but in Tests he still failed to nail the big score he needed to consolidate a regular place.

THE FACTS Simmons made 282 for West Indies A v England in St Kitts in January 2009 ... He made 200 (his maiden century) for Trinidad & Tobago v Jamaica in Tobago in February 2006, after being out for 0 in the first innings: in March 2011 he made 204 not out for T&T v Guyana at Providence ... His uncle, Phil Simmons, won 26 Test caps for West Indies between 1988 and 1997 ...

THE FIGURES to 17.09.12   **ᴇsᴘncricinfo.com**

Batting & Fielding	M	Inns	NO	Runs	HS	Avge	S/R	100	50	4s	6s	Ct	St
Tests	8	16	0	278	49	17.37	46.88	0	0	28	4	5	0
ODIs	40	39	3	1130	122	31.38	68.98	1	10	92	26	16	0
T20Is	13	13	1	308	77	25.66	119.84	0	2	37	6	4	0
First-class	81	142	10	4375	282	33.14	–	9	19	–	–	86	4

Bowling	M	Balls	Runs	Wkts	BB	Avge	RpO	S/R	5i	10m
Tests	8	192	147	1	1–60	147.00	4.59	192.00	0	0
ODIs	40	90	82	1	1–3	82.00	5.46	90.00	0	0
T20Is	13	36	55	6	4–19	9.16	9.16	6.00	0	0
First-class	81	876	518	13	3–6	39.84	3.54	67.38	0	0

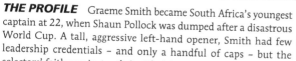

GRAEME **SMITH**

SOUTH AFRICA

Full name	**Graeme Craig Smith**
Born	**February 1, 1981, Johannesburg, Transvaal**
Teams	**Cape Cobras**
Style	**Left-hand bat, occasional offspinner**
Test debut	**South Africa v Australia at Cape Town 2001-02**
ODI debut	**South Africa v Australia at Bloemfontein 2001-02**
T20I debut	**South Africa v New Zealand at Johannesburg 2005-06**

THE PROFILE Graeme Smith became South Africa's youngest captain at 22, when Shaun Pollock was dumped after a disastrous World Cup. A tall, aggressive left-hand opener, Smith had few leadership credentials – and only a handful of caps – but the selectors' faith was instantly justified: in England in 2003 he collected back-to-back double-centuries. Reality bit back the following year, with Test-series defeats in Sri Lanka and India. There was also a run of 11 losses in 12 ODIs, a mixed time in New Zealand, and the start of an ultimately fruitless series against England. Yet Smith continued to crunch runs aplenty: his 125 to square the New Zealand series was a minor epic. He yields to no-one physically, but for a while he struggled against inswing bowling, frequently fumbling around his front pad. But he roared back in the Caribbean in 2005, with hundreds in three successive Tests. A baton-charge to 85 squared the home Test series against West Indies at the start of 2008, and later that year Smith achieved what he narrowly missed in 2003 – winning a Test series in England, his unbeaten 154 in a stiff run-chase at Edgbaston being one of the great captain's innings. In 2008-09 he presided over South Africa's first Test-series victory in Australia. He stood down as one-day captain after a subdued time at the 2011 World Cup, but remains firmly at the helm in Tests, and led South Africa to the top of the Test rankings in August 2012, after another victory in England – a series he started with a century at The Oval in his 100th Test.

THE FACTS In the first Test against England in 2003 Smith scored 277 at Birmingham, the highest score by a South African in Tests: in the second he made 259, the highest Test score by a visiting player at Lord's, beating Don Bradman's 254 in 1930 ... He has captained in a record 94 Test matches, beating Allan Border's 93 ... Smith played four matches for Somerset in 2005, scoring 311 against Leicestershire in one of them ... His record includes one Test for the World XI (as captain) and one ODI for the Africa XI ...

THE FIGURES *to 17.09.12*

ESPncricinfo.com

Batting & Fielding	M	Inns	NO	Runs	HS	Avge	S/R	100	50	4s	6s	Ct	St
Tests	102	179	12	8314	277	49.78	59.85	25	34	1055	23	137	0
ODIs	186	183	10	6698	141	38.71	81.20	9	46	758	43	98	0
T20Is	33	33	2	982	89*	31.67	127.53	0	5	123	26	18	0
First-class	144	244	17	11522	311	50.75	–		34	44	–	–	194	0

Bowling	M	Balls	Runs	Wkts	BB	Avge	RpO	S/R	5i	10m
Tests	102	1358	839	8	2–145	104.87	3.70	169.75	0	0
ODIs	186	1026	951	18	3–30	52.83	5.56	57.00	0	0
T20Is	33	24	57	0	–	–	14.25	–	0	0
First-class	144	1726	1086	11	2–145	98.72	3.77	156.90	0	0

STEVEN **SMITH**

Full name	**Steven Peter Devereux Smith**
Born	**June 2, 1989, Sydney**
Teams	**New South Wales, Pine Warriors**
Style	**Right-hand bat, legspinner**
Test debut	**Australia v Pakistan at Lord's 2010**
ODI debut	**Australia v West Indies at Melbourne 2009-10**
T20I debut	**Australia v Pakistan at Melbourne 2009-10**

THE PROFILE Steven Smith was initially seen as a possible new Warne, but as his legspin has regressed he will have to depend more on his batting. By the time he was 21 Smith was in all of Australia's senior squads. There were words of caution about his early elevation, but there was no hiding the excitement about a player who gives the ball air, hits it hard, catches it well, and seems unbothered by pressure. Smith became an international player in 2009-10 after starring with New South Wales, striking four Sheffield Shield centuries and finishing the season with career-best figures of 7 for 64. After only 13 first-class matches he was picked for the Test tour of New Zealand, but didn't get to play. He had already been tried in the limited-overs sides, impressing with his attitude, and was used more as a legspinner than a batsman. Two for 78 in his first one-dayer against West Indies doesn't sound very special, but he convinced Ricky Ponting to keep the field up to build pressure: not many 20-year-olds – Smith looked even younger – win arguments like that. His maiden Test series, against Pakistan in England in 2010, was encouraging: there were three wickets in the two games, and a muscular 77 at Headingley. But then he played three Tests in the 2010-11 Ashes without achieving much, and was similarly anonymous in the World Cup, although his fielding stood out. He continued to struggle to make an impact, and dropped out of the side after two quiet matches in England in July 2012. Smith started his state career in 2007-08, making his biggest impact in the Twenty20 Big Bash, in which he took nine wickets at the remarkable average of 5.33.

THE FACTS Smith's first four first-class hundreds – including his highest of 177 for NSW v Tasmania at Hobart – came during the 2009-10 Australian season ... He took 7 for 64 for NSW v South Australia at Adelaide in March 2010, after scoring 100 in the first innings ... Smith played in the Under-19 World Cup in 2008, alongside Phillip Hughes and Josh Hazlewood ...

THE FIGURES to 17.09.12   **ESPNcricinfo.com**

Batting & Fielding	M	Inns	NO	Runs	HS	Avge	S/R	100	50	4s	6s	Ct	St
Tests	5	10	1	259	77	28.77	56.79	0	2	27	2	3	0
ODIs	32	21	4	372	46*	21.88	87.11	0	0	26	3	14	0
T20Is	20	15	4	165	34	15.00	108.55	0	0	12	3	16	0
First-class	32	57	7	2100	177	42.00	58.84	5	10	268	21	43	0

Bowling	M	Balls	Runs	Wkts	BB	Avge	RpO	S/R	5i	10m
Tests	5	372	220	3	3–51	73.33	3.54	124.00	0	0
ODIs	32	875	764	22	3–33	34.72	5.23	39.77	0	0
T20Is	20	285	373	17	3–20	21.94	7.85	16.76	0	0
First-class	32	3683	2495	45	7–64	55.44	4.06	81.84	1	0

TIM **SOUTHEE**

Full name	**Timothy Grant Southee**
Born	**December 11, 1988, Whangarei**
Teams	**Northern Districts**
Style	**Right-hand bat, right-arm fast-medium bowler**
Test debut	**New Zealand v England at Napier 2007-08**
ODI debut	**New Zealand v England at Chester-le-Street 2008**
T20I debut	**New Zealand v England at Auckland 2007-08**

THE PROFILE Few players have made such a remarkable Test debut as 19-year-old Tim Southee in March 2008. First, swinging the ball at a healthy pace, he took 5 for 55 as England were restricted to 253, his victims including Andrew Strauss for 0 and Kevin Pietersen for 129. Later, with New Zealand in a hopeless position, he strolled in and smashed 77 not out from just 40 balls, with nine sixes, five of them off an unamused Monty Panesar. His second Test, at Lord's in May 2008, was rather more mundane – one run, no wickets – then he fell ill. Later that year he shook up the Aussies with three wickets in his first four overs at Brisbane, but further Test success proved elusive until he grabbed 7 for 64 to take New Zealand tantalisingly close to a rare Test victory over India. In the second innings in Bangalore he castled Sachin Tendulkar. By then Southee had become a consistent one-day force: in New Zealand's march to the semi-finals of the 2011 World Cup he took 18 wickets, a number exceeded only by Shahid Afridi and Zaheer Khan (21 apiece). Southee made his first-class debut for Northern Districts at 18 in February 2007, and the following season claimed 6 for 68 in a particularly impressive effort against Auckland. He was chosen for the Under-19 World Cup, but had to interrupt his preparations when he was drafted into the senior set-up for the Twenty20 games against England early in 2008. He ended the Under-19 World Cup as the second-highest wicket-taker, with 17, and was named Player of the Tournament. After that he barely had time to unpack before the Test call came.

THE FACTS Southee hit nine sixes in his first Test innings, a number only ever exceeded by four players, none of whom was making his debut: he had earlier become only the sixth New Zealander to take a five-for on Test debut ... He conceded 105 runs in ten overs against India at Christchurch in March 2009, a number exceeded in ODIs only by Australia's Mick Lewis, with 113 v South Africa at Johannesburg in 2005-06 ... Southee took 8 for 27 from 25 overs for Northern Districts v Wellington at Hamilton in November 2009 ...

THE FIGURES *to 17.09.12*   **ESPN**cricinfo.com

Batting & Fielding	M	Inns	NO	Runs	HS	Avge	S/R	100	50	4s	6s	Ct	St
Tests	19	32	4	526	77*	18.78	82.31	0	2	49	28	8	0
ODIs	60	35	12	232	32	10.08	89.23	0	0	13	10	10	0
T20Is	25	10	3	51	23	7.28	98.07	0	0	2	3	11	0
First-class	45	62	7	884	77*	16.07	74.85	0	3	81	37	12	0

Bowling	M	Balls	Runs	Wkts	BB	Avge	RpO	S/R	5i	10m
Tests	19	3698	2112	53	7–64	39.84	3.42	69.77	2	0
ODIs	60	2939	2550	82	5–33	31.09	5.20	35.84	1	0
T20Is	25	546	773	28	5–18	27.60	8.49	19.50	1	0
First-class	45	8615	4445	148	8–27	30.03	3.09	58.20	5	0

SREESANTH

Full name	**Shanthakumaran Sreesanth**
Born	**February 6, 1983, Kothamangalam, Kerala**
Teams	**Kerala, Rajasthan Royals**
Style	**Right-hand bat, right-arm fast-medium bowler**
Test debut	**India v England at Nagpur 2005-06**
ODI debut	**India v Sri Lanka at Nagpur 2005-06**
T20I debut	**India v South Africa at Johannesburg 2006-07**

THE PROFILE Punchy fast bowler Sreesanth, from unfashionable Kerala, started as a legspinner, idolising Anil Kumble, then once he turned to pace his rise was rapid although, since he played for a weak side, almost unnoticed. Not many bowlers play in the Duleep Trophy in their first season, but Sreesanth did, after taking 22 wickets in his first seven games in 2002-03. A couple of years later, now equipped with a more side-on action and increased pace, a superb display at the Challenger Trophy (trial matches for the national squad) propelled him into the side for the Sri Lanka series. Later he snapped up 6 for 55 against England, still the best one-day figures by an Indian fast bowler at home. Idiosyncratic, with an aggressive approach – to the stumps and the game – he can be expensive, but is also a wicket-taking bowler: in Antigua in June 2006 he fired out Ramnaresh Sarwan and Brian Lara (both for 0) in successive overs. He sometimes rubs opponents up the wrong way, but there is talent among the tantrums: Sreesanth took 19 wickets in the inaugural IPL in 2007-08, although his international form tailed off a little. A back injury in the second IPL didn't help, then more injuries – thigh and knee this time – disrupted the first half of 2010. He played in the first and last matches of the 2011 World Cup – failing to take a wicket in either – and was inconsistent on the England tour that followed, disappointing his many fans (and further upsetting his many critics). After that he was sidelined by a toe injury that needed surgery, which kept him out of action for most of 2012. Rising 30, he will need to regain form quickly to reclaim his place.

THE FACTS Sreesanth took a hat-trick for Kerala v Himachal Pradesh in the Ranji Trophy in November 2004 ... He is only the second Indian Test player from Kerala, after Tinu Yohannan, another fast-medium bowler ... Sreesanth did not score a run in ODIs until his 16th match, although that was only his fourth innings ...

THE FIGURES to 17.09.12   **espncricinfo.com**

Batting & Fielding	M	Inns	NO	Runs	HS	Avge	S/R	100	50	4s	6s	Ct	St
Tests	27	40	13	281	35	10.40	52.13	0	0	38	4	5	0
ODIs	53	21	10	44	10*	4.00	36.36	0	0	2	0	7	0
T20Is	10	3	2	20	19*	20.00	142.85	0	0	4	0	2	0
First-class	69	93	29	593	35	9.26	43.89	0	0	–	–	16	0

Bowling	M	Balls	Runs	Wkts	BB	Avge	RpO	S/R	5i	10m
Tests	27	5419	3271	87	5–40	37.59	3.62	62.28	3	0
ODIs	53	2476	2508	75	6–55	33.44	6.07	33.01	1	0
T20Is	10	204	288	7	2–12	41.14	8.47	29.14	0	0
First-class	69	12336	7251	201	5–40	36.07	3.52	61.37	6	0

MITCHELL **STARC**

Full name	**Mitchell Aaron Starc**
Born	**January 30, 1990, Baulkham Hills, Sydney**
Teams	**New South Wales, Yorkshire**
Style	**Left-hand bat, left-arm fast-medium bowler**
Test debut	**Australia v New Zealand at Brisbane 2011-12**
ODI debut	**Australia v India at Visakhapatnam 2010-11**
T20I debut	**Australia v Pakistan at Dubai 2012-13**

THE PROFILE One of several promising fast bowlers who have emerged in New South Wales in recent years, Mitchell Starc has a couple of advantages: he's very tall (6ft 4½), and he's a left-armer, a readymade replacement for the odd occasion when the other Mitchell, Johnson, goes walkabout. Starc turned heads with his speed and bounce during 2009-10, his first full season, during which he took 21 wickets – but he was restricted by injury the following summer, so missed the Ashes embarrassment, which might have been a blessing. He did make his ODI debut in October 2010, and took 4 for 27 in his second match, against Sri Lanka at Brisbane, before picking up a side strain. Starc was back in 2011-12, taking 27 wickets and earning a first Test cap against New Zealand after injuries to others. He looked slightly diffident in his early Tests, but a pep talk from Wasim Akram early in 2012 worked wonders: Starc even moved the ball around in unhelpful conditions in the UAE during a limited-overs series in September, taking 5 for 42 in the first match and 4 for 51 in the third one. "He bowled with good pace," enthused his captain Michael Clarke. "He's such a tall guy and he swung the ball beautifully in conditions where there wasn't much there for the fast bowlers." This followed an educational stint with Yorkshire – which started in farce when he was sent straight back to Australia on arrival at Heathrow because of a problem with his visa – and more experience of English conditions with Australia A later in the 2012 season. The new more confident Starc seems set for greater things in 2013.

THE FACTS Starc took 5 for 66 for NSW v Queensland at Brisbane in November 2011 ... He took 5 for 42 in an ODI against Pakistan in Sharjah in August 2012 ... Starc joined Yorkshire in 2012, but a visa problem meant he had to return to Australia immediately on arrival in the UK ...

THE FIGURES to 17.09.12   ᴇSᴘᴨcricinfo.com

Batting & Fielding	M	Inns	NO	Runs	HS	Avge	S/R	100	50	4s	6s	Ct	St
Tests	4	6	2	107	35	26.75	56.31	0	0	10	2	1	0
ODIs	11	4	2	43	17	21.50	89.58	0	0	5	0	2	0
T20Is	2	0	–	–	–	–	–	–	–	–	–	0	0
First-class	26	29	13	379	54*	23.68	53.75	0	1	41	6	12	0

Bowling	M	Balls	Runs	Wkts	BB	Avge	RpO	S/R	5i	10m
Tests	4	610	325	10	2–29	32.50	3.19	61.00	0	0
ODIs	11	543	461	22	5–42	20.95	5.09	24.68	1	0
T20Is	2	43	28	4	3–11	7.00	3.90	10.75	0	0
First-class	26	4019	2332	71	5–66	32.84	3.48	56.60	2	0

DALE **STEYN**

SOUTH AFRICA

Full name	**Dale Willem Steyn**
Born	**June 27, 1983, Phalaborwa, Limpopo Province**
Teams	**Titans, Deccan Chargers**
Style	**Right-hand bat, right-arm fast bowler**
Test debut	**South Africa v England at Port Elizabeth 2004-05**
ODI debut	**Africa XI v Asia XI at Centurion 2005-06**
T20I debut	**South Africa v New Zealand at Johannesburg 2007-08**

THE PROFILE Dale Steyn's rise to the South African side was as rapid as his bowling: he was picked for his first Test little more than a year after his first-class debut. A rare first-class cricketer from the Limpopo province close to the Kruger National Park and the Zimbabwe border, Steyn is genuinely fast, and moves the ball away. He played three Tests against England in 2004-05 before returning to domestic cricket, but was recalled in April 2006 and claimed 5 for 47 as New Zealand were routed at Centurion. He rattled a few helmets for Warwickshire in 2007, and really came of age the following winter, taking 40 wickets in five home Tests against New Zealand and West Indies, then 14 on Bangladesh's traditionally slow tracks. Finally he blew India away with 5 for 23 as they subsided to 76 all out and defeat at Ahmedabad. After a subdued time in England in 2008, Steyn claimed 34 victims in the home-and-away series against Australia, including ten wickets – and a rollicking 76 during a match-turning stand of 180 with J-P Duminy – in the Melbourne win that sealed South Africa's first-ever series win Down Under. He had a quiet 2009, but roared back the following year: after 13 wickets in the last two Tests against England in January, his 7 for 51 helped sink India at Nagpur, then 15 wickets in the Caribbean helped seal a 2-0 series win. In 2012 Steyn took 15 wickets in the three Tests in England which lifted South Africa to the top of the Test rankings – and was in sight of 300 wickets, at a phenomenal strike-rate.

THE FACTS Steyn's strike-rate in Tests has been bettered only by the 19th-century bowlers George Lohmann (34.19 balls per wicket) and John Ferris (37.73), Shane Bond of New Zealand (38.75) and his current team-mate Vernon Philander (33.19) ... Steyn took 8 for 41 (14 for 110 in the match) for Titans v Eagles in December 2007 ... He took 10 for 93 and 10 for 91 in successive home Tests v New Zealand in November 2007 ... Steyn made his ODI debut for the Africa XI, and his record includes two matches for them ...

THE FIGURES to 17.09.12   **ESPN**cricinfo.com

Batting & Fielding	M	Inns	NO	Runs	HS	Avge	S/R	100	50	4s	6s	Ct	St
Tests	57	71	16	808	76	14.69	43.30	0	1	79	20	15	0
ODIs	66	25	7	146	35	8.11	71.56	0	0	9	4	15	0
T20Is	23	4	2	8	5	4.00	80.00	0	0	0	0	8	0
First-class	99	118	28	1316	82	14.62	48.45	0	3	–	–	21	0

Bowling	M	Balls	Runs	Wkts	BB	Avge	RpO	S/R	5i	10m
Tests	57	11921	6745	287	7–51	23.50	3.39	41.53	18	4
ODIs	66	3225	2708	96	5–50	28.20	5.03	33.59	1	0
T20Is	23	498	554	31	4–9	17.87	6.67	16.06	0	0
First-class	99	19479	10797	442	8–41	24.42	3.32	44.07	26	6

GRAEME **SWANN**

Full name	**Graeme Peter Swann**
Born	**March 24, 1979, Northampton**
Teams	**Nottinghamshire**
Style	**Right-hand bat, offspinner**
Test debut	**England v India at Chennai 2008-09**
ODI debut	**England v South Africa at Bloemfontein 1999-2000**
T20I debut	**England v New Zealand at Auckland 2007-08**

THE PROFILE Self-confident and gregarious, Graeme Swann is an aggressive offspinner, not afraid to give the ball a real tweak, and also a hard-hitting lower-order batsman. He claimed a place in the revamped England squad which toured South Africa in 1999-2000 under new coach Duncan Fletcher, but Swann found life outside the Test side frustrating, although he bravely continued to give the ball a rip. However, he was less impressive off the field – what some saw as confidence, others interpreted as arrogance or cheek – and slid out of the reckoning. After marking time with Northamptonshire for a while, not helped by Monty Panesar's rise, Swann moved to Nottinghamshire in 2005 – a decision immediately justified when he helped them win the Championship. He was recalled for the Sri Lankan tour late in 2007, and took 4 for 34 in a one-day win at Dambulla, but he was soon on the outer again. However, with Panesar in something of a slump, Swann finally won his first Test cap in India in December 2008, making up for lost time by dismissing Gambhir and Dravid in his first over. He soon developed a reputation for troubling left-handers: half his Test wickets to date have been lefties, an unprecedented percentage. He also continued his enviable knack of taking wickets in the first over of a spell. Swann was underwhelming in the 2009 Ashes, but after that he blossomed, playing his part in the stunning 2010-11 victory Down Under with 5 for 91 at Adelaide, and spinning England to their 2011 whitewash over India with nine wickets at The Oval. By then he was ranked the No. 3 bowler in the world in Tests – and top in ODIs, although he slipped a little during a patchy 2012, when he was dropped for one of the home Tests against South Africa.

THE FACTS Swann took two wickets in his first over in Test cricket: the only other bowler to do this was England's Richard Johnson (v Zimbabwe at Chester-le-Street in 2003) ... Exactly half of Swann's Test wickets have been left-handers, an unprecedented percentage: Mohammad Aamer (48%) is next ... Swann took 7 for 33 for Northamptonshire v Derbyshire in June 2003 ... He made 183 for Northants v Gloucestershire at Bristol in August 2002 ...

THE FIGURES *to 17.09.12*   **ESPncricinfo.com**

Batting & Fielding	M	Inns	NO	Runs	HS	Avge	S/R	100	50	4s	6s	Ct	St
Tests	46	55	8	1078	85	22.93	79.67	0	4	141	14	39	0
ODIs	73	45	12	468	34	14.18	89.48	0	0	43	4	26	0
T20Is	34	14	11	70	18*	23.33	106.06	0	0	5	0	5	0
First-class	233	316	29	7369	183	25.67	–		4	35	–	–	176	0

Bowling	M	Balls	Runs	Wkts	BB	Avge	RpO	S/R	5i	10m
Tests	46	11594	5681	192	6–65	29.58	2.93	60.38	13	2
ODIs	73	3456	2579	98	5–28	26.31	4.47	35.26	1	0
T20Is	34	696	742	44	3–14	16.86	6.39	15.81	0	0
First-class	233	42790	21266	663	7–33	32.07	2.98	64.53	28	5

TATENDA **TAIBU**

ZIMBABWE

Full name	**Tatenda Taibu**
Born	**May 14, 1983, Harare**
Teams	**Southern Rocks**
Style	**Right-hand bat, wicketkeeper**
Test debut	**Zimbabwe v West Indies at Bulawayo 2001**
ODI debut	**Zimbabwe v West Indies at Harare 2001**
T20I debut	**Zimbabwe v Australia at Cape Town 2007-08**

THE PROFILE Diminutive and light on his feet, Tatenda Taibu is a throwback to the traditional style of wicketkeeper, and he has also been one of Zimbabwe's most dependable batsmen. He was vice-captain in England in 2003, when only 19, and the following year against Sri Lanka became the youngest-ever Test skipper, a week short of his 21st birthday. Taibu was plucked from Churchill High School to tour the West Indies and England early in 2000: he had not then played any domestic first-class cricket, but he was one of Zimbabwe's few bright spots in the 2003 World Cup and the subsequent England tour. In April 2004, he inherited the captaincy during a damaging dispute, and led a woefully inexperienced side by example in the face of repeated heavy defeats before Zimbabwe withdrew from Test cricket. Taibu had his own battles with authority, briefly threatening to settle in South Africa, but his class meant that he could not be ignored when he returned home. He reclaimed his place in the national side – although not as captain – in August 2007, and hit an ODI century against South Africa in his third match back; he made another ton against them two years later. He made 23 and 59 in Zimbabwe's comeback Test, the victory over Bangladesh in August 2011, and added 44 and 58 against Pakistan. Then he scored 53 as Zimbabwe chased down 329 to win an ODI against New Zealand, and added 53 in the close-run Test that followed. But Taibu picked up a finger injury on the tour of NZ early in 2012, then in July stunned supporters and team-mates by announcing his retirement, at 29, to devote himself to the church. He has revoked a previous retirement, though, so may yet be seen again in Zimbabwean colours.

THE FACTS Taibu was the youngest Test captain in history – 20 years 358 days v Sri Lanka at Harare in May 2004 ... In his first Test as captain, he took off the pads and took the first wicket to fall, ending an opening stand of 281 by dismissing Sanath Jayasuriya ... For Mashonaland v Midlands at Kwekwe in 2003-04 Taibu scored 175 not out and then took 8 for 43 ... His record includes one ODI for the African XI ...

THE FIGURES to 17.09.12   **ESPNcricinfo.com**

Batting & Fielding	M	Inns	NO	Runs	HS	Avge	S/R	100	50	4s	6s	Ct	St
Tests	28	54	3	1546	153	30.31	41.42	1	12	182	7	57	5
ODIs	150	137	21	3393	107*	29.25	67.58	2	22	235	32	114	33
T20Is	17	15	6	259	45*	28.77	100.77	0	0	19	2	6	5
First-class	114	198	20	6804	175*	38.22	–	12	39	–	–	297	30

Bowling	M	Balls	Runs	Wkts	BB	Avge	RpO	S/R	5i	10m
Tests	28	48	27	1	1–27	27.00	3.37	48.00	0	0
ODIs	150	84	61	2	2–42	30.50	4.35	42.00	0	0
T20Is	17	24	41	0	–	–	10.25	–	0	0
First-class	114	924	431	22	8–43	19.59	2.79	42.00	1	0

TAMIM IQBAL

Full name	**Tamim Iqbal Khan**
Born	**March 20, 1989, Chittagong**
Teams	**Chittagong**
Style	**Left-hand bat**
Test debut	**Bangladesh v New Zealand at Dunedin 2007-08**
ODI debut	**Bangladesh v Zimbabwe at Harare 2006-07**
T20I debut	**Bangladesh v Kenya at Nairobi 2007-08**

THE PROFILE A flamboyant left-hander, Tamim Iqbal is particularly strong square of the wicket, and also has a lovely straight drive. Selected for the 2007 World Cup after just four ODIs, he ignited the competition with 51 off 53 balls to ensure Bangladesh's reply to India's modest 191 got off to a flying start. Shrugging off a blow on the neck from Zaheer Khan, Tamim jumped down the track and smashed him over midwicket for six ... all this three days before his 18th birthday. He struggled to reproduce this form afterwards: it wasn't until his 18th match, in July 2007, that he reached 50 again. But the following year he made a hundred against Ireland, then in August 2009 rounded off a consistent run by hammering 154 – a national one-day record – against Zimbabwe. It was a similar story in Tests: great start (53 and 84 v New Zealand), quieter phase (17 innings with a best of 47), exciting flowering (128 as West Indies were beaten in St Vincent in July 2009). And by 2010 Tamim was clearly Bangladesh's star batsman: a superb 151 forced India to bat again despite amassing 554 at Mirpur in January, then twin eighties at home against England were followed by centuries in both Tests of the return series, at Lord's and Old Trafford. He was rewarded by becoming the first Bangladeshi to be named as one of *Wisden's* Five Cricketers of the Year. Tamim started the 2011 World Cup with another cameo against India, although this time his 70 could not bring victory. He continued to fire fitfully, and had a quieter time in 2012 – being signed for Pune Warriors in the IPL but not getting a game – but the opposition's celebrations whenever he departs cheaply speak volumes for the danger he poses.

THE FACTS Tamim Iqbal scored 154, Bangladesh's highest in ODIs, against Zimbabwe at Bulawayo in August 2009 ... He made 53 and 84 on his Test debut, against New Zealand in January 2008 ... Only Sachin Tendulkar and Mohammad Ashraful reached 1000 Test runs at a younger age than Tamim (a week short of his 21st birthday in 2010) ... His brother, Nafees Iqbal, and their uncle, Akram Khan, both played for Bangladesh too ...

THE FIGURES to 17.09.12   **espncricinfo.com**

Batting & Fielding	M	Inns	NO	Runs	HS	Avge	S/R	100	50	4s	6s	Ct	St
Tests	24	46	0	1748	151	38.00	60.15	4	10	241	12	8	0
ODIs	113	113	1	3368	154	30.07	79.17	3	23	379	45	30	0
T20Is	21	21	1	419	69*	20.95	100.23	0	2	49	3	5	0
First-class	45	83	1	3231	151	39.40	–	6	22	–	–	20	0

Bowling	M	Balls	Runs	Wkts	BB	Avge	RpO	S/R	5i	10m
Tests	24	24	10	0	–	–	2.50	–	0	0
ODIs	113	6	13	0	–	–	13.00	–	0	0
T20Is	21	0	–	–	–	–	–	–	–	–
First-class	45	132	77	0	–	–	3.50	–	0	0

TANVIR AHMED

Full name	**Tanvir Ahmed**
Born	**December 20, 1978, Kuwait City, Kuwait**
Teams	**Karachi, Sind**
Style	**Right-hand bat, right-arm fast-medium bowler**
Test debut	**Pakistan v South Africa at Abu Dhabi 2010-11**
ODI debut	**Pakistan v West Indies at Bridgetown 2010-11**
T20I debut	**Pakistan v New Zealand at Christchurch 2010-11**

THE PROFILE Tanvir Ahmed had to stand in line for a Test cap. A fast-medium bowler who was born in Kuwait (his father was working there at the time), Tanvir has played for numerous teams in Pakistan, most of them based around Karachi. He first made a mark in 2001-02 with 75 wickets, but did not pass 50 in the following seven seasons. International cricket seemed to have passed him by, but in 2009-10 – by now in his thirties – Tanvir rocketed into contention by topping the domestic wicket-taking lists with 97 at 20.22 apiece. That included 8 for 53 and 5 for 86 for Karachi Blues against Abbottabad, and ten wickets in each of the next two matches as well. "Tanvir's biggest asset is his perseverance," said the former Pakistan captain Rashid Latif. "He pitches the ball up compared to other Pakistani bowlers who bowl short." He could no longer be ignored, and was thrilled when he was selected to tour England in 2010 – but his only bowl came in a two-day game against Leicestershire. However, when the new-ball pair Mohammad Asif and Mohammad Aamer were banned after the spot-fixing scandal, Tanvir was finally given a chance. He made his Test debut in November 2010, and made up for lost time by dismissing Alviro Petersen with his third ball. He soon had 3 for 19 – but, with AB de Villiers making 278, South Africa recovered to 584: Tanvir finished with 6 for 120, still a fine effort. He added eight wickets in two Tests in New Zealand, and hit an important 57 in victory over West Indies in May 2011 – but seemed to fall off the radar after that, despite another consistent home season in 2011-12 (41 wickets at 29).

THE FACTS Tanvir Ahmed was only the second Test cricketer born in Kuwait: Shakeel Ahmed, a left-arm spinner, played one Test for Pakistan, against Australia at Karachi in October 1998 ... Tanvir took the wicket of South Africa's Alviro Petersen with his third ball in a Test, and dismissed Jesse Ryder of New Zealand with his fourth delivery in T20Is ... He took 8 for 53 (13 for 139 in the match) for Karachi Blues at Abbottabad in October 2009 ...

THE FIGURES to 17.09.12 ᴇSᴨᴨcricinfo.com

Batting & Fielding	M	Inns	NO	Runs	HS	Avge	S/R	100	50	4s	6s	Ct	St
Tests	4	5	1	116	57	29.00	61.70	0	1	21	0	1	0
ODIs	2	1	0	18	18	18.00	150.00	0	0	1	2	1	0
T20Is	1	0	–	–	–	–	–	–	–	–	–	0	0
First-class	120	187	26	3245	90	20.15	–	0	14	–	–	37	0

Bowling	M	Balls	Runs	Wkts	BB	Avge	RpO	S/R	5i	10m
Tests	4	617	393	16	6–120	24.56	3.82	38.56	1	0
ODIs	2	60	83	2	1–38	41.50	8.30	30.00	0	0
T20Is	1	18	13	1	1–13	13.00	4.33	18.00	0	0
First-class	120	22179	13048	462	8–53	28.24	3.52	48.00	25	7

TAUFEEQ UMAR

PAKISTAN

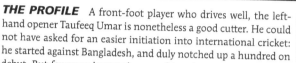

Full name	**Taufeeq Umar**
Born	**June 20, 1981, Lahore**
Teams	**Lahore, Habib Bank**
Style	**Left-hand bat, occasional offspinner**
Test debut	**Pakistan v Bangladesh at Multan 2001**
ODI debut	**Pakistan v Sri Lanka at Sharjah 2001-02**
T20I debut	**No T20Is yet**

THE PROFILE A front-foot player who drives well, the left-hand opener Taufeeq Umar is nonetheless a good cutter. He could not have asked for an easier initiation into international cricket: he started against Bangladesh, and duly notched up a hundred on debut. But far more impressive were his subsequent performances – 88 against a top-class Australian attack was followed by a flawless 135 against South Africa at Cape Town. On those bouncy pitches, Taufeeq had ample time to play the seamers. He did not get much opportunity in the 2003 World Cup, but proved himself an asset in the home series against South Africa shortly afterwards, with a hundred and three fifties in his four innings. But he was axed a few Tests later after a moderate run, then was in and out – more out – of the team. When he was given a chance, he looked understandably nervous ... but given that Pakistan's openers are rarely allowed to settle, the door remained ajar. He seemed to have been dumped for good after a double failure in the 2006 Headingley Test, but was recalled late in 2010, after the disastrous England tour, and initially did well in Tests against South Africa and New Zealand. But after three low scores in the West Indies his international future was on the line – then he was let off twice in the second innings in St Kitts, and went on to make 135, his first Test hundred for more than seven years. Taufeeq added a monumental 236 (in 712 minutes) against Sri Lanka in Abu Dhabi in October 2011, but a poor run the following year – only one fifty in 11 innings after starting with 58 against England in Dubai – left him looking over his shoulder again.

THE FACTS Taufeeq Umar was the eighth Pakistani to score a century on Test debut, with 104 against Bangladesh in August 2001 ... His fifth Test century (v West Indies in May 2011) came more than seven years after his fourth (in October 2003): only Mushtaq Mohammad, with almost nine years between 1962 and 1971, has a longer gap between Test hundreds for Pakistan ... Taufeeq made 236 against Sri Lanka in Abu Dhabi in October 2011 ...

THE FIGURES to 17.09.12   **ESP̄n**cricinfo.com

Batting & Fielding	M	Inns	NO	Runs	HS	Avge	S/R	100	50	4s	6s	Ct	St
Tests	43	81	5	2943	236	38.72	44.74	7	14	401	4	47	0
ODIs	22	22	1	504	81*	24.00	56.31	0	3	51	2	9	0
T20Is	0	0	–	–	–	–	–	–	–	–	–	0	0
First-class	137	238	13	8597	236	38.20	–	18	46	–	–	140	0

Bowling	M	Balls	Runs	Wkts	BB	Avge	RpO	S/R	5i	10m
Tests	43	78	44	0	–	–	3.38	–	0	0
ODIs	22	72	85	1	1–49	85.00	7.08	72.00	0	0
T20Is	0	0	–	–	–	–	–	–	–	–
First-class	137	880	481	14	3–33	34.35	3.27	62.85	0	0

BRENDAN **TAYLOR**

Full name	**Brendan Ross Murray Taylor**
Born	**February 6, 1986, Harare**
Teams	**Mid West Rhinos, Wellington**
Style	**Right-hand bat, occasional wicketkeeper**
Test debut	**Zimbabwe v Sri Lanka at Harare 2004**
ODI debut	**Zimbabwe v Sri Lanka at Bulawayo 2004**
T20I debut	**Zimbabwe v Bangladesh at Khulna 2006-07**

THE PROFILE Brendan Taylor was fast-tracked into the national team at 18 after the withdrawal of several senior players. He shot to international prominence at Cape Town on September 12, 2007, when his ice-cool 60 not out carried Zimbabwe to victory over Australia in the inaugural World Twenty20. Taylor marshalled a tense run-chase with the sort of sang froid that few had ever credited him with. But actually it wasn't the first time he had displayed a calm head in a pressure situation: in August 2006 he smoked 17 from the last over – including a six to win off the last ball – to beat Bangladesh. Early on, Taylor had often showed the ability to build an innings, but was frustratingly dismissed trying to play too aggressively: he passed 90 three times in ODIs before finally reaching 100. In Tests he made 77 against New Zealand in August 2005 when he was 19, but shortly after that Zimbabwe withdrew from Test cricket for six years. When they returned in August 2011, Taylor was captain, having put a chequered disciplinary record behind him. He had been Zimbabwe's outstanding batsman at the 2011 World Cup, his uppercut to third man one of the tournament's enduring images. He celebrated his elevation in style by scoring his first century – and leading Zimbabwe to victory – in their comeback Test, against Bangladesh at Harare. Another century followed soon afterwards against New Zealand. He may be more disciplined now, but still produces the trademark full-blooded front-foot cover-drives which make him an attractive batsman to watch. Taylor had a spell as wicketkeeper, and is now a reliable slip fielder.

THE FACTS Taylor scored 217 for Mid West Rhinos v Southern Rocks at Masvingo in February 2010 ... After three scores in the nineties, he finally reached his first ODI hundred against Bangladesh at Chittagong in November 2009 ... Taylor made his first Test century in his first match as captain, against Bangladesh at Harare in August 2011 ... He averages 46 in ODIs against India, but only 13 against England ... Taylor averages 39.17 in ODIs in which he has kept wicket, but only 28.48 as a specialist batsman ...

THE FIGURES to 17.09.12   **ESPncricinfo.com**

Batting & Fielding	M	Inns	NO	Runs	HS	Avge	S/R	100	50	4s	6s	Ct	St
Tests	14	28	1	791	117	29.29	51.76	2	5	89	9	14	0
ODIs	132	131	13	4112	145*	34.84	72.36	6	26	342	56	65	18
T20Is	15	15	4	373	75*	33.90	121.89	0	4	30	12	4	1
First-class	69	127	7	4730	217	39.41	–	14	19	–	–	83	4

Bowling	M	Balls	Runs	Wkts	BB	Avge	RpO	S/R	5i	10m
Tests	14	42	38	0	–	–	5.42	–	0	0
ODIs	132	396	406	9	3–54	45.11	6.15	44.00	0	0
T20Is	15	30	17	1	1–16	17.00	3.40	30.00	0	0
First-class	69	366	213	4	2–36	53.25	3.49	91.50	0	0

JAMES **TAYLOR**

Full name	**James William Arthur Taylor**
Born	**January 6, 1990, Nottingham**
Teams	**Nottinghamshire**
Style	**Right-hand bat, occasional legspinner**
Test debut	**England v South Africa at Leeds 2012**
ODI debut	**England v Ireland at Dublin 2011**
T20I debut	**No T20Is yet**

THE PROFILE A compact and correct batsman who is only 5ft 6ins (167cm) tall – his father was a jockey – James Taylor was long tipped for stardom. Unfazed by short-pitched bowling despite his small stature, he scored more than 1200 runs in 2009, his first full season, at an average of 57: that included a double-century against Surrey, and earned him the Cricket Writers' Club's young player of the year award. There was little drop-off in the often-significant second season – 1095 runs at 43, and another double-ton – which resulted in an England Lions tour to the West Indies, where he took 186 off Barbados and their Test new-ball pairing of Pedro Collins and Fidel Edwards. In 2011 Taylor didn't make a Championship century till August, but he had scored 168 not out against Sri Lanka A for the Lions, which led to a place in an experimental squad to face Ireland in an official one-day international in Dublin. In 2011-12 Taylor had a lean time as captain of the Lions in Sri Lanka, and started the 2012 home season indifferently too – by now he'd followed the road previously travelled by Stuart Broad and moved from lowly Leicestershire to Nottinghamshire. But another Lions century, against the West Indians, ushered in a run of better form, and when Jonny Bairstow was dropped for the start of the South African series after looking vulnerable to the short stuff, Taylor made his Test debut at Headingley. He made a composed 34, batting for two and a half hours and sharing a stand of 147 with Kevin Pietersen, but was outshone by the returning Bairstow at Lord's, not helped by a calamitous run-out, and missed the tour of India that followed.

THE FACTS Taylor scored 237 for Leicestershire v Loughborough University in April 2011, after coming in at 2 for 2 ... In 2008 he was the second winner of the Wisden Schools Cricketer of the Year Award, following Jonny Bairstow ... Taylor made 207 not out for Leicestershire v Surrey at The Oval in July 2009, and 206 not out against Middlesex at Leicester in May 2010 ...

THE FIGURES *to 17.09.12*   **ESPMcricinfo.com**

Batting & Fielding	M	Inns	NO	Runs	HS	Avge	S/R	100	50	4s	6s	Ct	St
Tests	2	3	0	48	34	16.00	31.57	0	0	6	0	2	0
ODIs	1	1	0	1	1	1.00	12.50	0	0	0	0	0	0
T20Is	0	0	–	–	–	–	–	–	–	–	–	–	–
First-class	81	134	19	5409	237	47.03	–	13	24	–	–	58	0

Bowling	M	Balls	Runs	Wkts	BB	Avge	RpO	S/R	5i	10m
Tests	2	0	–	–	–	–	–	–	–	–
ODIs	1	0	–	–	–	–	–	–	–	–
T20Is	0	0	–	–	–	–	–	–	–	–
First-class	81	228	176	0	–	–	4.63	–	0	0

ROSS **TAYLOR**

Full name **Luteru Ross Poutoa Lote Taylor**
Born **March 8, 1984, Lower Hutt, Wellington**
Teams **Central Districts, Delhi Daredevils**
Style **Right-hand bat, offspinner**
Test debut **New Zealand v South Africa at Johannesburg 2007-08**
ODI debut **New Zealand v West Indies at Napier 2005-06**
T20I debut **New Zealand v Sri Lanka at Wellington 2006-07**

THE PROFILE Ross Taylor was singled out for attention from an early age – he captained New Zealand in the 2001-02 Under-19 World Cup – but it was some time before he made the big breakthrough. In March 2005 he extended his maiden first-class century to 184, then began the following season with five sixes in a century against Otago. He then cracked 121 against Wellington, 114 off long-suffering Otago in the semi, then 50 in the final against Canterbury. He rounded off a fine season with 106 as CD won the State Championship final at Wellington. It all led to a call-up for the final two ODIs of West Indies' tour early in 2006, and a regular place the following season. Taylor flogged Sri Lanka – Murali and all – for an unbeaten 128 in only his third match, and added an equally muscular 117 against Australia at Auckland in February 2007. A belated Test debut followed in November, and he scored 120 against England in his third match, before entrancing Old Trafford with an unbeaten 154 in the return series in 2008, during which he also took some fine slip catches. Highlights since have included a fine 151 against India at Napier in March 2009, and a defiant 138 against Australia at Hamilton a year later. He also entertained the IPL's crowds with some big hitting. Taylor scored consistently in the 2011 World Cup, the highlight coming against Pakistan – on his 27th birthday – when he clattered 55 from his last 13 deliveries to reach 131. After the tournament he was appointed New Zealand's captain after Daniel Vettori stood down. Responsibility didn't seem to affect him: Taylor made a brace of 76s in his first Test in charge, in Zimbabwe, then in August 2012 stroked a superb 113 at Bangalore, as New Zealand came close to a rare Test victory in India.

THE FACTS Only Martin Donnelly and Bevan Congdon (twice) have made higher Test scores for New Zealand in England than Taylor's 154 not out at Manchester in 2008 ... He and Jesse Ryder put on 271, a record for NZ's fourth wicket, against India at Napier in March 2009 ... Taylor made 217 for Central Districts v Otago at Napier in December 2006 ...

THE FIGURES to 17.09.12   **ESPNcricinfo.com**

Batting & Fielding	M	Inns	NO	Runs	HS	Avge	S/R	100	50	4s	6s	Ct	St
Tests	41	75	4	3025	154*	42.60	57.86	7	16	393	29	67	0
ODIs	112	101	14	3323	131*	38.19	82.08	6	20	268	88	80	0
T20Is	41	37	6	702	63	22.64	117.19	0	3	42	32	27	0
First-class	91	154	6	6096	217	41.18	–	13	34	–	–	112	0

Bowling	M	Balls	Runs	Wkts	BB	Avge	RpO	S/R	5i	10m
Tests	41	90	43	2	2–4	21.50	2.86	45.00	0	0
ODIs	112	42	35	0	–	–	5.00	–	0	0
T20Is	41	–	–	–	–	–	–	–	–	–
First-class	91	660	359	6	2–4	59.83	3.26	110.00	0	0

SACHIN **TENDULKAR**

INDIA

Full name	**Sachin Ramesh Tendulkar**
Born	**April 24, 1973, Bombay (now Mumbai)**
Teams	**Mumbai, Mumbai Indians**
Style	**Right-hand bat, occasional medium-pace/legspin**
Test debut	**India v Pakistan at Karachi 1989-90**
ODI debut	**India v Pakistan at Gujranwala 1989-90**
T20I debut	**India v South Africa at Johannesburg 2006-07**

THE PROFILE You only have to attend a one-dayer at the Wankhede Stadium, and watch the lights flicker and the floor tremble as the applause echoes around the ground when he comes in, to realise what Sachin Tendulkar means to Mumbai ... and India. Age, and niggling injuries, may have dimmed the light a little – he's now more of an accumulator than an artist – but he is still light-footed with bat in hand, the nearest thing to Bradman, as The Don himself recognised. Sachin seems to have been around for ever: he made his Test debut at 16, shrugging off a blow on the head against Pakistan, captivated England in 1990, with a maiden Test century, and similarly enchanted Australia in 1991-92. Two more big hundreds lit up the 2007-08 series Down Under, and Tendulkar now has 11 Test tons against the Aussies. He leads the list of ODI runscorers by a country mile, and owns the records for most runs, centuries and appearances in Tests too. Early in 2010 he stroked the first ODI double-century, then most of the talk after an immensely satisfying victory in the 2011 World Cup was of his quest for 100 international hundreds, a landmark he finally reached in March 2012. Until he throttled back in his thirties, Tendulkar usually looked to attack: now he's more circumspect, but no less destructive when in form. Small, steady at the crease before a decisive move forward or back, he remains a master, his whipped flick to fine leg an object of wonder. He could have starred as a bowler: he can do offbreaks, leggies or dobbly medium-pacers, although he doesn't bowl much these days.

THE FACTS Tendulkar passed his childhood idol Sunil Gavaskar's record of 34 Test centuries in December 2005 ... No-one is close to his 100 international centuries (Ricky Ponting is next with 71) ... Tendulkar has hit 11 Test centuries against Australia, and nine in ODIs ... His first mention in *Wisden* came when he was 14, after a stand of 664 in a school game with another future Test batsman, Vinod Kambli ...

THE FIGURES *to 17.09.12*

cricinfo.com

Batting & Fielding	M	Inns	NO	Runs	HS	Avge	S/R	100	50	4s	6s	Ct	St
Tests	190	314	32	15533	248*	55.08	–	51	65	2005	67	113	0
ODIs	463	452	41	18426	200*	44.83	86.23	49	96	2016	195	140	0
T20Is	1	1	0	10	10	10.00	83.33	0	0	2	0	1	0
First-class	294	467	48	24452	248*	58.35	–	78	111	–	–	181	0

Bowling	M	Balls	Runs	Wkts	BB	Avge	RpO	S/R	5i	10m
Tests	190	4180	2451	45	3–10	53.68	3.50	91.82	0	0
ODIs	463	8054	6850	154	5–32	44.48	5.10	52.29	2	0
T20Is	1	15	12	1	1–12	12.00	4.80	15.00	0	0
First-class	294	7545	4343	70	3–10	62.04	3.45	107.78	0	0

UPUL **THARANGA**

Full name	**Warushavithana Upul Tharanga**
Born	**February 2, 1985, Balapitiya**
Teams	**Nondescripts, Ruhuna**
Style	**Left-hand bat, occasional wicketkeeper**
Test debut	**Sri Lanka v India at Ahmedabad 2005-06**
ODI debut	**Sri Lanka v West Indies at Dambulla 2005-06**
T20I debut	**Sri Lanka v England at Southampton 2006**

THE PROFILE Upul Tharanga's international call-up in July 2005 brightened a year marred by the Indian Ocean tsunami, which washed away his family home in Ambalangoda, a fishing town on the west coast. Tharanga, a wispy left-hander blessed with natural timing, had played premier-league cricket at 15 and passed seamlessly through the national age-group squads. He hit 105 against Bangladesh in only his fifth match – he celebrated modestly, aware that stiffer challenges lay ahead – then pummelled 165 against them in his third Test. During 2006 he lit up Lord's with 120 in the first of five successive defeats of England: he added 109 in the last of those, at Headingley, sharing a record opening stand of 286 with Sanath Jayasuriya. The feature of those innings was the way he made room to drive through the off side. In the 2007 World Cup Tharanga made 73 in the semi-final, but struggled the following season and lost his place. He emerged from the doldrums in 2008-09, passing 150 twice for the A team in South Africa then making his maiden double-century in a domestic match. In August 2009 he scored 76 against New Zealand (his first international fifty for more than two years), celebrated with 80 in the next game, and has been a 50-overs regular ever since, although he hasn't played a Test since December 2007. He scored centuries in the 2011 World Cup against England and Zimbabwe, but made only 2 in the final, and was then hit with a three-month ban after taking a herbal remedy for a shoulder injury which contained a banned drug. He was back later in the year, stroked another ODI hundred against Australia at Hambantota, and scored consistently during 2012.

THE FACTS Tharanga and Sanath Jayasuriya put on 286 (in 31.5 overs) against England at Leeds in July 2006, a first-wicket record for all ODIs ... There have been 24 opening stands of 200-plus in ODIs: Tharanga has been involved in a record six of them ... He averages 57.80 in ODIs against England, but 0 v Ireland ... Tharanga carried his bat for 265 for Ruhuna v Basnahira South in March 2009 ... His record includes one ODI for the Asia XI ...

THE FIGURES *to 17.09.12*   **ESPncricinfo.com**

Batting & Fielding	M	Inns	NO	Runs	HS	Avge	S/R	100	50	4s	6s	Ct	St
Tests	15	26	1	713	165	28.52	49.51	1	3	99	5	11	0
ODIs	155	148	8	4838	133	34.55	73.87	12	27	552	25	30	0
T20Is	10	10	0	131	37	13.10	113.91	0	0	12	3	1	0
First-class	83	138	4	4726	265*	35.26	–	10	19	–	–	62	1

Bowling	M	Balls	Runs	Wkts	BB	Avge	RpO	S/R	5i	10m
Tests	15	0	–	–	–	–	–	–	–	–
ODIs	155	0	–	–	–	–	–	–	–	–
T20Is	10	0	–	–	–	–	–	–	–	–
First-class	83	18	4	0	–	–	1.33	–	0	0

LAHIRU **THIRIMANNE**

Full name	**Hettige Don Rumesh Lahiru Thirimanne**
Born	**September 8, 1989, Moratuwa**
Teams	**Ragama, Uva**
Style	**Left-hand bat, occ. right-arm medium-pacer**
Test debut	**Sri Lanka v England at Southampton 2011**
ODI debut	**Sri Lanka v India at Dhaka 2010-11**
T20I debut	**Sri Lanka v Pakistan at Hambantota 2012**

THE PROFILE Left-hander Lahiru Thirimanne was long considered one of the best young batsmen in Sri Lanka, and it was no great surprise when he was named in the senior team for a tri-series in Bangladesh early in 2010. He made 22 in his first match, opening against India's experienced new-ball attack of Zaheer Khan and Ashish Nehra, but slipped out of the team after two more outings and was not required for the 2011 World Cup. He was back for the England tour that followed, when after Tillekeratne Dilshan broke a finger in the second Test, the match against Essex boiled down to a shootout between Thirimanne and Dinesh Chandimal for the vacant opening spot for the third Test at the Rose Bowl. Chandimal was out for 16 – but Thirimanne booked his place with a fine 104. On his Test debut at 21 he survived an hour for 10 in the first innings, then applied himself well for 38 in the second as Sri Lanka – nearly 200 behind – dug in for the draw. In *The Guardian*, David Hopps wrote: "Thirimanne's hundred against Essex before this Test was his first outside Sri Lanka, but his application against the moving ball suggested that it will not be the last." Dilshan naturally displaced him when the Australians toured later in 2011, but when Thilan Samaraweera was dropped it was Thirimanne who replaced him. He scored 68 in his third Test, against Pakistan in Abu Dhabi, but lost his place early in 2012 after a couple of failures. He had better luck in ODIs, though, making 47 and 77 in successive matches against India later in the year. Thirimanne, who played in the Under-19 World Cup in 2008 and made his first-class debut later that year, now faces a fight for a middle-order place with some other talented youngsters – including that man Chandimal.

THE FACTS Thirimanne made 148 (one of four centuries in a total of 720) for Basnahira South against Ruhuna in Colombo in May 2010 ... He scored 108 for Sri Lanka Under-19s against England (whose opening bowler was Steven Finn) in a one-day international in Kuala Lumpur in February 2007 ...

THE FIGURES to 17.09.12   **ESPNcricinfo.com**

Batting & Fielding	M	Inns	NO	Runs	HS	Avge	S/R	100	50	4s	6s	Ct	St
Tests	7	14	1	258	68	19.84	34.26	0	1	19	0	3	0
ODIs	27	20	1	591	77	31.10	75.47	0	4	34	5	12	0
T20Is	3	3	0	68	30	22.66	115.25	0	0	9	0	3	0
First-class	52	91	9	3347	148	40.81	48.94	9	17	341	24	44	0

Bowling	M	Balls	Runs	Wkts	BB	Avge	RpO	S/R	5i	10m
Tests	7	6	7	0	–	–	7.00	–	0	0
ODIs	27	25	25	1	1–25	25.00	6.00	25.00	0	0
T20Is	3	0	–	–	–	–	–	–	–	–
First-class	52	66	56	0	–	–	5.09	–	0	0

MANOJ **TIWARY**

INDIA

Full name	**Manoj Kumar Tiwary**
Born	**November 14, 1985, Howrah, Bengal**
Teams	**Bengal, Kolkata Knight Riders**
Style	**Right-hand bat, legspinner**
Test debut	**No Tests yet**
ODI debut	**India v Australia at Brisbane 2007-08**
T20I debut	**India v England at Kolkata 2011-12**

THE PROFILE Manoj Tiwary, an aggressive batsman from Bengal who idolises Kevin Pietersen, has developed an unwanted reputation as the unluckiest man in Indian cricket. In 2006-07 he piled up 796 runs at 99.50 in the Ranji Trophy, and forced his way into the party for the Bangladesh tour. He was all set to play at Mirpur ... but badly injured his shoulder during fielding practice the day before. Then when his debut did finally come, at Brisbane early in 2008 in the first match of the annual Australian one-day tri-series, he was suffering from jetlag and failed to cope with the pace of Brett Lee, who worked him over then yorked him for 2. Tiwary had to wait three years, and the 2011 West Indian tour, for another international chance – but was pushed up to open and struggled again. Bengal's cricket-lovers nicknamed him *chhota dada* (echoing Sourav Ganguly's nickname, *dada*), and patiently awaited the sort of comeback Ganguly made six years after his own debut, coincidentally also at Brisbane. Finally, in December 2011 Tiwary, who had remained a heavy scorer at domestic level, produced the goods on the big stage, hitting a one-day hundred against West Indies at Chennai. A run in the team? Not a bit of it ... Tiwary was stuck on the bench until July, biting his tongue during a Sri Lankan tour in which Rohit Sharma hardly got a run: possibly Tiwary's penchant for working the ball to leg was held against him. Finally included, he made an important 21 after taking four wickets with his unsung legspin in the fourth match, then hit an attractive 65 in the final game, which should guarantee him an extended trial.

THE FACTS Tiwary scored 104 not out against West Indies at Chennai in December 2011 – and then wasn't selected for another ODI for more than seven months ... He made 267 for Bengal v Madhya Pradesh in Kolkata in November 2011 ... Tiwary extended his maiden first-class hundred, against Mumbai at Kolkata in December 2006, to 210 ...

THE FIGURES to 17.09.12   **ESPNcricinfo.com**

Batting & Fielding	M	Inns	NO	Runs	HS	Avge	S/R	100	50	4s	6s	Ct	St
Tests	0	0	–	–	–	–	–	–	–	–	–	–	–
ODIs	8	8	1	251	104*	35.85	77.46	1	1	24	2	3	0
T20Is	3	1	0	15	15	15.00	88.23	0	0	0	0	2	0
First-class	57	82	8	4335	267	58.58	55.65	16	11	–	–	55	0

Bowling	M	Balls	Runs	Wkts	BB	Avge	RpO	S/R	5i	10m
Tests	0	0	–	–	–	–	–	–	–	–
ODIs	8	126	144	5	4–61	28.80	6.85	25.20	0	0
T20Is	3	0	–	–	–	–	–	–	–	–
First-class	57	1985	1093	18	2–38	60.72	3.30	110.27	0	0

JAMES **TREDWELL**

Full name	**James Cullum Tredwell**
Born	**February 27, 1982, Ashford, Kent**
Teams	**Kent**
Style	**Left-hand bat, offspinner**
Test debut	**England v Bangladesh at Mirpur 2009-10**
ODI debut	**England v Bangladesh at Mirpur 2009-10**
T20I debut	**No T20Is yet**

ENGLAND

THE PROFILE James "Pingu" Tredwell made steady progress after making his Kent debut in 2001. Initially seen as a containing offspinner in one-day cricket, it took him a while to establish himself in the Championship side. After he did that, in 2007, he was soon making his way steadily up the batting order: pushed up to No. 4, he made a maiden century against Yorkshire at Tunbridge Wells. He made another hundred against the New Zealand tourists from first drop the following year and, now settled around No. 7 in the order, reminded the selectors of his batting prowess with 115 against eventual champions Nottinghamshire in June 2010. Tredwell had a place at the ECB National Academy in 2003-04, and made the Performance squad in the winter of 2007. The following year he was part of the one-day squad in New Zealand, although he didn't get a game, but 69 Championship wickets in 2009 kept him in the frame. He was called up as cover for Graeme Swann during that winter's South African tour, and although again he did not feature in the internationals, his consistent performances booked him a place on the trip to Bangladesh which followed. Finally he won an England cap: after a quiet one-day debut he played in the second Test at Mirpur, dismissed the danger men Tamim Iqbal and Shakib Al Hasan in the first innings, and followed that with four more wickets in the second. However, with Swann firmly entrenched, chances were limited after that, although Tredwell continues to feature in England's one-day plans – and at Lord's in September 2012 took three wickets (all stumpings by Craig Kieswetter) as South Africa were downed by six wickets.

THE FACTS Tredwell took 8 for 66 for Kent v Glamorgan at Canterbury in May 2009 ... On his World Cup debut, against West Indies at Chennai in March 2011, Tredwell took 4 for 48 ... He scored 123 not out for Kent against the New Zealanders at Canterbury in April 2008 ... Tredwell took 7 for 22, including a hat-trick, as Kent beat Yorkshire at Leeds in September 2010 ...

THE FIGURES to 17.09.12   **ESPN** cricinfo.com

Batting & Fielding	M	Inns	NO	Runs	HS	Avge	S/R	100	50	4s	6s	Ct	St
Tests	1	1	0	37	37	37.00	58.73	0	0	6	0	1	0
ODIs	9	5	2	34	16	11.33	46.57	0	0	1	0	1	0
T20Is	0	0	–	–	–	–	–	–	–	–	–	–	–
First-class	128	182	23	3599	123*	22.63	43.09	3	14	–	–	136	0

Bowling	M	Balls	Runs	Wkts	BB	Avge	RpO	S/R	5i	10m
Tests	1	390	181	6	4–82	30.16	2.78	65.00	0	0
ODIs	9	408	337	11	4–48	30.63	4.95	37.09	0	0
T20Is	0	0	–	–	–	–	–	–	–	–
First-class	128	22628	11621	335	8–66	34.68	3.08	67.54	11	3

JONATHAN **TROTT**

Full name	**Ian Jonathan Leonard Trott**
Born	**April 22, 1981, Cape Town, South Africa**
Teams	**Warwickshire**
Style	**Right-hand bat, right-arm medium-pacer**
Test debut	**England v Australia at The Oval 2009**
ODI debut	**England v Ireland at Belfast 2009**
T20I debut	**England v West Indies at The Oval 2007**

THE PROFILE The story sounds familiar: aggressive right-hander, born in South Africa, reputation for cockiness on the county circuit. But no, we're not talking Kevin Pietersen here, rather Jonathan Trott, who moved to England in 2003. His grandparents were British, which meant he could play as a non-overseas player for Warwickshire, although he didn't actually become eligible for England until 2006. He was consistent from the start, following up 763 runs from ten matches in 2003 with 1000 in each of the next three seasons. His form dipped in 2007 although, contrarily, he was a left-field pick for that summer's two Twenty20 games against West Indies. Trott managed only 9 and 2, and returned post haste to county cricket. But when he continued to make eye-catchingly forthright runs in 2009, he was called up for the fifth and final Test against Australia at The Oval, the first to make his debut for England in an Ashes decider since 1896. He duly silenced the doubters with a seemingly nerveless century. After a quiet time in South Africa, Trott returned to form with 226 against Bangladesh in May 2010, and against Pakistan later in the summer added 184, sharing a Test-record eighth-wicket stand of 332 with Stuart Broad. And the runs just kept coming: 445 in the Ashes success, including two fine hundreds, then England's leading batsman in the ODI series there and in the World Cup. Another double-century followed against Sri Lanka at Cardiff, before a shoulder injury kept him out for a while. Trott was named the ICC's cricketer of the year for 2011, and continued to do well the following year, although big scores were more elusive – he went through the home summer with a highest international score of 71.

THE FACTS Trott was the 18th batsman to score a century on Test debut for England ... He averages 86.42 in Tests against Australia, but 24.50 v India ... At Lord's in 2010 Trott shared a Test-record eighth-wicket stand of 332 with Stuart Broad ... Trott took 7 for 39 for Warwickshire v Kent at Canterbury in September 2003 ...

THE FIGURES to 17.09.12   **ESPncricinfo.com**

Batting & Fielding	M	Inns	NO	Runs	HS	Avge	S/R	100	50	4s	6s	Ct	St
Tests	34	59	6	2676	226	50.49	47.56	7	12	302	0	12	0
ODIs	54	51	6	2208	137	49.06	74.89	3	18	169	2	12	0
T20Is	7	7	1	138	51	23.00	95.83	0	1	9	3	0	0
First-class	186	311	36	12343	226	44.88	–	29	60	–	–	163	0

Bowling	M	Balls	Runs	Wkts	BB	Avge	RpO	S/R	5i	10m
Tests	34	576	339	3	1–5	113.00	3.53	192.00	0	0
ODIs	54	183	166	2	2–31	83.00	5.44	91.50	0	0
T20Is	7	0	–	–	–	–	–	–	–	–
First-class	186	4886	2777	58	7–39	47.87	3.41	84.24	1	0

LONWABO **TSOTSOBE**

Full name	**Lonwabo Lopsy Tsotsobe**
Born	**March 7, 1984, Port Elizabeth**
Teams	**Warriors**
Style	**Right-hand bat, left-arm fast-medium**
Test debut	**South Africa v West Indies at Port-of-Spain 2010**
ODI debut	**South Africa v Australia at Perth 2008-09**
T20I debut	**South Africa v Australia at Melbourne 2008-09**

THE PROFILE   A tall left-arm swing bowler, Lonwabo Tsotsobe had a dream start to his ODI career in January 2009, when after removing Shaun Marsh he had Ricky Ponting caught behind. Later on he nabbed Mike Hussey and Mitchell Johnson as well, to finish with debut figures of 4 for 50 as South Africa romped to the 4-1 series victory which helped them pinch the No. 1 one-day ranking from the Aussies. This put him in the frame for a Test cap when the Australians toured shortly afterwards, but a knee injury kept him out, allowing his Warriors team-mate Wayne Parnell – quicker through the air and a better batsman – to take his chance. But in the West Indies early in 2010, with Parnell injured, Tsotsobe did well in the one-dayers and played two of the Tests. Three more caps followed against India in 2010-11: he took five wickets in the second game. He remains in the one-day mix – a superb yorker accounted for Alastair Cook second ball at the Rose Bowl in August 2012 – but others are ahead in the Test queue. Tsotsobe made his first-class debut for Eastern Province in 2004-05, taking 7 for 44 in his first match. He moved to the Warriors in 2006-07, and again did well, following a solid debut season for them with 49 wickets at 23.59 the next summer, before 12 wickets in two matches against Sri Lanka A in September 2008 earned him that trip to Australia. But he had an unhappy spell at Essex in 2011, being dropped to the second team before a Twitter outburst resulted in him being sent home. He is seen in South Africa as a talisman for the black population – the natural successor to the now-retired Makhaya Ntini – but it remains to be seen whether Tsotsobe is worth his place in the side on merit.

THE FACTS   Tsotsobe took 7 for 44 (9 for 96 in the match) on his first-class debut for Eastern Province against Boland at Paarl in November 2004, and took 10 for 72 in the match for EP v South Western Districts in Port Elizabeth in October 2006 ... He took 7 for 39 for Warriors v Lions at Johannesburg in October 2007 ... Tsotsobe's first victim in both Twenty20 internationals and ODIs was the Australian batsman Shaun Marsh ...

THE FIGURES to 17.09.12   **cricinfo.com**

Batting & Fielding	M	Inns	NO	Runs	HS	Avge	S/R	100	50	4s	6s	Ct	St
Tests	5	5	2	19	8*	6.33	35.84	0	0	2	0	1	0
ODIs	35	8	5	14	4*	4.66	73.68	0	0	3	0	5	0
T20Is	11	1	0	1	1	1.00	14.28	0	0	0	0	0	0
First-class	56	74	30	268	27*	6.09	29.94	0	0	35	3	13	0

Bowling	M	Balls	Runs	Wkts	BB	Avge	RpO	S/R	5i	10m
Tests	5	870	448	9	3–43	49.77	3.08	96.66	0	0
ODIs	35	1669	1301	59	4–22	22.05	4.67	28.28	0	0
T20Is	11	222	232	10	3–16	23.20	6.27	22.20	0	0
First-class	56	9423	5040	185	7–39	27.24	3.20	50.93	5	1

UMAR AKMAL

Full name	**Mohammad Umar Akmal**
Born	**May 26, 1990, Lahore, Punjab**
Teams	**Lahore, Sui Northern Gas**
Style	**Right-hand batsman, occasional wicketkeeper**
Test debut	**Pakistan v New Zealand at Dunedin 2009-10**
ODI debut	**Pakistan v Sri Lanka at Dambulla 2009**
T20I debut	**Pakistan v Sri Lanka at Colombo 2009**

THE PROFILE Umar Akmal, the brother of Pakistan's wicketkeepers Kamran and Adnan Akmal, started his international career with a flourish. Only 19, he hit a run-a-ball 66 in only his second one-dayer, in Sri Lanka in August 2009, and bettered that with a superb century in the next match. He entered with Pakistan a wobbly 130 for 4 in the 26th over, and hurtled to his hundred from just 70 balls: he outscored Younis Khan in a stand of 176, and looked comfortable from the start. He refused to be tied down, swinging his seventh delivery – from Ajantha Mendis – over long-on for the first of four sixes. In November 2009 Akmal marked his Test debut, in New Zealand, with 129 and 75, and he continued to look the part throughout 2010, scoring consistently in all three formats, although impetuosity often got the better of him. People started to lose patience, though, as he kept trying the big shots too soon and the tall scores refused to come: in 15 further Tests after his debut he reached 30 on 11 occasions but never progressed beyond 79, and eventually that cost him his place, although he remained a one-day regular throughout 2012. Akmal's international start mirrored his domestic one. In a triumphant 2007-08 season, he amassed 855 runs at 77.72 in nine Quaid-e-Azam Trophy matches, at an impressive strike-rate of 90.18. He extended his maiden century – in his sixth match – to 248 (off 225 balls) against Karachi Blues, and two matches later clattered 186 not out from 170 balls against Quetta.

THE FACTS Umar Akmal made 129 and 75 on his Test debut, against New Zealand in November 2009: only KS Ranjitsinhji, with 216 for England v Australia in 1896, scored more runs in his debut Test yet finished on the losing side ... Umar made 248 for Sui Northern Gas v Karachi Blues in December 2007 ... He hit a century, from only 70 balls, in his fourth ODI, against Sri Lanka in Colombo in August 2009 ... His brothers Kamran and Adnan Akmal have also kept wicket for Pakistan, as Umar has occasionally done ...

THE FIGURES to 17.09.12   **ESPNcricinfo.com**

Batting & Fielding	M	Inns	NO	Runs	HS	Avge	S/R	100	50	4s	6s	Ct	St
Tests	16	30	2	1003	129	35.82	65.98	1	6	117	17	12	0
ODIs	70	61	9	1976	102*	38.00	84.77	1	16	156	32	28	2
T20Is	34	32	4	714	64	25.50	117.04	0	4	54	19	26	2
First-class	51	86	7	3787	248	47.93	72.53	8	22	472	56	43	0

Bowling	M	Balls	Runs	Wkts	BB	Avge	RpO	S/R	5i	10m
Tests	16	0	–	–	–	–	–	–	–	–
ODIs	70	0	–	–	–	–	–	–	–	–
T20Is	34	0	–	–	–	–	–	–	–	–
First-class	51	96	54	1	1–0	54.00	3.37	96.00	0	0

UMAR GUL

Full name	**Umar Gul**
Born	**April 14, 1984, Peshawar, North-Western Frontier Province**
Teams	**Peshawar, Habib Bank**
Style	**Right-hand bat, right-arm fast-medium bowler**
Test debut	**Pakistan v Bangladesh at Karachi 2003-04**
ODI debut	**Pakistan v Zimbabwe at Sharjah 2002-03**
T20I debut	**Pakistan v Kenya at Nairobi 2007-08**

THE PROFILE Umar Gul was called up by Pakistan at 19, after their miserable 2003 World Cup. He usually keeps a good line, and obtains appreciable outswing with the new ball, while he can also nip the ball back in. His first real challenge in Tests came against India at Lahore in April 2004. Disparaged by some as the "Peshawar Rickshaw" to Shoaib Akhtar's "Rawalpindi Express", Gul tore through India's imposing top order, moving the ball both ways off the seam at a sharp pace. His 5 for 31 gave Pakistan the early initiative, and they went on to level the series. Stress fractures in the back then kept him out for two years, but he did well in England in 2006, particularly enjoying the conditions at Headingley. Nine wickets followed against West Indies at Lahore, but then he injured his knee. He was back for the 2007 World Cup, and was one of the few to return with reputation intact, but injuries intruded again before he started 2009 with a superb six-for against Sri Lanka on a Lahore batting paradise. Gul has proved a Twenty20 star, usually coming on after the initial overs and firing in yorkers on demand. He was the leading wicket-taker in the first two World Twenty20s, and it was a blow when a shoulder injury ruled him out of the third one in 2010. But in England later that year he revealed unexpected talent with the bat and bowled with his old fire, then led the attack well at the 2011 World Cup. He remained a regular in all three formats in 2012, starting the year with 11 wickets on spin-friendly tracks against England in the UAE.

THE FACTS Umar Gul was the first bowler to take five wickets in a Twenty20 international, with 5 for 6 against New Zealand at The Oval in June 2009: he also took 4 for 8 against Australia in Dubai in May 2009 ... He took 6 for 42 in an ODI against England at The Oval in September's 2010 ... Gul's best first-class figures are 8 for 78 for Peshawar v Karachi Urban in October 2005 ...

THE FIGURES *to 17.09.12*   **ESPNcricinfo.com**

Batting & Fielding	M	Inns	NO	Runs	HS	Avge	S/R	100	50	4s	6s	Ct	St
Tests	45	63	9	554	65*	10.25	48.21	0	1	60	20	9	0
ODIs	111	55	16	384	39	9.84	70.07	0	0	31	10	14	0
T20Is	43	19	7	108	30	9.00	103.84	0	0	7	6	15	0
First-class	77	99	15	1020	65*	12.14	–	0	1	–	–	17	0

Bowling	M	Balls	Runs	Wkts	BB	Avge	RpO	S/R	5i	10m
Tests	45	9233	5319	158	6–135	33.66	3.45	58.43	4	0
ODIs	111	5179	4392	158	6–42	27.79	5.08	32.77	2	0
T20Is	43	892	985	59	5–6	16.69	6.62	15.11	1	0
First-class	77	15058	8604	301	8–78	28.58	3.42	50.02	14	1

PROSPER **UTSEYA**

Full name	**Prosper Utseya**
Born	**March 26, 1985, Harare**
Teams	**Mountaineers**
Style	**Right-hand bat, offspinner**
Test debut	**Zimbabwe v Sri Lanka at Harare 2004**
ODI debut	**Zimbabwe v Sri Lanka at Bulawayo 2004**
T20I debut	**Zimbabwe v Bangladesh at Khulna 2006-07**

THE PROFILE   A diminutive offspinner, Prosper Utseya was unexpectedly thrust into the national team in 2004, aged 19, after several senior players withdrew as a damaging dispute rumbled on. Utseya made 45 in his first Test, but failed to take a wicket, and it soon became clear that the selectors considered him a one-day specialist. He was given a long run in the 50-overs side, but failed to make a consistent mark with either bat or ball ... until the West Indian tour early in 2006, when his mature bowling was a rare highlight. His flight was widely praised, and at times his economy rate was remarkable, which became a trademark. Utseya was consistently able to stifle the runs in the middle overs, and he provided two of the series highlights – comprehensively beating Brian Lara with successive deliveries in the first match in Trinidad, and taking a remarkable diving, juggling boundary catch in the second. In 2006 Utseya took over as captain, and at first continued to keep the runs down. But as opponents grew used to his flattish delivery his economy-rate diminished a little, and after a disappointing World Twenty20 campaign in May 2010 he resigned as skipper. Ironically, as his bowling had lost its sparkle his batting improved, to the point where he made a dozen successive double-figure scores in ODIs in 2010-11. He might struggle to take wickets at international level, but Utseya is a force to be reckoned with in domestic cricket. His spin partnership with Timycen Maruma has brought their teams several titles: in 2008-09 his ten-wicket haul helped Easterns clinch the Logan Cup with a thrilling one-wicket victory in a low-scoring contest against Northerns.

THE FACTS   Utseya has played more than 130 ODIs – but only one Test, in May 2004 ... He took 7 for 56 (11 for 110 in the match) for Easterns v Centrals in Harare in April 2009: in his next game he had match figures of 10 for 93 against Northerns in the Logan Cup final ... Utseya made 115 not out from No. 9 for Zimbabwe against a South African XI at Potchefstroom in November 2007...

THE FIGURES to 17.09.12

ᴇSᴨ cricinfo.com

Batting & Fielding	M	Inns	NO	Runs	HS	Avge	S/R	100	50	4s	6s	Ct	St
Tests	1	2	0	45	45	22.50	77.58	0	0	5	1	2	0
ODIs	139	113	42	1192	68*	16.78	59.60	0	3	74	16	42	0
T20Is	18	12	5	41	13*	5.85	71.92	0	0	2	0	5	0
First-class	72	121	8	2498	115*	22.10	42.22	1	14	–	–	28	0

Bowling	M	Balls	Runs	Wkts	BB	Avge	RpO	S/R	5i	10m
Tests	1	72	55	0	–	–	4.58	–	0	0
ODIs	139	7161	5103	111	4–38	45.97	4.27	64.51	0	0
T20Is	18	383	433	16	3–25	27.06	6.78	23.93	0	0
First-class	72	12562	5630	193	7–56	29.17	2.68	65.08	8	2

KRUGER **VAN WYK**

Full name	**Cornelius Francois Kruger van Wyk**
Born	**February 7, 1980, Wolmaransstad, South Africa**
Teams	**Central Districts**
Style	**Right-hand bat, wicketkeeper**
Test debut	**New Zealand v South Africa at Dunedin 2011-12**
ODI debut	**No ODIs yet**
T20I debut	**No T20Is yet**

THE PROFILE A polished wicketkeeper-batsman, Kruger van Wyk learned his cricket in South Africa, where for a while he was viewed as a potential replacement for Mark Boucher behind the stumps. Van Wyk started with Northerns, but had trouble getting a game for the senior Centurion team, Titans, behind Heino Kuhn in first-class cricket and AB de Villiers, when available, in one-dayers. So in 2006 van Wyk took up an offer from Canterbury, and moved to New Zealand: "If I'm brutally honest," he says, "at that time I was probably not consistent enough to make the South Africa side." The feisty van Wyk proved his worth by leading Canterbury to their first State Championship title for ten years in 2007-08 – but two seasons later he was stripped of the captaincy after falling out with the hierarchy, and joined Central Districts. The move landed him with more batting responsibility, and he has averaged 76 for CD since. That piqued the interest of New Zealand's selectors, and after Brendon McCullum gave up the gloves and Reece Young failed to provide the requisite runs, van Wyk's name began to be mentioned in despatches. When Zimbabwe toured early in 2012 van Wyk faced them in a warm-up game as a specialist batsman – and scored 61 after opening – but B-J Watling (who was also born in South Africa) was given the gloves for the solitary Test. However, when South Africa visited shortly afterwards, van Wyk was named to face his former countrymen. He did little wrong with bat or gloves in his first three Tests, then later in the year scored 71 and 31 at Bangalore as New Zealand came close to a rare victory in India.

THE FACTS Van Wyk scored 178* for Canterbury v Central Districts at New Plymouth in March 2010, sharing a sixth-wicket stand of 379* with Shanan Stewart ... Van Wyk played as a specialist batsman for a New Zealand XI against the touring Zimbabweans in January 2012, opened, and scored 61 ... He was the first person to make his Test debut against the country of his birth since the Hollioakes for England v Australia in 1997 ...

THE FIGURES *to 17.09.12*   **ESPncricinfo.com**

Batting & Fielding	M	Inns	NO	Runs	HS	Avge	S/R	100	50	4s	6s	Ct	St
Tests	7	13	0	300	71	23.07	50.08	0	1	37	0	17	1
ODIs	0	0	–	–	–	–	–	–	–	–	–	–	–
T20Is	0	0	–	–	–	–	–	–	–	–	–	–	–
First-class	107	164	36	4981	178*	38.91	–	6	27	–	–	308	16

Bowling	M	Balls	Runs	Wkts	BB	Avge	RpO	S/R	5i	10m
Tests	7	–	–	–	–	–	–	–	–	–
ODIs	0	0	–	–	–	–	–	–	–	–
T20Is	0	0	–	–	–	–	–	–	–	–
First-class	107	18	9	1	1–7	9.00	3.00	18.00	0	0

NEW ZEALAND

DANIEL **VETTORI**

Full name	**Daniel Luca Vettori**
Born	**January 27, 1979, Auckland**
Teams	**Northern Districts, Royal Challengers Bangalore**
Style	**Left-hand bat, left-arm orthodox spinner**
Test debut	**New Zealand v England at Wellington 1996-97**
ODI debut	**New Zealand v Sri Lanka at Christchurch 1996-97**
T20I debut	**New Zealand v Kenya at Durban 2007-08**

THE PROFILE Daniel Vettori, the first slow left-armer to take 300 Test wickets, has been arguably the best bowler of his type in international cricket for almost a decade – an assessment reinforced by his selection for the World XI in Australia late in 2005 – and the only cloud on his horizon is a susceptibility to injury, particularly in the bowler's danger area of the back. He seemed to have recovered from one stress fracture, which led to a dip in form in 2003, but after a couple of matches for Warwickshire in 2006 he was on the plane home nursing another one. Apart from a run of aches and pains in 2012, which restricted his appearances and reduced his effectiveness, Vettori has usually been fit since – which was just as well for New Zealand, as he carried a huge burden as captain (until standing down after the 2011 World Cup), key batsman and senior bowler. His early Tests in charge were notable for some superb personal performances: two fifties and nine wickets to stave off an embarrassing defeat by Bangladesh in October 2008, and two similar allround efforts which could not prevent defeat in Sri Lanka the following August. Vettori still has the enticing flight and guile that made him New Zealand's youngest Test player at 18 in 1996-97, and he remains economical in limited over games. After his mini-slump he returned to form in England in 2004, then butchered Bangladesh with 20 wickets in two Tests. He has improved his batting – after starting at No. 11, blinking nervously through his glasses – to the point that his six centuries include New Zealand's fastest in Tests, an 82-ball effort against the admittedly hopeless Zimbabweans at Harare in August 2005.

THE FACTS Vettori made his first-class debut at 17 in 1996-97, for Northern Districts against the England tourists: his maiden first-class victim was Nasser Hussain ... Three weeks later Vettori became NZ's youngest-ever Test player, at 18 years 10 days: his first wicket was Hussain again ... Vettori averages 23.62 with the ball in Tests against Sri Lanka, but 73.28 v South Africa ... His record includes a Test and four ODIs for the World XI ...

THE FIGURES to 17.09.12   **espncricinfo.com**

Batting & Fielding	M	Inns	NO	Runs	HS	Avge	S/R	100	50	4s	6s	Ct	St
Tests	112	173	23	4516	140	30.10	58.10	6	23	553	17	58	0
ODIs	272	172	51	2105	83	17.39	81.93	0	4	156	14	77	0
T20Is	29	20	6	187	38	13.35	109.35	0	0	13	2	8	0
First-class	169	249	31	6531	140	29.95	–	9	33	–	–	94	0

Bowling	M	Balls	Runs	Wkts	BB	Avge	RpO	S/R	5i	10m
Tests	112	28670	12392	360	7–87	34.42	2.59	79.63	20	3
ODIs	272	12903	8880	282	5–7	31.48	4.12	45.75	2	0
T20Is	29	673	617	35	4–20	17.62	5.50	19.22	0	0
First-class	169	40130	17549	552	7–87	31.79	2.62	72.69	32	3

MURALI **VIJAY**

Full name	**Murali Vijay Krishna**
Born	**April 1, 1984, Chennai**
Teams	**Tamil Nadu, Chennai Super Kings**
Style	**Right-hand bat, occasional offspinner**
Test debut	**India v Australia at Nagpur 2008-09**
ODI debut	**India v West Indies at Roseau 2011**
T20I debut	**India v Afghanistan at Gros Islet 2008-09**

THE PROFILE   All batsmen want to go in to their first Test in good form, and Murali Vijay was in better nick than most: when Gautam Gambhir was banned against Australia in November 2008, Vijay was hoicked out of a Ranji Trophy match in which he'd just scored 243. While the Ranji game went on without him, Vijay made a sound debut, sharing useful opening stands of 98 and 116 with Virender Sehwag as India set about what became a series-clinching 172-run victory. Vijay helped in the field too, running out Matthew Hayden and Michael Hussey, and taking a catch at short leg. Once Gambhir returned Vijay sat out the Tests in New Zealand early in 2009, but later that year made 87 in an opening stand of 221 with Sehwag against Sri Lanka in Mumbai. His next five Tests did not produce anything special, but he remained a consistent runscorer for Tamil Nadu – and upped his short game in the 2010 IPL, hammering a rapid hundred against Rajasthan Royals, and 458 runs overall as Chennai Super Kings lifted the title for the first time. Tall and solid, Vijay was an instant success in first-class cricket, despite being a late starter (he only switched to "proper" cricket from the soft-ball variety at 17): he hit 179 against Andhra in his second match, and finished his first season (2006-07) with 628 runs at 52 – only two others made more. There was no second-season dip, either: 667 runs, including a double-century against Saurashtra. But he had a quiet time in the West Indies in mid-2011, scoring only 72 runs in six Test innings, and found himself overtaken in the pecking order. Vijay did well in the 2012 IPL, cracking a 51-ball century for Chennai against Delhi ... but an international return proved elusive.

THE FACTS   Vijay made 243 for Tamil Nadu v Maharashtra in November 2008, sharing an opening stand of 462 with Abhinav Mukund (300 not out) ... Vijay also scored 230 not out for Tamil Nadu v Saurashtra in December 2007: this time the opening stand with Mukund was worth 256 ... He hit a 46-ball century against Rajasthan Royals in the 2010 IPL ... Vijay made 179 against Andhra in his second first-class match, at Chennai in December 2006 ...

THE FIGURES *to 17.09.12*   ESPncricinfo.com

Batting & Fielding	M	Inns	NO	Runs	HS	Avge	S/R	100	50	4s	6s	Ct	St
Tests	12	20	0	609	139	30.45	48.48	1	2	68	3	10	0
ODIs	11	11	0	196	33	17.81	61.82	0	0	23	1	6	0
T20Is	7	7	0	122	48	17.42	98.38	0	0	8	6	3	0
First-class	52	86	5	3867	243	47.74	50.44	9	17	459	54	51	0

Bowling	M	Balls	Runs	Wkts	BB	Avge	RpO	S/R	5i	10m
Tests	12	0	–	–	–	–	–	–	–	–
ODIs	11	0	–	–	–	–	–	–	–	–
T20Is	7	0	–	–	–	–	–	–	–	–
First-class	52	282	182	2	1–16	91.00	3.87	141.00	0	0

VINAY KUMAR

Full name	**Ranganath Vinay Kumar**
Born	**February 12, 1984, Davanagere, Karnataka**
Teams	**Karnataka, Royal Challengers Bangalore**
Style	**Right-hand bat, right-arm fast-medium bowler**
Test debut	**India v Australia at Perth 2011-12**
ODI debut	**India v Zimbabwe at Bulawayo 2010**
T20I debut	**India v Sri Lanka at Gros Islet 2010**

THE PROFILE Vinay Kumar is a bowler in the mould of the former Indian stalwart Venkatesh Prasad, relying more on outswingers, legcutters and accuracy than outright speed. For a while, this lack of pace threatened to stymie his international ambitions, but eventually he made it to the full Indian side. "Vinay Kumar is one of the hardest-working cricketers I have worked with," said coach Eric Simons. "You get guys with natural skill, and you get guys who just do it through really hard work. He is one of those." Vinay, who is also a fine outfielder, made his Ranji Trophy debut in 2004-05 and, after the retirements of former internationals Dodda Ganesh and David Johnson, established himself as a key part of Karnataka's attack, taking more than 20 wickets in each of his first three seasons. He added an inducer to his stock outswinger, resulting in a superb 2007-08 season, when he was the country's leading wicket-taker with 47 at a shade over 20. Vinay improved that with 53 wickets in 2009-10, and also mentored Karnataka's young fast bowlers, Abhimanyu Mithun and Sreenath Aravind, as they reached the Ranji final for the first time for 11 years. Finally the national call came: after a successful start to the 2010 IPL, Vinay was named in the squad for the World Twenty20 in the Caribbean later in the year. He played only once there, but the highlight among some consistent performances afterwards was 4 for 30 against England at Delhi in October 2011. His Test debut at Perth, which followed injuries to others, was forgettable – 13-0-73-1 – but it didn't stop Royal Challengers Bangalore from shelling out a cool million dollars to secure his services for IPL5.

THE FACTS Vinay Kumar took 8 for 32 (11 for 102 in the match) for Karnataka v Delhi in November 2009... He took 6 for 38 (and 4 for 66) for Karnataka v Maharashtra at Ratnagiri in December 2007 ... His fourth ball in Test cricket was hit for six by Australia's David Warner ...

THE FIGURES to 17.09.12   **espncricinfo.com**

Batting & Fielding	M	Inns	NO	Runs	HS	Avge	S/R	100	50	4s	6s	Ct	St
Tests	1	2	0	11	6	5.50	45.83	0	0	2	0	0	0
ODIs	22	9	3	43	18	7.16	43.87	0	0	2	0	3	0
T20Is	8	1	1	2	2*	–	50.00	0	0	0	0	0	0
First-class	67	89	17	1240	57	17.22	43.20	0	5	–	–	25	0

Bowling	M	Balls	Runs	Wkts	BB	Avge	RpO	S/R	5i	10m
Tests	1	78	73	1	1–73	73.00	5.61	78.00	0	0
ODIs	22	989	925	28	4–30	33.03	5.61	35.32	0	0
T20Is	8	165	221	7	3–24	31.57	8.03	23.57	0	0
First-class	67	12343	5928	242	8–32	24.49	2.88	51.00	11	2

BRIAN **VITORI**

Full name	**Brian Vitalis Vitori**
Born	**February 22, 1990, Masvingo**
Teams	**Southern Rocks**
Style	**Left-hand bat, left-arm fast-medium bowler**
Test debut	**Zimbabwe v Bangladesh at Harare 2011**
ODI debut	**Zimbabwe v Bangladesh at Harare 2011**
T20I debut	**No T20Is yet**

THE PROFILE Like his near-namesake Daniel Vettori, Brian Vitori is a left-hander: unlike the New Zealander, though, this Vitori likes to bowl fast, and can move the ball in to the right-hander at a decent pace. He is a stocky youngster from the southern province of Masvingo: "I started playing street cricket when I was eight, at primary school," he says. He played a few one-day matches for Masvingo early in 2006 with mixed results – hardly surprising given that he was barely 16 – but the new franchise system, created in 2008, offered him an opportunity to improve under the guidance of the former Surrey batsman Monte Lynch, who recommended him for a national training camp early in 2011. Vitori had just taken 25 wickets in the season for Southern Rocks – a reasonable return, although his average (37.16) was nothing to write home about. But Alan Butcher, Zimbabwe's new coach and an old county colleague of Lynch's, was also impressed: "I knew we had found someone special." Butcher kept Vitori under wraps until Bangladesh toured in August 2011, for a series that included Zimbabwe's first Test for six years. He made an immediate impact, taking five wickets in a joyous victory, moving the ball around at a waspish pace, and seemed to work well in concert with the rapid right-armer Kyle Jarvis. Vitori then grabbed five wickets in each of his first two ODIs, a unique feat, to leave Zimbabweans licking their lips at the prospect of a combative new-ball partnership at last. He struggled a little in New Zealand early in 2012, but was back among the wickets against South Africa A later in the year.

THE FACTS Vitori took five wickets in each of his first two ODIs, an unprecedented feat (Ryan Harris of Australia took two in his first three): he had ten wickets after two ODIs, another record (previously eight) ... Only six bowlers had previously taken a five-for on ODI debut ... Vitori conceded 105 runs in nine overs v New Zealand at Napier in February 2012: only Mick Lewis of Australia had conceded more (115) in an ODI innings ... He took 6 for 55 for Southern Rocks against Mountaineers at Masvingo in March 2011 ...

THE FIGURES to 17.09.12   **ESPncricinfo.com**

Batting & Fielding	M	Inns	NO	Runs	HS	Avge	S/R	100	50	4s	6s	Ct	St
Tests	3	5	0	33	14	6.60	68.75	0	0	5	1	1	0
ODIs	6	2	1	3	3*	–	60.00	0	0	0	0	0	0
T20Is	0	0	–	–	–	–	–	–	–	–	–	–	–
First-class	23	35	12	217	71	9.43	50.70	0	0	21	6	5	0

Bowling	M	Balls	Runs	Wkts	BB	Avge	RpO	S/R	5i	10m
Tests	3	540	334	6	4–66	55.66	3.71	90.00	0	0
ODIs	6	333	305	13	5–20	23.46	5.49	25.61	2	0
T20Is	0	0	–	–	–	–	–	–	–	–
First-class	23	3082	1945	58	6–55	33.53	3.78	53.13	3	0

MATTHEW **WADE**

Full name	**Matthew Scott Wade**
Born	**December 26, 1987, Hobart**
Teams	**Victoria**
Style	**Right-hand bat, wicketkeeper**
Test debut	**Australia v West Indies at Bridgetown 2011-12**
ODI debut	**Australia v India at Melbourne 2011-12**
T20I debut	**Australia v South Africa at Cape Town 2011-12**

THE PROFILE Everything Matthew Wade achieves in his cricket career will be a bonus after the shocking diagnosis, when he was just 16, that he had testicular cancer. He underwent chemotherapy to beat the disease, and by the time he was 19 was playing first-class cricket – for Victoria, rather than his native Tasmania, as too many keepers were spoiling the broth in Hobart (his childhood mate Tim Paine, for one). Wade was an instant hit in Melbourne, scoring 83 and taking six catches on debut against South Australia. The following season he made 57 dismissals – a Victorian record – then in 2009-10 scored 677 Sheffield Shield runs, including a vital 96 in the final. He still looked a fair way off the international side, with Paine proving a capable understudy to Brad Haddin, but then Paine broke a finger, and Wade played the Twenty20 internationals in South Africa, Haddin having given up the format. An innings of 72 from 43 balls in a T20 match against India in February 2012 meant Wade stayed in when Haddin missed some of the 50-overs games shortly afterwards – and then he got his big break, in unfortunate circumstances, after Haddin returned home from the Caribbean when his daughter was stricken with cancer. Wade grabbed his chance with a century in the third Test at Roseau in April – and this batting form, together with some slick displays behind the stumps, means a return for Haddin is by no means automatic. "He's done everything in his power to put his hand up there and perform," said Michael Clarke.

THE FACTS Wade hit 106 against West Indies at Roseau in his third Test: he was only the sixth Australian wicketkeeper to score a Test hundred, after Rod Marsh, Wayne Philips, Ian Healy, Adam Gilchrist and Brad Haddin ... Wade made 57 dismissals in 2008-09, a record for Victoria ... He was a talented junior Aussie Rules footballer (his father Scott played in the VFL for Hawthorn) but at 170cm decided he was too short to make a career out of it and pursued cricket instead ...

THE FIGURES to 17.09.12   **ESPN**cricinfo.com

Batting & Fielding	M	Inns	NO	Runs	HS	Avge	S/R	100	50	4s	6s	Ct	St
Tests	3	6	1	198	106	39.60	47.82	1	0	16	3	7	1
ODIs	25	24	0	546	75	22.75	68.85	0	4	30	9	30	4
T20Is	9	8	2	150	72	25.00	114.50	0	1	7	6	4	0
First-class	53	80	13	2688	113*	40.11	49.38	5	17	317	31	190	6

Bowling	M	Balls	Runs	Wkts	BB	Avge	RpO	S/R	5i	10m
Tests	3	0	–	–	–	–	–	–	–	–
ODIs	25	0	–	–	–	–	–	–	–	–
T20Is	9	0	–	–	–	–	–	–	–	–
First-class	53	0	–	–	–	–	–	–	–	–

NEIL **WAGNER**

Full name	**Neil Wagner**
Born	**March 13, 1986, Pretoria, South Africa**
Teams	**Otago**
Style	**Left-hand bat, left-arm fast-medium bowler**
Test debut	**New Zealand v West Indies at North Sound 2012**
ODI debut	**No ODIs yet**
T20I debut	**No T20Is yet**

THE PROFILE   One of several South African-born imports currently plying their trade in New Zealand domestic cricket, left-arm seamer Neil Wagner was immediately called up to the national squad once his four-year qualification period was completed in 2012. He's not the quickest of bowlers, but does have the precious ability to swing the ball. He has recently learned reverse-swing, too, which made him a more complete bowler in all conditions. Wagner learnt his cricket in Pretoria, and made a splash on his first-class debut for the local Northerns side in 2005-06, with four wickets in each innings. He then toured Zimbabwe and Bangladesh with the National Academy, and even fielded as South Africa's 12th man in two Tests at Centurion. In 2006-07 he was the leading wicket-taker in the Provincial Challenge, but decided to look elsewhere as opportunities seemed limited. He came close to a county contract with Sussex, but eventually decided to try his luck in New Zealand. After 21 wickets in his first season with Otago, he topped the domestic wicket-taking charts in 2010-11 – when his 51 scalps uniquely included five, all bowled, in the same over against Wellington – and 2011-12. A national call was soon seen as inevitable, and it came as soon as his eligibility was confirmed. "He brings a lot of aggression," said an admiring Daniel Vettori. "He runs in hard all day and wants to compete the whole time – I think he's a welcome addition to our side." The early results weren't spectacular – four wickets in two Tests in the West Indies – but many New Zealanders are waiting to see how the much-hyped Wagner will perform on the home surfaces he has enjoyed at domestic level.

THE FACTS   Wagner took five wickets in an over – unique in first-class cricket – including four in four balls, for Otago v Wellington at Queenstown in April 2011: all of them were bowled ... For Otago against Wellington in the 2011-12 season Wagner took 7 for 96 at the Basin Reserve in November and a career-best 7 for 46 at Dunedin in March 2012 ...

THE FIGURES *to 17.09.12*   **ESPNcricinfo.com**

Batting & Fielding	M	Inns	NO	Runs	HS	Avge	S/R	100	50	4s	6s	Ct	St
Tests	2	4	0	46	23	11.50	22.43	0	0	6	0	1	0
ODIs	0	0	–	–	–	–	–	–	–	–	–	–	–
T20Is	0	0	–	–	–	–	–	–	–	–	–	–	–
First-class	57	73	18	1098	70	19.96	49.52	0	4	–	23	16	0

Bowling	M	Balls	Runs	Wkts	BB	Avge	RpO	S/R	5i	10m
Tests	2	360	209	4	2–24	52.25	3.48	90.00	0	0
ODIs	0	0	–	–	–	–	–	–	–	–
T20Is	0	0	–	–	–	–	–	–	–	–
First-class	57	10567	5786	242	7–46	23.90	3.28	43.66	11	1

MALCOLM **WALLER**

ZIMBABWE

Full name	**Malcolm Noel Waller**
Born	**September 28, 1984, Harare**
Teams	**Mid West Rhinos**
Style	**Right-hand bat, offspinner**
Test debut	**Zimbabwe v New Zealand at Bulawayo 2011-12**
ODI debut	**Zimbabwe v Bangladesh at Mirpur 2008-09**
T20I debut	**Zimbabwe v New Zealand at Harare 2011-12**

THE PROFILE A hard-hitting batsman and a handy offspinner, Malcolm Waller – whose father Andy captained Zimbabwe in pre-Test days, and did finally win a couple of Test caps at the age of 35 – played for Zimbabwe under-15s in 2000, and four years later appeared for Mashonaland in the domestic one-day competition. His appearances were sporadic until he finally broke into first-class cricket in 2007-08, although even then his performances – except for some eye-catching Twenty20 displays – were hardly spectacular. But good club form for Harare Sports Club helped win him selection for the tour of Bangladesh in 2008-09, and soon after that he hit 63 in a thumping win over Kenya in Mombasa. His offbreaks, though, proved unpenetrative at international level (and still are). Waller missed out on initial selection when Zimbabwe returned to the Test arena in August 2011, but he anchored a rare one-day victory over New Zealand a couple of months later with a mature 99 not out at Bulawayo: "I decided to take the team home rather than get a hundred," he said after Zimbabwe ran down a daunting target of 329 with a ball to spare. That ensured him a Test debut the following week, after which he boasted a batting average of 101 – he followed a battling 72 not out with 29 – but that took a bit of a knock in New Zealand early in 2012, when a technique tailored to Zimbabwe's usually trustworthy pitches came unstuck on seaming surfaces. But Waller remains very much one for the future, although he did endure a bit of a horror trot with the bat at home in the middle of 2012.

THE FACTS Waller became only the 11th batsman (and the third Zimbabwean after Andy Flower and Alistair Campbell) to be stranded on 99 not out in an ODI, against New Zealand at Bulawayo in October 2011 ... Waller made 174 for Mid West Rhinos v Southern Rocks at Masvingo in October 2011, putting on 341 with Gary Ballance (210): four of Waller's five first-class hundreds have come at the Rocks' expense ... His father, Andy "Bundu" Waller, also scored a half-century on his Test debut, against England at Bulawayo in 1996-97 ...

THE FIGURES to 17.09.12   ESPNcricinfo.com

Batting & Fielding	M	Inns	NO	Runs	HS	Avge	S/R	100	50	4s	6s	Ct	St
Tests	2	4	1	124	72*	41.33	51.88	0	1	15	1	1	0
ODIs	24	23	2	468	99*	22.28	84.78	0	3	50	3	7	0
T20Is	4	3	0	33	12	11.00	110.00	0	0	3	1	1	0
First-class	40	69	8	2457	174	40.27	57.56	5	13	314	14	28	0

Bowling	M	Balls	Runs	Wkts	BB	Avge	RpO	S/R	5i	10m
Tests	2	18	8	0	–	–	2.66	–	0	0
ODIs	24	174	178	2	1–17	89.00	6.13	87.00	0	0
T20Is	4	0	–	–	–	–	–	–	–	–
First-class	40	2617	1443	33	5–48	43.72	3.30	79.30	1	0

DAVID **WARNER**

Full name	**David Andrew Warner**
Born	**October 27, 1986, Paddington, Sydney**
Teams	**New South Wales, Delhi Daredevils**
Style	**Left-hand bat, occasional legspinner**
Test debut	**Australia v New Zealand at Brisbane 2011-12**
ODI debut	**Australia v South Africa at Hobart 2008-09**
T20I debut	**Australia v South Africa at Melbourne 2008-09**

THE PROFILE David Warner, a diminutive and dangerous opener, exploded onto the international scene in January 2009. His astonishing 89 from 43 balls, wielding the bat more like a club, on his Twenty20 debut at the MCG was all the more remarkable as he was the first man to play for the full Australian side before playing first-class cricket since the inaugural Test back in 1877. This was after he began the season by smashing nine sixes in 165 not out – a NSW one-day record – against Tasmania in Sydney, and added 97 from 54 balls the following week. After that jet-propelled start, things predictably slowed down: Warner was tried in 50-overs ODIs, without much success, although he did finally play a first-class match for NSW. For a couple of years he was pigeonholed as a Twenty20 blaster, in the IPL and elsewhere, but all that changed in 2011. After touring Zimbabwe with Australia A, and showing he could bat long with a 7½-hour double-century, Warner made the Test side later in the year. He still looked to attack, but treated decent balls with some respect and – playing a brand of cricket described by Greg Baum in *Wisden* as "Test20" – carried his bat in only his second Test, almost conjuring a victory over New Zealand at Hobart, then caned India for a majestic 180 – including five sixes – shortly afterwards at Perth. Suddenly, he was just about the first name on the teamsheet in all three formats. Warner is also an excellent fielder, and a handy legspinner too (as he should be with a name like his). A keen surfer, he was sent home from the Australian academy in 2007 for general untidiness.

THE FACTS Warner was the first man since John Hodges and Tom Kendall in the first Test of all in 1876-77 to represent Australia in a full international without having previously played first-class cricket: Warner won the match award for his 89 from 43 balls (seven fours and six sixes) v South Africa in January 2009 ... He finally made his first-class debut for NSW in March 2009 ... He carried his bat for 123 in his second Test, against New Zealand at Hobart in December 2011 ... Warner hit 211 for Australia A v Zimbabwe A at Harare in July 2011 ...

THE FIGURES to 17.09.12   **ESPNcricinfo.com**

Batting & Fielding	M	Inns	NO	Runs	HS	Avge	S/R	100	50	4s	6s	Ct	St
Tests	9	16	2	590	180	42.14	71.42	2	1	69	6	12	0
ODIs	35	34	0	1050	163	30.88	81.83	2	5	106	13	8	0
T20Is	36	36	0	978	89	27.16	140.71	0	7	91	46	20	0
First-class	20	33	3	1550	211	51.66	71.06	5	4	186	21	17	0

Bowling	M	Balls	Runs	Wkts	BB	Avge	RpO	S/R	5i	10m
Tests	9	132	94	3	2–45	31.33	4.27	44.00	0	0
ODIs	35	6	8	0	–	–	8.00	–	0	0
T20Is	36	0	–	–	–	–	–	–	–	–
First-class	20	349	234	4	2–45	58.50	4.02	87.25	0	0

B-J **WATLING**

Full name	**Bradley-John Watling**
Born	**July 9, 1985, Durban, South Africa**
Teams	**Northern Districts**
Style	**Right-hand bat, wicketkeeper**
Test debut	**New Zealand v Pakistan at Napier 2009-10**
ODI debut	**New Zealand v Sri Lanka at Dambulla 2010**
T20I debut	**New Zealand v Pakistan at Dubai 2009-10**

THE PROFILE A right-hand opening batsman who can also keep wicket, Bradley-John (usually known just by his initials) Watling spent his early years in South Africa before his family moved to New Zealand when he was ten. He was part of the squad for the Under-19 World Cup in Bangladesh in 2003-04 before making it to the Northern Districts team, but in 2006-07 – his third season – he made 564 runs at 37.60, and passed 500 again in 2009-10 and 2010-11. He also did well in one-dayers, and was rewarded with a place in New Zealand's squad against Pakistan in November 2009. He made his first appearances in the Twenty20 games in Dubai – a slight surprise, since he is not regarded at home as a terribly fast scorer (his overall one-day strike-rate is a modest 68 per 100 balls). However, that didn't bother Daniel Vettori: "He plays pace well, lets the ball come to him, and in the middle overs he is very adept at turning the strike over against spin." When Pakistan toured New Zealand later in 2009 Watling made his debut in the third Test at Napier, making an undefeated 60 in the second innings, and later resisted the Australian attack for more than two hours in making 46 at Hamilton. But he slipped out of the national side after a modest Indian tour late in 2010: he missed the following year's World Cup, although another good domestic season rescued his national contract. Watling is also a handy keeper, and was entrusted with the gloves for the Test against Zimbabwe at Napier in January 2012: he took four catches, and also made a maiden century. In the West Indies later in the year he made 60, 72 not out and 40 in successive ODIs, but then surrendered the wicketkeeping gloves to Kruger van Wyk.

THE FACTS Watling's highest score of 164 not out came as Northern Districts chased down 384 to beat Wellington by nine wickets at Whangarei in March 2011, after conceding a first-innings lead of 175 ... His first three first-class hundreds all came at Otago's expense ... Watling made 145 not out in the final of New Zealand's one-day competition against Auckland in February 2010 ...

THE FIGURES *to 17.09.12* **ESPNcricinfo.com**

Batting & Fielding	M	Inns	NO	Runs	HS	Avge	S/R	100	50	4s	6s	Ct	St
Tests	8	15	3	360	102*	30.00	43.74	1	1	44	1	14	0
ODIs	12	11	1	275	72*	27.50	72.94	0	3	26	3	6	0
T20Is	2	2	0	29	22	14.50	64.44	0	0	2	0	2	0
First-class	62	111	9	3547	164*	34.77	41.01	8	17	–	–	74	0

Bowling	M	Balls	Runs	Wkts	BB	Avge	RpO	S/R	5i	10m
Tests	8	0	–	–	–	–	–	–	–	–
ODIs	12	0	–	–	–	–	–	–	–	–
T20Is	2	0	–	–	–	–	–	–	–	–
First-class	62	47	39	2	2–31	19.50	4.97	23.50	0	0

SHANE **WATSON**

Full name	**Shane Robert Watson**
Born	**June 17, 1981, Ipswich, Queensland**
Teams	**New South Wales, Rajasthan Royals**
Style	**Right-hand bat, right-arm fast-medium bowler**
Test debut	**Australia v Pakistan at Sydney 2004-05**
ODI debut	**Australia v South Africa at Centurion 2001-02**
T20I debut	**Australia v South Africa at Johannesburg 2005-06**

THE PROFILE To conquer international cricket, Shane Watson first had to beat his fragile body. Despite an athletic figure made for photoshoots, Watson's frame was so brittle it threatened to break him. He refused to give up, despite back stress fractures, hamstring strains, calf and hip trouble, a dislocated shoulder and a suspected heart attack that turned out to be food poisoning. He changed his training, and gave up alcohol, but not his dream. It finally paid off when he was promoted to open in the middle of the 2009 Ashes. Many would have been uncomfortable with the elevation from the middle order, but Watson was used to reinventing himself. In his first eight Tests in the new role he scored seven fifties and a 120. His first Test century was a long time coming, but after two nineties (and an 89) he finally reached three figures against Pakistan at the MCG in December 2009 ... thanks to a single from a dropped catch. He had earned some luck. At the crease he is an aggressive brute with a broad chest, a right-handed disciple of Matthew Hayden. He's had some purple patches in ODIs – successive centuries in the semi and final of the 2009 Champions Trophy, and a rollicking 161 not out against England at Melbourne in January 2011, which was just a warm-up for an astonishing undefeated 185 – with a record 15 sixes – to bully Bangladesh three months later. As a bowler he is willing and speedy, if not quite as good as he thinks he is: he is prone to verbal exchanges with batsmen, but does pick up handy wickets – 11 of them in two Tests against Pakistan in England in 2010, and 5 for 17 against South Africa at Johannesburg the following November.

THE FACTS Watson made 185 not out, Australia's highest score in ODIs, v Bangladesh at Mirpur in April 2011: the innings included an ODI-record 15 sixes ... He hit 201 in the 2005-06 Pura Cup final demolition of Victoria before retiring hurt: uniquely, four batsmen passed 150 in Queensland's 900 for 6 ... Watson played for Hampshire, alongside Shane Warne: in 2005 he scored 203 not out for them v Warwickshire at the Rose Bowl ...

THE FIGURES *to 17.09.12*   **ESPn**cricinfo.com

Batting & Fielding	M	Inns	NO	Runs	HS	Avge	S/R	100	50	4s	6s	Ct	St
Tests	35	64	2	2328	126	37.54	50.46	2	18	310	14	25	0
ODIs	154	134	24	4563	185*	41.48	88.27	6	28	450	99	52	0
T20Is	30	29	2	731	81	27.07	147.97	0	7	55	47	10	0
First-class	104	185	18	7431	203*	44.49	–	17	42	–	–	82	0

Bowling	M	Balls	Runs	Wkts	BB	Avge	RpO	S/R	5i	10m
Tests	35	3404	1706	59	6–33	28.91	2.92	59.22	3	0
ODIs	154	5586	4470	155	4–36	28.83	4.80	36.03	0	0
T20Is	30	452	539	24	4–15	22.45	7.15	18.83	0	0
First-class	104	9791	5327	193	7–69	27.60	3.26	50.73	7	1

CHANAKA **WELAGEDARA**

Full name	**Uda Walawwe Mahim Bandaralage Chanaka Asanga Welagedara**
Born	**March 20, 1981, Matale**
Teams	**Tamil Union, Wayamba**
Style	**Right-hand bat, left-arm fast-medium bowler**
Test debut	**Sri Lanka v England at Galle 2007-08**
ODI debut	**Sri Lanka v India at Rajkot 2009-10**
T20I debut	**Sri Lanka v New Zealand at Providence 2009-10**

THE PROFILE   Chanaka Welagedara is a brisk left-armer with a sturdy action, who is shaping up as the long-term replacement for Chaminda Vaas. Welagedara, whose array of initials outdoes even Vaas's, swings the ball in nicely, and traps a lot of batsmen lbw. He had problems at first with consistency – against India at home in mid-2010 he sprayed the ball around and proved expensive. A few months earlier, he had reduced India to 31 for 3 at Ahmedabad without the aid of a fielder. He later dismissed Rahul Dravid too – but not before he had made 177. Shortly afterwards Welagedara took 5 for 66 in a one-dayer against India, again removing the top three before proving costly later on. He was dropped after only three wickets in four Tests following nine in his first two, but after missing the 2011 World Cup returned for the ensuing England tour. He added spark to the attack in the second Test at Lord's, dismissing Andrew Strauss early on and finishing with five wickets in the match. Later in 2011 he took 5 for 87 against Pakistan in Sharjah, then 5 for 52 against South Africa at Durban, but missed much of 2012 with injuries to groin and shoulder. Welagedara was a late starter to cricket, not playing seriously until he was 17. When he came to Colombo from Matale (a hill-country town not far from Kandy) in 2000 he was soon chosen for the national Pace Academy, headed by the former Test fast bowler Rumesh Ratnayake. Welagedara bowled Moors to the Premier League title in 2002-03, with 34 wickets at 24.14. An ankle injury, requiring an operation, kept him out for 18 months until the end of 2006, but he made his Test debut against England the following December and took four wickets, three of them top-five batsmen.

THE FACTS   Welagedara took 5 for 34 (10 for 95 in the match) for a Sri Lanka Cricket XI v Tamil Nadu in the Gopalan Trophy match in Colombo in September 2007 ... He took 5 for 66 in an ODI against India at Mirpur in January 2010 ... Welagedara scored 76 for Moors v Sinhalese SC in Colombo in October 2009 ...

THE FIGURES to 17.09.12   **ESPNcricinfo.com**

Batting & Fielding	M	Inns	NO	Runs	HS	Avge	S/R	100	50	4s	6s	Ct	St
Tests	18	25	4	191	48	9.09	50.00	0	0	25	4	4	0
ODIs	10	3	2	4	2*	4.00	44.44	0	0	0	0	2	0
T20Is	2	1	1	2	2*	–	66.66	0	0	0	0	0	0
First-class	92	115	38	775	76	10.06	43.71	0	1	–	–	19	0

Bowling	M	Balls	Runs	Wkts	BB	Avge	RpO	S/R	5i	10m
Tests	18	3261	1929	48	5–52	40.18	3.54	67.93	2	0
ODIs	10	457	433	15	5–66	28.86	5.68	30.46	1	0
T20Is	2	36	61	1	1–21	61.00	10.16	36.00	0	0
First-class	92	13145	7720	252	5–34	30.63	3.52	52.16	8	1

KANE **WILLIAMSON**

Full name	**Kane Stuart Williamson**
Born	**August 8, 1990, Tauranga**
Teams	**Northern Districts, Gloucestershire**
Style	**Right-hand bat, offspinner**
Test debut	**New Zealand v India at Ahmedabad 2010-11**
ODI debut	**New Zealand v India at Dambulla 2010**
T20I debut	**New Zealand v Zimbabwe at Harare 2011-12**

THE PROFILE Well balanced, with an enviably perpendicular bat in defence, Kane Williamson is the most exciting batting talent New Zealand have unearthed since Martin Crowe in the early 1980s. He's also a handy offspinner. He had a smooth ride through age-group cricket and made his first-class debut at 17 in December 2007. A slow start (2 and 0) was followed next season by innings of 82, 73 and 98, and the seemingly inevitable maiden century came up in his tenth match. He finished 2008-09 with 812 runs at 50.75, and collected 614 more the following season – at a slightly lower average (47.23) but with two eye-catching big scores, 170 against Wellington and 192 against Auckland. All this propelled him into the squad for the second Test against Australia at Hamilton in March 2010, and although he didn't play in the end it was a clear sign that his entry would not be long delayed. He made a quiet start in one-day internationals – a ninth-ball duck, courtesy of a peach from Praveen Kumar, in his first game, and another blob in his next match before finally getting off the mark in his third. But then he made 108 against Bangladesh, before marking his Test debut with a seemingly nerveless 131 against India at Ahmedabad in November 2010. He looked set for another in his second Test, too, before being cut off by an unlucky lbw for 69 in Hyderabad. He did well in the 2011 World Cup, then took New Zealand to safety in the Wellington Test against South Africa in March 2012 with an unbeaten century after coming in at 1 for 2.

THE FACTS Williamson is the youngest of eight New Zealanders to score a century on Test debut, with 131 v India at Ahmedabad in November 2010 ... He made 284 not out for Northern Districts v Wellington at Lincoln in November 2011 ... He hit 75 and 151 v England in an Under-19 Test at Worcester in August 2008 ... Williamson scored more first-class runs before he had turned 20 than Martin Crowe (1428 to 1127) ...

THE FIGURES to 17.09.12   ᴇsᴘɴcricinfo.com

Batting & Fielding	M	Inns	NO	Runs	HS	Avge	S/R	100	50	4s	6s	Ct	St
Tests	16	29	1	884	131	31.57	41.23	2	5	89	1	9	0
ODIs	29	27	4	796	108	34.60	74.95	2	3	57	6	9	0
T20Is	9	8	2	170	48	28.33	126.86	0	0	16	3	1	0
First-class	56	97	4	3890	284*	41.82	51.29	10	18	466	15	50	0

Bowling	M	Balls	Runs	Wkts	BB	Avge	RpO	S/R	5i	10m
Tests	16	665	413	8	2–47	51.62	3.72	83.12	0	0
ODIs	29	242	219	5	2–13	43.80	5.42	48.40	0	0
T20Is	9	0	–	–	–	–	–	–	–	–
First-class	56	3882	2233	51	5–75	43.78	3.45	76.11	1	0

CHRIS **WOAKES**

ENGLAND

Full name	**Christopher Roger Woakes**
Born	**March 2, 1989, Birmingham**
Teams	**Warwickshire**
Style	**Right-hand bat, right-arm fast-medium bowler**
Test debut	**No Tests yet**
ODI debut	**England v Australia at Sydney 2010-11**
ODI debut	**England v Australia at Adelaide 2010-11**

THE PROFILE   A tall quick bowler and a handy batsman, Chris Woakes hit the headlines in his first international, a Twenty20 game at Adelaide, when he kept his cool to hit the winning run off the last ball, after earlier striking the pacy Shaun Tait for a big six: not for nothing did the England coach Andy Flower describe him beforehand as "a serious batter". He almost did it again in the next game, keeping England in touch by hammering Brett Lee over long-on for six in the final over, but history didn't quite repeat itself there. Then, in only his second ODI, Woakes ripped through Australia's middle order to take 6 for 45 at Brisbane – although, just to ruin the fairytale, England eventually lost by 51 runs. It looked as if a star had been born – but, rather perplexingly, Woakes soon slid from view. He missed out on selection for the World Cup, and played only three full internationals in the 2011 home season, the ODI against Ireland and two Twenty20s, although he remained an England Lions regular. At county level Woakes remains a considerable force. He seems to like playing Hampshire: his first two first-class hundreds came against them – 131 at Southampton in 2009, and 136 at Edgbaston in 2010, both not out – then in August 2011 he took a career-best 7 for 20 against them at Edgbaston as Warwickshire continued their ultimately unsuccessful bid for the Championship title. Woakes played a big part in that campaign, with 56 wickets and 78 in all matches, and starred again as they *did* win the title in 2012, although he missed the first part of the season with an ankle injury. He was back in England colours at the end of the summer, making 33 not out against South Africa at Trent Bridge.

THE FACTS   Woakes took 6 for 45 against Australia at Brisbane in his second ODI, in January 2011: only Paul Collingwood (6 for 31 v Bangladesh at Trent Bridge in 2005) has recorded better figures for England ... Woakes took 5 for 18, including a hat-trick, for England Lions v Guyana at Providence in March 2011 ... He scored 136* against Hampshire in April 2010, and the following August took 7 for 20 against them, also at Edgbaston ...

THE FIGURES to 17.09.12   **ESPNcricinfo.com**

Batting & Fielding	M	Inns	NO	Runs	HS	Avge	S/R	100	50	4s	6s	Ct	St
Tests	0	0	–	–	–	–	–	–	–	–	–	–	–
ODIs	6	5	3	72	33*	36.00	74.22	0	0	5	0	1	0
T20Is	3	3	2	37	19*	37.00	123.33	0	0	1	2	1	0
First-class	71	94	26	2590	136*	38.08	–	6	10	–	–	35	0

Bowling	M	Balls	Runs	Wkts	BB	Avge	RpO	S/R	5i	10m
Tests	0	0	–	–	–	–	–	–	–	–
ODIs	6	194	169	7	6–45	24.14	5.22	27.71	1	0
T20Is	3	60	94	2	1–29	47.00	9.40	30.00	0	0
First-class	71	12302	6263	250	7–20	25.05	3.05	49.20	12	3

UMESH **YADAV**

Full name	**Umeshkumar Tilak Yadav**
Born	**October 25, 1987, Nagpur, Maharashtra**
Teams	**Vidarbha, Delhi Daredevils**
Style	**Right-hand bat, right-arm fast-medium bowler**
Test debut	**India v West Indies at Delhi 2011-12**
ODI debut	**India v Zimbabwe at Bulawayo 2010**
T20I debut	**India v Sri Lanka at Pallekele 2012**

THE PROFILE   Less than two seasons after Umesh Yadav first bowled with a leather ball, he was up against the likes of Rahul Dravid and VVS Laxman in the Duleep Trophy. What makes his ascent even more remarkable is that he plays in the lower reaches of the Ranji Trophy for unglamorous Vidarbha, which had never produced a Test cricketer before. Yadav is the son of a coalmine worker, and had been thinking of becoming a policeman before his cricket started to get him noticed. A fast bowler with a fine flowing action, he nudges 90mph, moves the ball both ways, and has an effective bouncer. These qualities helped him take 20 wickets in four matches in 2008-09, his first season. That made a few local headlines, but he really caught the eye with some pacey spells for Delhi Daredevils in the IPL: he was flown to the West Indies as a replacement for the injured Praveen Kumar during the World Twenty20 in May 2010, and toured South Africa later that year. A Test cap had to wait until the following November, when West Indies visited, but Yadav made his mark with 3 for 23 and 4 for 80 in the second Test at Kolkata, wrapping up victory by taking the last two wickets with successive balls. In the otherwise miserable Australian trip that followed, Yadav was "the find of the tour" according to Gautam Gambhir, after a five-for to stall Australia's progress in the Perth Test in January 2012 then some fine displays in the one-day series. He was less successful in Sri Lanka later in the year, but then took five wickets in two spin-dominated victories at home against New Zealand.

THE FACTS   Yadav took 7 for 74 for Vidarbha against Maharashtra at Nasik in November 2010 ... He is the first Test cricketer to emerge from Vidarbha, and claimed 5 for 93 against Australia at Perth in January 2012 ... Yadav took 6 for 40 for Vidarbha v Jharkhand at Ranchi in November 2009 ...

THE FIGURES *to 17.09.12*　　　　　　　　　　　　　　　**ESPA**cricinfo.com

Batting & Fielding	M	Inns	NO	Runs	HS	Avge	S/R	100	50	4s	6s	Ct	St
Tests	8	11	5	36	21	6.00	33.33	0	0	5	1	1	0
ODIs	17	8	8	26	11*	–	72.22	0	0	4	0	3	0
T20Is	1	0	–	–	–	–	–	–	–	–	–	0	0
First-class	28	36	21	157	24*	10.46	43.97	0	0	20	2	12	0

Bowling	M	Balls	Runs	Wkts	BB	Avge	RpO	S/R	5i	10m
Tests	8	1305	956	28	5–93	34.14	4.39	46.60	1	0
ODIs	17	806	841	18	3–38	46.72	6.26	44.77	0	0
T20Is	1	18	24	1	1–24	24.00	8.00	18.00	0	0
First-class	28	4693	2744	97	7–74	28.28	3.50	48.38	5	0

YOUNIS KHAN

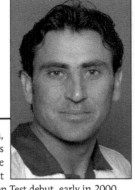

PAKISTAN

Full name	**Mohammad Younis Khan**
Born	**Nov 29, 1977, Mardan, North-West Frontier Province**
Teams	**NWFP, Peshawar, Habib Bank**
Style	**Right-hand bat, occasional legspinner**
Test debut	**Pakistan v Sri Lanka at Rawalpindi 1999-2000**
ODI debut	**Pakistan v Sri Lanka at Karachi 1999-2000**
T20I debut	**Pakistan v England at Bristol 2006**

THE PROFILE Younis Khan is a fearless middle-order batsman, as befits his Pathan ancestry. He plays with a flourish, and is especially strong in the arc from backward point to extra cover; he is prone to getting down on one knee and driving extravagantly. But this flamboyance is coupled with grit. He started with a century on Test debut, early in 2000, and scored well in bursts after that, including 153 against West Indies in Sharjah. He lost his place shortly after the 2003 World Cup following a modest run, but was soon back in favour, and made another century against Sri Lanka. He remained a heavy runmaker, especially against India: in March 2005 he hit 147 and 267 in successive Tests against them, then early the following year made 199, 83, 194, 0 and 77, before scoring consistently in England too, with 173 at Leeds. He flirted with the captaincy – theatrically resigning more than once – and started his reign as fulltime skipper with 313 in 760 minutes against Sri Lanka on a Karachi featherbed early in 2009. Later that year he led Pakistan to victory in the World Twenty20 in England ... but retired from 20-over cricket immediately afterwards. A short-lived ban for unspecified offences in Australia meant he missed the disastrous 2010 England tour, but he was welcomed back afterwards, scoring a century against South Africa in his first Test back. He had a quiet World Cup in 2011, then missed the West Indian tour after his brother died. But Younis was soon back in the runs, making 122 against Sri Lanka in Sharjah in November and caning Bangladesh for 200 a few weeks later. He rounded off the whitewash of England early in 2012 with 127 in Dubai. His one-day form dropped off later in the year, but he remains a class act.

THE FACTS Younis Khan scored 313, Pakistan's third Test triple-century, against Sri Lanka at Karachi in February 2009 ... He averages 88.06 in Tests against India – and more than 31 against everyone else ... Younis was the seventh Pakistani to score a century on Test debut, with 107 v Sri Lanka in February 2000 ... Against India at home early in 2006 he shared successive stands of 319, 142, 242, 0 and 158 with Mohammad Yousuf ...

THE FIGURES to 17.09.12   ESPncricinfo.com

Batting & Fielding	M	Inns	NO	Runs	HS	Avge	S/R	100	50	4s	6s	Ct	St
Tests	79	138	11	6565	313	51.69	52.75	20	26	754	37	88	0
ODIs	245	235	23	6824	144	32.18	75.61	6	47	548	52	127	0
T20Is	25	23	3	442	51	22.10	121.42	0	2	31	12	12	0
First-class	168	273	32	12262	313	50.87	–	38	50	–	–	179	0

Bowling	M	Balls	Runs	Wkts	BB	Avge	RpO	S/R	5i	10m
Tests	79	696	421	7	2–23	60.14	3.62	99.42	0	0
ODIs	245	272	271	3	1–3	90.33	5.97	90.66	0	0
T20Is	25	22	18	3	3–18	6.00	4.90	7.33	0	0
First-class	168	3030	1750	38	4–52	46.05	3.46	79.73	0	0

YUVRAJ SINGH

Full name	**Yuvraj Singh**
Born	**December 12, 1981, Chandigarh**
Teams	**Punjab, Pune Warriors**
Style	**Left-hand bat, left-arm orthodox spinner**
Test debut	**India v New Zealand at Mohali 2003-04**
ODI debut	**India v Kenya at Nairobi 2000-01**
T20I debut	**India v Scotland at Durban 2007-08**

THE PROFILE   Yuvraj Singh had swatted fast bowling all over the place – in the first World Twenty20 he collared Stuart Broad for six sixes in an over – but in 2012 he faced his biggest battle ... cancer. He conquered a rare germ-cell disorder with the aid of chemotherapy, and his return to fitness was crowned by inclusion in India's squad for the World Twenty20 in Sri Lanka in September 2012. Fingers will be crossed for him – not just in India. Yuvraj had made a lordly entry into international cricket at 18, toppling Australia in the ICC Knockout of October 2000 with a blistering 84 in his first innings and some scintillating fielding. He supplements those skills with loopy left-arm spin, with which he took two IPL hat-tricks in 2009. While his ability to hit the ball long and clean was instantly recognised, at first he was troubled by quality spin, and temporarily lost his place. But in 2002 his stand with Mohammad Kaif set up a memorable victory over England at Lord's. It still took another 15 months, and an injury to Sourav Ganguly, for Yuvraj to get a Test look-in. But in his third match, on a Lahore greentop, he stroked a stunning first-day century off 110 balls. A scintillating 169 against Pakistan at Bangalore in December 2007 seemed to have nailed down a Test place at last ... but a string of modest scores followed, and he was out again by the middle of 2008. He remained a one-day regular – and a fearsome sight (for bowlers, at least) in Twenty20 games – and was a star with bat and ball as the 2011 World Cup was won, lifting four match awards.

THE FACTS   Yuvraj hit England's Stuart Broad for six sixes in an over during the World Twenty20 at Durban in September 2007 ... He played 73 ODIs before winning his first Test cap ... He averages 63.55 in Tests against Pakistan, but 9.14 v Australia ... Yuvraj hit 358 for Punjab Under-19s against Bihar's in December 1999 ... His father, fast bowler Yograj Singh, played one Test in 1980-81 ... Yuvraj's record includes three ODIs for the Asia XI ...

THE FIGURES *to 17.09.12* **ESPNcricinfo.com**

Batting & Fielding	M	Inns	NO	Runs	HS	Avge	S/R	100	50	4s	6s	Ct	St
Tests	37	57	6	1775	169	34.80	58.33	3	10	247	19	31	0
ODIs	274	252	38	8051	139	37.62	87.58	13	49	827	144	84	0
T20Is	24	23	4	601	70	31.63	150.25	0	5	35	40	7	0
First-class	99	155	18	6114	209	44.62	–	18	30	–	–	93	0

Bowling	M	Balls	Runs	Wkts	BB	Avge	RpO	S/R	5i	10m
Tests	37	853	501	9	2–9	55.66	3.52	94.77	0	0
ODIs	274	4832	4060	109	5–31	37.24	5.04	44.33	1	0
T20Is	24	156	208	8	3–23	26.00	8.00	19.50	0	0
First-class	99	2143	1229	21	3–25	58.52	3.44	102.04	0	0

AFGHANISTAN

Samiullah Shenwari

Nawroz Mangal

Hamid Hassan

The improbable rise of war-torn Afghanistan as a cricket power was one of the great feelgood stories of 2008 and 2009. Starting in the lowly backwaters of world cricket's fifth division in May 2008, they won in Jersey to progress up the ladder a notch. They topped Division Four, too, in Tanzania, then emerged from Division Three, in Argentina at the end of January 2009. That put them into the World Cup qualifying series in South Africa, where they finished just one win short of a fairytale appearance in the main event itself in 2011. The decision to reduce the number of associate nations in the World Cup from six in 2007 to four next time ultimately cost Afghanistan a place, as they finished sixth – but that did bring the considerable consolation (and considerable funding) of official one-day international status for the next four years. They celebrated by walloping Scotland in their first ODI, and later in the year shared a short series in the unfamiliar surroundings of the Netherlands. They were also holding their own in the ICC's first-class Intercontinental Cup competition: also in Holland, Noor Ali became only the fourth man – after Test players in Arthur Morris of Australia, India's Nari Contractor and Aamer Malik of Pakistan – to score two centuries on his first-class debut. They qualified for the World Twenty20 in the West Indies early in 2010, and did not look out of place despite losing to India and South Africa, and qualified again in 2012. Some more impressive Intercontinental Cup performances followed, and soon the players were starting to bemoan their lack of opportunities against the senior Test nations in 50-overs matches. That's still the case, although they did play (and avoided embarrassment) against Australia late in 2012. Afghanistan's cricketers still have hurdles to overcome, but they have coped admirably with everything that has been thrown at them so far.

Afghanistan's ODI records *as at 17.09.12*

Highest total	295-8	v Scotland at Benoni 2008-09
Lowest total	88	v Kenya at Nairobi 2010-11
Most runs	743	Mohammad Shahzad (avge. 37.15)
Highest score	118	Moh'd Shahzad v Canada at Sharjah 2009-10
Most wickets	28	Samiullah Shenwari (avge. 27.42)
Best bowling	4-24	Shapoor Zadran v Netherlands at Amstelveen 2009
Most matches	23	Mohammad Nabi, Samiullah Shenwari (2009-12)
World Cup record		Have not qualified yet
Overall ODI record		Played 23: Won 12, Lost 11

AFGHANISTAN

ASGHAR STANIKZAI, Mohammad December 22, 1987, Kabul
RHB, RFM: 22 ODIs, 464 runs at 25.77, HS 66; 2 wickets at 42.00, BB 1-22.
Middle-order batsman who scored 66 against Australia at Sharjah in August 2012.

DAWLAT ZADRAN March 19, 1988, Khost
RHB, RFM: 6 ODIs, 36 runs at 7.20, HS 12; 8 wickets at 27.87, BB 3-49.
Hit for two sixes in his first ODI over – v Canada in 2011 – but took a wicket in his next one.

GULBODIN NAIB March 16, 1991, Peshawar, Pakistan
RHB, RFM: 6 ODIs, 49 runs at 9.80, HS 22; 1 wicket at 79.00, BB 1-37.
Hit 68 from 42 balls for Afghan Cheetahs in a 2011 Twenty20 match in Pakistan.

HAMID HASSAN June 1, 1987, Bati Kot, Nangrahar
RHB, RFM: 14 ODIs, 42 runs at 7.00, HS 17; 24 wickets at 21.91, BB 4-26.
Fast bowler who took 5-23 against Ireland in World Cup qualifier in South Africa in April 2009.

JAVED AHMADI, Mohammad January 2, 1992, Kunduz
RHB, OB: 10 ODIs, 139 runs at 15.44, HS 43; 1 wicket at 84.00; BB 1-47.
Batsman who appeared in the Under-19 World Cups of 2010 and 2012 (as captain).

KARIM SADIQ Khan February 18, 1984, Nangrahar
RHB, OB, WK: 21 ODIs, 458 runs at 25.44, HS 114*, 1x100: 4 wickets at 38.75, BB 2-22.
Scored 114 against Scotland at Ayr in August 2010.*

MIRWAIS ASHRAF June 30, 1988, Kunduz
RHB, RFM: 11 ODIs, 83 runs at 11.85, HS 17; 11 wickets at 29.81, BB 4-35.
Medium-pacer who took 4-35 v Kenya in Nairobi in October 2010.

MOHAMMAD NABI Eisakhil March 7, 1985, Loger
RHB, OB: 23 ODIs, 558 runs at 32.82, HS 62; 19 wickets at 38.89, BB 4-31.
Hard-hitting batsman who spent some time on the MCC cricket staff at Lord's.

MOHAMMAD SHAHZAD Mohammadi July 15, 1991, Nangrahar
RHB, WK: 21 ODIs, 743 runs at 37.15, HS 118, 3x100; 22 ct, 6 st.
Scored Afghanistan's first ODI hundred, against the Netherlands at Amstelveen in his second match.

NAJIBULLAH ZADRAN February 28, 1993, Loger
LHB, OB: 2 ODIs, 23 runs at 11.50, HS 23.
Promising allrounder who played against Australia in Sharjah in August 2012.

NAWROZ MANGAL, Khan July 15, 1984, Kabul
RHB, OB: 22 ODIs, 440 runs at 25.88, HS 70*; 7 wickets at 27.85, BB 3-35.
Afghanistan's captain throughout their astonishing rise. Took 5-24 v Malaysia in 2008.

NOOR ALI Zadran July 10, 1988, Khost
RHB, RM: 14 ODIs, 371 runs at 28.53, HS 114, 1x100.
Made 130 and 100 on first-class debut, for Afghanistan v Zimbabwe A in August 2009.*

SAMIULLAH SHENWARI February 3, 1987, Nangrahar
RHB, LBG: 23 ODIs, 376 runs at 26.85, HS 82; 28 wickets at 27.42, BB 4-31.
Improving legspinner who took 4-28 v Bermuda in World Cup qualifier in 2009.

SHABIR NOORI February 22, 1992, Nangrahar
RHB, OB: 9 ODIs, 182 runs at 20.22, HS 94.
Solid batsman who scored 94 against Canada at King City in August 2011.

SHAPOOR ZADRAN July 8, 1987, Loger
LHB, LFM: 16 ODIs, 21 runs at 4.20, HS 17; 22 wickets at 27.27, BB 4-24.
Left-armer who took 4-24 – including 3 for 1 in 8 balls – on ODI debut v Netherlands in Aug 2009.

CANADA

Ruvindu Gunasekera   *Harvir Baidwan*   *Rizwan Cheema*

Cricket has long been played in Canada: the first-ever international match was not England v Australia but Canada v the United States, in New York in 1844. But although the series continued fitfully over the years, cricket never quite took hold in north America – although the States had several handy teams around the turn of the 20th century, and the Canadians have long hosted visits by strong touring sides. Don Bradman made one such trip in the 1930s, and nominated the Brockton Point ground in Vancouver as the most beautiful he'd ever seen. In 1954 a Canadian side toured England, playing several first-class matches. In a portent of things to come, that team included several players who had moved to Canada from the West Indies for better job prospects. After a quiet period, Canadian cricket received a shot in the arm when they qualified for the 1979 World Cup in England, although the inexperienced team was embarrassed by the hosts, being hustled out for 45 at Old Trafford. Canada missed out on World Cup qualification until 2002-03, when a side largely made up of expats – and a few journeymen who happened to have been born in Canada – gave a decent account of themselves. John Davison, who had hovered on the fringes of the Victoria and South Australia sides, returned for the land of his birth and shocked everyone by hammering a century in 67 balls – the fastest in the World Cup at the time – against West Indies. Sri Lanka proved rather more ruthless, bowling them out for 36. Canada qualified again in 2007 and 2011, without upsetting any apple-carts. Their administration has been striving hard to become more professional, and in 2009 the first central contracts were introduced. Whether to accept them was simple for some, like the hard-hitting batsman Rizwan Cheema, who was serving behind the counter in a fast-food joint. But results since then have been dire, not helped by administrative squabbles. The shortage of home-grown talent remains a worry, so the next few years are vital.

Canada's ODI records *as at 17.09.12*

Highest total	312-4	v Ireland at Nairobi 2006-07
Lowest total	36	v Sri Lanka at Paarl 2002-03
Most runs	1961	A Bagai (avge. 38.45)
Highest score	137*	A Bagai v Scotland at Nairobi 2006-07
Most wickets	43	HS Baidwan (avge. 28.39)
Best bowling	5-27	A Codrington v Bangladesh at Durban 2002-03
Most matches	60	A Bagai (2003–2011)
World Cup record	First phase 1979, 2002-03, 2006-07, 2010-11	
Overall ODI record	Played 71: Won 17, Lost 53, No result 1	

CANADA

BAGAI, Ashish January 26, 1982, Delhi, India
RHB, WK: 60 ODIs, 1961 runs at 38.45, HS 137*, 2x100; 58 ct 9 st.
Tidy wicketkeeper/batsman who captained in 2011 World Cup: hundreds v Scotland and Ireland.

BAIDWAN, Harvir Singh July 31, 1987, Chandigarh, India
RHB, RM: 28 ODIs, 215 runs at 17.91, HS 33; 43 wickets at 28.39, BB 3-19.
Tidy medium-pacer who has a good economy-rate (just above five an over) in ODIs.

BALAJI RAO, Wandavasti Dorakanti March 4, 1978, Chennai, India
LHB, LB: 10 ODIs, 59 runs at 7.37, HS 24; 12 wickets at 37.33, BB 4-57.
Combative legspinner who took 4-57 v Zimbabwe in the 2011 World Cup.

DESAI, Parth Ajaykumar December 11, 1990, Navsari, Gujarat, India
RHB, SLA: 12 ODIs, 8 runs at 2.66, HS 3*; 11 wickets at 41.00, BB 3-35.
Young spinner who took 3-35 against Ireland in 2010.

GORDON, Tyson George January 31, 1982, St Mary, Jamaica
LHB, RFM: 5 ODIs, 27 runs at 5.40, HS 9; 0 wicket for 25.
Batsman who made his ODI debut against Sri Lanka in the 2011 World Cup.

GUNASEKERA, Ruvindu July 20, 1991, Colombo, Sri Lanka
LHB: 13 ODIs, 304 runs at 23.38, HS 71.
Batsman who played his first ODI at 17: in 2010 hit 71 and 59 v Ireland on successive days.

HANSRA, Amarbhir Singh ("Jimmy") December 29, 1984, Ludhiana, India
RHB, OB: 18 ODIs, 383 runs at 29.46, HS 70*; 7 wickets at 41.28, BB 3-27.
Scored 70 v Kenya and 70 v New Zealand in successive World Cup matches in 2011.*

KHURRAM CHOHAN February 22, 1980, Lahore, Pakistan
RHB, RFM: 23 ODIs, 142 runs at 12.90, HS 35*; 31 wickets at 29.90, BB 4-26.
Medium-pacer who took eight wickets in successive matches against Afghanistan in 2010.

KUMAR, Nitish Roenik May 21, 1994, Scarborough, Ontario
RHB: 11 ODIs, 144 runs at 14.40, HS 38.
Precocious batsman, nicknamed "Tendulkar", who made his ODI debut at 15.

OSINDE, Henry October 17, 1978, Uganda
RHB, RFM: 40 ODIs, 63 runs at 4.20, HS 21*; 42 wickets at 31.04, BB 4-26.
Experienced opening bowler who took 4-26 v Kenya in the 2011 World Cup.

PATEL, Hiral August 10, 1991, Ahmedabad, India
RHB, SLA: 19 ODIs, 398 runs at 20.94, HS 62; 9 wickets at 35.66, BB 4-28.
Aggressive batsman who hit 54 against Australia in the 2011 World Cup.

RIZWAN CHEEMA August 15, 1978, Pakistan
RHB, RM: 31 ODIs, 707 runs at 24.37, HS 94; 32 wickets at 32.15, BB 3-25.
Big-hitting batsman with an ODI strike-rate of 116.29 – and 33 sixes.

SURKARI, Zubin Eruch February 26, 1980, Toronto, Ontario
RHB: 23 ODIs, 328 runs at 17.26, HS 49.
Captained Canada on his ODI debut, against Bermuda in 2008.

USMAN LIMBADA October 2, 1989, Scarborough, Ontario
RHB, RM: 8 ODIs, 132 runs at 18.85, HS 50.
Young batsman who scored 50 against Ireland in September 2011.

IRELAND

Niall O'Brien

Tim Murtagh

William Porterfield

Cricket in Ireland was once so popular that Oliver Cromwell banned it in 1656. Since then, it has been something of a minority sport, although there were occasional big days, as in 1969 when the West Indians were skittled for 25 on a boggy pitch at Sion Mills in County Tyrone (rumours that the visitors enjoyed lavish hospitality at a nearby Guinness brewery the night before are thought to be unfounded). Cricket continued as an amateur pastime until the 1990s, when the Irish board left the auspices of the English one and attained independent ICC membership. Ireland became eligible to play in the World Cup, and narrowly missed out on the 1999 tournament, when they lost a playoff to Scotland. They made no mistake for 2007, though, winning the ICC Trophy (handily, it was played in Ireland) to ensure qualification. A change of captain to the Australian-born Trent Johnston ushered in a new, more professional set-up, and Ireland travelled to the Caribbean hopeful of making a mark. No-one, though, was quite prepared for what happened – except maybe Johnston himself, who packed enough for a seven-week stay when most were expecting a quiet return home in a week or two. In their first World Cup match, Ireland tied with Zimbabwe, then went one better on a Sabina Park greentop on St Patrick's Day, hanging on to beat Pakistan and eliminate one of the pre-tournament favourites. Ireland sailed on to the Super Eights, where they beat Bangladesh too. In 2011, the highlight of several good performances was a stunning victory over England, thanks to Kevin O'Brien's 50-ball hundred. But the better Irish players are already with English counties (Ed Joyce and Eoin Morgan have already played for England, and Boyd Rankin is trying to follow suit), and the others struggle to fit in ever-increasing international commitments around a steady job. Irish cricket is striving – against considerable odds – to build on World Cup success by planning a proper first-class structure, and may make a cheeky bid for Test status soon.

Ireland's ODI records *as at 17.09.12*

Highest total	329-7	v England at Bangalore 2010-11
Lowest total	77	v Sri Lanka at St George's 2006-07
Most runs	1752	WTS Porterfield (avge. 30.73)
Highest score	177	PR Stirling v Canada at Toronto 2010
Most wickets	63	DT Johnston (avge. 29.84)
Best bowling	5-14	DT Johnston v Canada at Centurion 2008-09
Most matches	68	KJ O'Brien (2006-2012)
World Cup record		Super Eights 2006-07, first phase 2010-11
Overall ODI record		Played 74: Won 34, Lost 35, Tied 1, No result 4

CUSACK, Alex Richard   October 29, 1980, Brisbane, Australia
RHB, RFM: 46 ODIs, 679 runs at 24.25, HS 71; 46 wickets at 22.04, BB 5-20.
Man of the Match on ODI debut for 36* and 3-15 v South Africa at Belfast in June 2007.

DOCKRELL, George Henry   July 22, 1992, Dublin
RHB, SLA: 30 ODIs, 80 runs at 10.00, HS 19; 37 wickets at 25.40, BB 4-35.
Precocious slow left-armer who did well in 2012 for Somerset.

JOHNSTON, David Trent   April 29, 1974, Wollongong, NSW, Australia
RHB, RFM: 61 ODIs, 668 runs at 19.08, HS 45*; 63 wickets at 29.84, BB 5-14.
Inspirational captain (and innovative chicken dancer) during Ireland's 2007 World Cup run.

JONES, Nigel Geoffrey   April 22, 1982, Timaru, New Zealand
RHB, RM: 14 ODIs, 74 runs at 14.80, HS 25*; 10 wickets at 23.40, BB 2-19.
Former New Zealander who appears to bowl off the wrong foot.

JOYCE, Edmund Christopher   September 22, 1978, Dublin
LHB: 32 ODIs (17 for England), 935 runs at 30.16, HS 107, 1×100.
Played for England in the 2006-07 World Cup, and Ireland in the 2010-11 one.

MOONEY, John Francis   February 10, 1982, Dublin
LHB, RM: 45 ODIs, 709 runs at 24.44, HS 55; 34 wickets at 28.55, BB 4-27.
Left-hander with a mean reverse-sweep; his brother Paul played for Ireland too.

MURTAGH, Timothy James   August 2, 1981, London
LHB, RFM: 2 ODIs, 15 runs at 15.00, HS 15; 0 wicket for 39.
Bustling Middlesex seamer with Irish grandparents – debut v Australia in 2012.

O'BRIEN, Kevin Joseph   March 4, 1984, Dublin
RHB, RFM: 68 ODIs, 1749 runs at 33.00, HS 142, 2×100; 49 wickets at 30.63, BB 4-71.
Well-built allrounder whose 50-ball century led to victory over England at the 2011 World Cup.

O'BRIEN, Niall John   November 8, 1981, Dublin
LHB, WK: 51 ODIs, 1215 runs at 26.41, HS 72; 38 ct, 7 st.
Feisty keeper who has played for Kent and Northants: made 72 in World Cup win over Pakistan.

PORTERFIELD, William Thomas Stuart   September 6, 1984, Londonderry
RHB: 60 ODIs, 1752 runs at 30.73, HS 112*, 5×100.
Solid opener: made two ODI hundreds in three days early in 2007; took over as captain in 2008.

POYNTER, Andrew David   April 25, 1987, Hammersmith, London
RHB, OB: 15 ODIs, 200 runs at 22.22, HS 78.
Clontarf batsman who played once for Middlesex in 2005: 78 v Afghanistan in 2010.

RANKIN, William Boyd   July 5, 1984, Derry
LHB, RFM: 37 ODIs, 35 runs at 7.00, HS 7*; 43 wickets at 32.34, BB 3-32.
Tall fast bowler who played for England Lions in 2011, after joining Warwickshire.

STIRLING, Paul Robert   September 3, 1990, Belfast
RHB: 38 ODIs, 1448 runs at 39.13, HS 177, 4×100; 20 wickets at 34.60, BB 4-11.
Batsman on Middlesex's books who slammed 177 against Canada in September 2010.

WHITE, Andrew Roland   July 3, 1980, Newtownards, Co. Down
RHB, OB: 56 ODIs, 769 runs at 18.75, HS 79; 25 wickets at 26.56, BB 4-44.
Offspinner, formerly with Northants, who hit 152* on first-class debut, for Ireland v Holland in 2004.

WILSON, Gary Craig   February 5, 1986, Dundonald, Northern Ireland
RHB, WK: 39 ODIs, 953 runs at 28.02, HS 113, 1×100; 23 ct, 7 st.
Handy keeper-batsman who is on the Surrey staff; scored 113 v Holland in Dublin in 2010.

KENYA

Rakep Patel

Alex Obanda

Nehemiah Odhiambo

The British Empire spread cricket to Kenya: the first notable match was played there in 1899, and English-style country clubs still flourish in Nairobi, which can claim one cricket record – six different grounds there have staged official one-day internationals, more than any other city. Strong MCC teams have made several visits to East Africa – one of them, in the early 1960s, unearthed Basharat Hassan, who went on to enjoy a long career with Nottinghamshire. Kenyan players formed the backbone of the East African side in the first World Cup, in 1975, but soon after that they struck out on their own, joining the ICC in their own right in 1981. Kenyan cricket continued to improve quietly until they qualified for the World Cup in 1995-96, where they amazed everyone by upsetting West Indies in a group game. Players reared on hard pitches struggled in early-season England at the 1999 Cup, but the 2003 version was different: it was held in Africa, and some of the matches were played in Kenya. Helped by outside events (England refused to go to Zimbabwe, while New Zealand boycotted Nairobi for security reasons), the Kenyans progressed to the semi-finals. It seemed like the start of a golden era: instead it ushered in a depressing time, marked by player strikes and arguments about administration. Peace broke out in time for the 2007 World Cup, but with several players approaching the veteran stage the results were poor, and Ireland comfortably usurped them as the leading non-Test nation: others have passed them since. More haggling over money intruded in 2010, before a resolution in time for the following year's World Cup. But more dreadful results there led to a clearout of the old guard, meaning farewells to stalwarts like Steve Tikolo – once seen as the best batsman outside Test cricket – and the chunky allrounder Thomas Odoyo, the first bowler from a non-Test nation to take 100 wickets in one-day internationals. Now a new young side is struggling to compete in international 50- and 20-overs cricket.

Kenya's ODI records *as at 17.09.12*

Highest total	347-3	v Bangladesh at Nairobi 1997-98
Lowest total	69	v New Zealand at Chennai 2010-11
Most runs	3362	SO Tikolo (avge. 29.49)
Highest score	144	KO Otieno v Bangladesh at Nairobi 1997-98
Most wickets	137	TM Odoyo (avge. 29.71)
Best bowling	5-24	CO Obuya v Sri Lanka at Nairobi 2002-03
Most matches	130	SO Tikolo (1996-2011)
World Cup record		Semi-finalists 2002-03; first phase 1995-96, 1999, 2006-07, 2010-11
Overall ODI record		Played 146: Won 39, Lost 102, No result 5

AGA, Ragheb Gul
July 10, 1984, Nairobi
RHB, RFM: 4 ODIs, 13 runs at 4.33, HS 12; 2 wickets at 48.50, BB 2-17.
Allrounder who reappeared after almost eight years in 2012: played for Sussex.

ALLAN, Duncan Iain
October 14, 1991, Brisbane, Australia
RHB, RFM: 4 ODIs, 53 runs at 13.25, HS 27; 2 wickets at 32.00, BB 1-22.
Promising allrounder: player of the tournament at the 2011 Under-19 World Cup qualifier.

MISHRA, Tanmay
December 22, 1986, Mumbai, India
RHB, RM: 38 ODIs, 979 runs at 31.58, HS 72; 0 wicket for 6.
Talented batsman who returned to Kenya in 2010 after studying in India: played in the IPL in 2012.

NGOCHE, James Otieno
January 29, 1988, Kenya
RHB, OB: 14 ODIs, 34 runs at 4.85, HS 21*; 18 wickets at 24.22, BB 3-18.
Offspinner who took 3-18 v Scotland in 2010: three brothers and two sisters have also played for Kenya.

NGOCHE , Shem Obado
June 6, 1989, Kenya
RHB, SLA: 10 ODIs, 43 runs at 6.14, HS 28; 9 wickets at 35.22, BB 2-28.
Slow left-armer who faced three balls at the 2011 World Cup – and was dismissed by all three.

OBANDA, Alex Ouma
December 25, 1987, Nairobi
RHB: 42 ODIs, 1151 runs at 31.97, HS 96*.
Strokeplaying batsman who was stranded four short of a century against Zimbabwe in Feb 2009.

OBUYA, Collins Omondi
July 27, 1981, Nairobi
RHB, LB: 96 ODIs, 1860 runs at 25.83, HS 98*; 33 wickets at 48.39, BB 5-24.
Made 98 v Australia in the 2011 World Cup – and took over as captain afterwards.*

OBUYA, David Oluoch
August 14, 1979, Nairobi
RHB, WK: 74 ODIs, 1355 runs at 19.35, HS 93; 39 ct, 5 st.
Opener, wicketkeeper, and brother of Collins Obuya and former Kenya keeper Kennedy Otieno.

ODHIAMBO, Nehemiah Ngoche
August 7, 1983, Nairobi, Kenya
RHB, RFM: 61 ODIs, 498 runs at 12.76, HS 66; 64 wickets at 35.85, BB 4-61.
Fast bowler who took 5-20 in T20 v Scotland in Feb 2010; three brothers have played for Kenya.

OTIENO, Elijah Asoyo
January 3, 1988, Nairobi
RHB, RFM: 22 ODIs, 40 runs at 4.44, HS 11; 17 wickets at 46.00, BB 3-39.
Promising young seamer – but with the bat collected five ducks in his first seven first-class innings.

OUMA, Maurice Akumu
November 8, 1982, Kiambli
RHB, WK: 72 ODIs, 1291 runs at 19.86, HS 61; 46 ct, 10 st.
Handy striker who often opens: took over as captain in 2009 but resigned in 2010.

PATEL, Rakep Rajendra
July 12, 1989, Nairobi
RHB, OB: 31 ODIs, 470 runs at 18.80, HS 92; 2 wickets at 54.00, BB 1-14.
Promising batsman who hit 92 against the Netherlands in February 2010.

VARAIYA, Hiren Ashok
April 9, 1984, Mumbai, India
RHB, SLA: 55 ODIs, 221 runs at 13.00, HS 34; 62 wickets at 28.56, BB 4-25.
Canny spinner who struck with his first ball in ODIs (v Canada in 2006).

WATERS, Seren Robert
April 11, 1990, Nairobi
RHB: 20 ODIs, 419 runs at 20.95, HS 74.
Young batsman who scored 74 v South Africa in November 2008 while still a schoolboy.

THE NETHERLANDS

Tom Cooper

Ryan ten Doeschate

Pieter Seelaar

Cricket was brought to The Netherlands by British soldiers during the Napoleonic War: by 1881 there was a Dutch team, and two years later a national board was set up, comprising 18 clubs, four of which still exist. A league system has long flourished, and there has been a tradition of foreign players coming over to coach. Dutch cricket received a boost in 1964 when Australia visited after an Ashes tour and lost by three wickets, and more noses were tweaked in 1989, with a win over England A. West Indies (1991) and South Africa (1994) also succumbed – it's safe to say they were more relaxed than they might have been for an official international – and another strongish England side was beaten in 1993. The Netherlands qualified for their first World Cup three years later, and weren't disgraced, and they were there again in 2003, when they beat Namibia. They just scraped in to the 2007 tournament, winning a playoff against the UAE, but again managed a consolation win, this time over Scotland, which made up for being pummelled by South Africa and Australia. Perhaps their biggest moment, though, came in the first match of the World Twenty20 in 2009, when they embarrassed England – at Lord's, too. Standout performers in recent years have included Roland Lefebvre, who played for Somerset and Glamorgan, and Bas Zuiderent, who had a spell with Sussex. Essex's Ryan ten Doeschate hammered four centuries in three ICC Intercontinental Cup games in 2006, while the Australian Tom Cooper, whose mother is Dutch, made a stunning start in 2010. Ten Doeschate hit two fine centuries in the 2011 World Cup, including 119 as the Netherlands nearly embarrassed England again. The local players are very keen, but there are not that many of them, fans are thin on the ground, and there's really no prospect of a proper first-class competition. The future might not be too bright but, for the Dutch one-day team at least, it's certainly orange.

The Netherlands' ODI records *as at 17.09.12*

Highest total	315-8	v Bermuda at Rotterdam 2007
Lowest total	80	v West Indies at Dublin 2007
Most runs	1541	RN ten Doeschate (avge. 67.00)
Highest score	134*	KJJ van Noortwijk v Namibia at Bloemfontein 2002-03
Most wickets	55	RN ten Doeschate (avge. 24.12)
Best bowling	4-23	E Schiferli v Kenya at Potchefstroom 2008-09
Most matches	57	B Zuiderent (1996-2011)
World Cup record		Eliminated in first round 1995-96, 2002-03, 2006-07 and 2010-11
Overall ODI record		Played 69: Won 26, Lost 41, No result 2

THE NETHERLANDS

AHSAN MALIK Jamil   August 29, 1989, Rotterdam
RHB, RFM: 5 ODIs, 0 runs; 4 wickets at 38.75, BB 3-38.
Energetic medium-pacer who took 4-24 against Lancashire in 2012 CB40.

BARRESI, Wesley   May 3, 1984, Johannesburg, South Africa
RHB, WK: 21 ODIs, 508 runs at 28.22, HS 67; 9 ct, 6 st.
Hard-hitting batsman who formerly played for Easterns in South Africa.

BORREN, Peter William   August 21, 1983, Christchurch, New Zealand
RHB, RM: 51 ODIs, 815 runs at 20.37, HS 96; 46 wickets at 32.17, BB 4-32.
Combative allrounder who made 105 and 96 v Canada in 2006: appointed captain in 2010.

BUKHARI, Mudassar   December 26, 1983, Gujrat, Pakistan
RHB, RFM: 39 ODIs, 465 runs at 18.60, HS 71; 46 wickets at 27.82, BB 3-17.
Primarily a bowler, he scored 71 (after opening) and took 3-24 against Ireland in July 2007.

BUURMAN, Atse Folkert   March 21, 1982, Dordrecht
RHB, WK: 17 ODIs, 140 runs at 15.55, HS 34; 17 ct, 3 st.
Found a place after the retirement of long-serving wicketkeeper Jeroen Smits in 2009.

COOPER, Tom Lexley William   November 26, 1986, Wollongong, NSW, Australia
RHB, OB: 20 ODIs, 916 runs at 53.88, HS 101, 1×100; 12 wickets at 27.66, BB 3-11.
Hard-hitting batsman who uniquely passed 50 in his first three ODIs, then made 101 in his fifth.

de GROOTH, Tom Nico   May 14, 1979, The Hague
RHB, OB: 33 ODIs, 472 runs at 17.48, HS 97; 1 wicket at 2.00, BB 1-2.
Made 98 (v Scotland), 196 and 97 (v Bermuda) in successive matches in August 2007.

KERVEZEE, Alexei Nicolaas   September 11, 1989, Walvis Bay, Namibia
RHB, RM: 39 ODIs, 924 runs at 28.00, HS 92; 0 wickets for 34.
World Cup debut at 17, later made 98 v Canada, and joined Worcestershire in 2007.

MYBURGH, Stephanus Johannes   February 28, 1984, Pretoria, South Africa
LHB, OB: 4 ODIs, 89 runs at 22.25, HS 56.
Import who scored 77, 74, 66 and 34 in successive CB40 matches in 2012.*

SEELAAR, Pieter Marinus   July 2, 1987, Schiedam
RHB, SLA: 33 ODIs, 95 runs at 9.50, HS 34*; 36 wickets at 33.08, BB 3-22.
Tidy spinner who took 5-57 in Intercontinental Cup match v Kenya at Amstelveen in 2008.

SWART, Michael Richard   October 1, 1982, Subiaco, Perth, Australia
RHB, OB: 6 ODIs, 140 runs at 28.00, HS 52; 1 wicket at 147.00, BB 1-21.
Batsman with a Sheffield Shield hundred: made 52 v Afghanistan in March 2012.

SZWARCZYNSKI, Eric Stefan   February 13, 1983, Vanderbijlpark, South Africa
RHB: 35 ODIs, 825 runs at 25.78, HS 84*.
Batsman whose favourite player is Allan Donald: made 84 v Canada in July 2010.*

ten DOESCHATE, Ryan Neil   June 30, 1980, Port Elizabeth, South Africa
RHB, RFM: 33 ODIs, 1541 runs at 67.00, HS 119, 5×100; 55 wickets at 24.12, BB 4-31.
Allrounder who reached 1000 ODI runs quicker than anyone bar Viv Richards and Gordon Greenidge.

VAN DER GUGTEN, Timm   Febraury 25, 1991, Sydney, Australia
RHB, RFM: 2 ODIs, 2 runs at 2.00, HS 2; 2 wickets at 25.50, BB 2-35.
Medium-pacer who set up CB40 victory over Essex in 2012 with two wickets in three balls.

WESTDIJK, Berend Arnold   March 5, 1985, The Hague
RHB, RFM: 4 ODIs, 1 run at 0.50, HS 1*; 1 wicket at 195.00, BB 1-56.
Medium-pacer whose first three ODIs were during the 2011 World Cup.

SCOTLAND

Gordon Drummond

Josh Davey

Majid Haq

Cricket crept over the border from England in the mid-18th century: soldiers played it near Perth in 1750, although the first recorded match in Scotland was not till 1785. More recently there has long been a strong amateur league system in the country, although – just as in Ireland – international aspirations have always been handicapped by the absence of a proper professional set-up, which has meant that the better players have always migrated south. One of them, the Ayr-born Mike Denness, captained England, while one of the few bowlers to trouble Don Bradman in 1930 was the Scottish legspinner Ian Peebles. More recently, offspinner Peter Such (born in Helensburgh) played for England, while Gavin Hamilton (born in Broxburn) also won an England Test cap after doing well for Scotland at the 1999 World Cup. Unfortunately, Hamilton bagged a pair, and was soon back playing for Scotland: he hit his maiden ODI century in 2008. At the 2007 World Cup, Hamilton appeared alongside another former England player in Dougie Brown, the combative allrounder who had a long career with Warwickshire and played nine ODIs in 1997-98. Scotland left the auspices of the English board and joined the ICC in 1994, but they failed to win a match – or reach 200 – in any of their World Cup games in 1999 or 2007. They also competed in the English counties' limited-overs league for many years, without managing more than the occasional upset, and the team failed to qualify for the World Twenty20 in 2010 or the following year's World Cup. The main problem lying in the way of Scotland's advancement – apart from the legendarily poor weather – remains the lack of a sound domestic structure which might support first-class cricket; local support is also patchy, despite the sterling efforts of a few diehards. Until this is addressed – if it ever can be – Scotland will continue to suffer from a player drain to English counties.

Scotland's ODI records *as at 17.09.12*

Highest total	323-5	v Ireland at Edinburgh 2011
Lowest total	68	v West Indies at Leicester 1999
Most runs	1231	GM Hamilton (avge. 35.17)
Highest score	123*	RR Watson v Canada at Mombasa 2006-07
Most wickets	41	JAR Blain (avge. 28.60)
Best bowling	5-9	JH Davey v Afghanistan at Ayr 2010
Most matches	43	NFI McCallum (2006-2011)
World Cup record	Eliminated in first round 1999 and 2006-07	
Overall ODI record	Played 55: Won 19, Lost 33, No result 3	

SCOTLAND

BERRINGTON, Richard Douglas April 3, 1987, Pretoria, South Africa
RHB, RFM: 21 ODIs, 396 runs at 22.00, HS 84; 11 wickets at 44.36, BB 2-14.
Handy allrounder who made a Twenty20 international hundred against Bangladesh in 2012.

COETZER, Kyle James April 14, 1984, Aberdeen
RHB, RM: 10 ODIs, 388 runs at 43.11, HS 89*; 1 wicket at 125.00, BB 1-35.
Attractive batsman who plays for Northamptonshire (and previously Durham).

DAVEY, Joshua Henry August 3, 1990, Aberdeen
RHB, RM: 9 ODIs, 170 runs at 21.25, HS 48*; 14 wickets at 18.35, BB 5-9.
Batsman on Middlesex's books: took 5-9 v Afghanistan at Ayr in August 2010.

DRUMMOND, Gordon David April 21, 1980, Meigle, Perthshire
RHB, RFM: 26 ODIs, 207 runs at 23.00, HS 35*; 24 wickets at 34.00, BB 4-41.
Watsonians fast bowler who took 4-41 v Canada in July 2009: appointed captain in 2010.

EVANS, Alasdair Campbell January 12, 1989, Tunbridge Wells
RHB, RFM: 3 ODIs, has not batted; 2 wickets at 56.00, BB 1-13.
Loughborough graduate, and fast bowler who joined Derbyshire in 2012.

GOUDIE, Gordon August 12, 1987, Aberdeen
RHB, RFM: 15 ODIs, 57 runs at 8.14, HS 17*; 23 wickets at 23.82, BB 5-73.
West of Scotland fast bowler who took 5-73 against Australia in 2009.

HAQ Khan, Rana Majid February 11, 1983, Paisley
LHB, OB: 32 ODIs, 445 runs at 18.54, HS 71; 40 wickets at 30.37, BB 4-28.
Hard-hitting allrounder, who plays for Ferguslie: took 4-28 v West Indies at Clontarf in 2007.

LYONS, Ross Thomas December 8, 1984, Greenock
LHB, SLA: 25 ODIs, 90 runs at 22.50, HS 28; 20 wickets at 45.05, BB 3-21.
Slow left-armer who dismissed Shahid Afridi in his first ODI.

MacLEOD, Calum Scott November 15, 1988, Glasgow
RHB, RFM: 9 ODIs, 179 runs at 29.83, HS 99*; 3 wickets at 46.33, BB 2-46.
Stranded on 99 in ODI against Canada at Ayr in 2012. Formerly with Warwickshire.*

MAIDEN, Gregor Ian July 22, 1979, Glasgow
RHB, WK: 7 ODIs, 84 runs at 21.00, HS 31; 5 ct.
Grange allrounder tried as Scotland's wicketkeeper in 2011.

MOMMSEN, Preston Luke October 14, 1987, Durban, South Africa
RHB, OB: 11 ODIs, 209 runs at 19.00, HS 80; 6 wickets at 17.50, BB 3-26.
Prolific schoolboy batsman who qualified for Scotland in 2010.

NEL, Johann Dewald June 6, 1980, Klerksdorp, South Africa
RHB, RFM: 19 ODIs, 31 runs at 15.50, HS 11*; 14 wickets at 46.35, BB 4-25.
Fast bowler who dismissed Inzamam-ul-Haq on his ODI debut, and both Australia's openers in 2009.

PARKER, Matthew Archibald March 2, 1990, Dundee
LHB, RFM: 10 ODIs, 59 runs at 9.83, HS 22; 12 wickets at 27.25, BB 4-33.
Fast bowler who took 5-47 v Warwickshire in 2011.

STANDER, Jan Hendrik January 4, 1982, Port Elizabeth, South Africa
RHB, RFM: 5 ODIs, 44 runs at 11.00, HS 22*; 6 wickets at 27.66, BB 2-25.
Allrounder who returned to the one-day side after three years in 2012.

WATTS, David Fraser June 5, 1979, King's Lynn, Norfolk
RHB: 36 ODIs, 974 runs at 28.64, HS 101, 1×100.
Banker-turned-batsman who scored 171 v Denmark in 2006, and 101 v Canada in July 2009.*

OFFICIALS

UMPIRE

ALEEM DAR

Aleem Dar played 17 first-class matches as an offspinning allrounder, but never surpassed the 39 he scored in his first innings, for Railways in February 1987. He took up umpiring in 1998-99, and stood in his first ODI the following season. He officiated at the 2003 World Cup, and a year later was the first Pakistani to join the ICC's elite panel. Calm and unobtrusive, he soon established a good reputation, and it was no surprise when he was chosen to stand in the 2007 World Cup final. What was a surprise was his part in the chaos in the dark at the end, for which all the officials were excluded from the World Twenty20 later in the year. But he was soon back in favour, and stood in the World Twenty20 final in Barbados in 2010 and the World Cup final in Mumbai in April 2011. He was the ICC's umpire of the year three times running from 2009.

Born *June 6, 1968, Jhang, Pakistan.* **Tests** *74*, **ODIs** *151*, **T20Is** *18*

COACH

MICKEY **ARTHUR**

A handy batsman who had a long career in South Africa – he scored 13 hundreds in more than 100 matches for Griquland West and Orange Free State – Mickey Arthur took over as Australia's coach (their first overseas one) at an awkward time, as the nation licked its wounds after Ashes humiliation at home in 2010-11. Arthur made a good start, as India were whitewashed Down Under, but an indication of his task came late in 2012 when the Australians briefly dipped below Ireland in the Twenty20 rankings. Arthur previously had a successful stint as South Africa's coach from 2005 to 2010, forming a good partnership with Graeme Smith.

Born *May 17, 1968, Johannesburg, Transvaal, South Africa. Appointed Australia's coach in 2011*

UMPIRE

ASAD RAUF

Asad Rauf was a right-hand batsman who enjoyed a solid if unspectacular first-class career in Pakistan in the 1980s, four times making more than 600 runs in a season and scoring three centuries, the highest 130 for Railways against National Bank in November 1981. He umpired his first first-class match in 1998-99, and stood in his first ODI early in 2000. It took a bit longer to crack the Test scene, but he advanced rapidly once he did, joining the ICC's elite panel in April 2006. A former offbreak bowler himself, he is more prepared than some to give spinners lbws when batsmen prop forward hiding bat behind pad.

Born *May 12, 1956, Lahore, Pakistan.* **Tests** *44*, **ODIs** *95*, **T20Is** *17*

DAVID **BOON**

David Boon, and his trademark bushy moustache, were Australian legends: he scored 7,422 runs in more than 100 Tests between 1984 and 1996, and was also a feared presence at short leg. He soon became a national selector, and also worked in cricket administration in his native Tasmania before replacing his fellow Aussie Alan Hurst as a match referee in 2011.

Born *December 29, 1960, Launceston, Tasmania, Australia.* **Tests** *10,* **ODIs** *18,* **T20Is** *3*

BILLY **BOWDEN**

Some eccentrics are born. Others thrust eccentricity upon themselves. Brent "Billy" Bowden shot to fame with a zany array of embellished signals and a preposterous eye for showmanship. Bowden turned to umpiring after the onset of arthritis in his early twenties, and earned a reputation for giving batsmen out with a curiously bent finger. The most celebrated of his antics is the hop-on-one-leg-and-reach-for-Jesus signal for six. For all the embellishments, though, his decision-making is usually spot-on.

Born *April 11, 1963, Henderson, Auckland, New Zealand.* **Tests** *70,* **ODIs** *173,* **T20Is** *19*

CHRIS **BROAD**

It was a classic case of poacher turned gamekeeper when Chris Broad became a match referee: he had several jousts with authority during a 25-Test career in the 1980s. A tall, angular left-hander, Broad did well in Australia, scoring four Test hundreds there. After a back injury hastened his retirement, he tried his hand at TV commentary, then in 2003 became a match referee keen on enforcing the Code of Conduct. His son, Stuart, made his England debut in 2006.

Born *September 29, 1957, Knowle, Bristol, England.* **Tests** *53,* **ODIs** *213,* **T20Is** *46*

ALAN **BUTCHER**

Alan Butcher played with distinction for Surrey and then Glamorgan – he was around for so long he once played against his son, the England batsman Mark – and won one England cap, opening with Geoff Boycott against India in 1979. After various coaching roles he took over the Zimbabwean national team in time for the 2011 World Cup, and oversaw their successful return to Test cricket against Bangladesh in August of that year.

Born *January 7, 1954, Croydon, Surrey, England. Appointed Zimbabwe's coach in 2011*

OFFICIALS

REFEREE

JEFF **CROWE**

Jeff Crowe might have played for Australia – he had several successful Sheffield Shield seasons in Adelaide – but he eventually returned to New Zealand, winning 39 Test caps, six as captain. Although he was often overshadowed by his younger brother Martin, Jeff managed three Test centuries of his own. After retirement he had a spell as New Zealand's manager, before becoming a referee in 2003. He oversaw the World Cup finals of 2007 and 2011.

Born *September 14, 1958, Auckland, New Zealand.* **Tests** *55,* **ODIs** *167,* **T20Is** *30*

UMPIRE

STEVE **DAVIS**

Steve Davis played club cricket in Adelaide before turning to umpiring. He had a rapid rise: appointed to the Australian first-class list in 1990-91, he joined the national panel two years later and stood in his first ODI the same season. He stood in three matches in the 2007 World Cup, and in the final two Tests in his native England in 2008, against South Africa, shortly after being elevated to the elite panel. He was one of the umpires in Lahore early the following year and was lucky to survive the terrorist attack on the Sri Lankan team coach.

Born *April 9, 1952, London, England.* **Tests** *42,* **ODIs** *111,* **T20Is** *14*

UMPIRE

KUMAR **DHARMASENA**

Kumar Dharmasena played 31 Tests for Sri Lanka as a brisk offspinner who could bat a bit. Although he was, almost inevitably overshadowed by the amazing feats of Muttiah Muralitharan, he still took 69 wickets, with a best of 6 for 72 against New Zealand at Galle in 1998, and also claimed 138 wickets in 141 one-day internationals. After retiring in 2006 he was fast-tracked into umpiring, standing in his first ODI less than three years later. He joined the ICC's elite panel in 2011, and was named Umpire of the Year in 2012.

Born *April 24, 1971, Colombo, Sri Lanka.* **Tests** *10,* **ODIs** *41,* **T20Is** *4*

MARAIS **ERASMUS**

The solidly built Marais Erasmus was a handy allrounder for Boland in South African domestic cricket, averaging just under 30 with the bat and also taking 131 wickets with some energetic medium-pace. That included 6 for 22 as the New Zealanders were bundled out for an embarrassing 86 on a sporting Paarl pitch in December 1994. Erasmus turned to umpiring on retirement and was speedily promoted: he stood in his first ODI in Kenya in 2007. Three years later he was appointed to the ICC's elite panel, stood in his first Test in Bangladesh in January 2010, and quietly established a fine reputation in the white coat.

Born *February 27, 1964, George, Cape Province, South Africa.* **Tests** *13,* **ODIs** *43,* **T20Is** *13*

DUNCAN **FLETCHER**

Duncan Fletcher was a gutsy allrounder for Zimbabwe in pre-Test days – he scored 69 not out and took four wickets when they upset Australia in the 1983 World Cup – and after a successful coaching career had a mixed time in charge of England, when the euphoric 2005 Ashes victory was followed by the 2006-07 whitewash Down Under. Fletcher replaced Gary Kirsten as India's coach after the 2011 World Cup, and endured a chastening return to England, which overshadowed his achievement in becoming the first international coach to oversee 100 Tests.

Born *September 27, 1948, Salisbury (now Harare), Zimbabwe. Appointed India's coach in 2011*

ANDY **FLOWER**

Andy Flower was often a lone beacon of class in an underpowered Zimbabwe side. A compact left-hander strong on the sweep, Flower scored 4,794 Tests runs at 51, and nearly 7,000 in ODIs. A deep thinker, Flower was hounded out of Zimbabwe after he and Henry Olonga wore black armbands mourning the "death of democracy" there during the 2003 World Cup. Flower moved to England, where he did well for Essex, then joined the England coaching set-up, taking over as fulltime coach in time for the successful 2009 Ashes series and – iron fist evident beneath the velvet glove – oversaw England's climb to No. 1 in the world Test rankings.

Born *April 28, 1968, Cape Town, South Africa. Appointed England coach in 2009*

GRAHAM **FORD**

A batsman who played a few matches for Natal B, Graham Ford has had a long coaching career, including spells at Natal (who won the Currie Cup under his stewardship) and Kent. He was South Africa's assistant coach at the 1999 World Cup, and replaced Bob Woolmer in the hot seat shortly afterwards, staying in charge until two series defeats cost him his job in 2002. After turning down an offer to coach India in 2009, he took on the Sri Lankan post in January 2012.

Born *November 16, 1960, Pietermaritzburg, South Africa. Appointed Sri Lanka's coach in 2012*

OFFICIALS

OTTIS **GIBSON**

COACH

Fast bowler Ottis Gibson was unlucky that his best years coincided with the pomp of Curtly Ambrose and Courtney Walsh: Gibson played only two Tests, and a few ODIs, in the 1990s. Still, he carved out a successful career in county cricket for Glamorgan, Leicestershire and for Durham. It was an inspired move: he made a career-best 155 for his new county in 2006, and the following year took all ten wickets in an innings against Hampshire. That winter he joined the England coaching staff, but early in 2010 Gibson was persuaded to return home and take on the big task of returning West Indies to Test cricket's top table.

Born *March 16, 1969, Sion Hill, St Peter, Barbados. Appointed West Indies coach in 2010*

IAN **GOULD**

UMPIRE

Ian "Gunner" Gould was a combative wicketkeeper/batsman who scored nearly 9000 runs and made more than 700 dismissals in first-class cricket. He started with Middlesex, then moved to Sussex, who he captained to the NatWest Trophy in 1986. Although he never won a Test cap, he did appear in 18 ODIs, all of them in 1983, including that year's World Cup in England. He joined the English first-class umpires' panel in 2002, was promoted to the international panel in April 2006, joined the elite panel three years later, and immediately looked at home.

Born *August 19, 1957, Taplow, Buckinghamshire, England.* **Tests** 31, **ODIs** 73, **T20Is** 15

MIKE **HESSON**

COACH

Mike Hesson took up coaching at the unusually early age of 22. He became Otago's head coach in 2004, and in six years converted a previously struggling team into one which regularly challenged for titles. He took over as Kenya's coach after their disappointing 2011 World Cup, but resigned less than a year later, citing security issues that affected his family. In July 2012, still only 37, Hesson replaced John Wright as New Zealand's coach.

Born *October 30, 1974, Dunedin, New Zealand. Appointed New Zealand's coach in 2012*

TONY **HILL**

UMPIRE

Tony Hill came into umpiring without any background in first-class cricket, but soon established himself as a competent and reliable official, being appointed to the ICC's international panel in 1998 – he stood in an ODI against Zimbabwe that March – and to the full elite panel in 2009, although he had umpired the occasional Test since 2001-02. A keen golfer, he is a regional training officer and mentor for umpires in the Northern Districts.

Born *June 26, 1951, Auckland, New Zealand.* **Tests** 31, **ODIs** 94, **T20Is** 17

RICHARD **KETTLEBOROUGH**

Richard Kettleborough had an unspectacular career as a batsman with Yorkshire and Middlesex, the highlight 108 for his native county against Essex in 1996. He became a first-class umpire in 2006, when only 33, and soon made a mark as a calm official who usually got things right. He stood in his first internationals in 2009, and joined the ICC's elite panel in 2011.

Born March 15, 1973, Sheffield, Yorkshire, England. **Tests** 10, **ODIs** 26, **T20Is** 4

GARY **KIRSTEN**

A gritty left-hander, Gary Kirsten played to his strengths in a career that brought him 7289 runs in 101 Tests for South Africa. Kirsten's methodical approach helped when he turned to coaching, first as a batting consultant, then as director of his own coaching academy in Cape Town. In 2007 he succeeded Greg Chappell in the hot seat as coach of India. He took them to World Cup glory in 2011 before returning home to coach South Africa, and soon had them top of the Test rankings.

Born November 23, 1967, Cape Town, South Africa. Appointed South Africa coach in 2011

NIGEL **LLONG**

A tall left-hander and part-time offspinner, Nigel Llong played for Kent throughout the 1990s, scoring six centuries. He joined the English umpires' panel in 2002, and in 2005 stood in the first Twenty20 international to be played in England. Quiet and undemonstrative, with a disarming smile that seems to calm the players, Llong stood in a few international matches, including the odd Test, before replacing Billy Doctrove on the ICC's elite panel in 2012.

Born February 11, 1969, Ashford, Kent, England. **Tests** 12, **ODIs** 57, **T20Is** 16

RANJAN **MADUGALLE**

A stylish right-hander, Ranjan Madugalle won 21 Test caps, the first of them in Sri Lanka's inaugural Test, against England in 1981-82, when he top-scored with 65. He also made 103 against India in Colombo in 1985, and captained Sri Lanka twice. Not long after retiring, he became one of the first match refs, and was appointed the ICC's chief referee in 2001. His easy-going exterior and charming personality are a mask for someone who has a reputation as a strict disciplinarian.

Born April 22, 1959, Kandy, Sri Lanka. **Tests** 136, **ODIs** 265, **T20Is** 46

OFFICIALS

ROSHAN **MAHANAMA**

Roshan Mahanama was part of the winning team in the 1996 World Cup, and the following year made 225 as he and Sanath Jayasuriya put on 576, then a record Test partnership, as Sri Lanka ran up 952 for 6 (another record) against India in Colombo. An attacking right-hander who made four Test centuries, he was also a fine fielder. He was jettisoned after the 1999 World Cup and quit not long afterwards. He joined the ICC's referees panel in 2003.

Born *May 31, 1966, Colombo, Sri Lanka.* **Tests** *38,* **ODIs** *181,* **T20Is** *21*

BRUCE **OXENFORD**

A legspinner who played eight times for Queensland, taking 5 for 91 against New South Wales at Sydney in January 1992 in only his third match, Bruce Oxenford soon turned to umpiring, and by 2001-02 was overseeing some of his former team-mates in the Sheffield Shield. He umpired his first Test in Sri Lanka late in 2010, and two years later was elevated to the elite panel when Simon Taufel retired to become the ICC's umpire performance and training manager.

Born *March 5, 1960, Southport, Queensland, Australia.* **Tests** *8,* **ODIs** *39,* **T20Is** *11*

RICHARD **PYBUS**

Injuries prevented Richard Pybus, a native Geordie, from having the first-class career he dreamed of, so he turned instead to coaching in his mid-twenties. He started with Border in South Africa before being poached by Pakistan ahead of the 1999 World Cup, but then lost his job – not surprisingly, perhaps, after he described the team manager, who was also the interim chairman of the board, as a "bumbling old idiot". He had a second attempt with Pakistan in 2003, and also had a brief stint in charge of Middlesex in 2007. After further successful spells with Titans and Cape Cobras in South Africa, Pybus took on the Bangladesh challenge in May 2012.

Born *July 5, 1964, Newcastle-upon-Tyne, England. Appointed Bangladesh's coach in 2012*

ANDY **PYCROFT**

A fine batsman, especially strong off the back foot, Andy Pycroft was a Zimbabwe regular throughout the 1980s, although he was slightly past his peak when they gained Test status in 1992-93. Still, he played in their first three Tests, scoring 60 against New Zealand at Harare in the last of them. The first and last of his 20 ODIs produced famous wins: over Australia in the 1983 World Cup and England in the 1991-92 one. He also found time to fit in the occasional spot of commentary. Outside cricket he was an attorney-at-law for 17 years, which stood him in good stead when he joined the ICC's referees' panel.

Born *June 6, 1956, Salisbury (now Harare), Zimbabwe.* **Tests** *22,* **ODIs** *63,* **T20Is** *19*

JAVAGAL **SRINATH**

Arguably the fastest bowler India has ever produced, Javagal Srinath took 236 wickets in Tests, and 315 more in ODIs. Unusually for a quick bowler, he did better in India than overseas, his bowling average of 26 at home being four runs lower than his overall one. He went out at the top: his last international match was the 2003 World Cup final. Sadly, there was no fairytale farewell – Srinath was caned (0 for 87) as Australia ran out easy winners. After a spell as a commentator he joined the referees' panel in 2006. "I'll have to concentrate more than I did during my playing days," he observed wryly.

Born *August 31, 1969, Mysore, Karnataka, India.* **Tests** *22,* **ODIs** *117,* **T20Is** *19*

ROD **TUCKER**

Allrounder Rod Tucker played 100 first-class matches for Tasmania over ten years from 1988-89. His seven hundreds included a satisfying 165 against his native NSW in March 1991. He was also a handy medium-pacer who took 123 wickets. On his first morning as a first-class umpire, in December 2004, South Australia were bowled out for 29, but by January 2009 he was standing in his first ODI. He officiated in the World Twenty20s of 2009 and 2010, in between making his Test debut in New Zealand, and was appointed to the ICC's elite panel in 2010.

Born *August 28, 1964, Auburn, Sydney, Australia.* **Tests** *20,* **ODIs** *26,* **T20Is** *8*

DAV **WHATMORE**

Stocky Dav (it's short for Davenell) Whatmore was a popular figure around the MCG, after scoring prolifically for Victoria in the Sheffield Shield. He won seven caps for Australia, with modest results, during the Packer schism. On turning to coaching he had two spells with Sri Lanka, and was in charge when they won the World Cup in 1996. He also won trophies with Lancashire, before the harder challenge of coaching Bangladesh (2003-07). Early in 2012 he took on the Pakistan job, starting with a flourish as his side won the Asia Cup.

Born *March 16, 1954, Colombo, Ceylon (now Sri Lanka). Appointed Pakistan's coach in 2012*

OVERALL RECORDS

Test Matches

Most appearances

190	SR Tendulkar I	
168	SR Waugh A	
165	RT Ponting A	
164	R Dravid I*	
156	AR Border A	
155	JH Kallis SA*	
147	MV Boucher SA*	
145	SK Warne A	
144	S Chanderpaul WI	
134	VVS Laxman I	

*The records for Boucher, Dravid and Kallis include one Test for the World XI

Most runs

		Avge
15533	SR Tendulkar I	55.08
13346	RT Ponting A	52.75
13288	R Dravid I*	52.31
12641	JH Kallis SA*	56.94
11953	BC Lara WI*	52.88
11174	AR Border A	50.56
10927	SR Waugh A	51.06
10540	DPMD J'wardene SL	50.43
10342	S Chanderpaul WI	50.20
10122	SM Gavaskar I	51.12

*The records for Dravid, Kallis and Lara include one Test for the World XI

Most wickets

		Avge
800	M Muralitharan SL*	22.72
708	SK Warne A	25.41
619	A Kumble I	29.65
563	GD McGrath A	21.64
519	CA Walsh WI	24.44
434	Kapil Dev I	29.64
431	RJ Hadlee NZ	22.29
421	SM Pollock SA	23.11
414	Wasim Akram P	23.62
406	Harbhajan Singh I	32.22

*Muralitharan's record includes one Test (5 wickets) for the World XI. CEL Ambrose (WI; 405) also passed 400

Highest scores

400*	BC Lara	WI v Eng at St John's	2003-04
380	ML Hayden	Aust v Zim at Perth	2003-04
375	BC Lara	WI v Eng at St John's	1993-94
374	DPMD Jayawardene	SL v SA at Colombo	2006
365*	GS Sobers	WI v Pak at Kingston	1957-58
364	L Hutton	Eng v Aust at The Oval	1938
340	ST Jayasuriya	SL v India at Colombo	1997-98
337	Hanif Mohammad	Pak v WI at Bridgetown	1957-58
336*	WR Hammond	Eng v NZ at Auckland	1932-33
334*	MA Taylor	Aust v Pak at Peshawar	1998-99
334	DG Bradman	Aust v Eng at Leeds	1930

In all 26 scores of 300 or more have been made in Tests

Best innings bowling

10-53	JC Laker	Eng v Aust at Manchester	1956
10-74	A Kumble	India v Pak at Delhi	1998-99
9-28	GA Lohmann	Eng v SA at Jo'burg	1895-96
9-37	JC Laker	Eng v Aust at Manchester	1956
9-51	M Muralitharan	SL v Zim at Kandy	2001-02
9-52	RJ Hadlee	NZ v Aust at Brisbane	1985-86
9-56	Abdul Qadir	Pak v Eng at Lahore	1987-88
9-57	DE Malcolm	Eng v SA at The Oval	1994
9-65	M Muralitharan	SL v Eng at The Oval	1998
9-69	JM Patel	India v Aust at Kanpur	1959-60

There have been seven further instances of a bowler taking nine wickets in an innings

Record wicket partnerships

1st	415	ND McKenzie (226) and GC Smith (232)	South Africa v Bangladesh at Chittagong	2007-08
2nd	576	ST Jayasuriya (340) and RS Mahanama (225)	Sri Lanka v India at Colombo	1997-98
3rd	624	KC Sangakkara (287) and DPMD Jayawardene (374)	Sri Lanka v South Africa at Colombo	2006
4th	437	DPMD Jayawardene (240) and TT Samaraweera (231)	Sri Lanka v Pakistan at Karachi	2008-09
5th	405	SG Barnes (234) and DG Bradman (234)	Australia v England at Sydney	1946-47
6th	351	DPMD Jayawardene (275) and HAPW Jayawardene (154*)	Sri Lanka v India at Ahmedabad	2009-10
7th	347	DS Atkinson (219) and CC Depeiaza (122)	West Indies v Australia at Bridgetown	1954-55
8th	332	IJL Trott (184) and SCJ Broad (169)	England v Pakistan at Lord's	2010
9th	195	MV Boucher (78) and PL Symcox (108)	South Africa v Pakistan at Johannesburg	1997-98
10th	151	BF Hastings (110) and RO Collinge (68*)	New Zealand v Pakistan at Auckland	1972-73
	151	Azhar Mahmood (128*) and Mushtaq Ahmed (59)	Pakistan v South Africa at Rawalpindi	1997-98

Figures to 17.09.12. Updated records can be found at **www.cricinfo.com/ci/engine/records**

Test Matches **OVERALL RECORDS**

Most catches

Fielders

210	R Dravid	*I/World*
194	RT Ponting	*A*
187	DPMD Jayawardene	*SL*
187	JH Kallis	*SA*
181	ME Waugh	*A*

Most dismissals

Wicketkeepers		*Ct/St*
555	MV Boucher *SA*	532/23
416	AC Gilchrist *A*	379/37
395	IA Healy *A*	366/29
355	RW Marsh *A*	343/12
270	PJL Dujon *WI*	265/5

Highest team totals

952-6d	**Sri Lanka** v India at Colombo	1997-98
903-7d	**Eng** v Australia at The Oval	1938
849	**Eng** v WI at Kingston	1929-30
790-3d	**WI** v Pakistan at Kingston	1957-58
765-6d	**Pak** v Sri Lanka at Karachi	2008-09
760-7d	**SL** v India at Ahmedabad	2009-10
758-8d	**Aust** v WI at Kingston	1954-55
756-5d	**Sri Lanka** v SA at Colombo	2006
751-5d	**WI** v England at St John's	2003-04
749-9d	**WI** v England at Bridgetown	2008-09

There have been 10 further totals of more than 700, three by Australia and India, and one each by England, Pakistan, Sri Lanka and West Indies

Lowest team totals

Completed innings

26	**NZ** v Eng at Auckland	1954-55
30	**SA** v Eng at Pt Elizabeth	1895-96
30	**SA** v Eng at Birmingham	1924
35	**SA** v Eng at Cape Town	1898-99
36	**Aust** v Eng at B'ham	1902
36	**SA** v Aust at M'bourne	1931-32
42	**Aust** v Eng at Sydney	1887-88
42	**NZ** v Aust at W'ton	1945-46
42*	**India** v England at Lord's	1974
43	**SA** v Eng at Cape Town	1888-89

* One batsmen absent hurt. There have been eight further totals of less than 50, the most recent Australia's 47 v S Africa at Cape Town in 2011-12

Best match bowling

19-90	JC Laker	Eng v Aust at Manchester	1956
17-159	SF Barnes	Eng v SA at Jo'burg	1913-14
16-136	ND Hirwani	India v WI at Madras	1987-88
16-137	RAL Massie	Aust v England at Lord's	1972
16-220	M Muralitharan	SL v England at The Oval	1998
15-28	J Briggs	Eng v SA at Cape Town	1888-89
15-45	GA Lohmann	Eng v SA at Pt Elizabeth	1895-96
15-99	C Blythe	Eng v SA at Leeds	1907
15-104	H Verity	England v Aust at Lord's	1934
15-123	RJ Hadlee	NZ v Aust at Brisbane	1985-86

Hirwani and Massie were making their Test debuts. W Rhodes (15-124) and Harbhajan Singh (15-217) also took 15 wickets in a match

Most centuries

		Tests
51	SR Tendulkar *India*	181
43	JH Kallis *South Africa/World XI*	145
41	RT Ponting *Australia*	154
36	R Dravid *India/World XI*	157
34	SM Gavaskar *India*	125
34	BC Lara *West Indies/World XI*	131
32	SR Waugh *Australia*	168
31	DPMD Jayawardene *Sri Lanka*	122
30	ML Hayden *Australia*	94
30	KC Sangakkara *Sri Lanka*	111

DG Bradman (Australia) scored 29 hundreds in 52 Test matches

Test match results

	Played	Won	Lost	Drawn	Tied	% win
Australia	744	350	194	198	2	47.04
Bangladesh	73	3	63	7	0	4.10
England	926	329	267	330	0	35.52
India	464	114	147	202	1	24.56
New Zealand	375	71	153	151	0	18.93
Pakistan	370	115	101	154	0	31.08
South Africa	369	131	126	112	0	35.50
Sri Lanka	215	64	76	75	0	29.76
West Indies	486	156	162	167	1	32.09
Zimbabwe	87	9	52	26	0	10.34
World XI	1	0	1	0	0	0.00
TOTAL	2055	1342	1342	711	2	

OVERALL RECORDS *One-day Internationals*

Most appearances

463	SR Tendulkar	*I*
445	ST Jayasuriya	*SL*
382	DPMD Jayawardene	*SL*
378	Inzamam-ul-Haq	*P*
375	RT Ponting	*A*
356	Wasim Akram	*P*
350	M Muralitharan	*SL*
349	Shahid Afridi	*P*
344	R Dravid	*I*
334	M Azharuddin	*I*

Seven further men have played in more than 300 ODIs, while BC Lara appeared in 299

Most runs

			Avge
18426	SR Tendulkar	*I*	44.83
13704	RT Ponting	*A*	42.03
13430	ST Jayasuriya	*SL*	32.36
11739	Inzamam-ul-Haq	*P*	39.52
11498	JH Kallis	*SA*	45.26
11363	SC Ganguly	*I*	41.02
10889	R Dravid	*I*	39.16
10842	KC Sangakkara	*SL*	38.72
10772	DPMD Jayawardene	*SL*	33.34
10405	BC Lara	*WI*	40.48

Mohammad Yousuf (9720), AC Gilchrist (9619), M Azharuddin (9378) and PA de Silva (9284) also reached 9000 runs

Most wickets

			Avge
534	M Muralitharan	*SL*	23.08
502	Wasim Akram	*P*	23.52
416	Waqar Younis	*P*	23.84
400	WPUJC Vaas	*SL*	27.53
393	SM Pollock	*SA*	24.50
381	GD McGrath	*A*	22.02
380	B Lee	*A*	23.36
348	Shahid Afridi	*P*	33.69
337	A Kumble	*I*	30.89
323	ST Jayasuriya	*SL*	36.75

J Srinath (315) also took 300 wickets. Eleven other bowlers have taken more than 250

Highest scores

219	V Sehwag	India v WI at Indore	2011-12
200*	SR Tendulkar	India v SA at Gwalior	2009-10
194*	CK Coventry	Zim v Bangladesh at Bulawayo	2008-09
194	Saeed Anwar	Pakistan v India at Chennai	1996-97
189*	IVA Richards	W Indies v England at Manchester	1984
189	ST Jayasuriya	Sri Lanka v India at Sharjah	2000-01
188*	G Kirsten	SA v UAE at Rawalpindi	1995-96
186*	SR Tendulkar	India v NZ at Hyderabad	1999-2000
185*	SR Watson	Aust v Bangladesh at Mirpur	2010-11
183*	MS Dhoni	India v Sri Lanka at Jaipur	2005-06
183	SC Ganguly	India v Sri Lanka at Taunton	1999

SR Tendulkar has scored 49 ODI centuries, RT Ponting 30, ST Jayasuriya 28, SC Ganguly 22 and HH Gibbs 21

Best innings bowling

8-19	WPUJC Vaas	SL v Zimbabwe at Colombo	2001-02
7-15	GD McGrath	Aust v Namibia at P'stroom	2002-03
7-20	AJ Bichel	Aust v Eng at Port Elizabeth	2002-03
7-30	M Muralitharan	Sri Lanka v India at Sharjah	2000-01
7-36	Waqar Younis	Pakistan v England at Leeds	2001
7-37	Aqib Javed	Pakistan v India at Sharjah	1991-92
7-51	WW Davis	West Indies v Australia at Leeds	1983
6-12	A Kumble	India v West Indies at Calcutta	1993-94
6-13	BAW Mendis	Sri Lanka v India at Karachi	2008
6-14	GJ Gilmour	Australia v England at Leeds	1975
6-14	Imran Khan	Pakistan v India at Sharjah	1984-85
6-14	MF Maharoof	Sri Lanka v W Indies at Mumbai	2006-07

Waqar Younis took five in an innings 13 times and Muralitharan 10

Record wicket partnerships

1st	286	WU Tharanga (109) and ST Jayasuriya (152)	Sri Lanka v England at Leeds	2006
2nd	331	SR Tendulkar (186*) and R Dravid (153)	India v New Zealand at Hyderabad	1999-2000
3rd	237*	R Dravid (104*) and SR Tendulkar (140*)	India v Kenya at Bristol	1999
4th	275*	M Azharuddin (153*) and A Jadeja (116*)	India v Zimbabwe at Cuttack	1997-98
5th	223	M Azharuddin (111*) and A Jadeja (119)	India v Sri Lanka at Colombo	1997-98
6th	218	DPMD Jayawardene (107) and MS Dhoni (139*)	Asia XI v Africa XI at Chennai	2007
7th	130	A Flower (142*) and HH Streak (56)	Zimbabwe v England at Harare	2001-02
8th	138*	JM Kemp (110*) and AJ Hall (56*)	South Africa v India at Cape Town	2006-07
9th	132	AD Mathews (77*) and SL Malinga (56)	Sri Lanka v Australia at Melbourne	2010-11
10th	106*	IVA Richards (189*) and MA Holding (12*)	West Indies v England at Manchester	1984

Figures to 17.09.12. Updated records can be found at **www.cricinfo.com/ci/engine/records**

One-day Internationals **OVERALL RECORDS**

Most catches

Fielders

192	DPMD Jayawardene	*SL*
160	RT Ponting	*A*
156	M Azharuddin	*I*
140	SR Tendulkar	*I*
133	SP Fleming	*NZ*

Most dismissals

Wicketkeepers		*Ct/St*
472	AC Gilchrist *A*	417/55
424	MV Boucher *SA*	402/22
390	KC Sangakkara *SL*	309/81
287	Moin Khan *P*	214/73
265	MS Dhoni *I*	199/66

Highest team totals

443-9	**SL** v N'lands at Amstelveen	2006
438-9	**SA** v Aust at Johannesburg	2005-06
434-4	**Australia** v SA at Jo'burg	2005-06
418-5	**SA** v Zim at P'stroom	2006-07
418-5	**India** v WI at Indore	2011-12
414-7	**India** v SL at Rajkot	2009-10
413-5	**Ind** v Bermuda at P-o-Spain	2006-07
411-8	**SL** v India at Rajkot	2009-10
402-2	**NZ** v Ireland at Aberdeen	2008
401-3	**India** v SA at Gwalior	2009-10

All these totals were made in 50 overs except SA's 438-9, when the winning run came off the fifth ball of the 50th over

Lowest team totals

Completed innings

35	**Zim** v SL at Harare	2003-04
36	**Canada** v SL at Paarl	2002-03
38	**Zim** v SL at Colombo	2001-02
43	**Pak** v WI at Cape Town	1992-93
43	**SL** v SA at Paarl	2011-12
44	**Zim** v B'desh at Ch'gong	2009-10
45	**Can** v Eng at Manchester	1979
45	**Nam** v Aust at P'stroom	2002-03
54	**India** v SL at Sharjah	2000-01
54	**WI** v SA at Cape Town	2003-04

The lowest total successfully defended in a non-rain-affected ODI is 125, by India v Pakistan (87) at Sharjah in 1984-85

Most sixes

298	Shahid Afridi	*P*
270	ST Jayasuriya	*SL*
195	SR Tendulkar	*I*
190	SC Ganguly	*I*
189	CH Gayle	*WI*
162	RT Ponting	*A*
153	CL Cairns	*NZ*
149	AC Gilchrist	*A*
144	Inzamam-ul-Haq	*P*
144	Yuvraj Singh	*I*

Eleven others have hit 100 sixes

Best strike rate

Runs per 100 balls		*Runs*
113.75	Shahid Afridi *P*	7075
104.60	V Sehwag *I*	8238
99.43	IDS Smith *NZ*	1055
97.86	KA Pollard *WI*	1419
96.94	AC Gilchrist *A*	9619
96.66	RL Powell *WI*	2085
96.21	PR Stirling *Ire*	1448
95.07	Kapil Dev *I*	3783
94.73	DR Smith *WI*	1098
93.71	JR Hopes *A*	1326

Qualification: 1000 runs

Most economical bowlers

Runs per over		*Wkts*
3.09	J Garner *WI*	146
3.28	RGD Willis *E*	80
3.30	RJ Hadlee *NZ*	158
3.32	MA Holding *WI*	142
3.37	SP Davis *A*	44
3.40	AME Roberts *WI*	87
3.48	CEL Ambrose *WI*	225
3.53	MD Marshall *WI*	157
3.54	ARC Fraser *E*	47
3.55	MR Whitney *A*	46

Qualification: 2000 balls bowled

One-day international results

	Played	Won	Lost	Tied	No result	% win
Australia	801	493	273	9	26	64.19
Bangladesh	262	72	188	0	2	27.69
England	587	286	274	7	20	51.05
India	809	401	367	6	35	52.19
Kenya	146	39	102	0	5	27.65
New Zealand	625	269	319	5	32	45.78
Pakistan	777	417	337	6	17	55.26
South Africa	475	296	161	5	13	64.61
Sri Lanka	672	313	328	4	27	48.83
West Indies	677	351	296	6	24	54.21
Zimbabwe	407	107	286	5	9	27.51
Others (see below)	370	122	235	1	12	34.21
TOTAL	**3304**	**3166**	**3166**	**27**	**111**	

Others: Afghanistan (P23, W12, L11), Africa XI (P6, W1, L4, NR1), Asia XI (P7, W4, L2, NR1), Bermuda (P35, W7, L28), Canada (P71, W17, L53, NR1), East Africa (P3, L3), Hong Kong (P4, L4), Ireland (P74, W34, L35, T1, NR4), Namibia (P6, L6), Netherlands (P69, W26, L41, NR2), Scotland (P55, W19, L33, NR3), UAE (P11, W1, L10), USA (P2, L2), World XI (P4, W1, L3).

OVERALL RECORDS *Twenty20 Internationals*

Most appearances

50	Shahid Afridi	P	
48	BB McCullum	NZ	
44	Shoaib Malik	P	
43	Umar Gul	P	
42	Saeed Ajmal	P	
41	Kamran Akmal	P	
41	LRPL Taylor	NZ	
39	AB de Villiers	SA	
39	Misbah-ul-Haq	P	
38	(four players)		

The first Twenty20 international was played in New Zealand in February 2005

Most runs

			Avge
1443	BB McCullum	NZ	36.07
1176	KP Pietersen	E	37.93
982	GC Smith	SA	31.67
981	DPMD Jayawardene	SL	30.65
978	DA Warner	A	27.16
917	TM Dilshan	SL	29.58
910	KC Sangakkara	SL	30.33
846	JP Duminy	SA	32.53
818	MJ Guptill	NZ	32.72
801	Shadid Afridi	P	18.20

The highest batting average (min. 200 runs) is 51.33, by ML Hayden (Aust)

Most wickets

			Avge
60	Saeed Ajmal	P	15.48
59	Umar Gul	P	16.69
58	Shahid Afridi	P	19.67
44	GP Swann	E	16.86
41	SCJ Broad	E	23.70
40	SL Malinga	SL	20.45
40	BAW Mendis	SL	11.12
36	J Botha	SA	20.19
36	MG Johnson	A	20.11
36	NL McCullum	NZ	16.58

Six further bowlers have taken 30 or more wickets

Highest Scores

117*	RE Levi	SA v NZ at Hamilton	2011-12
117	CH Gayle	WI v SA at Johannesburg	2007-08
116*	BB McCullum	NZ v A at Christchurch	2009-10
104*	TM Dilshan	SL v A at Pallekele	2011
101	SK Raina	India v SA at Gros Islet	2010
100	RD Berrington	Scot v Bang at The Hague	2012
100	DPMD J'wardene	SL v Zim at Providence	2010
99	AD Hales	Eng v WI at Nottingham	2012
98*	RT Ponting	A v NZ at Auckland	2004-05
98*	DPMD J'wardene	SL v WI at Bridgetown	2010
98	CH Gayle	WI v India at Bridgetown	2010

Levi's innings, on debut, included 13 sixes

Best innings bowling

6-16	BAW Mendis	SL v Australia at Pallekele	2011
5-6	Umar Gul	Pakistan v NZ at The Oval	2009
5-13	Elias Sunny	Bang v Ireland at Belfast	2012
5-18	TG Southee	NZ v Pakistan at Auckland	2010-11
5-19	R McLaren	SA v WI at N Sound	2010
5-20	NN Odhiambo	Ken v Scot at Nairobi	2009-10
5-26	DJG Sammy	WI v Zim at P-o-Spain	2009-10
4-6	SJ Benn	WI v Zim at P-o-Spain	2009-10
4-7	MR Gillespie	NZ v Kenya at Durban	2007-08
4-8	Umar Gul	Pak v Australia at Dubai	2009-09

Umar Gul has taken four wickets in an innings four times, BAW Mendis and Shahid Afridi three

Record wicket partnerships

1st	170	GC Smith (88) and LL Bosman (94)	South Africa v England at Centurion	2009-10
2nd	166	DPMD Jayawardene (98*) and KC Sangakkara (68)	Sri Lanka v West Indies at Bridgetown	2010
3rd	137	MJ Guptill (91*) and KS Williamson (48)	New Zealand v Zimbabwe at Auckland	2011-12
4th	112*	KP Pietersen (43*) and EJG Morgan (67*)	England v Pakistan at Dubai	2009-10
5th	119*	Shoaib Malik (52*) and Misbah-ul-Haq (66*)	Pakistan v Australia at Johannesburg	2007-08
6th	101*	CL White (85*) and MEK Hussey (39*)	Australia v Sri Lanka at Bridgetown	2010
7th	91	PD Collingwood (79) and MH Yardy (23*)	England v West Indies at The Oval	2007
8th	64*	WD Parnell (29*) and J Theron (31*)	South Africa v Australia at Johannesburg	2011-12
9th	47*	GC Wilson (41*) and MC Sorensen (12*)	Ireland v Bangladesh at Belfast	2012
10th	31*	Wahab Riaz (30*) and Shoaib Akhtar (8*)	Pakistan v New Zealand at Auckland	2010-11

Twenty20 Internationals **OVERALL RECORDS**

Most catches

Fielders
27	LRPL Taylor	*NZ*
24	DJ Hussey	*A*
22	AB de Villiers	*SA*
20	DA Warner	*A*
20	Shoaib Malik	*P*

Most dismissals

Wicketkeepers   *Ct/St*
47	Kamran Akmal	*P*	19/28
28	BB McCullum	*NZ*	21/7
28	KC Sangakkara	*SL*	17/11
26	D Ramdin	*WI*	21/5
24	Mushfiqur Rahim	*B*	10/14

Highest team totals

260-6	**Sri Lanka** v Kenya at Jo'burg	2007-08
241-6	**SA** v England at Centurion	2009-10
221-5	**Aust** v England at Sydney	2006-07
219-4	**SA** v India at Johannesburg	2011-12
218-4	**India** v England at Durban	2007-08
215-5	**Sri Lanka** v India at Nagpur	2009-10
214-5	**Australia** v NZ at Auckland	2004-05
214-6	**NZ** v Aust at Christchurch	2009-10
214-4	**Aust** v NZ at Christchurch	2009-10
211-4	**India** v Sri Lanka at Mohali	2009-10
211-5	**SA** v Scotland at The Oval	2009

There have been 12 further totals of 200+

Lowest team totals

Completed innings
67	**Kenya** v Ireland at Belfast	2008
68	**Ireland** v WI at Providence	2010
70	**Bermuda** v Can at Belfast	2008
71	**Kenya** v Ire at Dubai	2011-12
73	**Kenya** v NZ at Durban	2007-08
74	**India** v Aus at M'bourne	2007-08
74	**Pak** v Aus at Dubai	2012-13
75	**Can** v Zim at King City	2008-09
78	**B'desh** v NZ at Hamilton	2009-10
79	**Aust** v Eng at Southampton	2005

West Indies scored 79-7 in 20 overs v Zimbabwe at Port-of-Spain in 2009-10

Most sixes

57	BB McCullum	*NZ*
47	SR Watson	*A*
46	DA Warner	*A*
43	CH Gayle	*WI*
40	Yuvraj Singh	*I*
36	CL White	*A*
35	MJ Guptill	*NZ*
34	DJ Hussey	*A*
33	JA Morkel	*SA*
32	KP Pietersen	*E*
32	LRPL Taylor	*NZ*

Yuvraj's sixes included 6 in one over

Best strike rate

Runs per 100 balls   *Runs*
169.34	A Symonds *A*	337
159.82	CD McMillan *NZ*	187
152.46	V Sehwag *I*	340
152.31	E Chigumbura *Z*	329
150.25	Yuvraj Singh *I*	601
147.97	SR Watson *A*	731
147.76	KA Pollard *WI*	331
147.48	LE Bosman *SA*	323
147.22	Junaid Siddique *P*	159
146.58	YK Pathan *I*	236

Qualification: 100 balls faced

Meanest bowlers

Runs per over   *Wkts*
4.88	TM Odoyo *Kenya*	6
5.40	JAR Blain *Scot*	6
5.41	AC Botha *Ire*	21
5.45	JD Nel *Scot*	12
5.45	Samiullah Shenwari *Afg*	9
5.50	Elias Sunny *B*	9
5.50	DL Vettori *NZ*	35
5.54	GH Dockrell *Ire*	26
5.63	BAW Mendis *SL*	40
5.70	S Dhariram *Can*	6

Qualification: 120 balls bowled

Twenty20 international results

	Played	Won	Lost	Tied	No Result	% win
Australia	52	26	23	2	1	52.94
Bangladesh	24	8	16	0	0	33.33
England	48	25	20	0	3	55.55
India	36	18	16	1	1	52.85
New Zealand	53	25	25	3	0	50.00
Pakistan	58	34	22	2	0	60.34
South Africa	47	30	16	0	1	65.21
Sri Lanka	41	24	17	0	0	58.53
West Indies	38	16	20	2	0	44.73
Zimbabwe	20	3	16	1	0	17.50
Others (see below)	107	42	60	1	4	41.26
TOTAL	**262**	**251**	**251**	**6**	**5**	

Other teams: Afghanistan (P11, W6, L5), Bermuda (P3, L3), Canada (P15, W3, L11, T1), Ireland (P28, W15, L11, NR2),
Kenya (P17, W4, L13), Netherlands (P16, W9, L6, NR1), Scotland (P17, W5, L11, NR1). Matches decided by bowlouts are shown as tied

AUSTRALIA
Test Match Records

Most appearances

168	SR Waugh
165	RT Ponting
156	AR Border
145	SK Warne
128	ME Waugh
124	GD McGrath
119	IA Healy
107	DC Boon
105	JL Langer
104	MA Taylor

ML Hayden (103) also won more than 100 caps

Most runs

		Avge
13346	RT Ponting	52.75
11174	AR Border	50.56
10927	SR Waugh	51.06
8625	ML Hayden	50.73
8029	ME Waugh	41.81
7696	JL Langer	45.27
7525	MA Taylor	43.49
7422	DC Boon	43.65
7110	GS Chappell	53.86
6996	DG Bradman	99.94

RN Harvey (6149) and MJ Clarke (6097) have reached 6000 Test runs

Most wickets

		Avge
708	SK Warne	25.41
563	GD McGrath	21.64
355	DK Lillee	23.92
310	B Lee	30.81
291	CJ McDermott	28.63
259	JN Gillespie	26.13
248	R Benaud	27.03
246	GD McKenzie	29.78
228	RR Lindwall	23.03
216	CV Grimmett	24.21

MG Hughes (212), SCG MacGill (208) & JR Thomson (200) also reached 200

Highest scores

380	ML Hayden	v Zimbabwe at Perth	2003-04
334*	MA Taylor	v Pakistan at Peshawar	1998-99
334	DG Bradman	v England at Leeds	1930
329*	MJ Clarke	v India at Sydney	2011-12
311	RB Simpson	v England at Manchester	1964
307	RM Cowper	v England at Melbourne	1965-66
304	DG Bradman	v England at Leeds	1934
299*	DG Bradman	v South Africa at Adelaide	1931-32
270	DG Bradman	v England at Melbourne	1936-37
268	GN Yallop	v Pakistan at Melbourne	1983-84

At the time of his retirement in 1948 DG Bradman had made eight of Australia's highest ten Test scores

Best innings bowling

9-121	AA Mailey	v England at Melbourne	1920-21
8-24	GD McGrath	v Pakistan at Perth	2004-05
8-31	FJ Laver	v England at Manchester	1909
8-38	GD McGrath	v England at Lord's	1997
8-43	AE Trott	v England at Adelaide	1894-95
8-53	RAL Massie	v England at Lord's	1972
8-59	AA Mallett	v Pakistan at Adelaide	1972-73
8-61	MG Johnson	v South Africa at Perth	2008-09
8-65	H Trumble	v England at The Oval	1902
8-71	GD McKenzie	v West Indies at Melbourne	1968-69
8-71	SK Warne	v England at Brisbane	1994-95

Trott and Massie were making their Test debuts

Record wicket partnerships

1st	382	WM Lawry (210) and RB Simpson (205)	v West Indies at Bridgetown	1964-65
2nd	451	WH Ponsford (266) and DG Bradman (244)	v England at The Oval	1934
3rd	315	RT Ponting (206) and DS Lehmann (160)	v West Indies at Port-of-Spain	2002-03
4th	388	WH Ponsford (181) and DG Bradman (304)	v England at Leeds	1934
5th	405	SG Barnes (234) and DG Bradman (234)	v England at Sydney	1946-47
6th	346	JHW Fingleton (136) and DG Bradman (270)	v England at Melbourne	1936-37
7th	217	KD Walters (250) and GJ Gilmour (101)	v New Zealand at Christchurch	1976-77
8th	243	MJ Hartigan (116) and C Hill (160)	v England at Adelaide	1907-08
9th	154	SE Gregory (201) and JM Blackham (74)	v England at Sydney	1894-95
10th	127	JM Taylor (108) and AA Mailey (46*)	v England at Sydney	1924-25

Figures to 17.09.12. Updated records can be found at www.cricinfo.com/ci/engine/records

Test Match Records

AUSTRALIA

Most catches

Fielders

194	RT Ponting
181	ME Waugh
157	MA Taylor
156	AR Border
128	ML Hayden

Most dismissals

	Wicketkeepers	Ct/St
416	AC Gilchrist	379/37
395	IA Healy	366/29
355	RW Marsh	343/12
187	ATW Grout	163/24
164	BJ Haddin	160/4

Highest team totals

758-8d	v West Indies at Kingston	1954-55
735-6d	v Zimbabwe at Perth	2003-04
729-6d	v England at Lord's	1930
701	v England at The Oval	1934
695	v England at The Oval	1930
674-6d	v England at Cardiff	2009
674	v India at Adelaide	1947-48
668	v West Indies at Bridgetown	1954-55
659-4d	v India at Sydney	2011-12
659-8d	v England at Sydney	1946-47

Australia have reached 600 on 31 occasions in all, 16 of them against England

Lowest team totals

Completed innings

36	v England at Birmingham	1902
42	v England at Sydney	1887-88
44	v England at The Oval	1896
47	v SA at Cape Town	2011-12
53	v England at Lord's	1896
58*	v England at Brisbane	1936-37
60	v England at Lord's	1888
63	v England at The Oval	1882
65	v England at The Oval	1912
66*	v England at Brisbane	1928-29

*One or more batsmen absent.

Best match bowling

16-137	RAL Massie	v England at Lord's	1972
14-90	FR Spofforth	v England at The Oval	1882
14-199	CV Grimmett	v South Africa at Adelaide	1931-32
13-77	MA Noble	v England at Melbourne	1901-02
13-110	FR Spofforth	v England at Melbourne	1878-79
13-148	BA Reid	v England at Melbourne	1990-91
13-173	CV Grimmett	v South Africa at Durban	1935-36
13-217	MG Hughes	v West Indies at Perth	1988-89
13-236	AA Mailey	v England at Melbourne	1920-21
12-87	CTB Turner	v England at Sydney	1887-88

Massie was playing in his first Test, Grimmett (1935-36) in his last – he took 10 or more wickets in each of his last three

Hat-tricks

FR Spofforth	v England at Melbourne	1878-79
H Trumble	v England at Melbourne	1901-02
H Trumble	v England at Melbourne	1903-04
TJ Matthews	v South Africa at Manchester	1912
TJ Matthews	v South Africa at Manchester	1912
LF Kline	v South Africa at Cape Town	1957-58
MG Hughes	v West Indies at Perth	1988-89
DW Fleming	v Pakistan at Rawalpindi	1994-95
SK Warne	v England at Melbourne	1994-95
GD McGrath	v West Indies at Perth	2000-01
PM Siddle	v England at Brisbane	2010-11

Fleming was playing in his first Test, Trumble (1903-04) in his last. Matthews took two in the same Test

Australia's Test match results

	Played	Won	Lost	Drawn	Tied	% win
v Bangladesh	4	4	0	0	0	100.00
v England	326	133	102	91	0	40.79
v India	82	38	20	23	1	46.34
v New Zealand	52	27	8	17	0	51.92
v Pakistan	57	28	12	17	0	49.12
v South Africa	85	48	19	18	0	56.47
v Sri Lanka	23	14	1	8	0	60.86
v West Indies	111	54	32	24	1	48.64
v Zimbabwe	3	3	0	0	0	100.00
v World XI	1	1	0	0	0	100.00
TOTAL	**744**	**350**	**194**	**198**	**2**	**47.04**

Figures to 17.09.12. Updated records can be found at www.cricinfo.com/ci/engine/records

AUSTRALIA One-day International Records

Most appearances

374	RT Ponting
325	SR Waugh
286	AC Gilchrist
273	AR Border
249	GD McGrath
244	ME Waugh
232	MG Bevan
221	MJ Clarke
221	B Lee
208	DR Martyn

A total of 25 Australians have played in more than 100 ODIs

Most runs

		Avge
13589	RT Ponting	41.81
9595	AC Gilchrist	35.93
8500	ME Waugh	39.35
7569	SR Waugh	32.90
7278	MJ Clarke	45.48
6912	MG Bevan	53.58
6524	AR Border	30.62
6131	ML Hayden	44.10
6068	DM Jones	44.61
5964	DC Boon	37.04

MEK Hussey (5442), DR Martyn (5346) and A Symonds (5088) also reached 5000 runs

Most wickets

		Avge
380	GD McGrath	21.98
380	B Lee	23.36
291	SK Warne	25.82
203	CJ McDermott	24.71
195	SR Waugh	34.67
174	NW Bracken	24.36
174	MG Johnson	25.52
156	GB Hogg	26.84
155	SR Watson	28.83
142	JN Gillespie	25.42

Five further Australians have taken 100 wickets

Highest scores

185*	SR Watson	v Bangladesh at Mirpur	2010-11
181*	ML Hayden	v New Zealand at Hamilton	2006-07
173	ME Waugh	v West Indies at Melbourne	2000-01
172	AC Gilchrist	v Zimbabwe at Hobart	2003-04
164	RT Ponting	v South Africa at Johannesburg	2005-06
163	DA Warner	v Sri Lanka at Brisbane	2011-12
161*	SR Watson	v England at Melbourne	2010-11
158	ML Hayden	v West Indies at North Sound	2006-07
156	A Symonds	v New Zealand at Wellington	2005-06
154	AC Gilchrist	v Sri Lanka at Melbourne	1998-99

Ponting has scored 29 hundreds, ME Waugh 18, Gilchrist 16 and Hayden 10

Best innings bowling

7-15	GD McGrath	v Namibia at Potchefstroom	2002-03
7-20	AJ Bichel	v England at Port Elizabeth	2002-03
6-14	GJ Gilmour	v England at Leeds	1975
6-31	MG Johnson	v Sri Lanka at Pallekele	2011
6-39	KH MacLeay	v India at Nottingham	1983
5-13	SP O'Donnell	v New Zealand at Christchurch	1989-90
5-14	GD McGrath	v West Indies at Manchester	1999
5-14	JR Hopes	v Ireland at Dublin	2010
5-15	GS Chappell	v India at Sydney	1980-81
5-16	CG Rackemann	v Pakistan at Adelaide	1983-84

DK Lillee took 5-34 against Pakistan at Leeds in the 1975 World Cup, the first five-wicket haul in ODIs

Record wicket partnerships

1st	212	GR Marsh (104) and DC Boon (111)	v India at Jaipur	1986-87
2nd	252*	SR Watson (136*) and RT Ponting (111*)	v England at Centurion	2009-10
3rd	234*	RT Ponting (140*) and DR Martyn (88*)	v India at Johannesburg	2002-03
4th	237	RT Ponting (124) and A Symonds (151)	v Sri Lanka at Sydney	2005-06
5th	220	A Symonds (156) and MJ Clarke (82*)	v New Zealand at Wellington	2005-06
6th	165	MEK Hussey (109*) and BJ Haddin (70)	v West Indies at Kuala Lumpur	2006-07
7th	123	MEK Hussey (73) and B Lee (57)	v South Africa at Brisbane	2005-06
8th	119	PR Reiffel (58) and SK Warne (55)	v South Africa at Port Elizabeth	1993-94
9th	88	SE Marsh (110) and DE Bollinger (30)	v England at Hobart	2010-11
10th	63	SR Watson (35*) and AJ Bichel (28)	v Sri Lanka at Sydney	2002-03

Figures to 17.09.12. Updated records can be found at www.cricinfo.com/ci/engine/records

One-day International Records

Most catches

Fielders

159	RT Ponting	
127	AR Border	
111	SR Waugh	
108	ME Waugh	
105	MEK Hussey	

Most dismissals

Wicketkeepers — Ct/St

470	AC Gilchrist	416/54
233	IA Healy	194/39
136	BJ Haddin	127/9
124	RW Marsh	120/4
49	WB Phillips	42/7

Most sixes

159	RT Ponting
148	AC Gilchrist
103	A Symonds
99	SR Watson
87	ML Hayden
80	MEK Hussey
68	SR Waugh
64	DM Jones
57	ME Waugh
56	BJ Haddin

Ponting (3) and Gilchrist (1) also hit sixes for the World XI

Highest team totals

434-4	v South Africa at Johannesburg	2005-06
377-6	v South Africa at Basseterre	2006-07
368-5	v Sri Lanka at Sydney	2005-06
361-8	v Bangladesh at Mirpur	2010-11
359-2†	v India at Johannesburg	2002-03
359-5	v India at Sydney	2003-04
358-5	v Netherlands at Basseterre	2006-07
350-4	v India at Hyderabad	2009-10
349-6	v New Zealand at St George's	2006-07
348-6	v New Zealand at C'church	1999-2000

† In World Cup final. All scores made in 50 overs

Best strike rate

Runs per 100 balls — Runs

96.89	AC Gilchrist	9595
96.12	MG Johnson	720
93.71	JR Hopes	1326
92.44	A Symonds	5504
90.11	DJ Hussey	1668
88.27	SR Watson	4563
88.16	IJ Harvey	715
87.51	BJ Hodge	516
87.16	MEK Hussey	5442
85.71	WB Phillips	852

Qualification: 500 runs

Lowest team totals

Completed innings

70	v England at Birmingham	1977
70	v New Zealand at Adelaide	1985-86
91	v West Indies at Perth	1986-87
93	v S Africa at Cape Town	2005-06
101	v England at Melbourne	1978-79
101	v India at Perth	1991-92
107	v W Indies at Melbourne	1981-82
109	v England at Sydney	1982-83
120	v Pakistan at Hobart	1996-97
124	v New Zealand at Sydney	1982-83

Australia scored 101-9 in a 30-overs match against West Indies at Sydney in 1992-93 – and won by 14 runs

Most economical bowlers

Runs per over — Wkts

3.37	SP Davis	44
3.55	MR Whitney	46
3.58	DK Lillee	103
3.65	GF Lawson	88
3.65	TM Alderman	88
3.87	GD McGrath	380
3.92	PR Reiffel	106
3.94	CG Rackemann	82
3.94	RM Hogg	85
4.03	CJ McDermott	203

Qualification: 2000 balls bowled

Australia's one-day international results

	Played	Won	Lost	Tied	No Result	% win
v Bangladesh	19	18	1	0	0	94.73
v England	117	67	46	2	2	59.13
v India	109	64	37	0	8	63.36
v New Zealand	124	85	34	0	5	71.42
v Pakistan	89	54	31	1	3	63.37
v South Africa	80	41	36	0	3	53.12
v Sri Lanka	84	53	28	3	0	65.43
v West Indies	130	65	59	3	3	52.36
v Zimbabwe	28	26	1	0	1	96.29
v others (see below)	21	20	0	0	1	100.00
TOTAL	801	493	273	9	26	64.19

Other teams: Afghanistan (P1, W1), Canada (P2, W2), Ireland (P3, W2, NR1), Kenya (P5, W5), Namibia (P1, W1), Netherlands (P2, W2), Scotland (P3, W3), USA (P1, W1), World XI (P3, W3).

BANGLADESH *Test Match Records*

Most appearances

57	Mohammad Ashraful
50	Habibul Bashar
44	Khaled Mashud
40	Javed Omar
36	Mashrafe Mortaza
33	Mohammad Rafique
29	Shahadat Hossain
28	Mushfiqur Rahim
26	Shakib Al Hasan
24	Rajin Saleh
24	Tamim Iqbal

Habibul Bashar missed only two of Bangladesh's first 52 Tests

Most runs

		Avge
3026	Habibul Bashar	30.87
2419	Mohammad Ashraful	22.60
1748	Tamim Iqbal	38.00
1720	Javed Omar	22.05
1630	Shakib Al Hasan	34.68
1480	Mushfiqur Rahim	29.01
1409	Khaled Mashud	19.04
1141	Rajin Saleh	25.93
1126	Shahriar Nafees	26.80
1059	Mohammad Rafique	18.57

Habibul Bashar reached 2000 runs for Bangladesh before anyone else had made 1000

Most wickets

		Avge
100	Mohammad Rafique	40.76
96	Shakib Al Hasan	31.36
78	Mashrafe Mortaza	41.52
68	Shahadat Hossain	49.79
41	Enamul Haque jnr	39.24
36	Tapash Baisya	59.36
28	Manjural Islam	57.32
24	Mahmudullah	40.54
20	Mohammad Ashraful	59.40
18	Abdur Razzak	65.83
18	Enamul Haque snr	57.05

Moh'd Rafique completed the 1000-run 100-wicket double in his last Test

Highest scores

158*	Moh'd Ashraful	v India at Chittagong	2004-05
151	Tamim Iqbal	v India at Mirpur	2009-10
145†	Aminul Islam	v India at Dhaka	2000-01
144	Shakib Al Hasan	v Pakistan at Mirpur	2011-12
138	Shahriar Nafees	v Australia at Fatullah	2005-06
136	Moh'd Ashraful	v Sri Lanka at Chittagong	2005-06
129*	Moh'd Ashraful	v Sri Lanka at Colombo	2007
128	Tamim Iqbal	v West Indies at Kingstown	2009
121	Nafees Iqbal	v Zimbabwe at Dhaka	2004-05
119	Javed Omar	v Pakistan at Peshawar	2003-04

† On debut. Mohammad Ashraful has scored five Test centuries, Tamim Iqbal four, and Habibul Bashar three

Best innings bowling

7-36	Shakib Al Hasan	v NZ at Chittagong	2008-09
7-95	Enamul Haque jnr	v Zimbabwe at Dhaka	2004-05
6-27	Shahadat Hossain	v South Africa at Dhaka	2007-08
6-45	Enamul Haque jnr	v Zim at Chittagong	2004-05
6-77	Moh'd Rafique	v South Africa at Dhaka	2002-03
6-81	Manjural Islam	v Zim at Bulawayo	2000-01
6-82	Shakib Al Hasan	v Pakistan at Mirpur	2011-12
6-94	Elias Sunny	v WI at Chittagong	2011-12
6-99	Shakib Al Hasan	v SA at Centurion	2008-09
6-122	Moh'd Rafique	v New Zealand at Dhaka	2004-05

Shakib Al Hasan has taken five wickets in an innings on nine occasions, Mohammad Rafique seven, Shahadat Hossain four, and Enamul Haque jnr three

Record wicket partnerships

1st	185	Tamim Iqbal (103) and Imrul Kayes (75)	v England at Lord's	2010
2nd	200	Tamim Iqbal (151) and Junaid Siddique (55)	v India at Mirpur	2009-10
3rd	130	Javed Omar (119) and Mohammad Ashraful (77)	v Pakistan at Peshawar	2003-04
4th	120	Habibul Bashar (77) and Manjural Islam Rana (35)	v West Indies at Kingstown	2004
5th	180	Shahriar Nafees (97) and Shakib Al Hasan (144)	v West Indies at Mirpur	2011-12
6th	191	Mohammad Ashraful (129*) and Mushfiqur Rahim (80)	v Sri Lanka at Colombo	2007
7th	145	Shakib Al Hasan (87) and Mahmudullah (115)	v New Zealand at Hamilton	2009-10
8th	113	Mushfiqur Rahim (79) and Naeem Islam (38)	v England at Chittagong	2009-10
9th	77	Mashrafe Mortaza (79) and Shahadat Hossain (31)	v India at Chittagong	2006-07
10th	69	Mohammad Rafique (65) and Shahadat Hossain (3*)	v Australia at Chittagong	2005-06

Figures to 17.09.12. Updated records can be found at **www.cricinfo.com/ci/engine/records**

Test Match Records **BANGLADESH**

Most catches

Fielders

24	Mohammad Ashraful	
22	Habibul Bashar	
17	Shahriar Nafees	
16	Imrul Kayes	
14	Rajin Saleh	

Most dismissals

Wicketkeepers   *Ct/St*

87	Khaled Mashud	78/9
49	Mushfiqur Rahim	40/9
4	Mohammad Salim	3/1
2	Mehrab Hossain	2/0

Highest team totals

488	v Zimbabwe at Chittagong	2004-05
427	v Australia at Fatullah	2005-06
419	v England at Mirpur	2009-10
416	v West Indies at Gros Islet	2004
413	v Sri Lanka at Mirpur	2008-09
408	v New Zealand at Hamilton	2009-10
400	v India at Dhaka	2000-01
382	v England at Lord's	2010
361	v Pakistan at Peshawar	2003-04
350-9d	v West Indies at Chittagong	2011-12

The 400 against India came in Bangladesh's inaugural Test

Lowest team totals

Completed innings

62	v Sri Lanka at Colombo	2007
86	v Sri Lanka at Colombo	2005-06
87	v West Indies at Dhaka	2002-03
89	v Sri Lanka at Colombo	2007
90	v Sri Lanka at Colombo	2001-02
91	v India at Dhaka	2000-01
96	v Pakistan at Peshawar	2003-04
97	v Australia at Darwin	2003
102	v South Africa at Dhaka	2002-03
104	v Eng at Chester-le-Street	2005

The lowest all-out total by the opposition is 154, by Zimbabwe at Chittagong in 2004-05 (Bangladesh's first Test victory)

Best match bowling

12-200	Enamul Haque jnr	v Zimbabwe at Dhaka	2004-05
9-97	Shahadat Hossain	v South Africa at Dhaka	2007-08
9-115	Shakib Al Hasan	v NZ at Chittagong	2008-09
9-160	Moh'd Rafique	v Australia at Fatullah	2005-06
8-110	Mahmudullah	v W Indies at Kingstown	2009
8-129	Shakib Al Hasan	v W Indies at St George's	2009
7-105	Khaled Mahmud	v Pakistan at Multan	2003-04
7-116	Moh'd Rafique	v Pakistan at Multan	2003-04
7-128	Elias Sunny	v W Indies at Chittagong	2011-12
7-129	Shakib Al Hasan	v Pakistan at Mirpur	2011-12

Khaled Mahmud took only six other wickets in 11 more Tests

Hat-tricks

Alok Kapali	v Pakistan at Peshawar	2003-04

Alok Kapali's figures were 2.1-1-3-3; he ended Pakistan's innings by dismissing Shabbir Ahmed, Danish Kaneria and Umar Gul. He took only three other Test wickets.

Two bowlers have taken hat-tricks against Bangladesh: AM Blignaut for Zimbabwe at Harare in 2003-04, and JEC Franklin for New Zealand at Dhaka in 2004-05.

Shahadat Hossain and Abdur Razzak have taken ODI hat-tricks for Bangladesh

Bangladesh's Test match results

	Played	Won	Lost	Drawn	Tied	% win
v Australia	4	0	4	0	0	0.00
v England	8	0	8	0	0	0.00
v India	7	0	6	1	0	0.00
v New Zealand	9	0	8	1	0	0.00
v Pakistan	8	0	8	0	0	0.00
v South Africa	8	0	8	0	0	0.00
v Sri Lanka	12	0	12	0	0	0.00
v West Indies	8	2	4	2	0	25.00
v Zimbabwe	9	1	5	3	0	11.11
TOTAL	73	3	63	7	0	4.10

Figures to 17.09.12. Updated records can be found at **www.cricinfo.com/ci/engine/records**

BANGLADESH *One-day International Records*

Most appearances

169	Mohammad Ashraful
133	Abdur Razzak
126	Khaled Mashud
126	Shakib Al Hasan
123	Mohammad Rafique
122	Mashrafe Mortaza
113	Tamim Iqbal
111	Habibul Bashar
108	Mushfiqur Rahim
85	Aftab Ahmed

Habibul Bashar captained in 69 ODIs, Shakib Al Hasan in 47, and Mohammad Ashraful in 38

Most runs

		Avge
3635	Shakib Al Hasan	35.63
3397	Moh'd Ashraful	22.64
3368	Tamim Iqbal	30.07
2201	Shahriar Nafees	31.44
2168	Habibul Bashar	21.68
2047	Mushfiqur Rahim	25.27
1954	Aftab Ahmed	24.73
1818	Khaled Mashud	21.90
1427	Mahmudullah	31.02
1315	Imrul Kayes	27.97

Seven further batsmen have scored 1000 runs in ODIs for Bangladesh

Most wickets

		Avge
185	Abdur Razzak	28.12
160	Shakib Al Hasan	28.85
156	Mashrafe Mortaza	30.31
119	Mohammad Rafique	38.75
67	Khaled Mahmud	42.76
61	Syed Rasel	33.62
59	Tapash Baisya	41.55
51	Shafiul Islam	35.96
48	Rubel Hossain	32.77
46	Shahadat Hossain	45.04

Mohammad Rafique completed the 1000-run/100-wicket double in ODIs as well as Tests

Highest scores

154	Tamim Iqbal	v Zimbabwe at Bulawayo	2009
134*	Shakib Al Hasan	v Canada at St John's	2006-07
129	Tamim Iqbal	v Ireland at Dhaka	2007-08
125	Tamim Iqbal	v England at MIrpur	2009-10
123*	Shahriar Nafees	v Zimbabwe at Jaipur	2006
118*	Shahriar Nafees	v Zimbabwe at Harare	2006-07
115	Alok Kapali	v India at Karachi	2008
109	Moh'd Ashraful	v UAE at Lahore	2008
108*	Rajin Saleh	v Kenya at Fatullah	2005-06
108	Shakib Al Hasan	v Pakistan at Multan	2007-08

Shakib Al Hasan has scored five ODI hundreds, Shahriar Nafees four, Mohammad Ashraful and Tamim Iqbal three

Best bowling figures

6-26	Mashrafe Mortaza	v Kenya at Nairobi	2006
5-29	Abdur Razzak	v Zimbabwe at Mirpur	2009-10
5-30	Abdur Razzak	v Zimbabwe at Mirpur	2010-11
5-31	Aftab Ahmed	v NZ at Dhaka	2004-05
5-33	Abdur Razzak	v Zimbabwe at Bogra	2006-07
5-42	Farhad Reza	v Ireland at Dhaka	2007-08
5-47	Moh'd Rafique	v Kenya at Fatullah	2005-06
4-14	Abdur Razzak	v Zimbabwe at Mirpur	2010-11
4-16	Tapash Baisya	v West Indies at Kingstown	2004
4-16	Rajin Saleh	v Zimbabwe at Harare	2006
4-16	Shakib Al Hasan	v WI at Chittagong	2011-12

Aftab Ahmed took only seven more wickets in 84 other ODIs

Record wicket partnerships

1st	170	Shahriar Hossain (68) and Mehrab Hossain (101)	v Zimbabwe at Dhaka	1998-99
2nd	160	Imrul Kayes (66) and Junaid Siddique (97)	v Pakistan at Dambulla	2010
3rd	141	Mohammad Ashraful (109) and Raqibul Hassan (83)	v United Arab Emirates at Lahore	2008
4th	175*	Rajin Saleh (108*) and Habibul Bashar (64*)	v Kenya at Fatullah	2005-06
5th	119	Shakib Al Hasan (52) and Raqibul Hassan (63)	v South Africa at Dhaka	2007-08
6th	123*	Al Sahariar (62*) and Khaled Mashud (53*)	v West Indies at Dhaka	1999-2000
7th	101	Mushfiqur Rahim (86) and Naeem Islam (43)	v New Zealand at Dunedin	2009-10
8th	70*	Khaled Mashud (35*) and Mohammad Rafique (41*)	v New Zealand at Kimberley	2002-03
9th	97	Shakib Al Hasan (108) and Mashrafe Mortaza (38)	v Pakistan at Multan	2007-08
10th	54*	Khaled Mashud (39*) and Tapash Baisya (22*)	v Sri Lanka at Colombo	2005-06

Figures to 17.09.12. Updated records can be found at **www.cricinfo.com/ci/engine/records**

Most catches

Fielders

37	Mashrafe Mortaza	
35	Mohammad Ashraful	
35	Shakib Al Hasan	
30	Tamim Iqbal	
29	Abdur Razzak	

Most dismissals

	Wicketkeepers	*Ct/St*
126	Khaled Mashud	91/35
106	Mushfiqur Rahim	75/31
13	Dhiman Ghosh	9/4
4	Jahurul Islam	4/0

Highest team totals

320-8	v Zimbabwe at Bulawayo	2009
313-6	v Zimbabwe at Bulawayo	2009
301-7	v Kenya at Bogra	2005-06
300-8	v UAE at Lahore	2008
296-6	v India at Mirpur	2009-10
295-6	v Australia at Mirpur	2010-11
293-7	v Ireland at Dhaka	2007-08
285-7	v Pakistan at Lahore	2007-08
283-6	v India at Karachi	2008
283-9	v India at Mirpur	2010-11

Bangladesh passed 300 for the first time in their 119th one-day international

Lowest team totals

Completed innings

58	v West Indies at Mirpur	2010-11
74	v Australia at Darwin	2008
76	v Sri Lanka at Colombo	2002
76	v India at Dhaka	2002-03
77	v NZ at Colombo	2002-03
78	v S Africa at Mirpur	2010-11
86	v NZ at Chittagong	2004-05
87*	v Pakistan at Dhaka	1999-2000
91	v Pakistan at Mirpur	2011-12
92	v Zimbabwe at Nairobi	1997-98

* One batsman absent hurt

Most sixes

49	Aftab Ahmed	
45	Tamim Iqbal	
40	Mashrafe Mortaza	
29	Mohammad Ashraful	
29	Mohammad Rafique	
25	Shakib Al Hasan	
24	Mushfiqur Rahim	
16	Abdur Razzak	
13	Mahmudullah	
12	Imrul Kayes	
12	Naeem Islam	

Best strike rate

Runs per 100 balls		*Runs*
87.10	Mashrafe Mortaza	1182
83.04	Aftab Ahmed	1954
79.17	Tamim Iqbal	3368
78.07	Shakib Al Hasan	3635
71.81	Mohammad Rafique	1190
71.41	Abdur Razzak	657
70.14	Mohammad Ashraful	3397
69.84	Mahmudullah	1427
69.49	Shahriar Nafees	2201
68.22	Junaid Siddique	1196

Qualification: 500 runs

Most economical bowlers

Runs per over		*Wkts*
4.29	Shakib Al Hasan	160
4.39	Mohammad Rafique	119
4.42	Mushfiqur Rahman	19
4.48	Abdur Razzak	185
4.62	Mashrafe Mortaza	156
4.63	Syed Rasel	61
4.77	Naeem Islam	33
4.84	Manjural Islam	24
4.95	Naimur Rahman	10
5.04	Nazmul Hossain	44

Qualification: 1000 balls bowled

Bangladesh's one-day international results

	Played	Won	Lost	Tied	No Result	% win
v Australia	19	1	18	0	0	5.26
v England	15	2	13	0	0	13.33
v India	24	3	21	0	0	12.50
v New Zealand	21	5	16	0	0	23.80
v Pakistan	31	1	30	0	0	3.22
v South Africa	14	1	13	0	0	7.14
v Sri Lanka	30	3	27	0	0	10.00
v West Indies	20	4	14	0	2	22.22
v Zimbabwe	56	30	26	0	0	53.57
v others (see below)	32	22	10	0	0	68.75
TOTAL	262	72	188	0	2	27.69

Other teams: Bermuda (P2, W2), Canada (P2, W1, L1), Hong Kong (P1, W1), Ireland (P7, W5, L2), Kenya (P14, W8, L6), Netherlands (P2, W1, L1), Scotland (P3, W3), UAE (P1, W1).

ENGLAND

Test Match Records

Most appearances

133	AJ Stewart
118	GA Gooch
117	DI Gower
115	MA Atherton
114	MC Cowdrey
108	G Boycott
102	IT Botham
100	AJ Strauss
100	GP Thorpe
96	N Hussain

Cowdrey was the first man to reach 100 Tests, in 1968

Most runs

		Avge
8900	GA Gooch	42.58
8463	AJ Stewart	39.54
8231	DI Gower	44.25
8114	G Boycott	47.72
7728	MA Atherton	37.69
7624	MC Cowdrey	44.06
7249	WR Hammond	58.45
7076	KP Pietersen	49.48
7037	AJ Strauss	40.91
6971	L Hutton	56.67

KF Barrington (6806), GP Thorpe (6744) and AN Cook (6655) have also passed 6000 runs

Most wickets

		Avge
383	IT Botham	28.40
325	RGD Willis	25.20
307	FS Trueman	21.57
297	DL Underwood	25.83
276	JM Anderson	30.40
252	JB Statham	24.84
248	MJ Hoggard	30.50
236	AV Bedser	24.89
234	AR Caddick	29.91
229	D Gough	28.39

SJ Harmison (222), A Flintoff (219) and JA Snow (202) have also taken more than 200 wickets

Highest scores

364	L Hutton	v Australia at The Oval	1938
336*	WR Hammond	v New Zealand at Auckland	1932-33
333	GA Gooch	v India at Lord's	1990
325	A Sandham	v West Indies at Kingston	1929-30
310*	JH Edrich	v New Zealand at Leeds	1965
294	AN Cook	v India at Birmingham	2011
287	RE Foster	v Australia at Sydney	1903-04
285*	PBH May	v West Indies at Birmingham	1957
278	DCS Compton	v Pakistan at Nottingham	1954
262*	DL Amiss	v West Indies at Kingston	1973-74

Foster was playing in his first Test, Sandham in his last

Best innings bowling

10-53	JC Laker	v Australia at Manchester	1956
9-28	GA Lohmann	v South Africa at Johannesburg	1895-96
9-37	JC Laker	v Australia at Manchester	1956
9-57	DE Malcolm	v South Africa at The Oval	1994
9-103	SF Barnes	v S Africa at Johannesburg	1913-14
8-7	GA Lohmann	v S Africa at Port Elizabeth	1895-96
8-11	J Briggs	v South Africa at Cape Town	1888-89
8-29	SF Barnes	v South Africa at The Oval	1912
8-31	FS Trueman	v India at Manchester	1952
8-34	IT Botham	v Pakistan at Lord's	1978

Botham also scored 108 in England's innings victory

Record wicket partnerships

1st	359	L Hutton (158) and C Washbrook (195)	v South Africa at Johannesburg	1948-49
2nd	382	L Hutton (364) and M Leyland (187)	v Australia at The Oval	1938
3rd	370	WJ Edrich (189) and DCS Compton (208)	v South Africa at Lord's	1947
4th	411	PBH May (285*) and MC Cowdrey (154)	v West Indies at Birmingham	1957
5th	254	KWR Fletcher (113) and AW Greig (148)	v India at Bombay	1972-73
6th	281	GP Thorpe (200*) and A Flintoff (137)	v New Zealand at Christchurch	2001-02
7th	197	MJK Smith (96) and JM Parks (101*)	v West Indies at Port-of-Spain	1959-60
8th	332	IJL Trott (184) and SCJ Broad (169)	v Pakistan at Lord's	2010
9th	163*	MC Cowdrey (128*) and AC Smith (69*)	v New Zealand at Wellington	1962-63
10th	130	RE Foster (287) and W Rhodes (40*)	v Australia at Sydney	1903-04

Figures to 17.09.12. Updated records can be found at www.cricinfo.com/ci/engine/records

Test Match Records   ENGLAND

Most catches

Fielders

121	AJ Strauss	
120	IT Botham	
120	MC Cowdrey	
110	WR Hammond	
105	GP Thorpe	

Most dismissals

Wicketkeepers		*Ct/St*
269	APE Knott	250/19
241	AJ Stewart	227/14
219	TG Evans	173/46
179	MJ Prior	167/12
174	RW Taylor	167/7

Highest team totals

903-7d	v Australia at The Oval	1938
849	v West Indies at Kingston	1929-30
710-7d	v India at Birmingham	2011
658-8d	v Australia at Nottingham	1938
654-5	v South Africa at Durban	1938-39
653-4d	v India at Lord's	1990
652-7d	v India at Madras	1984-85
644	v Australia at Sydney	2010-11
636	v Australia at Sydney	1928-29
633-5d	v India at Birmingham	1979

England have made nine other totals of 600 or more

Lowest team totals

Completed innings

45	v Australia at Sydney	1886-87
46	v WI at Port-of-Spain	1993-94
51	v WI at Kingston	2008-09
52	v Australia at The Oval	1948
53	v Australia at Lord's	1888
61	v Aust at Melbourne	1901-02
61	v Aust at Melbourne	1903-04
62	v Australia at Lord's	1888
64	v NZ at Wellington	1977-78
65*	v Australia at Sydney	1894-95

*One batsman absent

Best match bowling

19-90	JC Laker	v Australia at Manchester	1956
17-159	SF Barnes	v S Africa at Johannesburg	1913-14
15-28	J Briggs	v S Africa at Cape Town	1888-89
15-45	GA Lohmann	v S Africa at Port Elizabeth	1895-96
15-99	C Blythe	v South Africa at Leeds	1907
15-104	H Verity	v Australia at Lord's	1934
15-124	W Rhodes	v Australia at Melbourne	1903-04
14-99	AV Bedser	v Australia at Nottingham	1953
14-102	W Bates	v Australia at Melbourne	1882-83
14-144	SF Barnes	v South Africa at Durban	1913-14

Barnes took ten or more wickets in a match a record seven times for England

Hat-tricks

W Bates	v Australia at Melbourne	1882-83
J Briggs	v Australia at Sydney	1891-92
GA Lohmann	v S Africa at Port Elizabeth	1895-96
JT Hearne	v Australia at Leeds	1899
MJC Allom	v New Zealand at Christchurch	1929-30
TWJ Goddard	v S Africa at Johannesburg	1938-39
PJ Loader	v West Indies at Leeds	1957
DG Cork	v West Indies at Manchester	1995
D Gough	v Australia at Sydney	1998-99
MJ Hoggard	v West Indies at Bridgetown	2003-04
RJ Sidebottom	v New Zealand at Hamilton	2007-08
SCJ Broad	v India at Nottingham	2011

England's Test match results

	Played	Won	Lost	Drawn	Tied	% win
v Australia	326	102	133	91	0	31.28
v Bangladesh	8	8	0	0	0	100.00
v India	103	38	19	46	0	36.89
v New Zealand	94	45	8	41	0	47.87
v Pakistan	74	22	16	36	0	29.72
v South Africa	141	56	31	54	0	39.71
v Sri Lanka	26	10	7	9	0	38.46
v West Indies	148	45	53	50	0	30.40
v Zimbabwe	6	3	0	3	0	50.00
TOTAL	**926**	**329**	**267**	**330**	**0**	**35.52**

Figures to 17.09.12. Updated records can be found at **www.cricinfo.com/ci/engine/records**

ENGLAND
One-day International Records

Most appearances

197	PD Collingwood	
170	AJ Stewart	
164	JM Anderson	
158	D Gough	
138	A Flintoff	
127	AJ Strauss	
125	GA Gooch	
125	KP Pietersen	
123	ME Trescothick	
122	AJ Lamb	

Six further men have played 100 or more ODIs for England

Most runs

		Avge
5092	PD Collingwood	35.36
4677	AJ Stewart	31.60
4335	ME Trescothick	37.37
4290	GA Gooch	36.98
4205	AJ Strauss	35.63
4166	KP Pietersen	42.51
4010	AJ Lamb	39.31
3846	GA Hick	37.33
3783	IR Bell	36.02
3637	NV Knight	40.41

A Flintoff (3293) and DI Gower (3170) have also passed 3000 runs in ODIs

Most wickets

		Avge
234	D Gough	26.29
222	JM Anderson	30.54
168	A Flintoff	23.61
145	IT Botham	28.54
137	SCJ Broad	27.08
115	PAJ DeFreitas	32.82
111	PD Collingwood	38.68
98	GP Swann	26.31
81	TT Bresnan	35.76
80	RGD Willis	24.60

Nine further bowlers have taken 50 wickets in ODIs for England

Highest scores

167*	RA Smith	v Australia at Birmingham	1993
158	DI Gower	v New Zealand at Brisbane	1982-83
158	AJ Strauss	v India at Bangalore	2010-11
154	AJ Strauss	v Bangladesh at Birmingham	2010
152	AJ Strauss	v Bangladesh at Nottingham	2005
142*	CWJ Athey	v New Zealand at Manchester	1986
142	GA Gooch	v Pakistan at Karachi	1987-88
137	DL Amiss	v India at Lord's	1975
137	AN Cook	v Pakistan at Abu Dhabi	2011-12
137	ME Trescothick	v Pakistan at Lord's	2001
137	IJL Trott	v Australia at Sydney	2010-11

Trescothick scored 12 centuries in ODIs, KP Pietersen 9, Gooch 8, Gower 7, and Strauss 6

Best innings bowling

6-31	PD Collingwood	v B'desh at Nottingham	2005
6-45	CR Woakes	v Australia at Brisbane	2010-11
5-15	MA Ealham	v Zim at Kimberley	1999-2000
5-19	A Flintoff	v WI at Gros Islet	2008-09
5-20	VJ Marks	v NZ at Wellington	1983-84
5-21	C White	v Zim at Bulawayo	1999-2000
5-23	SCJ Broad	v S Africa at Nottingham	2008
5-23	JM Anderson	v SA at Port Elizabeth	2009-10
5-26	RC Irani	v India at The Oval	2002
5-28	GP Swann	v Aust at Chester-le-Street	2009

Collingwood also scored 112* in the same match.
All Ealham's five wickets were lbw, an ODI record

Record wicket partnerships

1st	200	ME Trescothick (114*) and VS Solanki (106)	v South Africa at The Oval	2003
2nd	250	AJ Strauss (154) and IJL Trott (110)	v Bangladesh at Birmingham	2010
3rd	213	GA Hick (86*) and NH Fairbrother (113)	v West Indies at Lord's	1991
4th	226	AJ Strauss (100) and A Flintoff (123)	v West Indies at Lord's	2004
5th	174	A Flintoff (99) and PD Collingwood (79*)	v India at The Oval	2004
6th	150	MP Vaughan (90*) and GO Jones (80)	v Zimbabwe at Bulawayo	2004-05
7th	110	PD Collingwood (100) and C White (48)	v Sri Lanka at Perth	2002-03
8th	99*	RS Bopara (43*) and SCJ Broad (45*)	v India at Manchester	2007
9th	100	LE Plunkett (56) and VS Solanki (39*)	v Pakistan at Lahore	2005-06
10th	53	JM Anderson (20*) and ST Finn (35)	v Australia at Brisbane	2010-11

Figures to 17.09.12. Updated records can be found at **www.cricinfo.com/ci/engine/records**

One-day International Records — ENGLAND

Most catches

Fielders

108	PD Collingwood	
64	GA Hick	
57	AJ Strauss	
46	A Flintoff	
45	GA Gooch/ME Tres'thick	

Most dismissals

	Wicketkeepers	Ct/St
163	AJ Stewart	148/15
77	MJ Prior	69/8
72	GO Jones	68/4
62	C Kieswetter	50/12
47	RC Russell	41/6

Highest team totals

391-4	v Bangladesh at Nottingham	2005
363-7	v Pakistan at Nottingham	1992
347-7	v Bangladesh at Birmingham	2010
340-6	v New Zealand at Napier	2007-08
338-8	v India at Bangalore	2010-11
334-4	v India at Lord's	1975
333-6	v Australia at Sydney	2010-11
333-9	v Sri Lanka at Taunton	1983
328-7	v West Indies at Birmingham	2009
327-4	v Pakistan at Lahore	2005-06
327-8	v Ireland at Bangalore	2010-11

England have reached 300 on 16 other occasions in ODIs

Lowest team totals

Completed innings

86	v Australia at Manchester	2001
88	v SL at Dambulla	2003-04
89	v NZ at Wellington	2001-02
93	v Australia at Leeds	1975
94	v Aust at Melbourne	1978-79
101	v NZ at Chester-le-Street	2004
103	v SA at The Oval	1999
104	v SL at Colombo	2007-08
107	v Zim at Cape Town	1999-2000
110	v Aust at Melbourne	1998-99
110	v Aust at Adelaide	2006-07

The lowest totals against England are 45 by Canada (1979), and 70 by Australia (1977)

Most sixes

92	A Flintoff*	
74	PD Collingwood	
72	KP Pietersen*	
44	IT Botham	
41	GA Hick	
41	ME Trescothick	
31	EJG Morgan	
30	C Kieswetter	
30	AJ Lamb	
26	OA Shah	
26	AJ Stewart	

*Also hit one six for the World XI

Best strike rate

Runs per 100 balls		Runs
92.53	TT Bresnan	694
91.90	EJG Morgan	1861
91.08	C Kieswetter	1012
89.29	LJ Wright	701
89.14	A Flintoff	3293
86.90	KP Pietersen	4166
85.21	ME Trescothick	4335
83.83	PAJ DeFreitas	690
80.94	AJ Strauss	4205
79.28	AN Cook	2121

Qualification: 500 runs

Most economical bowlers

Runs per over		Wkts
3.28	RGD Willis	80
3.54	ARC Fraser	47
3.79	GR Dilley	48
3.84	AD Mullally	63
3.96	IT Botham	145
3.96	PAJ DeFreitas	115
4.01	AR Caddick	69
4.08	MA Ealham	67
4.10	JE Emburey	76
4.17	GC Small	58

Qualification: 2000 balls bowled

England's one-day international results

	Played	Won	Lost	Tied	No result	% win
v Australia	117	46	67	2	2	40.86
v Bangladesh	15	13	2	0	0	86.66
v India	81	33	43	2	3	43.58
v New Zealand	70	29	35	2	4	45.45
v Pakistan	72	42	28	0	2	60.00
v South Africa	50	21	25	1	3	45.74
v Sri Lanka	50	26	24	0	0	52.00
v West Indies	85	40	41	0	4	49.38
v Zimbabwe	30	21	8	0	1	72.41
v others (see below)	17	15	1	0	1	93.75
TOTAL	587	286	274	7	20	51.05

Other teams: Canada (P2, W2), East Africa (P1, W1), Ireland (P5, W4, L1), Kenya (P2, W2), Namibia (P1, W1), Netherlands (P3, W3), Scotland (P2, W1, NR1), United Arab Emirates (P1, W1).

INDIA   *Test Match Records*

Most appearances

190	SR Tendulkar	
163	R Dravid	
134	VVS Laxman	
132	A Kumble	
131	Kapil Dev	
125	SM Gavaskar	
116	DB Vengsarkar	
113	SC Ganguly	
99	M Azharuddin	
98	Harbhajan Singh	

Gavaskar played 106 consecutive matches between 1974-75 and 1986-87

Most runs

		Avge
15533	SR Tendulkar	55.08
13265	R Dravid	52.63
10122	SM Gavaskar	51.12
8781	VVS Laxman	45.97
8223	V Sehwag	50.75
7212	SC Ganguly	42.17
6868	DB Vengsarkar	42.13
6215	M Azharuddin	45.03
6080	GR Viswanath	41.74
5248	Kapil Dev	31.05

Tendulkar has scored 51 centuries, Dravid 36, Gavaskar 34, Azharuddin and Sehwag 22

Most wickets

		Avge
619	A Kumble	29.65
434	Kapil Dev	29.64
406	Harbhajan Singh	32.22
291	Z Khan	32.06
266	BS Bedi	29.74
242	BS Chandrasekhar	29.74
236	J Srinath	30.49
189	EAS Prasanna	30.38
162	MH Mankad	32.32
156	S Venkataraghavan	36.11

In all 17 Indians have taken 100 wickets in Tests

Highest scores

319	V Sehwag	v South Africa at Chennai	2007-08
309	V Sehwag	v Pakistan at Multan	2003-04
293	V Sehwag	v Sri Lanka at Mumbai	2009-10
281	VVS Laxman	v Australia at Kolkata	2000-01
270	R Dravid	v Pakistan at Rawalpindi	2003-04
254	V Sehwag	v Pakistan at Lahore	2005-06
248*	SR Tendulkar	v Bangladesh at Dhaka	2004-05
241*	SR Tendulkar	v Australia at Sydney	2003-04
239	SC Ganguly	v Pakistan at Bangalore	2007-08
236*	SM Gavaskar	v West Indies at Madras	1983-84

Sehwag and Tendulkar have scored six double-centuries, Dravid five, and Gavaskar four

Best innings bowling

10-74	A Kumble	v Pakistan at Delhi	1998-99
9-69	JM Patel	v Australia at Kanpur	1959-60
9-83	Kapil Dev	v WI at Ahmedabad	1983-84
9-102	SP Gupte	v W Indies at Kanpur	1958-59
8-52	MH Mankad	v Pakistan at Delhi	1952-53
8-55	MH Mankad	v England at Madras	1951-52
8-61	ND Hirwani	v W Indies at Madras	1987-88
8-72	S Venkataraghavan	v N Zealand at Delhi	1964-65
8-75	ND Hirwani	v W Indies at Madras	1987-88
8-76	EAS Prasanna	v NZ at Auckland	1975-76

Hirwani's two performances were in the same match, his Test debut

Record wicket partnerships

1st	413	MH Mankad (231) and P Roy (173)	v New Zealand at Madras	1955-56
2nd	344*	SM Gavaskar (182*) and DB Vengsarkar (157*)	v West Indies at Calcutta	1978-79
3rd	336	V Sehwag (309) and SR Tendulkar (194*)	v Pakistan at Multan	2003-04
4th	353	SR Tendulkar (241*) and VVS Laxman (178)	v Australia at Sydney	2003-04
5th	376	VVS Laxman (281) and R Dravid (180)	v Australia at Calcutta	2000-01
6th	298*	DB Vengsarkar (164*) and RJ Shastri (121*)	v Australia at Bombay	1986-87
7th	259*	VVS Laxman (143*) and MS Dhoni (132*)	v South Africa at Kolkata	2009-10
8th	161	M Azharuddin (109) and A Kumble (88)	v South Africa at Calcutta	1996-97
9th	149	PG Joshi (52*) and RB Desai (85)	v Pakistan at Bombay	1960-61
10th	133	SR Tendulkar (248*) and Z Khan (75)	v Bangladesh at Dhaka	2004-05

Figures to 17.09.12. Updated records can be found at **www.cricinfo.com/ci/engine/records**

Test Match Records

Most catches

Fielders

209	R Dravid	
135	VVS Laxman	
113	SR Tendulkar	
108	SM Gavaskar	
105	M Azharuddin	

Most dismissals

Wicketkeepers | | Ct/St

224	MS Dhoni	194/30
198	SMH Kirmani	160/38
130	KS More	110/20
107	NR Mongia	99/8
82	FM Engineer	66/16

Highest team totals

726-9d	v Sri Lanka at Mumbai	2009-10
707	v Sri Lanka at Colombo	2010
705-7d	v Australia at Sydney	2003-04
676-7	v Sri Lanka at Kanpur	1986-87
675-5d	v Pakistan at Multan	2003-04
664	v England at The Oval	2007
657-7d	v Australia at Kolkata	2000-01
644-7d	v West Indies at Kanpur	1978-79
643-6d	v South Africa at Kolkata	2009-10
642	v Sri Lanka at Kampur	2009-10

India have reached 600 on 13 further occasions

Lowest team totals

Completed innings

42*	v England at Lord's	1974
58	v Australia at Brisbane	1947-48
58	v England at Manchester	1952
66	v S Africa at Durban	1996-97
67	v Aust at Melbourne	1947-48
75	v West Indies at Delhi	1987-88
76	v SA at Ahmedabad	2007-08
81*	v NZ at Wellington	1975-76
81	v W Indies at Bridgetown	1996-97
82	v England at Manchester	1952

*One or more batsmen absent

Best match bowling

16-136	ND Hirwani	v West Indies at Madras	1987-88
15-217	Harbhajan Singh	v Australia at Chennai	2000-01
14-124	JM Patel	v Australia at Kanpur	1959-60
14-149	A Kumble	v Pakistan at Delhi	1998-99
13-131	MH Mankad	v Pakistan at Delhi	1952-53
13-132	J Srinath	v Pakistan at Calcutta	1998-99
13-181	A Kumble	v Australia at Chennai	2004-05
13-196	Harbhajan Singh	v Australia at Kolkata	2000-01
12-85	R Ashwin	v NZ at Hyderabad	2011-12
12-104	BS Chandrasekhar	v Australia at Melbourne	1977-78

Hirwani's feat was on his Test debut

Hat-tricks

Harbhajan Singh   v Australia at Kolkata   2000-01

The wickets of RT Ponting, AC Gilchrist and SK Warne, as India fought back to win after following on.

IK Pathan   v Pakistan at Karachi   2005-06

Salman Butt, Younis Khan and Mohammad Yousuf with the fourth, fifth and sixth balls of the match – Pakistan still won the match by 341 runs.

India had never conceded a hat-trick in a Test match until SCJ Broad took one for England at Nottingham in 2011

India's Test match results

	Played	Won	Lost	Drawn	Tied	% win
v Australia	82	20	38	23	1	24.39
v Bangladesh	7	6	0	1	0	85.71
v England	103	19	38	46	0	18.44
v New Zealand	52	18	9	25	0	34.61
v Pakistan	59	9	12	38	0	15.25
v South Africa	27	7	12	8	0	25.92
v Sri Lanka	35	14	6	15	0	40.00
v West Indies	88	14	30	44	0	15.90
v Zimbabwe	11	7	2	2	0	63.63
TOTAL	**464**	**114**	**147**	**202**	**1**	**24.56**

Figures to 17.09.12. Updated records can be found at **www.cricinfo.com/ci/engine/records**

One-day International Records

Most appearances

463	SR Tendulkar
340	R Dravid
334	M Azharuddin
308	SC Ganguly
271	Yuvraj Singh
269	A Kumble
229	J Srinath
227	Harbhajan Singh
226	V Sehwag
225	Kapil Dev

Robin Singh played 136 ODIs for India – but only one Test match

Most runs

		Avge
18426	SR Tendulkar	44.83
11221	SC Ganguly	40.95
10768	R Dravid	39.15
9378	M Azharuddin	36.92
7960	V Sehwag	35.53
7959	Yuvraj Singh	37.54
6734	MS Dhoni	50.63
5359	A Jadeja	37.47
5077	G Gambhir	40.94
4413	NS Sidhu	37.08

K Srikkanth (4091) has also scored more than 4000 runs

Most wickets

		Avge
334	A Kumble	30.83
315	J Srinath	28.08
288	AB Agarkar	27.85
269	Z Khan	30.11
255	Harbhajan Singh	33.52
253	Kapil Dev	27.45
196	BKV Prasad	32.30
173	IK Pathan	29.72
157	M Prabhakar	28.87
155	A Nehra	31.60

SR Tendulkar (154), RJ Shastri (129), Yuvraj Singh (108) and SC Ganguly (100) have also taken 100 wickets

Highest scores

219	V Sehwag	v West Indies at Indore	2011-12
200*	SR Tendulkar	v South Africa at Gwalior	2009-10
186*	SR Tendulkar	v N Zealand at Hyderabad	1999-2000
183*	MS Dhoni	v Sri Lanka at Jaipur	2005-06
183	SC Ganguly	v Sri Lanka at Taunton	1999
183	V Kohli	v Pakistan at Dhaka	2011-12
175*	Kapil Dev	v Zimbabwe at Tunbridge Wells	1983
175	SR Tendulkar	v Australia at Hyderabad	2009-10
175	V Sehwag	v Bangladesh at Mirpur	2010-11
163*	SR Tendulkar	v NZ at Christchurch	2008-09

Tendulkar has scored 49 centuries, Ganguly 22, Sehwag 15, Kohli and Yuvraj Singh 13, R Dravid 12 and G Gambhir 11

Best bowling figures

6-12	A Kumble	v West Indies at Calcutta	1993-94
6-23	A Nehra	v England at Durban	2002-03
6-27	M Kartik	v Australia at Mumbai	2007-08
6-42	AB Agarkar	v Australia at Melbourne	2003-04
6-55	S Sreesanth	v England at Indore	2005-06
6-59	A Nehra	v Sri Lanka at Colombo	2005
5-6	SB Joshi	v South Africa at Nairobi	1999-2000
5-15	RJ Shastri	v Australia at Perth	1991-92
5-16	SC Ganguly	v Pakistan at Toronto	1997-98
5-21	Arshad Ayub	v Pakistan at Dhaka	1988-89
5-21	N Chopra	v West Indies at Toronto	1999-2000

Agarkar took four wickets in an ODI innings 12 times, J Srinath and A Kumble 10

Record wicket partnerships

1st	258	SC Ganguly (111) and SR Tendulkar (146)	v Kenya at Paarl	2001-02
2nd	331	SR Tendulkar (186*) and R Dravid (153)	v New Zealand at Hyderabad	1999-2000
3rd	237*	R Dravid (104*) and SR Tendulkar (140*)	v Kenya at Bristol	1999
4th	275*	M Azharuddin (153*) and A Jadeja (116*)	v Zimbabwe at Cuttack	1997-98
5th	223	M Azharuddin (111*) and A Jadeja (119)	v Sri Lanka at Colombo	1997-98
6th	158	Yuvraj Singh (120) and MS Dhoni (67*)	v Zimbabwe at Harare	2005-06
7th	102	HK Badani (60*) and AB Agarkar (53)	v Australia at Melbourne	2003-04
8th	84	Harbhajan Singh (49) and P Kumar (40*)	v Australia at Vadodara	2009-10
9th	126*	Kapil Dev (175*) and SMH Kirmani (24*)	v Zimbabwe at Tunbridge Wells	1983
10th	64	Harbhajan Singh (41*) and L Balaji (18)	v England at The Oval	2004

Figures to 17.09.12. Updated records can be found at **www.cricinfo.com/ci/engine/records**

One-day International Records

Most catches

Fielders

156	M Azharuddin
140	SR Tendulkar
124	R Dravid
99	SC Ganguly
88	V Sehwag

Most dismissals

Wicketkeepers		Ct/St
235	MS Dhoni	178/57
154	NR Mongia	110/44
90	KS More	63/27
86	R Dravid	72/14
36	SMH Kirmani	27/9

Highest team totals

418-5	v West Indies at Indore	2011-12
414-7	v Sri Lanka at Rajkot	2009-10
413-5	v Bermuda at Port-of-Spain	2006-07
401-3	v South Africa at Gwalior	2009-10
392-4	v N Zealand at Christchurch	2008-09
387-5	v England at Rajkot	2008-09
376-2	v N Zealand at Hyderabad	1999-2000
374-4	v Hong Kong at Karachi	2008
373-6	v Sri Lanka at Taunton	1999
370-4	v Bangladesh at Mirpur	2010-11

All scored in 50 overs

Lowest team totals

Completed innings

54	v Sri Lanka at Sharjah	2000-01
63	v Australia at Sydney	1980-81
78	v Sri Lanka at Kanpur	1986-87
79	v Pakistan at Sialkot	1978-79
88	v NZ at Dambulla	2010
91	v South Africa at Durban	2006-07
100	v WI at Ahmedabad	1993-94
100	v Australia at Sydney	1999-2000
103	v Sri Lanka at Colombo	2008-09
103	v Sri Lanka at Dambulla	2010

The lowest score against India is
Zimbabwe's 65 at Harare in 2005

Most sixes

195	SR Tendulkar
189	SC Ganguly
142	Yuvraj Singh
132	MS Dhoni
131	V Sehwag
85	A Jadeja
80	SK Raina
77	M Azharuddin
67	Kapil Dev
44	NS Sidhu

Dhoni hit 10 sixes in one innings

Best strike rate

Runs per 100 balls		Runs
113.60	YK Pathan	810
104.72	V Sehwag	7960
95.07	Kapil Dev	3783
93.66	SK Raina	3699
91.92	RV Uthappa	786
89.43	SB Joshi	584
87.76	MS Dhoni	6734
87.32	Yuvraj Singh	7959
86.43	V Kohli	3886
86.23	SR Tendulkar	18426

Qualification: 500 runs

Most economical bowlers

Runs per over		Wkts
3.71	Kapil Dev	253
3.95	Maninder Singh	66
4.05	Madan Lal	73
4.21	RJ Shastri	129
4.27	M Prabhakar	157
4.29	Harbhajan Singh	255
4.29	A Kumble	334
4.33	M Amarnath	46
4.36	SLV Raju	63
4.44	SB Joshi	69
4.44	J Srinath	315

Qualification: 2000 balls bowled

India's one-day international results

	Played	Won	Lost	Tied	No result	% win
v Australia	109	37	64	0	8	36.63
v Bangladesh	24	21	3	0	0	87.50
v England	81	43	33	2	3	56.41
v New Zealand	88	46	37	0	5	55.42
v Pakistan	121	48	69	0	4	41.02
v South Africa	66	24	40	0	2	37.50
v Sri Lanka	139	75	52	1	11	58.98
v West Indies	106	46	57	1	2	44.71
v Zimbabwe	51	39	10	2	0	78.43
v others (see below)	24	22	2	0	0	91.66
TOTAL	809	401	367	6	35	52.19

Other teams: Bermuda (P1, W1), East Africa (P1, W1), Hong Kong (P1, W1), Ireland (P2, W2), Kenya (P13, W11, L2), Namibia (P1, W1), Netherlands (P2, W2), Scotland (P1, W1), United Arab Emirates (P2, W2).

NEW ZEALAND *Test Match Records*

Most appearances

111	SP Fleming
111	DL Vettori
86	RJ Hadlee
82	JG Wright
81	NJ Astle
78	AC Parore
77	MD Crowe
70	CS Martin
68	BB McCullum
63	IDS Smith

Vettori also played for the World XI against Australia in October 2005

Most runs

		Avge
7172	SP Fleming	40.06
5444	MD Crowe	45.36
5334	JG Wright	37.82
4702	NJ Astle	37.02
4508	DL Vettori	30.25
3978	BB McCullum	35.83
3448	BE Congdon	32.22
3428	JR Reid	33.28
3320	CL Cairns	33.53
3124	RJ Hadlee	27.16

CD McMillan (3116) and LRPL Taylor (3025) also scored more than 3000 runs

Most wickets

		Avge
431	RJ Hadlee	22.29
359	DL Vettori	34.20
230	CS Martin	33.97
218	CL Cairns	29.40
160	DK Morrison	34.68
130	BL Cairns	32.92
123	EJ Chatfield	32.17
116	RO Collinge	29.25
111	BR Taylor	26.60
102	JG Bracewell	35.81

RC Motz took exactly 100 Test wickets. Vettori also took one wicket for the World XI

Highest scores

299	MD Crowe	v Sri Lanka at Wellington	1990-91
274*	SP Fleming	v Sri Lanka at Colombo	2002-03
267*	BA Young	v Sri Lanka at Dunedin	1996-97
262	SP Fleming	v South Africa at Cape Town	2005-06
259	GM Turner	v West Indies at Georgetown	1971-72
239	GT Dowling	v India at Christchurch	1967-68
230*	B Sutcliffe	v India at Delhi	1955-56
225	BB McCullum	v India at Hyderabad	2010-11
224	L Vincent	v Sri Lanka at Wellington	2004-05
223*	GM Turner	v West Indies at Kingston	1971-72

There have been six other double-centuries, two by MS Sinclair and one each by NJ Astle, MP Donnelly, SP Fleming and JD Ryder

Best innings bowling

9-52	RJ Hadlee	v Australia at Brisbane	1985-86
7-23	RJ Hadlee	v India at Wellington	1975-76
7-27	CL Cairns	v West Indies at Hamilton	1999-2000
7-52	C Pringle	v Pakistan at Faisalabad	1990-91
7-53	CL Cairns	v Bangladesh at Hamilton	2001-02
7-64	TG Southee	v India at Bangalore	2012-13
7-65	SB Doull	v India at Wellington	1998-99
7-74	BR Taylor	v West Indies at Bridgetown	1971-72
7-74	BL Cairns	v England at Leeds	1983
7-87	SL Boock	v Pakistan at Hyderabad	1984-85
7-87	DL Vettori	v Australia at Auckland	1999-2000

Hadlee took five or more wickets in an innings 36 times

Record wicket partnerships

1st	387	GM Turner (259) and TW Jarvis (182)	v West Indies at Georgetown	1971-72
2nd	241	JG Wright (116) and AH Jones (143)	v England at Wellington	1991-92
3rd	467	AH Jones (186) and MD Crowe (299)	v Sri Lanka at Wellington	1990-91
4th	271	LRPL Taylor (151) and JD Ryder (201)	v India at Napier	2008-09
5th	222	NJ Astle (141) and CD McMillan (142)	v Zimbabwe at Wellington	2000-01
6th	339	MJ Guptill (189) and BB McCullum (185)	v Bangladesh at Hamilton	2009-10
7th	225	CL Cairns (158) and JDP Oram (90)	v South Africa at Auckland	2003-04
8th	256	SP Fleming (262) and JEC Franklin (122*)	v South Africa at Cape Town	2005-06
9th	136	IDS Smith (173) and MC Snedden (22)	v India at Auckland	1989-90
10th	151	BF Hastings (110) and RO Collinge (68*)	v Pakistan at Auckland	1972-73

Figures to 17.09.12. Updated records can be found at **www.cricinfo.com/ci/engine/records**

Test Match Records   NEW ZEALAND

Most catches

Fielders

171	SP Fleming
71	MD Crowe
70	NJ Astle
67	LRPL Taylor
64	JV Coney

Most dismissals

	Wicketkeepers	*Ct/St*
201	AC Parore	194/7
176	IDS Smith	168/8
172	BB McCullum	161/11
96	KJ Wadsworth	92/4
59	WK Lees	52/7

Highest team totals

671-4	v Sri Lanka at Wellington	1990-91
630-6d	v India at Chandigarh	2003-04
619-9d	v India at Napier	2008-09
595	v South Africa at Auckland	2003-04
593-8d	v South Africa at Cape Town	2005-06
586-7d	v Sri Lanka at Dunedin	1996-97
563	v Pakistan at Hamilton	2003-04
561	v Sri Lanka at Napier	2004-05
553-7d	v Australia at Brisbane	1985-86
553-7d	v Bangladesh at Hamilton	2009-10

671-4 is the record score in any team's second innings in a Test match

Lowest team totals

Completed innings

26	v England at Auckland	1954-55
42	v Australia at Wellington	1945-46
47	v England at Lord's	1958
54	v Australia at Wellington	1945-46
65	v England at Christchurch	1970-71
67	v England at Leeds	1958
67	v England at Lord's	1978
70	v Pakistan at Dacca	1955-56
73	v Pakistan at Lahore	2001-02
74	v W Indies at Dunedin	1955-56
74	v England at Lord's	1958

26 is the lowest all-out total by any team in a Test match

Best match bowling

15-123	RJ Hadlee	v Australia at Brisbane	1985-86
12-149	DL Vettori	v Australia at Auckland	1999-2000
12-170	DL Vettori	v Bangladesh at Chittagong	2004-05
11-58	RJ Hadlee	v India at Wellington	1975-76
11-102	RJ Hadlee	v West Indies at Dunedin	1979-80
11-152	C Pringle	v Pakistan at Faisalabad	1990-91
11-155	RJ Hadlee	v Australia at Perth	1985-86
11-169	DJ Nash	v England at Lord's	1994
11-180	CS Martin	v South Africa at Auckland	2003-04
10-88	RJ Hadlee	v India at Bombay	1988-89

Hadlee took 33 wickets at 12.15 in the three-Test series in Australia in 1985-86

Hat-tricks

PJ Petherick	v Pakistan at Lahore	1976-77
JEC Franklin	v Bangladesh at Dhaka	2004-05

Petherick's hat-trick was on Test debut: he dismissed Javed Miandad (who had made 163 on his debut), Wasim Raja and Intikhab Alam. Petherick won only five more Test caps.

Franklin is one of only six men to have scored a century and taken a hat-trick in Tests: the others are J Briggs and SCJ Broad of England, Abdul Razzaq and Wasim Akram of Pakistan, and IK Pathan of India

New Zealand's Test match results

	Played	Won	Lost	Drawn	Tied	% win
v Australia	52	8	27	17	0	15.38
v Bangladesh	9	8	0	1	0	88.88
v England	94	8	45	41	0	8.51
v India	52	9	18	25	0	17.30
v Pakistan	50	7	23	20	0	14.00
v South Africa	38	4	21	13	0	10.52
v Sri Lanka	26	9	7	10	0	34.61
v West Indies	39	9	12	18	0	23.07
v Zimbabwe	15	9	0	6	0	60.00
TOTAL	375	71	153	151	0	18.93

Figures to 17.09.12. Updated records can be found at www.cricinfo.com/ci/engine/records

NEW ZEALAND One-day International Records

Most appearances

279	SP Fleming
268	DL Vettori
250	CZ Harris
223	NJ Astle
214	CL Cairns
203	BB McCullum
197	CD McMillan
188	SB Styris
179	AC Parore
159	JDP Oram

Fleming (1), Vettori (4) and Cairns (1) also played in official ODIs for the World XI

Most runs

		Avge
8007	SP Fleming	32.41
7090	NJ Astle	34.92
4881	CL Cairns	29.22
4707	CD McMillan	28.18
4704	MD Crowe	38.55
4554	BB McCullum	30.36
4483	SB Styris	32.48
4379	CZ Harris	29.00
3891	JG Wright	26.46
3323	LRPL Taylor	38.19

AC Parore (3314) and KR Rutherford (3143) also passed 3000. Fleming also scored 30 runs and Cairns 69 for the World XI

Most wickets

		Avge
274	DL Vettori	31.75
205	KD Mills	25.99
203	CZ Harris	37.50
200	CL Cairns	32.78
173	JDP Oram	28.92
158	RJ Hadlee	21.56
147	SE Bond	20.88
140	EJ Chatfield	25.84
137	SB Styris	35.32
126	DK Morrison	27.53

MC Snedden (114), GR Larsen (113), DR Tuffey (110) and C Pringle (103) also took 100 wkts. Vettori also took 8 wickets, and Cairns 1, for the World XI

Highest scores

172	L Vincent	v Zimbabwe at Bulawayo	2005-06
171*	GM Turner	v East Africa at Birmingham	1975
166	BB McCullum	v Ireland at Aberdeen	2008
161	JAH Marshall	v Ireland at Aberdeen	2008
146	RJ Nicol	v Zimbabwe at Whangarei	2011-12
145*	NJ Astle	v USA at The Oval	2004
141	SB Styris	v Sri Lanka at Bloemfontein	2002-03
140	GM Turner	v Sri Lanka at Auckland	1982-83
139	JM How	v England at Napier	2007-08
134*	SP Fleming	v SA at Johannesburg	2002-03

Turner's 171 was the highest score in the first World Cup*

Best bowling figures

6-19	SE Bond	v India at Bulawayo	2005-06
6-23	SE Bond	v Australia at Port Elizabeth	2002-03
6-25	SB Styris	v West Indies at Port-of-Spain	2001-02
5-7	DL Vettori	v Bangladesh at Queenstown	2007-08
5-22	MN Hart	v West Indies at Margao	1994-95
5-22	AR Adams	v India at Queenstown	2002-03
5-23	RO Collinge	v India at Christchurch	1975-76
5-23	SE Bond	v Australia at Wellington	2006-07
5-25	RJ Hadlee	v Sri Lanka at Bristol	1983
5-25	SE Bond	v Australia at Adelaide	2001-02
5-25	KD Mills	v South Africa at Durban	2007-08

In all Hadlee took five wickets in an ODI on five occasions

Record wicket partnerships

1st	274	JAH Marshall (161) and BB McCullum (166)	v Ireland at Aberdeen	2008
2nd	157	MJ Guptill (105) and BB McCullum (87)	v Zimbabwe at Harare	2011-12
3rd	180	AC Parore (96) and KR Rutherford (108)	v India at Baroda	1994-95
4th	190	LRPL Taylor (95) and SB Styris (89)	v India at Dambulla	2010
5th	195	LRPL Taylor (119) and KS Williamson (100*)	v Zimbabwe at Bulawayo	2011-12
6th	165	CD McMillan (117) and BB McCullum (86*)	v Australia at Hamilton	2006-07
7th	123	NT Broom (71) and JDP Oram (83)	v Bangladesh at Napier	2009-10
8th	94	JEC Franklin (72*) and NL McCullum (43)	v India at Vadodara	2010-11
9th	83	KD Mills (54) and TG Southee (32)	v India at Christchurch	2008-09
10th	65	MC Snedden (40) and EJ Chatfield (19*)	v Sri Lanka at Derby	1983

Figures to 17.09.12. Updated records can be found at **www.cricinfo.com/ci/engine/records**

Most catches

Fielders

132	SP Fleming	
96	CZ Harris	
83	NJ Astle	
80	LRPL Taylor	
75	DL Vettori	

Most dismissals

Wicketkeepers		Ct/St
233	BB McCullum	218/15
136	AC Parore	111/25
85	IDS Smith	80/5
37	TE Blain	36/1
30	LK Germon	21/9
30	WK Lees	28/2

Highest team totals

402-2	v Ireland at Aberdeen	2008
397-5	v Zimbabwe at Bulawayo	2005-06
373-8	v Zimbabwe at Napier	2011-12
372-6	v Zimbabwe at Whangarei	2011-12
363-5	v Canada at St Lucia	2006-07
358-6	v Canada at Mumbai	2010-11
350-9	v Australia at Hamilton	2006-07
349-9	v India at Rajkot	1999-2000
348-8	v India at Nagpur	1995-96
347-4	v USA at The Oval	2004

The 397-5 came from 44 overs; all the others were from 50, except 350-9 (49.3)

Lowest team totals

Completed innings

64	v Pakistan at Sharjah	1985-86
73	v Sri Lanka at Auckland	2006-07
74	v Aust at Wellington	1981-82
74	v Pakistan at Sharjah	1989-90
94	v Aust at Christchurch	1989-90
97	v Aust at Faridabad	2003-04
103	v India at Chennai	2010-11
105	v Aust at Auckland	2005-06
108	v Pakistan at Wellington	1992-93
110	v Pakistan at Auckland	1993-94

The lowest totals against New Zealand are 69, by Kenya at Chennai in 2010-11, and 70, by Australia at Adelaide in 1985-86

Most sixes

151	CL Cairns	
130	BB McCullum	
88	LRPL Taylor	
86	NJ Astle	
84	CD McMillan	
81	JDP Oram	
68	SB Styris	
63	SP Fleming	
43	CZ Harris	
42	MJ Guptill	

Cairns also hit 2 for the World XI

Best strike rate

Runs per 100 balls		Runs
104.88	BL Cairns	987
99.43	IDS Smith	1055
89.72	JD Ryder	1100
89.55	BB McCullum	4554
86.67	JDP Oram	2432
83.76	CL Cairns	4881
82.35	NL McCullum	588
82.08	LRPL Taylor	3323
81.76	DL Vettori	2053
81.13	RJ Nicol	516

Qualification: 500 runs

Most economical bowlers

Runs per over		Wkts
3.30	RJ Hadlee	158
3.57	EJ Chatfield	140
3.76	GR Larsen	113
4.06	BL Cairns	89
4.12	DL Vettori	274
4.14	W Watson	74
4.17	DN Patel	45
4.17	JV Coney	54
4.28	SE Bond	147
4.28	CZ Harris	203

Qualification: 2000 balls bowled

New Zealand's one-day international results

	Played	Won	Lost	Tied	No result	% win
v Australia	124	34	85	0	5	28.57
v Bangladesh	21	16	5	0	0	76.19
v England	70	35	29	2	4	54.54
v India	88	37	46	0	5	44.57
v Pakistan	89	35	51	1	2	40.80
v South Africa	55	18	33	0	4	35.29
v Sri Lanka	74	35	34	1	4	50.71
v West Indies	56	21	28	0	7	42.85
v Zimbabwe	35	25	8	1	1	75.00
v others (see below)	13	13	0	0	0	100.00
TOTAL	625	269	319	5	32	45.78

Other teams: Canada (P3, W3), East Africa (P1, W1), Ireland (P2, W2), Kenya (P2, W2), Netherlands (P1, W1), Scotland (P2, W2), United Arab Emirates (P1, W1), United States of America (P1, W1).

PAKISTAN
Test Match Records

Most appearances

124	Javed Miandad
119	Inzamam-ul-Haq
104	Wasim Akram
103	Salim Malik
90	Mohammad Yousuf
88	Imran Khan
87	Waqar Younis
81	Wasim Bari
79	Younis Khan
78	Zaheer Abbas

Inzamam-ul-Haq also played one Test for the World XI

Most runs

		Avge
8832	Javed Miandad	52.57
8829	Inzamam-ul-Haq	50.16
7530	Mohammad Yousuf	52.29
6565	Younis Khan	51.69
5768	Salim Malik	43.69
5062	Zaheer Abbas	44.79
4114	Mudassar Nazar	38.09
4052	Saeed Anwar	45.52
3931	Majid Khan	38.92
3915	Hanif Mohammad	43.98

Mohammad Yousuf was known as Yousuf Youhana until September 2005

Most wickets

		Avge
414	Wasim Akram	23.62
373	Waqar Younis	23.56
362	Imran Khan	22.81
261	Danish Kaneria	34.79
236	Abdul Qadir	32.80
208	Saqlain Mushtaq	29.83
185	Mushtaq Ahmed	32.97
178	Shoaib Akhtar	25.69
177	Sarfraz Nawaz	32.75
171	Iqbal Qasim	28.11

Six further bowlers have taken 100 wickets

Highest scores

337	Hanif Mohammad	v WI at Bridgetown	1957-58
329	Inzamam-ul-Haq	v NZ at Lahore	2001-02
313	Younis Khan	v Sri Lanka at Karachi	2008-09
280*	Javed Miandad	v India at Hyderabad	1982-83
274	Zaheer Abbas	v Eng at Birmingham	1971
271	Javed Miandad	v NZ at Auckland	1988-89
267	Younis Khan	v India at Bangalore	2004-05
260	Javed Miandad	v England at The Oval	1987
257*	Wasim Akram	v Zim at Sheikhupura	1996-97
240	Zaheer Abbas	v England at The Oval	1974

Hanif batted for 970 minutes, a Test record. Wasim Akram's innings included 12 sixes, a record for any Test innings

Best innings bowling

9-56	Abdul Qadir	v England at Lahore	1987-88
9-86	Sarfraz Nawaz	v Australia at Melbourne	1978-79
8-58	Imran Khan	v Sri Lanka at Lahore	1981-82
8-60	Imran Khan	v India at Karachi	1982-83
8-69	Sikander Bakht	v India at Delhi	1979-80
8-164	Saqlain Mushtaq	v England at Lahore	2000-01
7-40	Imran Khan	v England at Leeds	1987
7-42	Fazal Mahmood	v India at Lucknow	1952-53
7-49	Iqbal Qasim	v Australia at Karachi	1979-80
7-52	Intikhab Alam	v NZ at Dunedin	1972-73
7-52	Imran Khan	v Eng at Birmingham	1982

Wasim Akram took five or more wickets in a Test innings on 25 occasions, Imran Khan 23, Waqar Younis 22

Record wicket partnerships

1st	298	Aamer Sohail (160) and Ijaz Ahmed (151)	v West Indies at Karachi	1997-98
2nd	291	Zaheer Abbas (274) and Mushtaq Mohammad (100)	v England at Birmingham	1971
3rd	451	Mudassar Nazar (231) and Javed Miandad (280*)	v India at Hyderabad	1982-83
4th	350	Mushtaq Mohammad (201) and Asif Iqbal (175)	v New Zealand at Dunedin	1972-73
5th	281	Javed Miandad (163) and Asif Iqbal (166)	v New Zealand at Lahore	1976-77
6th	269	Mohammad Yousuf (223) and Kamran Akmal (154)	v England at Lahore	2005-06
7th	308	Waqar Hasan (189) and Imtiaz Ahmed (209)	v New Zealand at Lahore	1955-56
8th	313	Wasim Akram (257*) and Saqlain Mushtaq (79)	v Zimbabwe at Sheikhupura	1996-97
9th	190	Asif Iqbal (146) and Intikhab Alam (51)	v England at The Oval	1967
10th	151	Azhar Mahmood (128*) and Mushtaq Ahmed (59)	v South Africa at Rawalpindi	1997-98

Figures to 17.09.12. Updated records can be found at **www.cricinfo.com/ci/engine/records**

Test Match Records

PAKISTAN

Most catches

Fielders

93	Javed Miandad
88	Younis Khan
81	Inzamam-ul-Haq
65	Majid Khan
65	Mohammad Yousuf
65	Salim Malik

Most dismissals

Wicketkeepers   *Ct/St*

228	Wasim Bari	201/27
206	Kamran Akmal	184/22
147	Moin Khan	127/20
130	Rashid Latif	119/11
104	Salim Yousuf	91/13

Highest team totals

765-6d	v Sri Lanka at Karachi	2008-09
708	v England at The Oval	1987
699-5	v India at Lahore	1989-90
679-7d	v India at Lahore	2005-06
674-6	v India at Faisalabad	1984-85
657-8d	v West Indies at Bridgetown	1957-58
652	v India at Faisalabad	1982-83
643	v New Zealand at Lahore	2001-02
636-8d	v England at Lahore	2005-06
624	v Australia at Adelaide	1983-84

Pakistan have made four other scores of 600 or more, and one of 599-7d

Lowest team totals

Completed innings

53*	v Australia at Sharjah†	2002-03
59	v Australia at Sharjah†	2002-03
62	v Australia at Perth	1981-82
72	v Australia at Perth	2004-05
72	v England at Birmingham	2010
74	v England at Lord's	2010
77*	v West Indies at Lahore	1986-87
80	v England at Nottingham	2010
87	v England at Lord's	1954
90	v England at Manchester	1954
90	v Sri Lanka at Colombo	2009

* One batsman retired hurt or absent hurt.

† Same match

Best match bowling

14-116	Imran Khan	v Sri Lanka at Lahore	1981-82
13-101	Abdul Qadir	v England at Lahore	1987-88
13-114	Fazal Mahmood	v Australia at Karachi	1956-57
13-135	Waqar Younis	v Zimbabwe at Karachi	1993-94
12-94	Fazal Mahmood	v India at Lucknow	1952-53
12-94	Danish Kaneria	v Bangladesh at Multan	2001-02
12-99	Fazal Mahmood	v England at The Oval	1954
12-100	Fazal Mahmood	v West Indies at Dacca	1958-59
12-130	Waqar Younis	v NZ at Faisalabad	1990-91
12-165	Imran Khan	v Australia at Sydney	1976-77

Imran Khan took ten or more wickets in a match six times, Abdul Qadir, Waqar Younis and Wasim Akram five each

Hat-tricks

Wasim Akram	v Sri Lanka at Lahore	1998-99
Wasim Akram	v Sri Lanka at Dhaka	1998-99
Abdul Razzaq	v Sri Lanka at Galle	1999-2000
Mohammad Sami	v Sri Lanka at Lahore	2001-02

Wasim Akram's hat-tricks came in successive matches: he also took Pakistan's first two hat-tricks in one-day internationals.

RS Kaluwitharana was the first victim in both Wasim Akram's first hat-trick and in Abdul Razzaq's

Pakistan's Test match results

	Played	Won	Lost	Drawn	Tied	% win
v Australia	57	12	28	17	0	21.05
v Bangladesh	8	8	0	0	0	100.00
v England	74	16	22	36	0	21.62
v India	59	12	9	38	0	20.33
v New Zealand	50	23	7	20	0	46.00
v South Africa	18	3	8	7	0	16.66
v Sri Lanka	43	16	10	17	0	37.20
v West Indies	46	16	15	15	0	34.78
v Zimbabwe	15	9	2	4	0	60.00
TOTAL	**370**	**115**	**101**	**154**	**0**	**31.08**

Figures to 17.09.12. Updated records can be found at **www.cricinfo.com/ci/engine/records**

PAKISTAN
One-day International Records

Most appearances

375	Inzamam-ul-Haq
356	Wasim Akram
344	Shahid Afridi
283	Salim Malik
281	Mohammad Yousuf
262	Waqar Younis
261	Abdul Razzaq
250	Ijaz Ahmed
247	Saeed Anwar
245	Younis Khan

Javed Miandad (233), Moin Khan (219) and Shoaib Malik (203) also played in more than 200 ODIs

Most runs

		Avge
11701	Inzamam-ul-Haq	39.53
9554	Mohammad Yousuf	42.08
8824	Saeed Anwar	39.21
7381	Javed Miandad	41.70
7170	Salim Malik	32.88
7038	Shahid Afridi	23.61
6824	Younis Khan	32.18
6564	Ijaz Ahmed	32.33
5841	Rameez Raja	32.09
5253	Shoaib Malik	33.03

Abdul Razzaq (5031) and Aamer Sohail (4780) also scored more than 4000 runs

Most wickets

		Avge
502	Wasim Akram	23.52
416	Waqar Younis	23.84
346	Shahid Afridi	33.71
288	Saqlain Mushtaq	21.78
268	Abdul Razzaq	31.53
241	Shoaib Akhtar	24.70
182	Aqib Javed	31.43
182	Imran Khan	26.61
161	Mushtaq Ahmed	33.29
158	Umar Gul	27.79

Seven further bowlers have taken 100 wickets for Pakistan ODIs

Highest scores

194	Saeed Anwar	v India at Chennai	1996-97
160	Imran Nazir	v Zimbabwe at Kingston	2006–07
144	Younis Khan	v Hong Kong at Colombo	2004
143	Shoaib Malik	v India at Colombo	2004
141*	Mohammad Yousuf	v Zim at Bulawayo	2002-03
140	Saeed Anwar	v India at Dhaka	1997-98
139*	Ijaz Ahmed	v India at Lahore	1997-98
139*	Mohammad Hafeez	v Zimbabwe at Harare	2011
137*	Inzamam-ul-Haq	v N Zealand at Sharjah	1993-94
137	Ijaz Ahmed	v England at Sharjah	1998-99

Saeed Anwar scored 20 centuries, Mohammad Yousuf 15, Ijaz Ahmed and Inzamam-ul-Haq 10

Best innings bowling

7-36	Waqar Younis	v England at Leeds	2001
7-37	Aqib Javed	v India at Sharjah	1991-92
6-14	Imran Khan	v India at Sharjah	1984-85
6-16	Shoaib Akhtar	v New Zealand at Karachi	2001-02
6-18	Azhar Mahmood	v W Indies at Sharjah	1999-2000
6-26	Waqar Younis	v Sri Lanka at Sharjah	1989-90
6-27	Naved-ul-Hasan	v India at Jamshedpur	2004-05
6-30	Waqar Younis	v N Zealand at Auckland	1993-94
6-35	Abdul Razzaq	v Bangladesh at Dhaka	2001-02
6-38	Shahid Afridi	v Australia at Dubai	2008-09

Waqar Younis took five or more wickets 13 times (the ODI record), Shahid Afridi 8, Saqlain Mushtaq and Wasim Akram 6

Record wicket partnerships

1st	228*	Mohammad Hafeez (139*) and Imran Farhat (75*)	v Zimbabwe at Harare	2011
2nd	263	Aamer Sohail (134) and Inzamam-ul-Haq (137*)	v New Zealand at Sharjah	1993-94
3rd	230	Saeed Anwar (140) and Ijaz Ahmed (117)	v India at Dhaka	1997-98
4th	206	Shoaib Malik (128) and Mohammad Yousuf (87)	v India at Centurion	2009-10
5th	176	Younis Khan (89) and Umar Akmal (102*)	v Sri Lanka at Colombo	2009
6th	144	Imran Khan (102*) and Shahid Mahboob (77)	v Sri Lanka at Leeds	1983
7th	124	Mohammad Yousuf (91*) and Rashid Latif (66)	v Australia at Cardiff	2001
8th	100	Fawad Alam (63*) and Sohail Tanvir (59)	v Hong Kong at Karachi	2008
9th	73	Shoaib Malik (52*) and Mohammad Sami (46)	v South Africa at Centurion	2006-07
10th	103	Mohammad Aamer (73*) and Saeed Ajmal (33)	v New Zealand at Abu Dhabi	2009-10

Figures to 17.09.12. Updated records can be found at www.cricinfo.com/ci/engine/records

One-day International Records

Most catches

Fielders

122	Younis Khan
113	Inzamam-ul-Haq
112	Shahid Afridi
90	Ijaz Ahmed
88	Wasim Akram

Most dismissals

Wicketkeepers

		Ct/St
287	Moin Khan	214/73
220	Rashid Latif	182/38
164	Kamran Akmal	137/27
103	Salim Yousuf	81/22
62	Wasim Bari	52/10

Highest team totals

385-7	v Bangladesh at Dambulla	2010
371-9	v Sri Lanka at Nairobi	1996-97
353-6	v England at Karachi	2005-06
351-4	v South Africa at Durban	2006-07
349	v Zimbabwe at Kingston	2006-07
347-5	v Zimbabwe at at Karachi	2007-08
344-5	v Zimbabwe at Bulawayo	2002-03
344-8	v India at Karachi	2003-04
343-5	v Hong Kong at Colombo	2004
338-5	v Sri Lanka at Swansea	1983

Pakistan have reached 300 on 44 further occasions

Lowest team totals

Completed innings

43	v W Indies at Cape Town	1992-93
71	v W Indies at Brisbane	1992-93
74	v England at Adelaide	1991-92
75	v Sri Lanka at Lahore	2008-09
81	v West Indies at Sydney	1992-93
85	v England at Manchester	1978
87	v India at Sharjah	1984-85
89	v S Africa at Mohali	2006-07
107	v S Africa at Cape Town	2006-07
108	v Australia at Nairobi	2002-03

Against India in 1984-85 Pakistan were chasing only 126 to win

Most sixes

296	Shahid Afridi
143	Inzamam-ul-Haq
124	Abdul Razzaq
121	Wasim Akram
97	Saeed Anwar
87	Ijaz Ahmed
87	Mohammad Yousuf
61	Moin Khan
59	Shoaib Malik
52	Younis Khan

Afridi hit 2 other sixes in official ODIs

Best strike rate

Runs per 100 balls

		Runs
113.69	Shahid Afridi	7038
94.82	Nasir Jamshed	714
89.60	Manzoor Elahi	741
88.33	Wasim Akram	3717
84.80	Zaheer Abbas	2572
84.77	Umar Akmal	1976
84.51	Naved-ul-Hasan	524
84.07	Kamran Akmal	2930
81.67	Abdul Razzaq	5031
81.30	Moin Khan	3266

Qualification: 500 runs

Most economical bowlers

Runs per over

		Wkts
3.63	Sarfraz Nawaz	63
3.71	Akram Raza	38
3.89	Imran Khan	182
3.89	Wasim Akram	502
4.04	Mohammad Hafeez	89
4.06	Abdul Qadir	132
4.14	Arshad Khan	56
4.14	Saeed Ajmal	109
4.14	Tauseef Ahmed	55
4.24	Mudassar Nazar	111

Qualification: 2000 balls bowled

Pakistan's one-day international results

	Played	Won	Lost	Tied	No result	% win
v Australia	89	31	54	1	3	36.62
v Bangladesh	31	30	1	0	0	96.77
v England	72	28	42	0	2	40.00
v India	121	69	48	0	4	58.97
v New Zealand	89	51	35	1	2	59.19
v South Africa	57	18	38	0	1	32.14
v Sri Lanka	132	77	50	1	4	60.54
v West Indies	120	52	66	2	0	44.16
v Zimbabwe	44	40	2	1	1	94.18
v others (see below)	22	21	1	0	0	95.45
TOTAL	777	417	337	6	17	55.26

Other teams: Afghanistan (P1, W1), Canada (P2, W2), Hong Kong (P2, W2), Ireland (P3, W2, L1), Kenya (P6, W6), Namibia (P1, W1), Netherlands (P3, W3), Scotland (P2, W2), United Arab Emirates (P2, W2).

SOUTH AFRICA *Test Match Records*

Most appearances

154	JH Kallis	
146	MV Boucher	
108	SM Pollock	
101	G Kirsten	
101	M Ntini	
101	GC Smith	
90	HH Gibbs	
77	AB de Villiers	
72	AA Donald	
70	DJ Cullinan	

Kallis, Boucher and Smith all also played one Test for the World XI against Australia

Most runs

		Avge
12558	JH Kallis	56.82
8302	GC Smith	50.31
7289	G Kirsten	45.27
6167	HH Gibbs	41.95
5618	AB de Villiers	48.85
5498	MV Boucher	30.54
4946	HM Amla	49.95
4554	DJ Cullinan	44.21
3781	SM Pollock	32.31
3714	WJ Cronje	36.41

Kallis (83 runs), Smith (12) and Boucher (17) also played one Test for the World XI against Australia

Most wickets

		Avge
421	SM Pollock	23.11
390	M Ntini	28.82
330	AA Donald	22.25
287	DW Steyn	23.50
279	JH Kallis	32.61
170	HJ Tayfield	25.91
150	M Morkel	30.36
134	PR Adams	32.87
123	TL Goddard	26.22
123	A Nel	31.86

Four other bowlers have also taken 100 wickets. Kallis also took one wicket for the World XI

Highest scores

311*	HM Amla	v England at The Oval	2012
278*	AB de Villiers	v Pakistan at Abu Dhabi	2010-11
277	GC Smith	v England at Birmingham	2003
275*	DJ Cullinan	v New Zealand at Auckland	1998-99
275	G Kirsten	v England at Durban	1999-2000
274	RG Pollock	v Australia at Durban	1969-70
259	GC Smith	v England at Lord's	2003
255*	DJ McGlew	v New Zealand at Wellington	1952-53
253*	HM Amla	v India at Nagpur	2009-10
236	EAB Rowan	v England at Leeds	1951

Smith's 277 and 259 were in consecutive matches

Best innings bowling

9-113	HJ Tayfield	v England at Johannesburg	1956-57
8-53	GB Lawrence	v N Zealand at Johannesburg	1961-62
8-64	L Klusener	v India at Calcutta	1996-97
8-69	HJ Tayfield	v England at Durban	1956-57
8-70	SJ Snooke	v England at Johannesburg	1905-06
8-71	AA Donald	v Zimbabwe at Harare	1995-96
7-23	HJ Tayfield	v Australia at Durban	1949-50
7-29	GF Bissett	v England at Durban	1927-28
7-37	M Ntini	v W Indies at Port-of-Spain	2004-05
7-51	DW Steyn	v India at Nagpur	2009-10

Klusener was making his Test debut

Record wicket partnerships

1st	415	ND McKenzie (226) and GC Smith (232)	v Bangladesh at Chittagong	2007-08
2nd	315*	HH Gibbs (211*) and JH Kallis (148*)	v New Zealand at Christchurch	1998-99
3rd	429*	JA Rudolph (222*) and HH Dippenaar (177*)	v Bangladesh at Chittagong	2002-03
4th	249	JH Kallis (177) and G Kirsten (137)	v West Indies at Durban	2003-04
5th	267	JH Kallis (147) and AG Prince (131)	v West Indies at St John's	2004-05
6th	271	AG Prince (162*) and MV Boucher (117)	v Bangladesh at Centurion	2008-09
7th	246	DJ McGlew (255*) and ARA Murray (109)	v New Zealand at Wellington	1952-53
8th	150	ND McKenzie (103) and SM Pollock (111)	v Sri Lanka at Centurion	2000-01
	150	G Kirsten (130) and M Zondeki (59)	v England at Leeds	2003
9th	195	MV Boucher (78) and PL Symcox (108)	v Pakistan at Johannesburg	1997-98
10th	107*	AB de Villiers (278*) and M Morkel (35*)	v Pakistan at Abu Dhabi	2010-11

*Figures to 17.09.12. Updated records can be found at **www.cricinfo.com/ci/engine/records***

Test Match Records — SOUTH AFRICA

Most catches

Fielders

183	JH Kallis	
134	GC Smith	
94	HH Gibbs	
89	AB de Villiers	
83	G Kirsten	

Most dismissals

Wicketkeepers — Ct/St

553	MV Boucher	530/23
152	DJ Richardson	150/2
141	JHB Waite	124/17
56	DT Lindsay	54/2
51	HB Cameron	39/12

Highest team totals

682-6d	v England at Lord's	2003
658-9d	v West Indies at Durban	2003-04
651	v Australia at Cape Town	2008-09
637-2d	v England at The Oval	2012
622-9d	v Australia at Durban	1969-70
621-5d	v New Zealand at Auckland	1998-99
620-4d	v India at Centurion	2010-11
620-7d	v Pakistan at Cape Town	2002-03
620	v Australia at Johannesburg	1966-67
604-6d	v West Indies at Centurion	2003-04

South Africa also scored 600-3d against Zimbabwe at Harare in 2001-02

Lowest team totals

Completed innings

30	v Eng at Port Elizabeth	1895-96
30	v Eng at Birmingham	1924
35	v Eng at Cape Town	1898-99
36	v Aust at Melbourne	1931-32
43	v Eng at Cape Town	1888-89
45	v Aust at Melbourne	1931-32
47	v Eng at Cape Town	1888-89
58	v England at Lord's	1912
72	v Eng at Johannesburg	1956-57
72	v Eng at Cape Town	1956-57

South Africa's lowest total since their return to Test cricket in 1991-92 is 84 against India at Johannesburg in 2006-07

Best match bowling

13-132	M Ntini	v W Indies at Port-of-Spain	2004-05
13-165	HJ Tayfield	v Australia at Melbourne	1952-53
13-192	HJ Tayfield	v England at Johannesburg	1956-57
12-127	SJ Snooke	v England at Johannesburg	1905-06
12-139	AA Donald	v India at Port Elizabeth	1992-93
12-181	AEE Vogler	v England at Johannesburg	1909-10
11-112	AE Hall	v England at Cape Town	1922-23
11-113	AA Donald	v Zimbabwe at Harare	1995-96
11-127	AA Donald	v England at Jo'burg	1999-2000
11-150	EP Nupen	v England at Jo'burg	1930-31

Hall was making his Test debut. His performance, and Vogler's, were at the old Wanderers ground in Johannesburg

Hat-tricks

GM Griffin	v England at Lord's	1960

Griffin achieved the feat in his second and final Test (he was no-balled for throwing in the same match).

GA Lohmann (for England at Port Elizabeth in 1895-96), TJ Matthews (twice in the same match for Australia at Manchester in 1912) and TWJ Goddard (for England at Johannesburg in 1938-39) have taken Test hat-tricks against South Africa

South Africa's Test match results

	Played	Won	Lost	Drawn	Tied	% win
v Australia	85	19	48	18	0	22.35
v Bangladesh	8	8	0	0	0	100.00
v England	141	31	56	54	0	21.98
v India	27	12	7	8	0	44.44
v New Zealand	38	21	4	13	0	55.26
v Pakistan	18	8	3	7	0	44.44
v Sri Lanka	20	10	5	5	0	50.00
v West Indies	25	16	3	6	0	64.00
v Zimbabwe	7	6	0	1	0	85.71
TOTAL	369	131	126	112	0	35.50

Figures to 17.09.12. Updated records can be found at www.cricinfo.com/ci/engine/records

SOUTH AFRICA *One-day International Records*

Most appearances

316	JH Kallis
294	SM Pollock
290	MV Boucher
248	HH Gibbs
245	JN Rhodes
188	WJ Cronje
185	G Kirsten
185	GC Smith
172	M Ntini
171	L Klusener

Kallis, Pollock, Boucher, Ntini and Smith also appeared in official ODIs for composite teams

Most runs

		Avge
11469	JH Kallis	46.06
8094	HH Gibbs	36.13
6798	G Kirsten	40.95
6698	GC Smith	38.94
5935	JN Rhodes	35.11
5565	WJ Cronje	38.64
5018	AB de Villiers	50.18
4523	MV Boucher	28.44
3860	DJ Cullinan	32.99
3576	L Klusener	41.10

Kallis (29 runs), Smith (0), Boucher (163) and de Villiers (150) also appeared in official ODIs for composite teams

Most wickets

		Avge
387	SM Pollock	24.31
272	AA Donald	21.78
266	JH Kallis	31.75
265	M Ntini	24.53
192	L Klusener	29.95
114	WJ Cronje	34.78
106	A Nel	27.68
100	CK Langeveldt	29.62
95	N Boje	35.27
95	PS de Villiers	27.74
95	AJ Hall	26.47

Pollock, Ntini, Kallis and Boje also appeared in ODIs for composite teams

Highest scores

188*	G Kirsten	v UAE at Rawalpindi	1995-96
175	HH Gibbs	v Australia at Johannesburg	2005-06
169*	DJ Callaghan	v N Zealand at Verwoerdburg	1994-95
161	AC Hudson	v Netherlands at Rawalpindi	1995-96
153	HH Gibbs	v B'desh at Potchefstroom	2002-03
150	HM Amla	v England at Southampton	2012
147*	MV Boucher	v Zimbabwe at Potchefstroom	2006-07
146	AB de Villiers	v West Indies at St George's	2006-07
143	HH Gibbs	v N Zealand at Johannesburg	2002-03
141	GC Smith	v England at Centurion	2009-10

Gibbs has scored 21 one-day hundreds, Kallis 17, de Villiers and Kirsten 13, and Amla 10

Best bowling figures

6-22	M Ntini	v Australia at Cape Town	2005-06
6-23	AA Donald	v Kenya at Nairobi	1996-97
6-35	SM Pollock	v W Indies at East London	1998-99
6-49	L Klusener	v Sri Lanka at Lahore	1997-98
5-18	AJ Hall	v England at Bridgetown	2006-07
5-20	SM Pollock	v Eng at Johannesburg	1999-2000
5-21	L Klusener	v Kenya at Amstelveen	1999
5-21	N Boje	v Australia at Cape Town	2001-02
5-21	M Ntini	v Pakistan at Mohali	2006-07
5-23	SM Pollock	v Pakistan at Johannesburg	2006-07

Klusener has taken five wickets in an ODI innings six times, Pollock five and Ntini four

Record wicket partnerships

1st	235	G Kirsten (115) and HH Gibbs (111)	v India at Kochi	1999-2000
2nd	209	G Kirsten (124) and ND McKenzie (131*)	v Kenya at Cape Town	2001-02
3rd	221	HM Amla (113) and AB de Villiers (134)	v Netherlands at Mohali	2010-11
4th	232	DJ Cullinan (124) and JN Rhodes (121)	v Pakistan at Nairobi	1996-97
5th	183*	JH Kallis (109*) and JN Rhodes (94*)	v Pakistan at Durban	1997-98
6th	137	WJ Cronje (70*) and SM Pollock (75)	v Zimbabwe at Johannesburg	1996-97
7th	114	MV Boucher (68) and L Klusener (75*)	v India at Nagpur	1999-2000
8th	138*	JM Kemp (100*) and AJ Hall (56*)	v India at Cape Town	2006-07
9th	65	WD Parnell (49) and DW Steyn (35)	v India at Jaipur	2009-10
10th	67*	JA Morkel (23*) and M Ntini (42*)	v New Zealand at Napier	2003-04

Figures to 17.09.12. Updated records can be found at **www.cricinfo.com/ci/engine/records**

Most catches

Fielders

125	JH Kallis
108	HH Gibbs
105	JN Rhodes
104	SM Pollock
98	GC Smith

Most dismissals

	Wicketkeepers	*Ct/St*
415	MV Boucher	394/21
165	DJ Richardson	148/17
71	AB de Villiers	68/3
9	SJ Palframan	9/0
8	MN van Wyk	7/1

Highest team totals

438-9	v Australia at Johannesburg	2005-06
418-5	v Zimbabwe at Potchefstroom	2006-07
399-6	v Zimbabwe at Benoni	2010-11
392-6	v Pakistan at Centurion	2006-07
365-2	v India at Ahmedabad	2009-10
363-3	v Zimbabwe at Bulawayo	2001-02
358-4	v Bangladesh at Benoni	2008-09
356-4	v West Indies at St George's	2006-07
354-3	v Kenya at Cape Town	2001-02
354-6	v England at Cape Town	2009-10

438-9 was the highest total in all ODIs at the time, and came from 49.5 overs; all the others above were scored in 50 overs, apart from 353-3 (40)

Lowest team totals

Completed innings

69	v Australia at Sydney	1993-94
83	v England at Nottingham	2008
101*	v Pakistan at Sharjah	1999-2000
106	v Australia at Sydney	2001-02
107	v England at Lord's	2003
107	v England at Lord's	2003
108	v NZ at Mumbai	2006-07
119	v Eng at Port Elizabeth	2009-10
123	v Aust at Wellington	1994-95
129	v Eng at East London	1995-96
129	v Aust at Centurion	2011-12

* One batsman retired hurt

Most sixes

136	JH Kallis
128	HH Gibbs
94	WJ Cronje
84	AB de Villiers
81	MV Boucher
76	L Klusener
55	SM Pollock
52	JM Kemp
47	JN Rhodes
43	GC Smith

Boucher (2), Pollock (3), Kemp (1) and de Villiers (4) also hit sixes for the Africa XI

Best strike rate

Runs per 100 balls		*Runs*
101.33	JA Morkel	760
93.21	AB de Villiers	5018
91.72	HM Amla	3216
89.91	L Klusener	3576
89.29	N Boje	1410
88.38	F du Plessis	563
85.55	SM Pollock	3193
84.66	MV Boucher	4523
83.61	PL Symcox	694
83.60	JP Duminy	2601

Qualification: 500 runs

Most economical bowlers

Runs per over		*Wkts*
3.57	PS de Villiers	95
3.65	SM Pollock	387
3.94	CR Matthews	79
4.15	AA Donald	272
4.15	PL Symcox	72
4.28	BM McMillan	70
4.44	WJ Cronje	114
4.50	RP Snell	44
4.51	N Boje	95
4.51	AJ Hall	95
4.51	M Ntini	265

Qualification: 2000 balls bowled

South Africa's one-day international results

	Played	Won	Lost	Tied	No result	% win
v Australia	80	36	41	3	0	46.87
v Bangladesh	14	13	1	0	0	92.85
v England	50	25	21	1	3	54.25
v India	66	40	24	0	2	62.50
v New Zealand	55	33	18	0	4	64.70
v Pakistan	57	38	18	0	1	67.85
v Sri Lanka	51	25	24	1	1	51.00
v West Indies	51	38	12	0	1	76.00
v Zimbabwe	32	29	2	0	1	93.54
v others (see below)	19	19	0	0	0	100.00
TOTAL	**475**	**296**	**161**	**5**	**13**	**64.61**

Other teams: Canada (P1, W1), Ireland (P3, W3), Kenya (P10, W10), Netherlands (P3, W3), Scotland (P1, W1), United Arab Emirates (P1, W1).

SRI LANKA
Test Match Records

Most appearances

133	DPMD Jayawardene	
132	M Muralitharan	
111	KC Sangakkara	
111	WPUJC Vaas	
110	ST Jayasuriya	
93	PA de Silva	
93	A Ranatunga	
90	MS Atapattu	
83	HP Tillekeratne	
81	TM Dilshan	

Ranatunga uniquely played in his country's first Test and their 100th

Most runs

		Avge
10540	DPMD Jayawardene	50.43
9872	KC Sangakkara	56.73
6973	ST Jayasuriya	40.07
6361	PA de Silva	42.97
5502	MS Atapattu	39.02
5283	TT Samaraweera	51.29
5105	A Ranatunga	35.69
5028	TM Dilshan	41.21
4545	HP Tillekeratne	42.87
3089	WPUJC Vaas	24.32

RS Mahanama (2576) and AP Gurusinha (2452) also scored 2000 runs

Most wickets

		Avge
795	M Muralitharan	22.67
355	WPUJC Vaas	29.58
154	HMRKB Herath	31.72
101	SL Malinga	33.15
100	CRD Fernando	37.84
98	ST Jayasuriya	34.34
85	GP Wickremasinghe	41.87
73	RJ Ratnayake	35.10
69	HDPK Dharmasena	42.31
64	DNT Zoysa	33.70

Muralitharan also took 5 wickets for the World XI

Highest scores

374	DPMD Jayawardene	v SA at Colombo	2006
340	ST Jayasuriya	v India at Colombo	1997-98
287	KC Sangakkara	v SA at Colombo	2006
275	DPMD Jayawardene	v Ind at Ahmedabad	2009-10
270	KC Sangakkara	v Zim at Bulawayo	2003-04
267	PA de Silva	v NZ at Wellington	1990-91
253	ST Jayasuriya	v Pak at Faisalabad	2004-05
249	MS Atapattu	v Zim at Bulawayo	2003-04
242	DPMD Jayawardene	v India at Colombo	1998-99
240	DPMD Jayawardene	v Pak at Karachi	2008-09

Jayawardene has made 31 Test centuries, Sangakkara 30, de Silva 20 and Atapattu 16

Best innings bowling

9-51	M Muralitharan	v Zimbabwe at Kandy	2001-02
9-65	M Muralitharan	v England at The Oval	1998
8-46	M Muralitharan	v West Indies at Kandy	2005
8-70	M Muralitharan	v England at Nottingham	2006
8-83	JR Ratnayeke	v Pakistan at Sialkot	1985-86
8-87	M Muralitharan	v India at Colombo	2001-02
7-46	M Muralitharan	v England at Galle	2003-04
7-71	WPUJC Vaas	v West Indies at Colombo	2001-02
7-84	M Muralitharan	v South Africa at Galle	2000-01
7-94	M Muralitharan	v Zimbabwe at Kandy	1997-98

Muralitharan took five or more wickets in an innings a record 67 times

Record wicket partnerships

1st	335	MS Atapattu (207*) and ST Jayasuriya (188)	v Pakistan at Kandy	2000
2nd	576	ST Jayasuriya (340) and RS Mahanama (225)	v India at Colombo	1997-98
3rd	624	KC Sangakkara (287) and DPMD Jayawardene (374)	v South Africa at Colombo	2006
4th	437	DPMD Jayawardene (240) and TT Samaraweera (231)	v Pakistan at Karachi	2008-09
5th	280	TT Samaraweera (138) and TM Dilshan (168)	v Bangladesh at Colombo	2005-06
6th	351	DPMD Jayawardene (275) and HAPW Jayawardene (154*)	v India at Ahmedabad	2009-10
7th	223*	HAPW Jayawardene (120*) and WPUJC Vaas (100*)	v Bangladesh at Colombo	2007
8th	170	DPMD Jayawardene (237) and WPUJC Vaas (69)	v South Africa at Galle	2004-05
9th	118	TT Samaraweera (83) and BAW Mendis (78)	v India at Colombo	2010
10th	79	WPUJC Vaas (68*) and M Muralitharan (43)	v Australia at Kandy	2003-04

*Figures to 17.09.12. Updated records can be found at **www.cricinfo.com/ci/engine/records***

Test Match Records

SRI LANKA

Most catches

Fielders

187	DPMD Jayawardene	
89	HP Tillekeratne	
78	ST Jayasuriya	
75	TM Dilshan	
70	M Muralitharan	

Most dismissals

Wicketkeepers		Ct/St
151	KC Sangakkara	131/20
120	HAPW Jayawardene	93/27
119	RS Kaluwitharana	93/26
35	HP Tillekeratne	33/2
34	SAR Silva	33/1

Highest team totals

952-6d	v India at Colombo	1997-98
760-7d	v India at Ahmedabad	2009-10
756-5d	v South Africa at Colombo	2006
713-3d	v Zimbabwe at Bulawayo	2003-04
644-7d	v Pakistan at Karachi	2008-09
642-4d	v India at Colombo	2010
628-8d	v England at Colombo	2003-04
627-9d	v West Indies at Colombo	2001-02
610-6d	v India at Colombo	2001-02
606	v Pakistan at Lahore	2008-09

952-6d is the highest total in all Tests. In all
Sri Lanka have reached 500 on 27 occasions

Lowest team totals

Completed innings

71	v Pakistan at Kandy	1994-95
73*	v Pakistan at Kandy	2005-06
81	v England at Colombo	2000-01
82	v India at Chandigarh	1990-91
82	v England at Cardiff	2011
93	v NZ at Wellington	1982-83
95	v S Africa at Cape Town	2000-01
97	v N Zealand at Kandy	1983-84
97	v Australia at Darwin	2004
101	v Pakistan at Kandy	1985-86

* One batsman absent hurt

Best match bowling

16-220	M Muralitharan	v England at The Oval	1998
14-191	WPUJC Vaas	v West Indies at Colombo	2001-02
13-115	M Muralitharan	v Zimbabwe at Kandy	2001-02
13-171	M Muralitharan	v South Africa at Galle	2000
12-82	M Muralitharan	v Bangladesh at Kandy	2007
12-117	M Muralitharan	v Zimbabwe at Kandy	1997-98
12-171	HMRKB Herath	v England at Galle	2011-12
12-225	M Muralitharan	v South Africa at Colombo	2006
11-93	M Muralitharan	v England at Galle	2003-04
11-110	M Muralitharan	v India at Colombo	2008

Muralitharan took ten or more wickets in a match a record
22 times; the only others to do it for Sri Lanka are Vaas (twice),
UDU Chandana, Herath and BAW Mendis

Hat-tricks

DNT Zoysa	v Zimbabwe at Harare	1999-2000

He dismissed TR Gripper, MW Goodwin and NC
Johnson with the first three balls of his first over, the
second of the match.

Four hat-tricks have been taken against Sri Lanka in
Tests, all of them for Pakistan: two by Wasim Akram (in
successive Tests in the Asian Test Championship at
Lahore and Dhaka in 1998-99), Abdul Razzaq (at Galle
in 2000-01) and Mohammad Sami (at Lahore in
2001-02)

Sri Lanka's Test match results

	Played	Won	Lost	Drawn	Tied	% win
v Australia	23	1	14	8	0	4.34
v Bangladesh	12	12	0	0	0	100.00
v England	26	7	10	9	0	26.92
v India	35	6	14	15	0	17.14
v New Zealand	26	7	9	10	0	26.92
v Pakistan	43	10	16	17	0	23.25
v South Africa	20	5	10	5	0	25.00
v West Indies	15	6	3	6	0	40.00
v Zimbabwe	15	10	0	5	0	66.66
TOTAL	215	64	76	75	0	29.76

Figures to 17.09.12. Updated records can be found at **www.cricinfo.com/ci/engine/records**

SRI LANKA
One-day International Records

Most appearances

441	ST Jayasuriya	
377	DPMD Jayawardene	
343	M Muralitharan	
326	KC Sangakkara	
321	WPUJC Vaas	
308	PA de Silva	
269	A Ranatunga	
268	MS Atapattu	
248	TM Dilshan	
213	RS Mahanama	

HP Tillekeratne also played in 200 ODIs

Most runs

		Avge
13664	ST Jayasuriya	32.51
10583	KC Sangakkara	38.62
10503	DPMD Jayawardene	32.92
9284	PA de Silva	34.90
8529	MS Atapattu	37.57
7456	A Ranatunga	35.84
6715	TM Dilshan	35.15
5162	RS Mahanama	29.49
4828	WU Tharanga	34.73
3950	RP Arnold	35.26

AP Gurnsinha (3902), HP Tillekeratne (3789) and RS Kaluwitharana (3711) also scored 3000 runs

Most wickets

		Avge
523	M Muralitharan	23.07
399	WPUJC Vaas	27.45
320	ST Jayasuriya	36.67
200	SL Malinga	26.57
183	CRD Fernando	30.66
151	UDU Chandana	31.72
138	HDPK Dharmasena	36.21
133	MF Maharoof	26.80
132	KMDN Kulasekara	33.74
109	GP Wickremasinghe	39.64

DNT Zoysa (108) and PA de Silva (106) also took 100 wickets

Highest scores

189	ST Jayasuriya	v India at Sharjah	2000-01
160*	TM Dilshan	v India at Hobart	2011-12
160	TM Dilshan	v India at Rajkot	2009-10
157	ST Jayasuriya	v Netherlands at Amstelveen	2006
152	ST Jayasuriya	v England at Leeds	2006
151*	ST Jayasuriya	v India at Mumbai	1996-97
145	PA de Silva	v Kenya at Kandy	1995-96
144	TM Dilshan	v Zimbabwe at Pallekele	2010-11
144	DPMD J'dene	v England at Leeds	2011
140	ST Jayasuriya	v N Zealand at Bloemfontein	1994-95

Jayasuriya has scored 28 centuries, Jayawardene and KC Sangakkara 14, Dilshan 13, WU Tharanga 12, MS Atapattu and de Silva 11

Best bowling figures

8-19	WPUJC Vaas	v Zimbabwe at Colombo	2001-02
7-30	M Muralitharan	v India at Sharjah	2000-01
6-13	BAW Mendis	v India at Karachi	2008
6-14	MF Maharoof	v West Indies at Mumbai	2006-07
6-20	AD Mathews	v India at Colombo	2008-09
6-25	WPUJC Vaas	v B'desh at P'maritzburg	2002-03
6-27	CRD Fernando	v England at Colombo	2007-08
6-29	ST Jayasuriya	v England at Moratuwa	1992-93
6-29	BAW Mendis	v Zimbabwe at Harare	2008-09
6-38	SL Malinga	v Kenya at Colombo	2010-11

Vaas's 8-19 are the best bowling figures in all ODIs. In his 6-25 Vaas took a hat-trick with the first three balls of the match, and four wickets in all in the first over

Record wicket partnerships

1st	286	WU Tharanga (109) and ST Jayasuriya (152)	v England at Leeds	2006
2nd	200	TM Dilshan (160*) and KC Sangakkara (105)	v India at Hobart	2011-12
3rd	226	MS Atapattu (102*) and DPMD Jayawardene (128)	v India at Sharjah	2000-01
4th	171*	RS Mahanama (94*) and A Ranatunga (87*)	v West Indies at Lahore	1997-98
5th	166	ST Jayasuriya (189) and RP Arnold (52*)	v India at Sharjah	2000-01
6th	159	LPC Silva (67) and CK Kapugedera (95)	v West Indies at Port-of-Spain	2007-08
7th	126*	DPMD Jayawardene (94*) and UDU Chandana (44*)	v India at Dambulla	2005-06
8th	91	HDPK Dharmasena (51*) and DK Liyanage (43)	v West Indies at Port-of-Spain	1996-97
9th	132	AD Mathews (77*) and SL Malinga (56)	v Australia at Melbourne	2010-11
10th	51	RP Arnold (103) and KSC de Silva (2*)	v Zimbabwe at Bulawayo	1999-2000

Figures to 17.09.12. Updated records can be found at **www.cricinfo.com/ci/engine/records**

One-day International Records

SRI LANKA

Most catches

Fielders
186	DPMD Jayawardene
128	M Muralitharan
123	ST Jayasuriya
109	RS Mahanama
95	PA de Silva

Most dismissals

Wicketkeepers
		Ct/St
381	KC Sangakkara	303/78
206	RS Kaluwitharana	131/75
45	HP Tillekeratne	39/6
34	DSBP Kuruppu	26/8
30	RG de Alwis	27/3

Highest team totals

443-9	v Netherlands at Amstelveen	2006
411-8	v India at Rajkot	2009-10
398-5	v Kenya at Kandy	1995-96
357-9	v Bangladesh at Lahore	2008
349-9	v Pakistan at Singapore	1995-96
343-5	v Australia at Sydney	2002-03
339-4	v Pakistan at Mohali	1996-97
332-7	v Canada at Hambantota	2010-11
332-8	v Bangladesh at Karachi	2008
329	v West Indies at Sharjah	1995-96

Sri Lanka scored 324-2 in 37.3 overs against England at Leeds in 2006

Lowest team totals

Completed innings
43	v S Africa at Paarl	2011-12
55	v W Indies at Sharjah	1986-87
78*	v Pakistan at Sharjah	2001-02
86	v W Indies at Manchester	1975
91	v Australia at Adelaide	1984-85
96	v India at Sharjah	1983-84
98	v S Africa at Colombo	1993-94
98	v India at Sharjah	1998-99
99	v England at Perth	1998-99
102	v W Indies at Brisbane	1995-96

* One batsman absent hurt

Most sixes

268	ST Jayasuriya
102	PA de Silva
64	A Ranatunga
58	DPMD Jayawardene
54	KC Sangakkara
44	TM Dilshan
42	AP Gurusinha
27	CK Kapugedera
23	MF Maharoof

Jayasuriya also hit 2 for the Asia XI

Best strike rate

Runs per 100 balls
		Runs
91.27	ST Jayasuriya	13364
86.80	RJ Ratnayake	612
86.54	TM Dilshan	6715
84.44	MF Maharoof	1042
83.43	AD Mathews	1642
81.13	PA de Silva	9284
77.91	A Ranatunga	7456
77.84	DPMD Jayawardene	10503
77.73	KMDN Kulasekara	880
77.73	M Muralitharan	674

Qualification: 500 runs

Most economical bowlers

Runs per over
		Wkts
3.92	M Muralitharan	523
4.18	WPUJC Vaas	399
4.18	SD Anurasiri	32
4.27	HDPK Dharmasena	138
4.29	VB John	34
4.29	CPH Ramanayake	68
4.33	BAW Mendis	96
4.50	DS de Silva	32
4.50	RS Kalpage	73
4.52	DNT Zoysa	108

Qualification: 2000 balls bowled

Sri Lanka's one-day international results

	Played	Won	Lost	Tied	No result	% win
v Australia	84	28	53	0	3	34.56
v Bangladesh	30	27	3	0	0	90.00
v England	50	24	26	0	0	48.00
v India	139	52	75	1	11	41.01
v New Zealand	74	34	35	1	4	49.28
v Pakistan	132	50	77	1	4	39.45
v South Africa	51	24	25	1	1	49.00
v West Indies	49	20	26	0	3	43.47
v Zimbabwe	47	39	7	0	1	84.78
v others (see below)	16	15	1	0	0	93.75
TOTAL	672	313	328	4	27	48.83

Other teams: Bermuda (P1, W1), Canada (P2, W2), Ireland (P1, W1), Kenya (P6, W5, L1), Netherlands (P3, W3), Scotland (P1, W1), United Arab Emirates (P2, W2).

WEST INDIES   *Test Match Records*

Most appearances

144	S Chanderpaul
132	CA Walsh
130	BC Lara
121	IVA Richards
116	DL Haynes
110	CH Lloyd
108	CG Greenidge
102	CL Hooper
98	CEL Ambrose
93	CH Gayle
93	GS Sobers

Sobers played 85 successive Tests between 1954-55 and 1971-72

Most runs

		Avge
11912	BC Lara	53.17
10342	S Chanderpaul	50.20
8540	IVA Richards	50.23
8032	GS Sobers	57.78
7558	CG Greenidge	44.72
7515	CH Lloyd	46.67
7487	DL Haynes	42.29
6603	CH Gayle	42.32
6227	RB Kanhai	47.53
5949	RB Richardson	44.39

Greenidge and Haynes put on 6482 runs together, the Test record by any pair of opening batsmen

Most wickets

		Avge
519	CA Walsh	24.44
405	CEL Ambrose	20.99
376	MD Marshall	20.94
309	LR Gibbs	29.09
259	J Garner	20.97
249	MA Holding	23.68
235	GS Sobers	34.03
202	AME Roberts	25.61
192	WW Hall	26.38
161	IR Bishop	24.27

In all 18 West Indians have reached 100 Test wickets

Highest scores

400*	BC Lara	v England at St John's	2003-04
375	BC Lara	v England at St John's	1993-94
365*	GS Sobers	v Pakistan at Kingston	1957-58
333	CH Gayle	v Sri Lanka at Galle	2010-11
317	CH Gayle	v South Africa at St John's	2004-05
302	LG Rowe	v England at Bridgetown	1973-74
291	IVA Richards	v England at The Oval	1976
291	RR Sarwan	v England at Bridgetown	2008-09
277	BC Lara	v Australia at Sydney	1992-93
270*	GA Headley	v England at Kingston	1934-35

Lara scored 34 Test centuries, Sobers 26, S Chanderpaul 25, Richards 24, CG Greenidge and CH Lloyd 19

Best innings bowling

9-95	JM Noreiga	v India at Port-of-Spain	1970-71
8-29	CEH Croft	v Pakistan at Port-of-Spain	1976-77
8-38	LR Gibbs	v India at Bridgetown	1961-62
8-45	CEL Ambrose	v England at Bridgetown	1989-90
8-92	MA Holding	v England at The Oval	1976
8-104	AL Valentine	v England at Manchester	1950
7-22	MD Marshall	v England at Manchester	1988
7-25	CEL Ambrose	v Australia at Perth	1992-93
7-37	CA Walsh	v New Zealand at Wellington	1994-95
7-49	S Ramadhin	v England at Birmingham	1957

Valentine was playing in his first Test, Croft and Noreiga in their second

Record wicket partnerships

1st	298	CG Greenidge (149) and DL Haynes (167)	v England at St John's	1989-90
2nd	446	CC Hunte (260) and GS Sobers (365*)	v Pakistan at Kingston	1957-58
3rd	338	ED Weekes (206) and FMM Worrell (167)	v England at Port-of-Spain	1953-54
4th	399	GS Sobers (226) and FMM Worrell (197*)	v England at Bridgetown	1959-60
5th	322	BC Lara (213) and JC Adams (94)	v Australia at Kingston	1998-99
6th	282*	BC Lara (400*) and RD Jacobs (107*)	v England at St John's	2003-04
7th	347	DS Atkinson (219) and CC Depeiaza (122)	v Australia at Bridgetown	1954-55
8th	148	JC Adams (101*) and FA Rose (69)	v Zimbabwe at Kingston	1999-2000
9th	161	CH Lloyd (161*) and AME Roberts (68)	v India at Calcutta	1983-84
10th	143	D Ramdin (107*) and TL Best (95)	v England at Birmingham	2012

Figures to 17.09.12. Updated records can be found at **www.cricinfo.com/ci/engine/records**

Test Match Records — WEST INDIES

Most catches

Fielders

164	BC Lara	
122	IVA Richards	
115	CL Hooper	
109	GS Sobers	
96	CG Greenidge	

Most dismissals

Wicketkeepers		*Ct/St*
270	PJL Dujon	265/5
219	RD Jacobs	207/12
189	DL Murray	181/8
138	D Ramdin	135/3
101	JR Murray	98/3

Highest team totals

790-3d	v Pakistan at Kingston	1957-58
751-5d	v England at St John's	2003-04
749-9d	v England at Bridgetown	2008-09
747	v South Africa at St John's	2004-05
692-8d	v England at The Oval	1995
687-8d	v England at The Oval	1976
681-8d	v England at Port-of-Spain	1953-54
660-5d	v New Zealand at Wellington	1994-95
652-8d	v England at Lord's	1973
644-8d	v India at Delhi	1958-59

West Indies have passed 600 in Tests on nine further occasions, six of them coming against India

Lowest team totals

Completed innings

47	v England at Kingston	2003-04
51	v Aust at Port-of-Spain	1998-99
53	v Pakistan at Faisalabad	1986-87
54	v England at Lord's	2000
61	v England at Leeds	2000
76	v Pakistan at Dacca	1958-59
77	v NZ at Auckland	1955-56
78	v Australia at Sydney	1951-52
82	v Australia at Brisbane	2000-01
86*	v England at The Oval	1957

*One batsman absent hurt. West Indies have been dismissed for less than 100 on seven further occasions

Best match bowling

14-149	MA Holding	v England at The Oval	1976
13-55	CA Walsh	v N Zealand at Wellington	1994-95
12-121	AME Roberts	v India at Madras	1974-75
11-84	CEL Ambrose	v England at Port-of-Spain	1993-94
11-89	MD Marshall	v India at Port-of-Spain	1988-89
11-107	MA Holding	v Australia at Melbourne	1981-82
11-120	MD Marshall	v N Zealand at Bridgetown	1984-85
11-126	WW Hall	v India at Kanpur	1958-59
11-134	CD Collymore	v Pakistan at Kingston	2004-05
11-147	KD Boyce	v England at The Oval	1973

Marshall took ten or more wickets in a Test four times, Ambrose and Walsh three

Hat-tricks

WW Hall	v Pakistan at Lahore	1958-59

The first Test hat-trick not for England or Australia.

LR Gibbs	v Australia at Adelaide	1960-61

Gibbs had taken three wickets in four balls in the previous Test, at Sydney.

CA Walsh	v Australia at Brisbane	1988-89

The first Test hat-trick to be split over two innings.

JJC Lawson	v Australia at Bridgetown	2002-03

Also split over two innings

West Indies' Test match results

	Played	Won	Lost	Drawn	Tied	% win
v Australia	111	32	54	24	1	28.82
v Bangladesh	8	4	2	2	0	50.00
v England	148	53	45	50	0	35.81
v India	88	30	14	44	0	34.09
v New Zealand	39	12	9	18	0	30.76
v Pakistan	46	15	16	15	0	32.60
v South Africa	25	3	16	6	0	12.00
v Sri Lanka	15	3	6	6	0	20.00
v Zimbabwe	6	4	0	2	0	66.66
TOTAL	486	156	162	167	1	32.09

Figures to 17.09.12. Updated records can be found at www.cricinfo.com/ci/engine/records

WEST INDIES One-day International Records

Most appearances

295	BC Lara
268	S Chanderpaul
238	DL Haynes
231	CH Gayle
227	CL Hooper
224	RB Richardson
205	CA Walsh
187	IVA Richards
176	CEL Ambrose
173	RR Sarwan

25 West Indians have played more than 100 ODIs. Lara and Gayle also played for the World XI

Most runs

		Avge
10348	BC Lara	40.90
8778	S Chanderpaul	41.60
8648	DL Haynes	41.37
8305	CH Gayle	39.73
6721	IVA Richards	47.00
6248	RB Richardson	33.41
5761	CL Hooper	35.34
5644	RR Sarwan	43.41
5134	CG Greenidge	45.03
3675	PV Simmons	28.93

Gayle has scored 20 ODI hundreds, Lara 19, Haynes 17, Greenidge, Richards and Chanderpaul 11

Most wickets

		Avge
227	CA Walsh	30.47
225	CEL Ambrose	24.12
193	CL Hooper	36.05
157	MD Marshall	26.96
156	CH Gayle	34.71
146	DJ Bravo	30.73
146	J Garner	18.84
142	MA Holding	21.36
130	M Dillon	32.44
118	IR Bishop	26.50
118	IVA Richards	35.83

WKM Benjamin (100) and RA Harper (100) also reached 100 wickets

Highest scores

189*	IVA Richards	v England at Manchester	1984
181	IVA Richards	v Sri Lanka at Karachi	1987-88
169	BC Lara	v Sri Lanka at Sharjah	1995-96
157*	XM Marshall	v Canada at King City	2008-09
156	BC Lara	v Pakistan at Adelaide	2004-05
153*	IVA Richards	v Australia at Melbourne	1979-80
153*	CH Gayle	v Zimbabwe at Bulawayo	2003-04
153	BC Lara	v Pakistan at Sharjah	1993-94
152*	DL Haynes	v India at Georgetown	1988-89
152*	CH Gayle	v S Africa at Johannesburg	2003-04
152	CH Gayle	v Kenya at Nairobi	2001-02

S Chanderpaul scored 150 v SA at East London in 1998-99

Best bowling figures

7-51	WW Davis	v Australia at Leeds	1983
6-15	CEH Croft	v England at Kingstown	1980-81
6-22	FH Edwards	v Zimbabwe at Harare	2003-04
6-27	KAJ Roach	v Netherlands at Delhi	2010-11
6-29	BP Patterson	v India at Nagpur	1987-88
6-41	IVA Richards	v India at Delhi	1989-90
6-50	AH Gray	v Aust at Port-of-Spain	1990-91
5-1	CA Walsh	v Sri Lanka at Sharjah	1986-87
5-17	CEL Ambrose	v Australia at Melbourne	1988-89
5-22	AME Roberts	v England at Adelaide	1979-80
5-22	WKM Benjamin	v Sri Lanka at Bombay	1993-94

Edwards's feat was in his first ODI

Record wicket partnerships

1st	200*	SC Williams (78*) and S Chanderpaul (109*)	v India at Bridgetown	1996-97
2nd	221	CG Greenidge (115) and IVA Richards (149)	v India at Jamshedpur	1983-84
3rd	195*	CG Greenidge (105*) and HA Gomes (75*)	v Zimbabwe at Worcester	1983
4th	226	S Chanderpaul (150) and CL Hooper (108)	v South Africa at East London	1998-99
5th	154	CL Hooper (112*) and S Chanderpaul (67)	v Pakistan at Sharjah	2001-02
6th	154	RB Richardson (122) and PJL Dujon (53)	v Pakistan at Sharjah	1991-92
7th	115	PJL Dujon (57*) and MD Marshall (66)	v Pakistan at Gujranwala	1986-87
8th	101	AD Russell (41) and DJG Sammy (84)	v Australia at Gros Islet	2011-12
9th	77	RR Sarwan (65) and IDR Bradshaw (37)	v New Zealand at Christchurch	2005-06
10th	106*	IVA Richards (189*) and MA Holding (12*)	v England at Manchester	1984

Figures to 17.09.12. Updated records can be found at www.cricinfo.com/ci/engine/records

One-day International Records — **WEST INDIES**

Most catches

Fielders

120	CL Hooper
117	BC Lara
102	CH Gayle
100	IVA Richards
75	RB Richardson

Most dismissals

	Wicketkeepers	*Ct/St*
204	PJL Dujon	183/21
189	RD Jacobs	160/29
131	D Ramdin	125/6
68	CO Browne	59/9
51	JR Murray	44/7

Highest team totals

360-4	v Sri Lanka at Karachi	1987-88
347-6	v Zimbabwe at Bulawayo	2003-04
339-4	v Pakistan at Adelaide	2004-05
333-6	v Zimbabwe at Georgetown	2005-06
333-7	v Sri Lanka at Sharjah	1995-96
333-8	v India at Jamshedpur	1983-84
330-8	v Netherlands at Delhi	2010-11
324-4	v India at Ahmedabad	2002-03
324-8	v India at Nagpur	2006-07
319	v India at Kingston	2009

All these totals came from 50 overs except the 333-8 (45)

Lowest team totals

Completed innings

54	v S Africa at Cape Town	2003-04
61	v B'desh at Chittagong	2011-12
80	v Sri Lanka at Mumbai	2006-07
87	v Australia at Sydney	1992-93
91	v Zimbabwe at Sydney	2000-01
93	v Kenya at Pune	1995-96
103	v Pak at Melbourne	1996-97
110	v Australia at Manchester	1999
111	v Pak at Melbourne	1983-84
112	v Pakistan at Dhaka	2010-11

The 87 was in a match reduced to 30 overs: Australia made 101-9

Most sixes

188	CH Gayle
133	BC Lara
126	IVA Richards
85	S Chanderpaul
81	CG Greenidge
75	RL Powell
70	KA Pollard
65	CL Hooper
57	MN Samuels
56	RR Sarwan

XM Marshall holds the West Indian record for sixes in an innings (12)

Best strike rate

Runs per 100 balls		*Runs*
123.62	AD Russell	586
104.15	DJG Sammy	978
97.86	KA Pollard	1419
96.66	RL Powell	2085
94.73	DR Smith	1098
90.20	IVA Richards	6721
84.40	CH Gayle	8305
81.22	CH Lloyd	1977
80.54	DJ Bravo	2165
79.62	BC Lara	10348

Qualification: 500 runs

Most economical bowlers

Runs per over		*Wkts*
3.09	J Garner	146
3.32	MA Holding	142
3.40	AME Roberts	87
3.48	CEL Ambrose	225
3.53	MD Marshall	157
3.83	CA Walsh	227
3.97	RA Harper	100
4.00	CE Cuffy	41
4.09	EAE Baptiste	36
4.15	WKM Benjamin	100

Qualification: 2000 balls bowled

West Indies' one-day international results

	Played	Won	Lost	Tied	No result	% win
v Australia	130	59	65	3	3	47.63
v Bangladesh	20	14	4	0	2	77.77
v England	85	41	40	0	4	50.61
v India	106	57	46	1	2	55.28
v New Zealand	56	28	21	0	7	57.14
v Pakistan	120	66	52	2	0	55.83
v South Africa	51	12	38	0	1	24.00
v Sri Lanka	49	26	20	0	3	56.52
v Zimbabwe	41	31	9	0	1	77.50
v others (see below)	19	17	1	0	1	89.47
TOTAL	**677**	**351**	**296**	**6**	**24**	**54.21**

Other teams: Bermuda (P1, W1), Canada (P4, W4), Ireland (P4, W3, NR1), Kenya (P6, W5, L1), Netherlands (P2, W2), Scotland (P2, W2).

ZIMBABWE
Test Match Records

Most appearances

67	GW Flower	
65	HH Streak	
63	A Flower	
60	ADR Campbell	
46	GJ Whittall	
37	SV Carlisle	
30	HK Olonga	
29	DD Ebrahim	
28	T Taibu	
27	CB Wishart	

Zimbabwe played no Test cricket between September 2005 and August 2011

Most runs

		Avge
4794	A Flower	51.54
3457	GW Flower	29.54
2858	ADR Campbell	27.21
2207	GJ Whittall	29.42
1990	HH Streak	22.35
1615	SV Carlisle	26.91
1546	T Taibu	30.31
1464	DL Houghton	43.05
1414	MW Goodwin	42.84
1225	DD Ebrahim	22.68

CB Wishart (1098) and GJ Rennie (1023) also reached 1000 runs

Most wickets

		Avge
216	HH Streak	28.14
79	RW Price	35.92
70	PA Strang	36.02
68	HK Olonga	38.52
56	BC Strang	39.33
53	AM Blignaut	37.05
51	GJ Whittall	40.94
32	M Mbangwa	31.43
30	DH Brain	30.50
26	EA Brandes	36.57

GW Flower, TJ Friend and AG Huckle all took 25 wickets

Highest scores

266	DL Houghton	v Sri Lanka at Bulawayo	1994-95
232*	A Flower	v India at Nagpur	2000-01
203*	GJ Whittall	v New Zealand at Bulawayo	1997-98
201*	GW Flower	v Pakistan at Harare	1994-95
199*	A Flower	v South Africa at Harare	2001-02
188*	GJ Whittall	v New Zealand at Harare	2000-01
183*	A Flower	v India at Delhi	2000-01
166*	MW Goodwin	v Pakistan at Bulawayo	1997-98
163*	TMK Mawoyo	v Pakistan at Bulawayo	2011
156*	GW Flower	v Pakistan at Bulawayo	1997-98
156	A Flower	v Pakistan at Harare	1994-95

Andy Flower scored 12 Test centuries, Grant Flower 6, Dave Houghton and Guy Whittall 4

Best innings bowling

8-109	PA Strang	v New Zealand at Bulawayo	2000-01
6-59	DT Hondo	v Bangladesh at Dhaka	2004-05
6-73	RW Price	v West Indies at Harare	2003-04
6-73	HH Streak	v India at Harare	2005-06
6-87	HH Streak	v England at Lord's	2000
6-90	HH Streak	v Pakistan at Harare	1994-95
6-109	AG Huckle	v New Zealand at Bulawayo	1997-98
6-121	RW Price	v Australia at Sydney	2003-04
5-27	HH Streak	v WI at Port-of-Spain	1999-2000
5-31	TJ Friend	v Bangladesh at Dhaka	2001-02

AJ Traicos took 5-86 in Zimbabwe's inaugural Test, against India in 1992-93: he was 45, and had played three Tests for South Africa 22 years previously

Record wicket partnerships

1st	164	DD Ebrahim (71) and ADR Campbell (103)	v West Indies at Bulawayo	2001
2nd	135	MH Dekker (68*) and ADR Campbell (75)	v Pakistan at Rawalpindi	1993-94
3rd	194	ADR Campbell (99) and DL Houghton (142)	v Sri Lanka at Harare	1994-95
4th	269	GW Flower (201*) and A Flower (156)	v Pakistan at Harare	1994-95
5th	277*	MW Goodwin (166*) and A Flower (100*)	v Pakistan at Bulawayo	1997-98
6th	165	DL Houghton (121) and A Flower (59)	v India at Harare	1992-93
7th	154	HH Streak (83*) and AM Blignaut (92)	v West Indies at Harare	2001
8th	168	HH Streak (127*) and AM Blignaut (91)	v West Indies at Harare	2003-04
9th	87	PA Strang (106*) and BC Strang (42)	v Pakistan at Sheikhupura	1996-97
10th	97*	A Flower (183*) and HK Olonga (11*)	v India at Delhi	2000-01

Figures to 17.09.12. Updated records can be found at **www.cricinfo.com/ci/engine/records**

Test Match Records **ZIMBABWE**

Most catches

Fielders

60	ADR Campbell	
43	GW Flower	
34	SV Carlisle	
19	GJ Whittall	
17	DL Houghton/HH Streak	

Most dismissals

	Wicketkeepers	*Ct/St*
151	A Flower	151/9
60	T Taibu	55/5
16	WR James	16/0

Flower also took 9 catches when not keeping wicket

Highest team totals

563-9d	v West Indies at Harare	2001
544-4d	v Pakistan at Harare	1994-95
542-7d	v Bangladesh at Chittagong	2001-02
507-9d	v West Indies at Harare	2003-04
503-6	v India at Nagpur	2000-01
462-9d	v Sri Lanka at Bulawayo	1994-95
461	v New Zealand at Bulawayo	1997-98
457	v Bangladesh at Bulawayo	2000-01
456	v India at Harare	1992-93
441	v Bangladesh at Harare	2003-04

Zimbabwe's 456 in 1992-93 is the highest by any country in their first Test match

Lowest team totals

Completed innings

51	v N Zealand at Napier	2011-12
54	v SA at Cape Town	2004-05
59	v N Zealand at Harare	2005-06
63	v WI at Port-of-Spain	1999-2000
79	v Sri Lanka at Galle	2001-02
83	v England at Lord's	2000
94	v Eng at Chester-le-Street	2003
99	v N Zealand at Harare	2005-06
102	v S Africa at Harare	1999-2000
102	v WI at Kingston	1999-2000
102	v Sri Lanka at Harare	2003-04

At Harare in 2005-06 and Napier in 2011-12 Zimbabwe were bowled out twice on the same day by New Zealand

Best match bowling

11-255	AG Huckle	v N Zealand at Bulawayo	1997-98
10-158	PA Strang	v N Zealand at Bulawayo	2000-01
10-161	RW Price	v West Indies at Harare	2003-04
9-72	HH Streak	v WI at Port-of-Spain	1999-2000
9-105	HH Streak	v Pakistan at Harare	1994-95
9-235	RW Price	v W Indies at Bulawayo	2003-04
8-104	GW Flower	v Pakistan at Chittagong	2001-02
8-105	HH Streak	v Pakistan at Harare	1994-95
8-110	AM Blignaut	v Bangladesh at Bulawayo	2000-01
8-114	HH Streak	v Pakistan at Rawalpindi	1993-94

Blignaut was playing in his first Test, Huckle in his second

Hat-tricks

AM Blignaut	v Bangladesh at Harare	2003-04

Blignaut dismissed Hannan Sarkar, Mohammad Ashraful and Mushfiqur Rahman to reduce Bangladesh to 14-5.

The only Test hat-trick against Zimbabwe was taken by DNT Zoysa for Sri Lanka at Harare in 1999-2000, when he removed TR Gripper, MW Goodwin and NC Johnson with the first three balls he bowled, in the second over of the match

Zimbabwe's Test match results

	Played	Won	Lost	Drawn	Tied	% win
v Australia	3	0	3	0	0	0.00
v Bangladesh	9	9	1	3	0	55.55
v England	6	0	3	3	0	0.00
v India	11	2	7	2	0	18.18
v New Zealand	15	0	9	6	0	0.00
v Pakistan	15	2	9	4	0	13.33
v South Africa	7	0	6	1	0	0.00
v Sri Lanka	15	0	10	5	0	0.00
v West Indies	6	0	4	2	0	0.00
TOTAL	87	9	52	26	0	10.34

Figures to 17.09.12. Updated records can be found at **www.cricinfo.com/ci/engine/records**

ZIMBABWE
One-day International Records

Most appearances

221	GW Flower	
213	A Flower	
188	ADR Campbell	
187	HH Streak	
149	T Taibu	
147	GJ Whittall	
139	E Chigumbura	
139	P Utseya	
132	BRM Taylor	
115	H Masakadza	

S Matsikenyeri (112) SV Carlisle (111) and RW Price (102) have also played in more than 100 ODIs

Most runs

		Avge
6786	A Flower	35.34
6571	GW Flower	33.52
5185	ADR Campbell	30.50
4112	BRM Taylor	34.84
3383	T Taibu	29.41
3006	H Masakadza	27.08
2901	HH Streak	28.44
2786	E Chigumbura	24.01
2740	SV Carlisle	27.67
2705	GJ Whittall	22.54

S Matsikenyeri (2205) and V Sibanda (2194) have also scored more than 2000 runs

Most wickets

		Avge
237	HH Streak	29.81
111	P Utseya	45.97
104	GW Flower	40.62
100	RW Price	35.75
96	PA Strang	33.05
88	GJ Whittall	39.55
85	E Chigumbura	40.84
75	GB Brent	37.01
70	EA Brandes	32.37
68	CB Mpofu	37.75

Brandes took Zimbabwe's only ODI hat-trick, against England at Harare in 1996-97

Highest scores

194*	CK Coventry	v Bangladesh at Bulawayo	2009
178*	H Masakadza	v Kenya at Harare	2009-10
172*	CB Wishart	v Namibia at Harare	2002-03
156	H Masakadza	v Kenya at Harare	2009-10
145*	BRM Taylor	v S Africa at Bloemfontein	2010-11
145	A Flower	v India at Colombo	2002-03
142*	GW Flower	v Bangladesh at Bulawayo	2000-01
142*	A Flower	v England at Harare	2001-02
142	DL Houghton	v New Zealand at Hyderabad	1987-88
140	GW Flower	v Kenya at Dhaka	1998-99

ADR Campbell made seven ODI centuries for Zimbabwe, GW Flower and BRM Taylor six

Best bowling figures

6-19	HK Olonga	v England at Cape Town	1999-2000
6-20	BC Strang	v Bangladesh at Nairobi	1997-98
6-28	HK Olonga	v Kenya at Bulawayo	2002-03
6-46	AG Cremer	v Kenya at Harare	2009-10
6-52	CB Mpofu	v Kenya at Nairobi	2008-09
5-20	BV Vitori	v Bangladesh at Harare	2011
5-21	PA Strang	v Kenya at Patna	1995-96
5-22	PA Strang	v Kenya at Dhaka	1998-99
5-28	EA Brandes	v England at Harare	1996-97
5-30	BV Vitori	v Bangladesh at Harare	2011

Vitori took five wickets in each of his first two ODIs, a unique feat

Record wicket partnerships

1st	167	V Sibanda (96) and H Masakadza (80)	v West Indies at Bulawayo	2007-08
2nd	150	GW Flower (78) and GJ Rennie (76)	v Kenya at Nairobi	1997-98
3rd	181	T Taibu (98) and CR Ervine (85)	v Canada at Nagpur	2010-11
4th	202	SV Carlisle (109) and SM Ervine (100)	v India at Adelaide	2003-04
5th	186*	MW Goodwin (112*) and GW Flower (96*)	v West Indies at Chester-le-Street	2000
6th	188	T Taibu (103*) and S Matsikenyeri (86)	v South Africa at Benoni	2009-10
7th	130	A Flower (142*) and HH Streak (56)	v England at Harare	2001-02
8th	117	DL Houghton (142) and IP Butchart (54)	v New Zealand at Hyderabad	1987-88
9th	55	KM Curran (62) and PWE Rawson (19)	v West Indies at Birmingham	1983
10th	60	SW Masakadza (45*) and IA Nicolson (14)	v Ireland at Harare	2010-11

Figures to 17.09.12. Updated records can be found at www.cricinfo.com/ci/engine/records

One-day International Records

ZIMBABWE

Most catches

Fielders

86	GW Flower	
74	ADR Campbell	
49	H Masakadza	
45	E Chigumbura	
45	HH Streak	

Most dismissals

Wicketkeepers		*Ct/St*
165	A Flower	133/32
143	T Taibu	111/32
59	BRM Taylor	41/18
31	DL Houghton	29/2
6	F Mutizwa	4/2

Highest team totals

351-7	v Kenya at Mombasa	2008-09
340-2	v Namibia at Harare	2002-03
338-7	v Bermuda at Port-of-Spain	2005-06
329-3	v Kenya at Harare	2009-10
325-6	v Kenya at Dhaka	1998-99
323-7	v Bangladesh at Bulawayo	2009
313-4	v Kenya at Harare	2009-10
312-4	v Sri Lanka at New Plymouth	1991-92
312-8	v Bangladesh at Bulawayo	2009
310-6	v Bangladesh at Dhaka	1998-99

Zimbabwe have made nine further totals of 300 or more

Lowest team totals

Completed innings

35	v Sri Lanka at Harare	2003-04
38	v Sri Lanka at Colombo	2001-02
44	v Bang at Chittagong	2009-10
65	v India at Harare	2005-06
67	v Sri Lanka at Harare	2008-09
69	v Kenya at Harare	2005-06
80	v Sri Lanka at Mirpur	2008-09
85	v WI at Ahmedabad	2006-07
92	v England at Bristol	2003
94	v Pakistan at Sharjah	1996-97

Zimbabwe have also been bowled out for 99 twice

Most sixes

77	E Chigumbura
48	HH Streak
45	BRM Taylor
44	ADR Campbell
38	H Masakadza
37	GW Flower
30	T Taibu
28	SV Carlisle
28	CK Coventry
26	A Flower
26	GJ Whittall

Best strike rate

Runs per 100 balls		*Runs*
106.28	AM Blignaut	626
88.37	CK Coventry	821
85.54	SM Ervine	698
82.63	E Chigumbura	2622
75.94	CN Evans	764
75.69	TJ Friend	548
75.65	CR Ervine	581
74.59	A Flower	6786
73.94	H Masakadza	2938
73.61	HH Streak	2901

Qualification: 500 runs

Most economical bowlers

*Runs per over**		*Wkts*
3.88	AJ Traicos	19
3.89	RW Price	97
4.13	BC Strang	46
4.23	P Utseya	106
4.37	PA Strang	96
4.37	AR Whittall	45
4.40	EC Rainsford	45
4.50	HH Streak	237
4.52	AH Shah	18
4.64	GW Flower	104
4.66	DH Brain	21

**Qualification: 1000 balls bowled*

Zimbabwe's one-day international results

	Played	Won	Lost	Tied	No result	% win
v Australia	28	1	26	0	1	3.70
v Bangladesh	56	26	30	0	0	46.42
v England	30	8	21	0	1	27.58
v India	51	10	39	2	0	21.56
v New Zealand	35	8	25	1	1	25.00
v Pakistan	44	2	40	1	1	5.81
v South Africa	32	2	29	0	1	6.45
v Sri Lanka	47	7	39	0	1	15.21
v West Indies	41	9	31	0	1	22.50
v others (see below)	43	34	6	1	2	79.06
TOTAL	407	107	286	5	9	27.51

Other teams: Bermuda (P2, W2), Canada (P2, W2), Ireland (P5, W3, L1, T1), Kenya (P32, W25, L5, NR 2), Namibia (P1, W1), Netherlands (P1, W1).

INTERNATIONAL SCHEDULE 2012-13

	Tests	ODIs	T20Is
October 2012			
Sri Lanka v New Zealand	2	5	1
November 2012			
India v England	4	5	2
Australia v South Africa	3	–	–
Sri Lanka v New Zealand	2	5	1
Bangladesh v West Indies	3	5	1
December 2012			
South Africa v New Zealand	2	3	3
Australia v Sri Lanka	3	5	2
Zimbabwe v Pakistan	2	3	2
January 2013			
South Africa v Pakistan	3	5	2
February 2013			
Australia v West Indies	–	5	1
New Zealand v England	3	3	3
Sri Lanka v Bangladesh	2	3	–
March 2013			
India v Australia	4	–	–
West Indies v Zimbabwe	2	3	2
April 2013			
West Indies v Sri Lanka	2	3	2

	Tests	ODIs	T20Is
May 2013			
England v New Zealand	2	3	2
June 2013			
Champions Trophy in England	–	15	–
West Indies v Pakistan	2	5	2
July 2013			
England v Australia	5	5	2
Zimbabwe v India	–	3	–
Sri Lanka v South Africa	3	5	3
September 2013			
Scotland v Australia	–	1	–
October 2013			
India v Australia	–	7	1
Bangladesh v New Zealand	2	3	1
Pakistan v South Africa	2	5	3
Zimbabwe v Sri Lanka	2	3	–
November 2013			
Australia v England	5	5	3
South Africa v India	3	7	2
Sri Lanka v New Zealand	–	3	1
December 2013			
New Zealand v West Indies	3	5	1
Pakistan v Sri Lanka	3	5	2

Details subject to change. Some tours may continue into the month(s) after the one shown above